Striving to Save

Striving to Save

Creating Policies for Financial
Security of Low-Income Families

MARGARET SHERRARD SHERRADEN

AND AMANDA MOORE MCBRIDE

WITH SONDRA G. BEVERLY

The University of Michigan Press

Ann Arbor

Copyright © by the University of Michigan 2010
All rights reserved
Published in the United States of America by
The University of Michigan Press
Manufactured in the United States of America
⊗ Printed on acid-free paper

2013   2012   2011   2010   4   3   2   1

A CIP catalog record for this book is available from the British Library.

Library of Congress Cataloging-in-Publication Data

Sherraden, Margaret S.
    Striving to save : creating policies for financial security of
low-income families / Margaret Sherrard Sherraden and Amanda Moore
McBride with Sondra G. Beverly.
        p.   cm.
    Includes bibliographical references and index.
    ISBN 978-0-472-11712-3 (cloth : alk. paper)
    ISBN 978-0-472-02181-9 (e-book)
    1. Individual development accounts.   2. Poor—Finance, Personal.
I. McBride, Amanda Moore, 1971–   II. Beverly, Sondra G.   III. Title.
HG1660.A3S53 2010
332.0240086'942—dc22   2009038397

Savings plans are a necessity for a working family, you know. They need some kind of savings. Everyone should be able to save something. It's difficult to save when your paycheck is very limited, you know. . . . Tax-free savings and automatic deductions . . . would help families to save. There has to be some kind of something there that would make it just a little bit difficult for them to just pull it out . . . just any little extra step they would have to take that would keep them from going in that direction. That would help them to save. But if it's too accessible, it's too much temptation. And so a lot of times that's why people do not save.

LaVonne, age 46

Since I joined the program maybe [my focus] has changed a little bit because since I've joined the program I've managed to save a little bit of money every month for going on a year now. And so of course that's made me feel a little better and it's made me know that you can save money, you know, if you just really work hard and really strive hard.

Kenneth, age 46

Contents

Acknowledgments

This in-depth study of saving in low-income households is part of the American Dream Demonstration (ADD), an experimental test of Individual Development Accounts. The CFED designed and implemented ADD, while the Center for Social Development (CSD) designed and led the research agenda. Our gratitude goes to the twelve foundations that provided support, including The Ford Foundation, Charles Stewart Mott Foundation, Joyce Foundation, F. B. Heron Foundation, John D. and Catherine T. MacArthur Foundation, Citigroup Foundation, Fannie Mae Foundation, Levi Strauss Foundation, Ewing Marion Kauffman Foundation, Rockefeller Foundation, Metropolitan Life Foundation, and Moriah Fund.

We are also grateful to the host organization, Community Action Project (CAP), of Tulsa, Oklahoma, for facilitating the interviews. Throughout, the executive director, Steven Dow, and the dedicated staff at CAP, including Jennifer Robey, Rachel Trares, Virilyaih Davis, Kimberly Cowden, and Leisa Crawford, provided support and assistance in recruiting respondents, clarifying program guidelines, and keeping track of program and participant information that helped inform our research. Their contributions made this study possible.

From the start, this study has been a team effort. First, we express our appreciation to the entire in-depth interview research team. The project's talented interviewers, Shannon Collier-Tennison, Philip Rozario, Trina Williams Shanks, Fred Ssewamala, Rebecca Vonderlack-Navarro, and Michal Grinstein-Weiss, not only engaged respondents in in-depth conversations about their financial lives and saving but also provided extensive comments and helpful suggestions regarding interpretation and analysis. Throughout, Lissa Johnson at the Center for Social Development kept the project going, managing analysis and savings data, supervising human subjects reviews, and making valuable contributions to qualitative data analysis. Thanks also to Philip Hong who contributed to the interview instrument. Julie Bliss carefully transcribed the interviews. Jami Curley checked transcriptions and profiles for accuracy. Suzie Fragale provided helpful assistance throughout the interview process, including organizing correspondence with research participants. Ella Boyd ably managed interview tapes and correspondence.

Stacie Hanson played a key role in analysis. She listened to all the interviews, created case profiles, and extracted vignettes of key cases; but more important, she conducted thoughtful analyses that inform this volume. Fred Ssewamala carefully reviewed qualitative files and contributed to qualitative analysis. Trina Williams Shanks analyzed the effects of saving on children's welfare. Mark Schreiner provided data and analysis from other parts of ADD research. Kwofie Danso and Chang-Keun Han also helped with quantitative analysis of monitoring and survey data. Beatriz Castaño helped to organize and categorize the data, Catherine Sherraden extracted expense data, and Shelby Schroeder, Lisa Waddell, and Jason Wead extracted data from the interviews. We are grateful to each for their help.

Deepest appreciation also goes to the editorial team beginning with Julia Stevens who supervised the editorial process, edited the entire manuscript, and improved clarity. Luisa Leme and Wei Chang checked references and calculations, and Carrie Freeman made the manuscript look right. Lissa Johnson, Margaret Clancy, Michael Sherraden, Rajiv Prabhakar, and two anonymous reviewers read the manuscript and offered constructive and helpful suggestions. Sondra Beverly gave extensive guidance on revisions during the final stage of editing, making the volume conceptually cleaner and more concise. Amanda Moore McBride managed data collection, including supervising the research team and support staff, conducted quantitative analyses, and provided advice during analysis and writing. Margaret Sherraden led research design, analysis, and writing.

Over the years, many people have enhanced our thinking about saving and financial decision making in low-income households, including Deb Adams, Ray Boshara, Kathy Edin, Willie Elliott, Bill Emmons, Steve Fazzari, Bob Friedman, Jeanne Hogarth, David Lander, Duncan Lindsey, Howard Karger, Julian LeGrand, Annamaria Lusardi, Yves Moury, Yunju Nam, Melvin Oliver, Shirley Porterfield, Will Rainford, Mark Rank, Herb and Irene Rubin, Cynthia Sanders, Ed Scanlon, Mark Schreiner, Tom Shapiro, Michael Sherraden, Fred Ssewamala, David Stoesz, Carolina Trivelli, and Min Zhan. We thank each of them.

This book would not have been possible without Camille, Anne, Tonya, Ella, Becky, Fred, LaVonne, Debra, Heather, Theresa, Cynthia, and the others in the study who allowed us to learn about their families' financial lives. Although the book is about the ostensibly rational topic of savings, it is in reality a complex and often emotional matter. The credit for insights into saving in low-income households explored in this book goes to them.

Amanda would like to dedicate this book to Lewis and Eula Bracy, her maternal grandparents, who never had much materially but pinched their pennies—in many of the same ways discussed in this book—which led to the down payment for her first house.

Margaret thanks Michael, Catherine, and Sam for their love and encouragement, and dedicates this book to her parents, Connie and Tom, who didn't teach us about money, but taught us about people.

M.S.S.
A.M.M.
September 2008

Saving in Low-Income Households

Low-income Americans face significant challenges in their efforts to accumulate wealth. They often lack even the most basic transaction and savings instruments (Caskey 1997; Barr 2004). Furthermore, savings vehicles with more favorable terms, such as Individual Retirement Accounts (IRAs), 529 college savings plans, or defined contribution schemes such as 401(k)s, are not financially attractive to families working in the low-wage sector of the economy (Sherraden 1991; OECD 2003).

In this book, we look at the experiences of 59 low-income families participating in a groundbreaking savings program. The families saved in Individual Development Accounts (IDAs), accounts that match the savings of poor families for long-term investments such as a house, postsecondary education, retirement, or a small business.[1] Looking at the experiences of a random sampling of low, medium, and high savers in the IDA program, we analyze whether low-income families can successfully accumulate savings and what difference it makes when they do. To understand their experiences, we begin by describing the realities of growing up in poor households, especially the economic socialization and tangible support individuals received from their families as they came of age. Following them into adulthood, we explore how successfully they manage their finances, earn a living, and save. We learn about their hopes and dreams for the future, and whether the savings program helped them meet their goals. Their successes and failures in the IDA program provide insight into saving in poor families and inform public policy debates on wealth building in low-income households.

As a useful comparison, we also examine the experiences of 25 low-income individuals who signed up for the IDA program but were not selected to participate. The experimental research framework allows us to contrast and compare the perspectives and motivations of IDA participants and nonparticipants. In-depth interviews with these 84 families, along with quantitative survey and account monitoring data, contribute to a better understanding of saving and the impact of a matched savings program on participants' expectations and achievements.

To set the stage, we introduce Camille.[2] Camille had always believed saving was important, so when she heard about the IDA program, she immediately signed on.[3] Unfortunately, she was not selected to participate. Through her story, however, we begin to understand why a savings program might be important to low-income families.

Camille

At 57 years of age, Camille had already raised one child, and, at the time we talked to her, she was caring for her five grandchildren. Growing up, Camille learned how to work hard. Her mother was a domestic worker, and the "foundation" of the family. Her father worked long and hard hours as a "common laborer," holding two or more jobs at a time throughout Camille's childhood. After a life of hard work and thrift, her father died, leaving the family with two small plots of land, a house, and a car. Camille's mother also found money hidden under a mattress and in a credit union savings account. Camille recalled, "[My father] always taught us, you know, you should save, save, save, save, save, save. He would drill that in our heads continuously, you know, because you'll never have anything if you spend everything you've got."

Camille married early. Her first marriage ended when the baby was young, but Camille soon remarried and moved out of state with her new husband. Eventually, she completed a GED, attended secretarial school, and began to get better jobs.

Camille had several jobs before she was able to save any money. She tried to follow her father's advice to save. "But I never could find a way to save because it took every dollar" just to pay the bills. She tried to save small amounts in a savings account, "but then for some reason I would always have to go get it." "I went from payday to payday. I didn't feel I had any to save, you know, with a baby. And I didn't want food stamps and all that crap . . . because we weren't raised that way, you know." She sometimes opened a savings account to deposit her income tax refund. "Every year I open it up, but something comes up and it's gone before the next year." Camille felt stymied by her inability to save. "My mother says—she still says it to this day—that we just live above our needs and this is why we can't save. So she may have a point because I still can't save."

There were two times in Camille's life when she accumulated some savings. The first time she saved enough to make a down payment on a small house. She was working at a credit union at the time. With her father in mind ("his voice never left me alone"), she had part of her wages automatically deposited in a savings account. She also had a job doing paperwork for a realtor and saw listings before they were released to the public. That way she found a house and bought it "at a steal."

Camille said that having the credit union savings account made her feel good. "It felt good, you know, to look and see that I actually had some money that belonged to me." Moreover, she said it was an easy process because they took it out of her check before she got it. She also had a retirement account at the credit union but left the job before she accumulated much money.

The second time she accumulated savings was through her job where the pay and the benefits were better than her previous jobs. "Things were going pretty good . . . and I did have savings. I had a little bit of money." But in 1989, she had to return to Oklahoma to care for her grandchildren. She sold all of her assets, setting the savings aside for what lay ahead.

> I was very fearful because I didn't know what to do "God, how I am going to take care of these five grandchildren? I don't know what to do." So everything that I had I sold because it was too expensive to bring. I had a house sale. I sold my car. I sold furniture. I sold goldfish, aquariums. Everything I had I sold so I could come here with as much cash as possible.

When she returned to Oklahoma she turned to public assistance for the first time "because of the kids." Unfortunately, Camille came up against the asset limit test in the welfare system. "When they found out that I had money, they told me that was considered as an asset. . . . Any money you have in savings is considered an asset. And if you have a certain amount of money you can't get help. I couldn't get housing. I couldn't get anything. So I had to go out on my own and find a place to stay. We couldn't stay with my mom. She was 70-something years old."

Within seven or eight months, Camille had spent down her life savings. When her savings were depleted, she began to receive state aid. Nonetheless, she still did not qualify for housing and had to pay her rent out of the monthly check. Camille reflected on her decision to tell the welfare worker about her savings.

> You can't lie and say you don't have it. I guess you could. Some people do, but I didn't. I was very honest, and they said, "Well, you have to use that up first and then come back because that's an asset." You have means to supply yourself. Why should we give you anything when you've got money? . . . I guess it makes sense, but it made me angry.

At the time she applied for the IDA program, Camille was living close to the margin, working two jobs, and raising five grandchildren, three still at home. All she had was what was in her checking account. She kept a small surplus in the account as a back up. "All I have is sitting in my checking account where I can go get it if I need it. I usually . . . maintain $200 or $300 monthly in my checking account. . . . I like to see a big number in my checkbook." She likes the checking account surplus because she can get to it if she needs it.

As she described the surplus in her checking account—which she later calculated as about $100 average—she felt bad that she hadn't saved more. "Talking to you is making me realize that, you know, I could save if I would just do it. But I always say, 'Oh no, I ain't got no money to save, girl. I need all my money, you know.'" She believed that she could not accumulate larger amounts because the money was so accessible. "I guess because it's just readily available. And you know, it's really a stupid thing . . . because that sitting over in savings could be drawing a little bit of interest. Whereas in checking, I'm not drawing any interest. I'm just writing it out, writing it out."

At the time of the interview, Camille was also saving in other ways. Through her job in the school district, she was saving in a retirement account and an annuity. She was not impressed with the amounts in either account. "Because this annuity, if you cash it in, you know it's less. You know, they show you the cash value and what it actually is, so the cash value is not that great. So it just, you know, sits there."

She is also saving in stock investments through her job. "That's right, I'm buying stock, five dollars a payday. . . . They take that out of my check. And then they have shareholding accounts. . . . They really, really, really push saving incentives there." She signed up for the stock option because "they put it out there for you and you'd just be kind of stupid not to take advantage of it." But, she laughed, she would not buy this stock if it was not coming directly out of her paycheck because it would be too easy to spend instead. "I doubt it—if I'm not working for them—I really doubt that I would write out a check and send it to them to purchase stock. But this way, by coming out of my check before I even see it, you know. Yeah."

Camille did not really think about these retirement accounts and the stocks as savings because she did not have easy access to them. She thought about them "as really belonging to someone else." She understood they belonged to her and money was deposited regularly, but they were not accessible. "Actually it's my money. But it's—you've got to go through channels to get it if you wanted it. Whereas the money in my checking account, I look at that as being mine because I don't have to go through channels. All I've got to do is stick the ATM card in the deal and get my money." Until speaking with the interviewer, she hadn't thought about these as savings. "You know, I don't know, because I had never really realized that—I mean, I know there's savings, and I know it comes out of my check. But until sitting here talking to you about it, I never even kept up with it, to tell you the truth. I know I can't get it."

Although Camille thought her small retirement savings were fairly insignificant, upon further reflection she commented that "at least it's a nest egg" for the grandchildren. "I doubt if I'll ever use it because it will never be large enough for me to use, but maybe it will benefit them." She only wished there was more. "I just feel like one day when I stop working, you know, whenever that day is, there should be something you could fall back on instead of just having absolutely nothing."

Camille was disappointed she was not selected for the IDA program because it was an opportunity to save for a house that would provide greater stability for her grandchildren and herself. Nonetheless, she is still determined to pursue this goal. "I'm not giving up." She planned to use her next tax refund (which she had planned to deposit in the IDA before she learned she was not accepted into the program) for a house down payment. "When I file my income tax this time, I'm going to try to already have it set up where I can go buy a house. And then if I could take the money and hurry and put it down, you know." However, her determination seemed to fade as her voice trailed off. "But those types of things . . ." As if trying to gather her energy, she once more expressed her desire to buy a home, concluding, "I do want a home, I really do, you know. I really do."

Despite a lack of schooling and an unsuccessful teenage marriage, Camille managed to land on her feet. She moved to another state with her second husband, raised her daughter, and worked her way up to a responsible job with decent benefits. Fortunately, Camille worked in jobs that provided opportunities to save. First, she worked at a credit union where she could automatically deduct a sum from each paycheck to deposit into a savings account. Later, in a job that offered a structured savings program, she saved even more. She accumulated some assets, and despite her divorce, Camille held onto her home, her most precious financial asset.

Unfortunately, life events intervened, and Camille became, like an increasing number of other grandparents in America, responsible for raising her grandchildren. Turning to public assistance, Camille found herself caught up in welfare regulations that deplete the assets of poor families, and she was forced to spend down her life savings before she could receive assistance for her grandchildren. Camille believes that owning a house would provide stability and a foundation for her grandchildren, but she has little money to make a down payment.

Camille tries, but it is difficult to save on a low income and without the support of a structured savings program. Therefore, she planned to start saving the way she had many years earlier using an automatic deduction from her paycheck to her savings account. She understands it is easier to save if she does not see it. Nonetheless, it is difficult to arrange because of her low income and high consumption needs. The hardships she confronts make saving difficult, even as lack of savings makes hardships more difficult to endure.

ASSET ACCUMULATION IN POOR HOUSEHOLDS

Why do assets and wealth matter for poor households?[4] Although income and assets are highly correlated, research suggests that assets have positive effects beyond those of income (Schreiner and Sherraden 2007). Assets may endow people with economic resources, offer psychological and social benefits, and shape opportunities for the future (Miller and Roby 1970; Henretta and Campbell 1978; Sherraden 1991; Oliver and Shapiro 1995; Midgley 1995; Scanlon and Page-Adams 2001; Shapiro and Wolff 2001; Miller-Adams 2002; Shapiro 2004; Glennerster 2006). As Seymour Spilerman observes, people may benefit from their assets without their losing value, in contrast to income, which is consumed (2001, 369; see also Spilerman 2000). A retirement account, for example, offers peace of mind about the future, tends to appreciate in value, and in bad economic times, can be sold and consumed. A house provides shelter, gives a family a stake in the neighborhood, and may be an object of pride, a tangible form of accomplishment, and a source of equity (Conley 2001). Thomas

Shapiro suggests that inherited wealth, in particular, is "transformative" in the sense that it lifts families "beyond their own achievements" (2001, 10) and therefore promotes social mobility (Shapiro and Johnson 2005). Assets can build opportunities and change perceptions about the future in ways that income alone cannot.

Assets are inaccessible to many low-income Americans, however, because their net worth (household assets minus liabilities) is low (Carasso and McKernan 2008). Net worth in the poorest 40 percent of U.S. households averaged only $2,200 in 2004 (Wolff 2007). Net worth among the poorest 10 percent of U.S. households was a negative $1,800 in 1999 (Caner and Wolff 2004; see also Kennickell 2006).[5] According to Robert Haveman and Edward Wolff, one quarter of Americans were asset poor in 1998. Their net worth (home, savings, and other assets minus debts) could not support them at a poverty level for three months, and one-half of the population had liquid assets of less than $5,000 (Haveman and Wolff 2005).

Some population groups have particularly low levels of net worth (Haveman and Wolff 2005; Nembhard and Chiteji 2006). Women, especially single heads of households, own fewer assets than men do, in part because of the consumption demands of raising children (Conley and Ryvicker 2005). Wealth is lower in families with lower levels of education (Lerman 2005). Middle-class families hold 9.5 times the net worth of low-income families (Carasso and McKernan 2008). Median wealth of those in the bottom 40 percent of the income distribution declined between 2001 and 2004 (Bucks, Kennickell, and Moore 2006), and this trend may continue (Keister 2000b; Keister and Moller 2000; Wolff and Zacharias 2006; Smeeding and Thompson 2007). People who live in rural areas have lower levels of net financial and liquid assets (Fisher and Weber 2004).

Across ethnic and racial groups, there is a large and persistent disparity in wealth. A legacy of racism and discrimination contributes to low levels of assets (Terrell 1971; Massey and Denton 1993; Oliver and Shapiro 1995; Conley 1999; Denton 2001; Stern 2001; Masnick 2004; Shanks 2005; Lui et al. 2006). Median net worth in Native American households in 2002 was $5,700, in Black households it was $5,998, and in Hispanic households it was $7,932, fractions of the $88,651 median net worth in White non-Hispanic households (Kochhar 2004; Zagorski 2006). Approximately 31 percent of African Americans and 35 percent of Hispanics had zero or negative net worth in 2001, while in White households only 13 percent had zero or negative net worth (Caner and Wolff 2004).

Several factors contribute to lack of assets in poor households. First, low-wage employment and low levels of education contribute to low income that strains families' ability to accumulate assets, especially among women and families with children (Chang 2006). There is frequently little to save as families struggle to pay for basics and to cover emergencies (Waldron, Roberts, and Reamer 2004).

Second, low levels of wealth in one generation beget low levels of wealth in the next (Kotlikoff and Summers 1981; Gale and Scholz 1994; Shapiro 2004). Although estimates vary widely, inheritance helps to explain wealth holding (Kotlikoff and Summers 1981; Gale and Scholz 1994), with significant implications across social classes, and across race and ethnic groups (Shapiro 2001, 2004; Wilhelm 2001).

Third, many families living in poverty lack transaction accounts such as basic checking and savings accounts, which help to establish financial stability and build financial assets (Barr 2004; Sherraden and Barr 2005; Blank and Barr, 2009). An estimated 24 percent of low-income families lack a bank account (Carasso and McKernan 2008). These so-called unbanked are disproportionately poorer, younger, unemployed, less educated, and more likely to be non-White than their banked counterparts (Aizcorbe, Kennickell, and Moore 2003; Hogarth, Anguelov, and Lee 2004; Berry 2005).[6] Up to half of Latinos, for example, lack transaction accounts, and therefore lack one of the key building blocks for asset building (Muñiz, Rodriguez, and Pérez 2004).

Fourth, low-income families typically cannot take advantage of policies that structure and subsidize asset building in wealthier American households (Sherraden 1991). Tax expenditures, including the home mortgage interest deduction and tax-favored retirement savings accounts, build wealth in nonpoor households. The poor, because of their low tax liability, do not benefit, and they lack equivalent policies that build assets in poor households (Sherraden 2005). The federal government invests approximately $335 billion in asset subsidies (mostly through tax deductions), one-third of which goes to the wealthiest 1 percent of the population, while less than 5 percent goes to the bottom 60 percent (Woo, Schweke, and Buchholz 2004). Tax expenditures, which overwhelmingly benefit the nonpoor, contribute to what some have called a "hidden" welfare state (Howard 1999; Seidman 2001).

Finally, the poor not only lack access to subsidies for saving and other asset-building policies, but they also are discouraged from asset accumulation because of asset tests. Middle-class people can save for retirement in a tax deferred 401(k) plan, buy a home with a generous tax subsidy from the government, and save for their children's college education in a tax-benefited 529 college savings plan. In contrast, a typical poor family does not have access to these tax benefits and furthermore cannot save without risking the loss of welfare benefits, including cash, health care, and housing assistance (Hubbard, Skinner, and Zeldes 1995; Ziliak 2003). There is evidence that "asset limits" in means-tested social programs may reduce asset holdings of the poor (Nam 2008).

In 2001, only 30 percent of households in the bottom quintile of income reported saving, a proportion that had declined in the previous 10 years (Aizcorbe, Kennickell, and Moore 2003; Belsky and Calder 2005). Despite generally low savings in poor households, some studies report that the poor want to save and already do set aside money for their families' well-being and security (Newton 1977; Furnham 1985; Kennickell, Starr-McCluer, and Surrette 2000; Hogarth and Anguelov 2003). Many recipients of the Earned Income Tax Credit (EITC), a tax credit for low-income families, plan to use this money as a tool for economic mobility (e.g., invest in education), as well as to make ends meet (Romich and Weisner 2000; Smeeding, Phillips, and O'Connor 2000). Researchers point to the widespread use of self-run saving and lending groups in poor communities in the United States and around the world as further evidence that even the poorest want to and have the capacity to save when provided appropriate financial instruments (Rutherford 2000, 2005; Matin, Hulme, and Rutherford 2002; Collins et al. 2009).

ORGANIZATION OF THE BOOK

Little research exists on how families with low incomes save and how successful they are in accumulating savings. We know even less about the impact that saving may have on their lives and those of their families. This book follows a group of people who signed up for an Individual Development Account (IDA). The 84 respondents whose experiences fill these pages signed up for an IDA in the hopes that it would help them accumulate some savings they could use to make progress in their lives.

What we learn from the 59 IDA participants and 25 nonparticipants, including Camille, challenges traditional assumptions that the poor do not want to or cannot save. The findings suggest ways to understand the economic lives of low-income and low-wealth individuals and families, and offer valuable insights into approaches for future policy, programs, and savings products that will help build assets in poor households.

The first part of the book explores the context for saving and the efforts of Camille and 83 others to save in the absence of a savings program. The latter part of the book analyzes what happened when some of these families entered a savings program, what difference it made in their lives, and what these findings mean for savings theory and public policy. Because they signed up for a voluntary savings program, respondents in this study may be more motivated to save than the average person in their financial position. They may possess greater motivation and have more personal and economic resources. However, it is also possible that most low-income people who participate in a structured savings plan would respond similarly. A test of universal savings would be necessary to establish how the low-income population as a whole would react.

Following this introduction, chapter 1 describes the American Dream Demonstration and details the features of IDAs. For readers interested in the study's research methods, the second part of the chapter describes the sampling, interview content and format, and data analysis for the in-depth interviews that form the basis of this book.

Chapter 2 reviews economic and institutional theory about why and how people save, especially in low-income households. We focus on the major strands of thinking about saving, including neoclassical economics, behavioral economics, and institutional theory and perspectives. The second half of the chapter reviews evidence on the impacts and implications of saving in low-income households. For readers who prefer to skip this chapter, a rather dense discussion of theory and evidence, there is a list of key questions at the end of the chapter.

Chapter 3 continues Camille's story and introduces Anne and some of the 82 other respondents, including Cynthia, a nonparticipant. It explores their growing up and coming of age in working-poor families. Many respondents grew up in financially stretched and sometimes unstable families, struggling to provide for their children. Respondents' schooling was often unrewarding and interrupted. As children, they learned little about household financial management and saving; their economic socialization focused on getting a job. Several left home and assumed financial independence at a very young age. With low levels of education, they tried to obtain decent jobs at a time when good jobs were disappearing from the American landscape. They encountered obstacles and made mistakes. Most respondents, with a few important exceptions, sought to gain an economic foothold in the adult world with few tangible resources from their families of origin.

Chapter 4 begins with the experiences of two respondents who discuss how they manage their household finances on low incomes: IDA participant Tonya and Ella, a nonparticipant. Turning to the whole sample, we find that with high expenses and low incomes, families tend to adopt a perspective that they will make it through hard times with faith and hard work. They try to be economical and cut back on unnecessary expenses, but they also borrow, use their savings, and scramble to earn more when they must.

Despite respondents' efforts to make ends meet and cover expenses with available income, some accumulated problem debt. Debt, the topic of chapter 5, absorbs resources and saps respondents' energy and future expectations. Beginning with Ella's and Becky's stories of debt, the chapter explores how low incomes and unexpected events contribute to problem debt. When families are in problem debt, they find it difficult to build a good credit record, and for some, debt forecasts difficulty in accumulating savings.

Chapter 6 continues Ella's story and introduces another participant, Debra, as well as a nonparticipant, LaVonne. The chapter explores how these three women managed to save and invest over their lifetimes, chronicling savings goals, types of savings, and families' efforts to save, including sources, strategies, and patterns of saving. Although the focus is on those respondents who did not participate in the IDA program, we also hear from some IDA participants who describe their saving before they joined the IDA program. They relate their frustrations and difficulties saving and discuss how they tried to save in ways that would accumulate over the long term.

In chapter 7, we turn to the experience of participants in the IDA program. Here we continue Theresa's and Becky's stories and introduce two other participants, Heather and Denise. These four women, and other IDA participants, discuss what attracted them to the IDA program and how they perceive its features.

In chapter 8, these four women and the other 55 IDA participants reveal how they earmarked money for saving, how they deposited it in their IDA, and how they struggled to avoid spending their IDA savings. They also discuss how the IDA program affected their ability to set money aside. The chapter concludes with a discussion of the major barriers to saving in an IDA.

Chapter 9 examines evidence for potential effects of saving and savings,[7] including effects on participants' families and children. Beginning with Heather, Denise, and Becky, the chapter discusses cognitive, psychological, and economic effects of saving in an IDA. These reactions provide a glimpse into the possible meaning of saving and asset accumulation in low-income households.

Finally, the conclusion returns to Camille and her dream of stability for herself and her five grandchildren. It also continues Cynthia's narrative. She articulates the hopes, dreams, and frustrations of many of the 84 families as they try to get ahead and build opportunities for themselves and their families. After summarizing the book's findings, we propose a conceptual model for how families with low incomes save, and discuss how saving affects them and their families. We discuss some of the debates that arise throughout the book about saving in low-income families and raise key challenges for savings programs. The chapter concludes with theoretical, policy, and research implications.

CHAPTER 1

Research on Matched Savings in Low-Income Households

Camille and the other 83 respondents whose stories fill the pages of this book participated in a large research experiment, called the American Dream Demonstration (ADD), the first large test of Individual Development Accounts (IDAs) in low-income households. IDAs are savings accounts for designated purposes, such as buying a first home, going to college, building a small business, or retirement. Participants with IDAs receive match incentives designed to encourage saving and build savings faster. People of all ages can participate in IDAs, including children. IDAs for children usually are known as children's development accounts (CDAs) or children's savings accounts (CSAs) (Goldberg 2005; NAF 2008). Typically, IDA participants receive financial education. Funding for IDA savings matches and program operations comes from a variety of public and private sources.

IDAs were introduced by Michael Sherraden (1988, 1991), who suggested that saving and asset accumulation are largely the result of structures and incentives, not just personal preferences. Furthermore, he proposed that assets might have a range of economic, social, and psychological impacts. Because of their potential to promote household development, Sherraden proposed that asset building, along with more traditional forms of social welfare such as income support, should be a cornerstone of public policy for the poor.

Currently, low-income households have low or negligible tax obligations and therefore do not benefit from subsidized asset-building policies, such as Individual Retirement Accounts (IRAs) or 401(k) plans. IDAs provide a subsidy through a savings match rather than through a tax break. IDAs are a relatively simple policy instrument and are adaptable to a wide range of applications and circumstances (Sherraden 2001).

HOW IDAS WORK

Because IDA program design varies, what follows is a description of IDAs at the large research site where this study took place. The IDA program administered through ADD provided a bundle of program features (Schreiner and Sherraden 2007).

- *Savings goal.* Participants received a savings match when they saved for any of the following investment options: retirement, postsecondary education, house purchase or repair, and business development.
- *Savings incentive.* Participants received a savings match of 1:1 for all purposes except for a house purchase, for which they received a 2:1 match. Participants could withdraw matched savings after their accounts had been open at least six months and they had completed all required financial education.
- *Financial education.* The program required a total of twelve hours (six classes) of money management training, with at least four hours prior to opening the IDA. Topics included budgeting, credit and debt management, credit repair, financial planning, and saving. In addition, the program required asset-specific training: two hours for postsecondary education and training, two hours for retirement, five hours for house purchase, and sixteen hours for business development.
- *Annual and lifetime match caps.* The annual match cap was $750. Participants could save more, but the program would not provide a match on the extra savings. The lifetime match cap for most purposes was $4,500. For those saving for a house, the lifetime match cap was $6,750.
- *Time cap.* Participants had three years in which to save and receive a savings match.
- *Minimum monthly deposits.* The program expected participants to deposit at least $10 a month for at least nine months a year, although they were encouraged to save more.
- *IDA account statements.* Participants received a monthly IDA account statement from the financial institution that held the account. They also received a quarterly account statement from the program showing both the savings deposited and the match dollars accrued.

- *Saving reminders.* If participants fell behind in making deposits, they received postcards and occasional phone call reminders.
- *Limits on savings withdrawals.* When participants withdrew their savings for any purpose other than the savings goal, their savings were not eligible for a match. They could withdraw their money (unmatched), but the program discouraged unmatched savings withdrawals and limited them to three per year (although staff were lax about the exact number).

ADD RESEARCH METHODS

ADD, which took place from 1997 through 2005, was organized by CFED, a policy, education, and advocacy organization based in Washington, DC, and was funded by a consortium led by the Ford Foundation (CFED 2007). ADD included one large experimental site where researchers compared IDA participants with similar people who were eligible but were not selected for the IDA program. ADD also included 13 small-scale sites scattered across the United States. Research at these sites did not include nonparticipants (Schreiner and Sherraden 2007).

Field research for this book took place at the experimental site, Community Action Project of Tulsa County (CAPTC). CAPTC, now known as CAP, is a community action program originally funded in the 1960s by the War on Poverty's Office of Economic Opportunity. In the ensuing years, CAP adopted a broad antipoverty and community development agenda. Services include health care, early childhood education, screening for public benefits, tax assistance, affordable housing, policy analysis, and advocacy. Many of the people participating in ADD (as participants and nonparticipants) had made use of these other services offered by CAPTC.

The research, designed by the Center for Social Development (CSD) at Washington University in St. Louis, aimed to understand asset accumulation in low-income households and to inform development of asset policy and programs (Sherraden, Page-Adams, and Johnson 1999; Schreiner and Sherraden 2007). Researchers used four principal research approaches: (1) survey interviews (Abt Associates 2004), (2) savings tracking (Johnson, Hinterlong, and Sherraden 2001), (3) cost analyses (Schreiner 2005), and (4) in-depth interviews.

All research participants were employed (full- or part-time) and had an adjusted gross household income that did not exceed 150 percent of the federal poverty level in 1998 (average income was 130 percent of the poverty level). Individuals were randomly assigned to either the treatment (IDA program) or the control condition. In total, 1,103 people enrolled, with 537 in the treatment group (456 actually opened IDAs) and the remaining 566 in the control group (Schreiner and Sherraden 2007). When respondents signed up for the IDA program, they were aware that they would be participating in research with multiple methods, including in-depth interviews. The Institutional Review Board at Washington University in St. Louis reviewed and approved all phases of the research.

Field research for this book was conducted at CAP using in-depth interviews. A detailed description of the methodology follows.

In-depth Interviews

Program data and surveys provide an overall assessment of accomplishments and shortcomings of IDAs in ADD. In-depth interviews are semistructured long interviews with fewer numbers of respondents. They provide a more detailed and reflective assessment of the experiences and perspectives of respondents toward saving, the IDA program, and other key details and nuances of their lives (Merton, Lowenthal, and Kendall 1990; Rubin and Rubin 1995; Schwartz 2006).

Sample. We interviewed 59 IDA participants and 25 nonparticipants. Throughout the book, we refer to those selected for the IDA program as "participants," to those not selected as "nonparticipants," and generically, to all those interviewed as "respondents." Interviews with nonparticipants help sort out effects of the IDA program from other influences.

The sampling frame for IDA participants totaled 223 participants who had an IDA account open for at least six months. We used a stratified sample to ensure a comparable number of low, medium, and high savers, as measured by average monthly deposits (AMD).[1] Low savers had an AMD ranging from $0 to $27 ($n = 18$). Middle savers had an AMD ranging from $28 to $63 ($n = 22$). High savers had an AMD ranging from $65 to $513 ($n = 18$). Median AMD of selected participants was $54, and the mean was $60.

In addition, we randomly selected 30 people from the entire group of 566 nonparticipants at CAP, and after reviewing the sample to match the population of participants in terms of gender and race, we conducted interviews with 25 nonparticipants. We also drew 10 "replacements" for each group, so that we could randomly select replacements who would match the gender and ethnicity of respondents we were unable to interview. In the end, 6 IDA participants and 6 nonparticipants came from the replacement groups.

The sample of people interviewed tended to be female and middle-aged (see table 1.1). (Appendixes A and B provide details about IDA participants and nonparticipants.) Six respondents were over the age of 60, including two in their 70s. Most respondents self-identified as White or African American. Smaller numbers self-identified as Hispanic/Latino/a, Asian, or Native American. There were seven immigrants from three continents. Reflecting larger trends, many participants (52) reported they had either been divorced or separated at some point in their life. As a result, some respondents lived in blended families with children from previous marriages.

For the most part, sample characteristics of IDA participants are similar to the demographic profile of the larger sample at CAP, although compared to the entire group, IDA participants in the in-depth interview study are more likely to be married, white, older, and male.

Research Protocol. Interviews took place during two weeks in July 2000 in the Tulsa, Oklahoma, metropolitan area. Approximately one month prior to the two-week interview period, respondents received letters describing interview content and length, confidentiality, and incentives. One week later, interviewers called respondents to schedule the interviews. These calls also aimed to dispel anxiety and increase willingness to participate. During the week of the scheduled interview, interviewers contacted each respondent once more.[2]

We paid each respondent $50 for participating, an amount intended to cover transportation costs and time, and gave each one a coupon (worth approximately $5) for a popular local ice cream parlor as a token of appreciation.

Interview Content and Format. Interviews explored saving—including the importance of early experiences, sources of savings, savings instruments, financial education, and so forth. We used a chronological approach, beginning with childhood. Specific topics included economic well-being, education, financial management (and banking experiences), and savings attitudes and behaviors beginning in childhood and extending to the present. Closed-ended questions at the end of the interview addressed current household expenses. For IDA participants, the second half of the interview delved into experiences in the IDA program, including program access and evaluation, savings patterns, sources of savings, planned uses, aspirations and expectations, and perceived outcomes. For nonparticipants, we modified the same questions to refer to other savings instruments and programs they might have used (see table 1.2 for main topics).

For the in-depth interview study, we refined the instrument that had been developed for 16 case studies at five other ADD research sites (Sherraden, Moore, and Hong 2000). We tested the instrument with a volunteer who was an IDA participant in another program site.

TABLE 1.1. Demographic Characteristics of In-Depth Interview Respondents

	IDA Participants (n = 59) n (%)	Nonparticipants (n = 25) n (%)	Total (N = 84) n (%)
Gender			
Female	43 (73)	21 (84)	64 (76)
Male	16 (27)	4 (16)	20 (24)
Age			
Under 20	1 (2)	0 (0)	1 (1)
20–29	8 (14)	7 (28)	15 (18)
30–39	14 (24)	11 (44)	25 (30)
40–49	27 (46)	1 (4)	28 (33)
50–59	5 (8)	4 (16)	9 (11)
60+	4 (7)	2 (8)	6 (7)
Race/Ethnicity			
African American	21 (36)	9 (36)	30 (36)
White	31 (53)	12 (48)	43 (51)
Hispanic/Latino/a	2 (3)	2 (8)	4 (5)
Asian American	2 (3)	0 (0)	2 (2)
Native American	2 (3)	1 (4)	3 (4)
Other	1 (2)	1 (4)	2 (2)
Marital status			
Never married	10 (17)	11 (44)	21 (25)
Married	24 (41)	10 (40)	34 (40)
Divorced/Separated	19 (32)	4 (16)	23 (27)
Widowed	6 (10)	0 (0)	6 (7)
Education			
Grade school, middle school, junior high	3 (5)	0 (0)	3 (4)
Some high school	1 (2)	3 (12)	4 (5)
High school degree or GED	13 (22)	2 (8)	15 (18)
Some college	22 (37)	11 (44)	33 (39)
Two-year college degree	9 (15)	2 (8)	11 (13)
Four-year college degree	6 (10)	4 (16)	10 (12)
Some graduate school	4 (7)	2 (8)	6 (7)
Graduate school degree	1 (2)	1 (4)	2 (2)

Source: Abt Associates baseline survey.

TABLE 1.2. In-Depth Interview Topics: Family of Origin, Young Adulthood, and Current Household

A. Socioeconomic and demographic profile
   Education
   Employment
   Income
   Public assistance
   Community context and involvement
   Family decision making
   Approach to socioeconomic and other challenges

B. Asset ownership
   Home ownership and other asset ownership
   Investment decisions and opportunities
   Financing asset accumulation

C. Financial issues
   Attitudes about money and money matters
   Financial management and decision making
   Respondent autonomy or support from family
   Financial services (informal and formal)
   Consumption and expenses
   Surplus
   Financial strain and challenges
   Financial education training or counseling

D. Saving in family of origin and respondent household
   Saving, patterns, and sources
   Saving goals
   Saving strategies
   When savings occurred and how much

E. IDA experience (IDA participants only)
   Information and access
   Decision process and reasons for participation
   IDA goals
   IDA saving, patterns, and sources (facilitating factors and obstacles)
   Social network obligations and reciprocity effects
   Alternative uses of money
   IDA economic education/financial management
   Perception and assessment of IDA program
   Perceived value of IDAs
   Program improvements and recommendations

F. Saving, asset accumulation, and IDA perceived effects
   Economic
   Personal (emotional, cognitive)
   Family
   Intergenerational
   Social and civic

Interviews provided direction to respondents but did not restrict responses to discrete categories (Merton, Loewenthal, and Kendall 1990; Rubin and Rubin 1995). This open-ended quality allowed respondents to address a question or to bring up other issues that they thought were more relevant. Each question had several open-ended follow-up questions that helped respondents understand the questions better and recall their actions and thoughts. We designed the interviews to build trust and elicit forthright responses about potentially sensitive topics (e.g., childhood memories, income, and saving strategies). Interviewers, who memorized most of the interview guide, encouraged respondents to explore topics and to feel comfortable bringing up other issues.

With these aims in mind, we selected interviewers—doctoral or masters students in social work—who could engage respondents, communicate effectively, and understand the goals and objectives of the research. Each interviewer participated in training and conducted additional trial interviews and a taped pilot interview with an IDA participant at another ADD program site. We provided feedback and guidance based on these pilots. Prior to interviewing, interviewers also attended orientation with CAP program staff where they learned more about the organization, the IDA program, and Tulsa's social and economic environment.

Data Analysis. Qualitative interviewing generates a large amount of data that is systematically reduced during the analysis phase. After transcribing the taped interviews,[3] we used ATLAS.ti, a qualitative software program, to help code and analyze the interview transcripts (Lewis 1998). For descriptive and analytic purposes, we enumerated some of the qualitative data (e.g., counted the numbers of participants who mentioned the utility of financial education) and entered them into SPSS, a statistical program. For descriptive purposes, we also occasionally used data on the same respondents from the Management Information System for IDAs (MIS IDA) and from the experimental design survey implemented by Abt Associates.[4]

Although primarily an inductive study, we derived the initial code list from ADD case studies and included concepts from existing empirical and theoretical research (see chap. 2) and ADD research questions and hypotheses (Sherraden 2002). For example, we used concepts in Sondra Beverly, Amanda McBride, and Mark Schreiner's (2003) article on "asset-accumulation stages and strategies" in the initial code list, although in the final analysis, we dropped some categories, and modified and elaborated others. In order to safeguard against bias and validity problems, we paid attention to descriptive, interpretive, theoretical, and evaluative validity, as well as generalizability (Maxwell 1992).

We expanded the initial code list using open coding (Strauss and Corbin 1998), basing the final code list on line-by-line coding. In this way, the initial code list was transformed. Each step in coding included interrater reliability checks (MacQueen et al. 1998) until codes and coding patterns were substantially similar (i.e., root codes were the same, although subcodes sometimes differed).

Five researchers, including the two authors, an interviewer, a CSD staff member intimately familiar with program operations, and a research assistant, coded all the interviews. We began by coding the same five interviews. Using ATLAS.ti to merge the coded interviews, we discussed similarities and differences, modified the list (e.g., added new codes, eliminated and merged others), and agreed on coding conventions. We followed this with four more waves of coding (one was done by all five coders, three by pairs of coders) and checking until all coders largely agreed on coding categories. Finally, one analyst read all interviews, merged duplicative codes, and ensured that we conformed to coding conventions throughout.

Using ATLAS.ti, we extracted families of codes that collectively addressed key questions and concepts. Working from a tentative outline, we exported them into a word processing program for review. We constructed matrices divided into the major substantive or conceptual categories by respondent case number (Miles and Huberman 1994). Depending on several factors—including the relevance of questions, depth and breadth of interview coverage, respondents' responsiveness, and thoroughness of coding—matrices varied in comprehensiveness. When code families generated too much data to manage effectively, we reduced the size of code families and began the process again.

In addition, we created respondent profiles, organized by research questions and key demographic variables, and added data from surveys and savings account monitoring (Lincoln and Guba 1985). Matrices revealed themes and patterns across interviews, while profiles provided a way to check codes and categories against the coherence of respondents' actual life stories and experiences.

The matrices, profiles, and other material generated in these processes provide the raw material for the analyses in the chapters that follow. Prior to turning to the experiences of the 84 respondents in this study, we turn in the next chapter to a review of what we know about saving in low-income households.

CHAPTER 2

Theory and Evidence on Saving in Low-Income Households

Over the years, Camille and other respondents repeatedly tried to save, sometimes successfully, but often with little success. What do theory and existing research tell us about their efforts? Three approaches suggest economic, psychological, cognitive, and institutional factors that influence saving patterns and asset accumulation in poor households.

This chapter summarizes how theories of saving inform saving and asset accumulation in low-income households.[1] As noted in the introduction, the poor tend to have low levels of saving and asset holdings. The percentage gap in net worth between low- and upper-income households is growing wider, with similar disparities in wealth across ethnic and racial groups in the United States. We turn to theories and empirical studies of saving for explanations for low wealth in poor households.

In the second half of the chapter, we explore asset effects including the implications of saving and owning savings on people's well-being and development. In this section, we examine possible economic, psychological, cognitive, and social effects of assets.

The chapter concludes with research questions that guide the analysis in this book. What can we learn from Camille, and the other 83 respondents who participated in the American Dream Demonstration, that may shed light on why and how the poor save and the difference that saving and owning assets may make in their lives?

THEORIES OF SAVING AND ASSET ACCUMULATION

Beginning with the dominant views on saving from neoclassical economic theory, we turn next to behavioral economics to explore the possible influence of psychological and cognitive limitations on saving. Together, neoclassical economics and behavioral economics focus on the individual and the decision to save or spend. Finally, we look at how social institutions also help to shape individual decisions and outcomes related to saving and asset accumulation.

Neoclassical Economics and Saving by the Poor

Neoclassical economic theories assume that individuals behave rationally to maximize their utility by using their economic resources, including income and assets, to consume. Savings are considered delayed consumption; people save today so that they can spend later. In deciding whether to consume today or save for tomorrow, people seek stable consumption levels across their lifetime.

This last notion reflects the predominant model of saving, the life-cycle hypothesis (LCH) (Modigliani and Brumberg 1954), which suggests that people rationally determine how much they can consume over the remainder of their lives and smooth their consumption accordingly, taking their assets and future earnings into account. As Nyhus and Webley (2006) explain, "In any given year the difference between this level of consumption and income will be the amount saved (or the amount borrowed)" (308). As a result, over a lifetime, saving looks like an inverted U-shape (Harrod 1948). When people are young and have low incomes, they borrow; when they are middle-aged, they have higher incomes and save the surplus; and when they are old and their incomes decline, they spend their savings to pay for consumption.

Similar to the life-cycle hypothesis, Friedman's (1957) permanent income hypothesis suggests that people base their saving on an understanding of their mean permanent income and "life plan" (Douglas and Isherwood 1978, 49). Fluctuations in income and consumption are handled by saving during flush years and borrowing during slump years. Further, if people think their income is rising permanently, they will increase their standard for consumption, but if they think the increase is temporary, they will save the surplus.

According to neoclassical economics, income is an important determinant of saving. Low incomes support limited consumption, and so the cost of saving (i.e., forgone consumption) is high. Even when income increases somewhat, the relatively high cost of saving means that poor households are likely to consume rather than save the increase (Tin 2000). Nonetheless, the poor may save small amounts for short-term reasons, according to economic theory. Instead of saving for retirement, as the LCH suggests, the poor may save for precautionary purposes—to cover short income declines, for example, or unexpected expenses (Hubbard, Skinner, and Zeldes 1994, 1995). Some scholars propose that low-income people aim to have contingency funds or "buffer stocks" (Hrung 2002). Accordingly, people set target saving amounts for these emergency funds. Once they meet these targets, they are unlikely to save more (Carroll 1992; Deaton 1992; Carroll, Dynan, and Krane 1999).

Behavioral Economics and Saving by the Poor

Some economists (and economic psychologists) observe that people tend to behave less rationally than predicted by neoclassical theory (Simon 1957; Maital 1982; Lea and Webley 2005). It may be unrealistic to assume that people have much understanding of future income flows, prices, household consumption, and life span. To make this point, Richard Thaler writes that the LCH assumes that most people have the ability to "in any year compute the present value of your wealth, including current income, net assets, and future income; figure out the level annuity you could purchase with that money; then consume the amount you would receive if you in fact owned such an annuity" (1990, 193–94). While the LCH and PIH assume that individuals act rationally and maintain self-control as they plan their spending and saving over a lifetime, in reality, people's spending is likely to be strongly influenced by *current* income (Maital and Maital 1993, 1994).

Behavioral economic explanations attempt to bring together aspects of economics and psychology in an effort to better understand and predict economic behavior, including saving (Maital 1982; Tversky and Kahneman 1986; Wärneryd 1999). We next describe issues identified by behavioral economists to help explain saving behavior. These include psychological and cognitive limitations that affect saving and ways that people overcome and compensate for these limitations. Behavioral economics has not focused on explaining saving in poor households, but there is no reason to believe that people across the income and wealth spectrums behave in fundamentally different ways. Thus, we describe how behavioral economic theory might help explain limited saving in low-income households.

Psychological and Cognitive Limitations That Affect Saving. When people save, they are choosing to set aside money that they could spend today. Neoclassical economics assumes that people have a preference for current consumption and that future consumption is worth less; in other words, people discount saving for the future relative to spending now (Fisher 1930). Saving requires self-control, which behavioral economists suggest is difficult. However, while people prefer to spend today, they also try to control this tendency toward impulsiveness (Ainslie and Haslam 1992). Richard Thaler and Hersh Shefrin (1981) use metaphors to explain these two coexisting preferences: a "doer" who is a myopic or impulsive consumer and a "planner" who intends to save for the future (see also Schelling 1984; Shefrin and Thaler 1992).[2] The planner finds it easiest to restrict the choices of the doer through external controls and rules rather than through internal willpower, which people often lack.

Another cognitive factor that contributes to the difficulty people have in saving is loss aversion, or a human tendency to judge losses as more significant than gains (Kahneman and Tversky 1979). Loss aversion complicates saving decisions because it means that people find it very difficult to set aside savings in the present; in other words, even though funds will be available in the future, a person feels the pain of saving now more than they feel the joy of seeing their savings increase (Tversky and Kahneman 1986).

People also have a tendency to procrastinate, which contributes to the tendency to spend rather than save (Akerlof 1991). As Amos Tversky and Eldar Shafir write, "It is difficult to overestimate the significance of the tendency to delay decisions. Many things never get done not because someone has chosen not to do them, but because the person has chosen not to do them *now*" (1992, 361).

How Do People Overcome Limited Self-Control and a Tendency to Procrastinate? People adopt conscious and unconscious strategies to help them assert self-control and overcome procrastination.[3] People, for example, tend to think about and treat money in different ways. The likelihood of saving according to behavioral economists, is not the same for all types of money. In this way, money is not as "fungible," or fully exchangeable, as once assumed. Hersh Shefrin and Richard Thaler (1988) propose that people mentally divide income sources into separate "accounts." People think about these mental accounts differently, and "frame" or describe them in different ways that affect the likelihood of spending each (Tversky and Kahneman 1981; Lea, Tarpy, and Webley 1987; Shefrin and Thaler 1988; Zelizer 1989; Levin 1998).

What are the different accounts? In a simplified model, Hersh Shefrin and Richard Thaler (1992) suggest that individuals assign money to three mental accounts: current income (such as wage income), current assets (such as current discretionary savings), and future income (such as savings for a child's education or future retirement income).[4] Shefrin and Thaler (1988, 1992) also suggest that people are most tempted to spend out of the current-income account and less tempted to spend from assets and future-income accounts.

Different mental accounts may help people overcome problems of self-control and resist the temptation to spend (Kahneman and Tversky 1979; Shefrin and Thaler 1988; Thaler 1985; Xiao and Olson 1993). For example, people are more likely to save windfall income (e.g., an insurance settlement, lottery winning, end-of-year bonus, extraordinary investment return) when they assign it to an asset account than to a current income account. Poor people, like the wealthy, seem to understand this. As Romich and Weisner (2000) suggest, people with very low incomes often choose the lump-sum earned-income tax credit over the advance-payment option and view it as a separate account destined for large purchases and for saving.

In addition to mental accounts, people similarly often choose to separate their money into different physical accounts. David Laibson (1997) suggests that people are less likely to spend savings that are in illiquid forms. When invested in a retirement fund or in home equity, for example, people are less likely to withdraw savings to pay for current consumption. In fact, Laibson (1997) observes, people often persist in investing in the long-term asset even during periods of financial need. This helps to explain the counterintuitive finding that people accumulate illiquid savings even when they have credit card debt (Laibson, Repetto, and Tobacman 2003).

Sometimes people precommit to saving or investing money in ways that prevent them from being able to spend it (Laibson, Repetto, and Tobacman 1998). As Richard Thaler notes, "In real life, people realize that self-control is difficult, and so they take steps to constrain their future behavior" (1992b, 109). People do this by taking "irreversible" actions that restrict and guide their actions to help them maintain self-control and thwart procrastination (Thaler 1992b, 109; Tversky and Kahneman 1981; Akerlof 1991). One type of irreversible action is signing a savings contract that directs income from current consumption to a savings or investment vehicle, such as a home mortgage, car, or insurance (Katona 1975; Maital and Maital 1994). This type of contractual savings arrangement, according to George Katona (1975), helps people accumulate savings without individual effort (beyond the effort required to set up the arrangement).

To what extent do low-income households use mental accounting, and especially physical accounting and precommitment constraints to help themselves save? Several factors make it more difficult for the poor to capture savings in the ways just described. First, when income is irregular and comes in cash forms, such as tips, payments for odd jobs, and sales commissions, it is more difficult to convert into savings using contractual savings plans (O'Curry 1999; Beverly, McBride, and Schreiner 2003). For example, when a person is paid in cash, direct deposit—a key method in contractual saving—is not possible. Second, even when people (including many nonpoor) commit themselves to saving, the spread of easy credit, such as credit cards and home equity loans, may encourage people to separate the pleasure of buying from the pain of paying, making it more difficult to follow self-imposed constraints (Maital and Maital 1994).

Finally, people in low-wage employment typically do not have access to precommitment mechanisms like contractual savings plans such as 401(k)s. Instead, they turn to other ways to commit to saving their money. These include signing up for a Christmas club savings plan, buying on installment (Caplovitz 1967; Webley and Nyhus 2001), purchasing a house or other property, and deliberately overpaying income taxes to receive a lump-sum refund later (Neumark 1995; Laibson, Repetto, and Tobacman 1998; Romich and Weisner 2000). Unfortunately, these approaches to saving require considerable effort on the part of low-income families, and the financial payoff (e.g., interest rate) is not as beneficial in comparison to savings plans that are available to wealthier families.

Individuals, Households, and Society

Economic models typically assume an individual decision maker, but in reality, spending and saving decisions often occur in the context of households, cultures, and societies (Pahl 1989). Households, for example, consist of individuals of unequal decision-making power engaged in cooperation and in conflict (Folbre 1988; Lackman and Lanasa 1993). In contrast to an assumption of a cohesive family unit with an "altruistic male" head (Becker 1981), research on gender and household finance suggests that household members negotiate decision making and resource distribution (Berk and Berk 1983; Pahl 1989; Curtis 1986; Winnett and Lewis 1995). Bargaining power, according to feminist theory, is based in part on perceived economic contributions of members of the household (Folbre 1988). Empirical studies of lower-income households suggest that women are more likely than men to manage time-consuming day-to-day financial matters and less likely to be making larger financial decisions (Vogler and Pahl 1994; Pahl 1995). Moreover, gender roles and patterns of household financial decision making are changing, further complicating our understanding of economic behavior (Buss and Schaninger 1983).

Although most research on household financial decision making focuses on managing income and consumption, some examines saving and asset accumulation. Dalton Conley and Miriam Ryvicker, for example, find that women have lower net worth than men do, controlling for such factors as income, education, age, marital status, and number of children. They surmise that women are less able to save because of higher expenses (Conley and Ryvicker 2005). In a study of saving in Britain, Adrian Furnham reports that more women save than men, and that women are more likely to save for old age, children's education, holidays, and health care (1985, 367). Overall, we know relatively little about the effects of gender on household decision making and saving.

Traditional economic theory gives little attention to culture, socialization, values, and saving habits, despite considerable evidence that these phenomena matter (Maital and Maital 1994). In a summary of research on saving among the poor, Emily Lawrance assumes that culture and class of one's birth make the poor less future-oriented and more "impatient." Income constraints influence the poor as does a culture of "present-oriented behavior" (Lawrance 1987, 462; 1991). This suggests parallels to culture-of-poverty explanations for poverty (e.g., Lewis 1959). Skeptics of this thesis point out that impatience and present orientation among the poor are "a rational reaction to the expected high uncertainty of returns" because they lack a resource buffer (Sørensen 2000, 1539).

Others look more broadly at historical, social, and economic circumstances that may affect the way individuals save (Douglas and Isherwood 1978). For example, wealthier groups may have greater patience and be more future-oriented because they are more likely to benefit from unexpected wealth gains and better lending rates (Dynan 1993; Carney and Gale 2001). Paul Webley and colleagues suggest that "normative and ideological pressures, institutional arrangements, class, race, locality, and state of the local economy" affect saving (2001, 153). Newton (1977) suggests that the poor are likely to save when delay of gratification and self-control are related to control of one's life and ability to predict the future. Sociologists, for instance, suggest that racial discrimination and its myriad effects affect household saving, resulting in substantial inequities in wealth holding (Oliver and Shapiro 1995; Keister 2000a).

Sociologists further observe that the way people view money, including the mental accounts to which they assign their money, is embedded in organizations, culture, and social structure (Douglas and Isherwood 1978). As Bruce Carruthers explains,

Money is classified (budgetarily, normatively, or cognitively) into different categories, and these disrupt the fungibility of money. . . . Monetary distinctions reflect larger cultural distinctions and organizational commitments. The strength of these boundaries and the vigilance with which they must be maintained (e.g., sharp distinctions between "clean" and "dirty" money, or between monies earmarked for different budget items) derive from the underlying fungibility of modern money. *Modern money is not special money, so people have to make it special.* (Carruthers 2005, 369, emphasis added)

The meaning of money depends on where money comes from (e.g., "dirty" vs. "clean" money, earnings vs. windfalls) and where it goes (Rainwater, Coleman, and Handel 1959; Zelizer 1989; Carruthers and Espeland 1998; Carruthers 2005). In historical research, Viviana Zelizer (1994) finds that families treat "women's money," such as "pin money," differently than "men's money." These ideas further challenge the concept of perfect fungibility, a foundation of rational economic theory, and suggest a more complex and broader array of historical, economic, political, social, and cultural factors that affect how people spend and save money.

Institutions and Saving by the Poor

Thus far, we have identified several key influences on saving by the poor. Neoclassical economic theory suggests that the poor are unlikely to save other than precautionary savings; the cost of saving is high because they have low incomes. We also know that official data show low savings in low-income households. Nonetheless, we know that even in the poorest households in the world, the poor do save: for emergencies, for life-cycle needs, and also for opportunities (Rutherford 2000; Matin, Hulme, and Rutherford 2002; Collins et al. 2009). Qualitative evidence from the United States also suggests that the poor do accumulate some forms of assets and believe they are important to well-being (Edin 2001; Shapiro and Johnson 2005; Scanlon and Adams 2009).

Behavioral economists observe that people develop rules of thumb to set aside savings and they make commitments that help them save. They use mental accounting and framing techniques to counteract a desire to spend. In the United States, some may sign up for contractual savings plans that help them with savings deposits, although, as we note earlier, the poor are less likely to have access to beneficial contractual savings plans. It is possible that if savings programs were in place to help the poor save—to capture these flows, and make them more productive—people would respond positively (Schreiner and Sherraden 2007). Yet we have also noted that savings plans for the poor would have to address problems of low and volatile income, cash wages, and access to easy credit.

Further, the ability to accumulate savings is not simply an individual decision, as mentioned previously. Household gender relations and culture may complicate saving in ways that individual explanations do not take into account. Social institutions and the organizations that make them up give shape and meaning to human behavior (Hall and Taylor 1996). As Walter Powell and Paul DiMaggio explain, "Institutions do not just constrain options: they establish the very criteria by which people discover their preferences" (1991, 11). As a result, writes Samuel Bowles, "seemingly small differences in institutions can make large differences in outcomes" (2004, 124).

In saving by the poor, institutions may make a large difference. In his 1991 book *Assets and the Poor*, Michael Sherraden emphasizes that "asset accumulations are primarily the result of institutionalized mechanisms involving explicit connections, rules, incentives, and subsidies" (1991, 116). In a later publication, Mark Schreiner and Michael Sherraden underscore the importance of institutions, noting that they "shape rules of thumb and matter for behavior far beyond what economic theory predicts because the process of completely rational choice is too costly" (2007, 32; see also Bernheim 1991). Institutions influence saving behavior without requiring people to exert as much self-control and willpower. As behavioral economists suggest, a structure for saving significantly reduces the psychological cost of saving (Thaler and Shefrin 1981). People still have agency because institutions do not fully determine individual behavior. However, institutions make certain choices more desirable, more predictable, and more likely to facilitate opportunity. In this way, institutions structure choices by providing resources for the purposeful action of self-interested actors (Knight 1992).

Some scholars note that the bulk of asset accumulation in middle-class American households, for example, does not occur as a result of individual decisions to save in a savings account. Instead, these savings are the result of contractual agreements. When middle-class people buy a home, they simultaneously build home equity and receive a substantial tax subsidy to do so. Automatic monthly deductions from a bank account require little individual effort, and at tax time, the home mortgage tax deduction provides a subsidy for home ownership. Saving also occurs when employees enroll in an employment-based retirement plan that takes advantage of a government subsidy for retirement, creating "new opportunities for exercising self discipline" (Bernheim 1991, 71). Policies may also affect the decision to spend (and not save). For example, lack of regulation in the consumer credit industry may encourage borrowing too much, "tempting individuals to invade certain mentally 'reserved' accounts in order to spend" (Bernheim 1991, 71; see also Laibson 1997; Stegman and Faris 2003). Contractual savings plans represent institutional and often subsidized public policies, not simply individual preferences for saving or dissaving.

Institutional Dimensions

Although traditional economic theory holds that saving rates increase with income and expectations of more income over time, this theory generally has not paid much attention to low-income savers (Beverly and Sherraden 1999; Sherraden, Schreiner, and Beverly 2003). Institutional theory explicitly attempts to explain saving in low-income households.

As social psychologists point out, situational factors shape and constrain behavior (Ross and Nisbett 1991). Social and economic "channels" form the sociological context within which individuals act, and can direct behaviors in consequential ways, according to Kurt Lewin (1951, 185–86). An example is 401(k) contractual retirement savings plans that make saving automatic once savers are enrolled. Institutional theory suggests that a variety of institutional supports, including automatic deductions, help people save. It also calls attention to the fact that low-income households currently have limited access to these supports. The poor, after all, are less likely to be working at a company that offers a 401(k) plan, and even when a company offers such a plan, the poor are less able to take advantage of it.

Sherraden and colleagues propose seven institutional constructs that shape saving and asset accumulation, including access, security, information, incentives, facilitation, expectations, and restrictions (Sherraden 1991; Beverly and Sherraden 1999; Sherraden, Schreiner, and Beverly 2003; Sherraden and Barr 2005; Schreiner and Sherraden 2007; Beverly et al. 2008).[5] The first six are expected to increase saving, while the last one, by definition, constrains use of accumulated savings (Sherraden, Schreiner, and Beverly 2003, 97). The following sections describe each of these constructs and present examples of empirical evidence related to their impact on saving in low-income households.

Access. Access refers to the ability and right that people have to approach, enter, use, and communicate with an institution. An individual with access to institutional structures for saving is more likely to save than a person who has no such access. A historical perspective of savings policies in the United States shows that while the wealthy are connected to saving institutions and subsidies, the poor, especially racial and ethnic minorities and women, are not (Furnham 1985; Sherraden 1991). The poor are less likely than the middle class and wealthy to have access to automatic payroll transfer between places of employment and financial institutions. They lack access to inexpensive banking services, and they often rely on costly alternative financial services or relatively low-return informal financial arrangements (Caskey 1994; Matin, Hulme, and Rutherford 1999; Jacob, Hudson, and Bush 2000; Barr 2004).

Security. Security means that people's savings are safe. At the macro level, savings are less vulnerable in a growing and stable economy with low inflation risk, and a stable political context with low levels of corruption (Beverly et al. 2008). At a micro level, savings are secure when there is less risk of property loss (such as theft and mishandling) and investment risk (such as low rates of return) (Beverly et al. 2008). In this sense, security is related to institutional legitimacy and the historical relationship between financial institutions and low-income populations. While security may be of greater concern in poor countries (Rutherford 2000), these are significant issues in the United States, especially in minority communities that have been exploited by financial institutions (Oliver and Shapiro 1995; Keister 2000b; Squires, 2004).

Incentives. Incentives are the subsidies, financial returns, and nonfinancial rewards for saving. Economic and psychological theory and empirical research suggest that people respond positively to incentives. Tversky and Kahneman (1986, S274) explain, "Incentives do not operate by magic: they work by focusing attention and by prolonging deliberation." In the case of saving, incentives are usually financial (Sherraden, Schreiner, and Beverly 2003, 98).

Saving subsidies build savings directly (such as an IDA or a 401(k) savings match) and indirectly (such as a home mortgage tax deduction, which could be deposited in savings). The financial return to saving—or the rate of interest—is another type of incentive to save.

Some argue that saving incentives might encourage saving among affluent individuals but not among the poor. According to this view, the poor have different cultures, attitudes, and capacity for delayed gratification and therefore might not respond to incentives in the same way that wealthier people do (Lawrance 1987). In contrast, institutional theory suggests that existing saving incentives do not benefit poor households. The poor do not earn enough to benefit from most tax incentives, for example, and when they do, the returns are low (Beverly and Sherraden 1999). People with low incomes are less likely to benefit from other tax subsidies that result in substantial savings accumulation among the nonpoor, such as those incorporated into Individual Retirement Accounts (IRAs), 401(k) plans, and 529 college savings plans (Sherraden 1991; Abramovitz 2001). The poor are also less likely to enjoy tax benefits associated with home ownership, because they are less likely to own a home (Pratt 1986; Green and White 1997), and even if they are home owners, they are in a lower marginal tax bracket, making the subsidy worth little or perhaps nothing. Moreover, those living in low-income neighborhoods tend to receive lower rates of return on their home investments. In general, the poor reap lower returns on their generally smaller investments (Beverly and Sherraden 1999).

IDAs offer a high rate of return on deposits (typically one-to-one or two-to-one). Economists note this can have contradictory effects on saving (Thaler 1992a). On one hand, a savings match could increase saving because people may be motivated to take advantage of the incentive and to accumulate more than they otherwise could have. On the other hand, a savings match could decrease saving because individuals can achieve a savings goal by relying on the match to double or triple their accumulations (Bernheim and Scholz 1993). Moreover, incentives—such as tax subsidies or a savings match—may encourage "shifting" of assets from one savings vehicle to another to take advantage of an attractive incentive (Venti and Wise 1992; Hubbard and Skinner 1996; Schreiner and Sherraden 2007).

There is no consensus on whether generous subsidies actually increase savings, but existing empirical research seems to suggest that higher match rates increase participation and contributions in saving programs, even among low-income populations (Duflo et al. 2005; Beverly et al. forthcoming). The effect on net savings is less clear—because people may shift funds from another savings vehicle (Choi et al. 2004; Schreiner and Sherraden 2007, 216–17). Although more research is required to gauge the extent of asset shifting in response to incentives, low-income households are unlikely to have large stocks of wealth to shift from. Limited evidence from IDAs suggests that at least some of the savings are new and that the match increases both participation and deposits (Moore et al. 2001; Schreiner and Sherraden 2007).

The other side of the coin is disincentives, or factors that discourage and punish saving. Poor rates of return may discourage saving. Social policy may also deter saving among the poor. For example, asset tests for means-tested social assistance preclude saving above certain levels, imposing a ceiling on savings and asset holdings (Gruber and Yelowitz 1997; Edin 2001). One review of research in the post-1996 welfare reform era shows an inverse relationship between asset limits and wealth holdings of lower-income households. The authors conclude that "asset tests under [the] means-tested benefit represent perhaps the steepest implicit tax on retirement saving imposed by the federal government" (McDonald, Orszag, and Russell n.d., 7). Contributing to the problems, poor families may underestimate asset limits and, as a result, set low savings goals (Marlowe, Godwin, and Maddux 1996). Asset limits in other types of programs, such as for financial aid for college, may also be a disincentive for saving (Feldstein 1995). Overall, asset tests appear to reduce saving among the poor (Hubbard, Skinner, and Zeldes 1995). Although some dispute the negative impact of asset limits (Ziliak 2003; Hurst and Ziliak 2006), further analysis suggests that easing asset tests encourages financial asset accumulation and owning bank accounts (Nam 2008).

Information. Financial information may encourage people to enroll in savings plans and make better decisions regarding spending and saving. Those who have knowledge and understanding about the saving process and outcomes may be more likely to take advantage of opportunities presented to them and to increase their savings level (Smeeding, Phillips, and O'Connor 2000; Sherraden, Schreiner, and Beverly 2003).

While traditional economic theory suggests that people are rational optimizers and will learn when presented with information, behavioral economists are more skeptical. They suggest that real people are "quasi-rational," trying but not necessarily getting it quite right (Thaler 2000, 136). People tend to make financial decisions, writes B. Douglas Bernheim, "by extremely rough rules of thumb" (1994, 63). Information improves this ability. Education and early socialization for saving may affect people's ability to delay gratification and exercise self-control. Bernheim, Garrett, and Maki (2001), for example, find that people who received financial education and used a bank account in childhood report saving more than others as adults. Ellen Nyhus and Paul Webley (2006) find that parent saving, discussing financial matters with children, and future orientation also affect children's economic behavior during childhood and adulthood. Nonetheless, according to behavioral economists, information will not create a rational human being, and lack of financial knowledge by itself does not explain low rates of saving (Bernheim 1994, 1996).

Existing research suggests that financial knowledge, especially among the poor and among those with less education, is relatively low (Bernheim and Scholz 1993; Bernheim 1998; Hilgert, Hogarth, and Beverly 2003; OECD 2003; Mandell 2004). However, some evidence suggests that financial education increases knowledge and confidence in financial decision making among the poor and nonpoor. For example, in one study with a nationally representative sample, financial behaviors are associated with positive financial practices, including saving (Hilgert, Hogarth, and Beverly 2003). In other studies, there are indications that financial knowledge among low-income people increases with financial education and counseling, although there is variation depending on demographic characteristics and teaching methods (Hogarth and Swanson 1995; Shelton and Hill 1995; DeVaney et al. 1996; Grable and Joo 1999; Hirad and Zorn 2001; Braunstein and Welch 2002). In IDA programs and other matched savings programs, financial education is associated with financial knowledge and increased saving (Anderson, Zhan, and Scott 2004; Shockey and Seiling 2004; Rohe, Gorham, and Quercia 2005; Zhan, Anderson, and Scott 2006; Fry et al. 2008). In particular, some studies have found that each hour of financial education up to ten hours is associated with increased savings (Clancy, Grinstein-Weiss, and Schreiner 2001; Schreiner, Clancy, and Sherraden 2002; Schreiner and Sherraden 2007).

There is also some limited evidence that financial education may increase savings. For example, people who graduated from high school in states that mandate financial education are more likely to save and have higher net worth as young adults (Bernheim, Garrett, and Maki 2001). Another study found that employer-sponsored seminars on retirement increase assets in low-wealth and low-education samples (Lusardi 2000).

The role of information on saving is generally underresearched. Studies in this area, with few exceptions, are not rigorous enough to yield firm conclusions and often do not include low-income consumers (Bell and Lerman 2005; Hogarth 2006; Lyons, Chang, and Scherpf 2006; U.S. Department of Treasury 2006). Further, causality is difficult to determine; that is, more knowledge may lead to improved financial behavior, or more financial experience may lead to greater knowledge (Hilgert, Hogarth, and Beverly 2003; Bell and Lerman 2005). Finally, despite the potential benefits of financial information, there are time, energy, and financial costs to education. These costs may be especially salient for the poor (Romich and Weisner 2000), who often lack access to beneficial financial services (Dixon 2006; Watson 2006; Johnson and Sherraden 2007).

Facilitation. Savings plans that assist people with saving make it easier to save. Through mechanisms like automatic enrollment, automatic payroll deduction, and other forms of assistance, facilitation counteracts the human tendencies to spend and to procrastinate (Sherraden, Schreiner, and Beverly 2003, 97). From a behavioral economics perspective, facilitation is a key concept because it reduces the willpower required to save and introduces a structured way for an individual to impose self-control. In other words, individuals exert less effort to save with facilitation than they do when saving on their own. As behavioral economists and economic psychologists might say, facilitation reduces the cost of choosing future gain over current pleasure (Maital 1982; Maital and Maital 1994; Shefrin and Thaler 1988).

Automatic deposits into savings, a form of precommitment, is a key way to facilitate saving. A retirement plan, for example, in which employee earnings are automatically deducted from payroll and transferred into a savings instrument "produces saving at no psychic cost" (Thaler and Shefrin 1981, 399). Because deposits are automatically deducted from employees' paychecks, savings accumulate with little individual effort.

Default enrollment, where employees are automatically enrolled in a default savings plan unless they "opt out" or choose alternative investments, is another form of facilitation. Research has shown that the percentage of employees in a 401(k) plan dramatically increases under automatic enrollment, and that fewer employees have a zero balance (Choi, Laibson, and Madrian 2004; see also Thaler and Benartzi 2004). It takes great willpower and foresight to enroll in a savings program and make investment choices, and people find it easier to take the "path of least resistance" offered by the default plan (Madrian and Shea 2001; Choi et al. 2004, 2006). Lower-wage workers may be most affected by automatic enrollment because they are the least likely to sign up for savings programs on their own (Choi et al. 2004).

Unfortunately, there is also a strong tendency for people to remain in a default plan, even when it is a "bad default" (Madrian and Shea 2001; Choi et al. 2004, 2005).[6] Research findings, therefore, suggest that facilitation may have drawbacks as well as benefits, depending on how plans are implemented. Further, findings reveal the importance of transparency of processes and outcomes when defaults are used (along with financial education, as discussed earlier).

Even when there is a well-designed savings option for the poor, some may not participate because they are not comfortable making the financial decisions participation requires. People may perceive savings programs as threatening, stigmatizing, or confusing (Bertrand, Mullainathan, and Shafir 2004). "Small situational barriers" may reduce saving, especially by people with low incomes, who may be particularly uncomfortable making plan choices (Bertrand, Mullainathan, and Shafir 2004, 420). Facilitating factors, however, such as default options, simplicity, education, loans, and assistance may counteract barriers and inaction resulting from information overload, uncertainty, and emotional discomfort (Tversky and Shafir 1992; Choi et al. 2004; Choi, Laibson, and Madrian 2005; Botti and Iyendar 2006, 29).

We know relatively little about the impact of facilitation on saving in low-income populations; there have been few efforts to extend saving opportunities to the poor (Sherraden, Schreiner, and Beverly 2003). There is no reason to believe (without evidence) that poor people are less likely than others to respond to facilitation. In fact, some evidence suggests that the poor will respond. For example, millions of low-income families count on an EITC lump-sum refund for consumption and investment (Romich and Weisner 2000; Smeeding, Phillips, and O'Connor 2000). In IDA research, direct deposit into savings is associated with saving and a higher deposit frequency, although only a small percentage of participants chose or had access to this service (Grinstein-Weiss, Zhan, and Sherraden 2004; Grinstein-Weiss, Wagner, and Ssewamala 2006; Schreiner and Sherraden 2007, 228).

Expectations. Expectations set rules, norms, or goals related to participation in a savings program.[7] For example, IDA programs often ask participants to make minimum deposits every month. In this case, the expectation is explicit. Savings plans establish expectations in a number of other ways, too, and sometimes the expectations are implicit or even unintended.

For example, many savings plans have match caps, limits on the amount of personal deposits that will be matched. Researchers have found that people often turn these match caps into savings targets. When IDA participants face a match cap of $750 a year, for instance, data suggest they set their own annual savings target at that amount (Schreiner and Sherraden 2007, 220; Fry et al. 2008). Research on saving among the nonpoor also suggests that people have a tendency to see match caps set by a program (which in traditional economic theory are considered limits) as savings targets (Choi et al. 2004, 2005). Scholars have proposed that people "anchor" on a value that is provided to them because it helps economize decision making (Tversky and Kahneman 1974).

Time caps—limits on the time period when deposits will be matched or even allowed—also establish a time expectation for saving. Establishing time caps for saving in poor households is complex. On one hand, people may delay making savings deposits unless there is a time cap, especially in income-constrained households. On the other hand, people with low incomes may not have surpluses to save within a certain period and may need additional time to make deposits.

There is limited empirical evidence regarding the effect of expectations on saving. Case study interviews suggest that low-income IDA participants refer to program expectations when they talk about what helps them save (Sherraden, Moore, and Hong 2000). Research on 401(k) participation, for example, has shown that expected contribution rates and built-in increases in these expected contribution rates have bigger effects on savings contributions than do incentives (Choi, Laibson, and Madrian 2004).

Restrictions. Restrictions refer to limits on access and use of savings. In accord with behavioral economics, which suggests people have difficulty with self-control, restrictions help strengthen the saver's resolve to protect savings. Plans may enforce restrictions through rules that limit the type or frequency of withdrawals. For instance, withdrawals from 529 college savings plans can be used only to pay for education costs to qualified colleges. IDA programs permit withdrawals, but a withdrawal is matched only if the participant uses it for an approved purpose. This may encourage people to think carefully before dissaving, and it also may highlight choices, such as retirement security, house purchase, or higher education, that people may not have otherwise considered (Schreiner and Sherraden 2007, 34). Savings programs also may enforce restrictions through penalties on withdrawals, such as fees.

In qualitative research, people talk about the importance of keeping their savings safely out of the way where they cannot easily reach them (Kennickell, Starr-McCluer, and Sundén 1997; Kempson, Atkinson, and Collard 2006). In a field experiment in the Philippines, 28 percent of an experimental group chose to open an account with restricted access to withdrawals even though it offered the same interest rate as ordinary accounts, suggesting that a large proportion of people who opened savings accounts were seeking restrictions (Ashraf, Karlan, and Yin 2006). Further, the group eligible for the restricted accounts saved more, with no evidence that they had shifted these savings from other accounts in the same bank. Similarly, Mark Schreiner and Michael Sherraden (2007) conclude that when participants and the sponsoring organization jointly own an IDA account, savings are higher, suggesting that hard restrictions may discourage withdrawals.

In sum, institutional theory suggests that low savings by the poor may result, at least in part, from lack of access to programs that support saving (and sometimes from saving disincentives). Institutional theory also posits that low-income households would save more if they had access to well-designed saving programs, that is, programs that take into account barriers to saving and asset accumulation faced by these families. Findings from the American Dream Demonstration (ADD) demonstrate that incentives (savings match), restrictions (withdrawals matched only for approved uses; restrictions on unmatched withdrawals), expectations (match caps, time caps), facilitation (use of automatic transfer), and information (financial education), in particular, are associated with saving in IDAs (Schreiner and Sherraden 2007, 247–48). Overall, however, researchers are only beginning to gather empirical evidence on the relative importance of institutional constructs and how they might individually and in combination lead to saving in poor families.

THE POTENTIAL EFFECTS OF SAVING AND ASSET HOLDING IN LOW-INCOME HOUSEHOLDS

According to standard economic theory, income and consumption shape individual and family welfare. Asset theory proposes that what people own may have effects beyond the ability to pay for current and future consumption (Miller and Roby 1970; Sherraden 1991; Bourdieu 2001). Furthermore, the act of saving may have effects that are different from a condition in which a person owns savings or assets. In other words, when people save, they may feel better about themselves and feel engaged in building a better future for themselves and their families. However, owning savings may offer expanded opportunities.

Relatively little research specifies these effects. While scholars have studied income effects for many years, asset effects have been largely overlooked. This section explores theory and empirical evidence related to asset effects. The focus here is on the more inclusive category of assets (savings, investments, home ownership, and so forth) rather than savings alone, because there is relatively little research on savings effects, especially among the poor, and because savings programs aim to increase assets overall.

In *Assets and the Poor,* Michael Sherraden proposed several possible effects of assets on individual and family well-being: improved household stability, greater future orientation, development of human capital and other assets, enhanced focus and specialization, more stable foundation for risk taking, improved outlook for offspring, and increased self-efficacy, social influence, and political participation (1991, 148). Next we discuss some of these effects, including related empirical evidence.[8] We begin with economic effects then discuss psychological, social, and political effects. Several times, we point out that studies suggest that there is a relationship between saving or asset holding and a particular outcome, but relatively few studies establish causality. In some cases, causality could in fact be in the opposite direction (e.g., household stability may contribute to greater asset holding). Moreover, few studies distinguish between the effects of *obtaining* an asset (especially saving, i.e., setting aside money) and the effects of *owning* an asset.

Economic Effects of Savings

Scholars propose that owning assets has direct and indirect economic effects. A person may be able to rely on assets to make it through financial crises, including illness, unemployment, death, and divorce (Miller and Roby 1970; Sherraden 1991; Haveman and Wolff 2005). Savings can provide liquid resources to help finance household expenses. Even illiquid assets can have economic benefits in times of crisis. Home owners, for example, can use home equity as collateral to borrow at lower rates, while families without assets often have no choice but to turn to high-priced credit. Low-income home ownership provided protection and stability during the mid-1970s, a period of economic turmoil characterized by high inflation and recession (Caplovitz 1979). Without assets, those near poverty and those who experience a lengthy crisis may experience real hardship.

Owning assets may also contribute to tangible support for children's current and future health, safety, and education, as well as to their learning about how to acquire and manage assets (Sherraden 1991; Conley 1999). Intergenerational transfers constitute a significant portion of household wealth in the United States, especially when gifts during the life of the donor are included (Kotlikoff and Summers 1981; Gale and Scholz 1994). Children of savers are more likely to earn more (Conley 1999; Boehm and Schlottman 2001) and be savers (Pritchard, Myers, and Cassidy 1989). Children of home owners are more likely to become home owners, controlling for other social and economic factors (Henretta 1984, 1987; Mulder and Wagner 1998; Mulder and Smits 1999; Boehm and Schlottman 1999, 2001; Kurz 2004; Mulder 2006). Families with assets transfer more to their less well-off children (McGarry and Schoeni 1995). When poor single mothers have assets, their adult children are less likely to be poor (Cheng and Page-Adams 1996).

Owning assets also may lead to the development of additional assets. For example, owning physical assets may lead people to learn about and care for these assets, which in turn, may increase the value of the assets. Research suggests, for example, that owner-occupants of property are more likely to invest in it (especially when they believe in the future quality of the neighborhood) and to be committed to the surrounding neighborhood, which may increase the value of the property and overall household wealth (Mayer 1981; Galster 1983, 1987; Rohe and Stewart 1996; Rohe, McCarthy, and van Zandt 2000). Savings also can lead to investment in productive assets, such as self-employment (Lindh and Ohlsson 1998; Sherraden, Sanders, and Sherraden 2004). Owning assets may also make it possible to invest in human capital, such as higher educational attainment, which will result in higher future income (Conley 2001).

Evidence suggests that assets help explain the White-Black gap in earnings over time (Morillas 2007). Empirical studies show that financial assets provide a cushion for women who have experienced separation or divorce, and for other single mothers (Rocha 1997; Cho 1999). However, most of the evidence on the economic effects of asset holding focuses on home ownership, the single most valuable asset held by U.S. households. Research reports largely positive effects of home ownership (Rohe, Van Zandt, and McCarthy 2001; Scanlon and Page-Adams 2001). For example, home ownership is associated with higher net worth, ownership of other assets, such as savings and investments (Oliver and Shapiro 1995; Rossi and Weber 1996), and a lower likelihood of declaring bankruptcy (Domowitz and Sartain 1999).

Foundation for Diversification and Positive Risk Taking. With assets, families may also have enhanced ability to act on future economic opportunity. Households with more assets may be able to take risks that increase the possibility of improved future outcomes because they have a safety net in the present (Chen and Dunn 1996). People with few assets have to pursue short-term survival strategies, while families who can diversify assets and invest resources have the latitude to pursue future mobility (Chen and Dunn 1996). Although there is little empirical research, this proposition suggests that assets may enhance people's ability to take constructive economic risks (Sherraden 1991, 160; Morillas 2007).

The economic benefits of home ownership, however, tend to accrue faster in wealthier households, particularly in deregulated financial markets (Burbidge 2000), in part because appreciation is lower in minority and low-income neighborhoods (Oliver and Shapiro 1995; Gyourko, Linneman, and Wachter 1999). The positive effects associated with home ownership may be an indicator of the presence of other resources or of unmeasured forms of household efficiency (Mayer and Jencks 1989). Home owners also have higher maintenance costs and higher debt (Rossi and Weber 1996), which may impose undue burdens on the poor.

Psychological, Social, and Political Effects of Saving and Assets

Michael Sherraden (1991) suggests that assets may have not only economic effects but also psychological, social, and political effects. Simply put, saving and having savings may "spark hope" and help change a person's worldview and patterns of interaction with society (Schreiner and Sherraden 2007, 21). Further, an individual's current well-being depends in part on their future outlook. To take an example, saving for a house and expecting to own a house in the future may produce a positive psychological effect for the saver today. Traditional economic theory focuses only on eventual consumption, but in a psychological and cognitive model, assets generate the idea of future opportunity, which is a benefit to the saver, perhaps even if the opportunity is not fully realized (Schreiner and Sherraden 2007).

Sense of Security. Owning assets and knowing that these can be used to help make it though hard times have implications for a person's feelings of safety and security. Owning assets may also confer a sense of stability and permanence (Rakoff 1977). With a reserve of assets, families may perceive less financial strain even when income streams are uneven or relatively low (Shobe and Boyd 2005; Dew 2007). Home owners, for example, may experience less financial strain during episodes of unemployment, financial shocks, hardship, or ill health, and for some people, during retirement (Page-Adams and Vosler 1996; Rasmussen, Megbolugbe, and Morgan 1997; Domowitz and Sartain 1999; Mirowsky and Ross 1999).

Self-Esteem, Well-Being, and Control. Assets may impart a sense of well-being, confidence in one's own abilities, and a feeling of control over one's life and future. For example, home ownership may make people feel "worthy," feel that they are conforming to social norms, feel privileged in relation to others, feel a sense of control over an asset, or believe they are getting ahead (building equity, making improvements) (Perin 1977; Rakoff 1977; Lassarre 1986; Saunders 1990; Megbolugbe and Linneman 1993; Rohe and Stegman 1994a; Rohe et al. 2001). Assets are relatively predictable compared to income, which may explain why people feel in greater control when they own assets (Sherraden 1991). Asset ownership may lead to greater self-efficacy and sense of control because the owner has more choices and is not as vulnerable to the whims of others (Rohe et al. 2001). Yet ownership suggests more responsibility and accountability, which could increase stress and reduce feelings of control (Rohe et al. 2001). There are many recent examples of people losing a house due to foreclosure (Morgenson 2007).

On the empirical side, researchers find an association between assets and health and mental health. Home ownership, for example, is associated with physical and emotional well-being in several studies (Pugh et al. 1991; Rodgers 1991; Arber and Ginn 1993; Hahn 1993; Page-Adams and Vosler 1996; Baker, Taylor, and the Alspac Survey Team 1997). A longitudinal study finds an increase in life satisfaction among a nonrandom sample of home owners, but no increase in self-esteem and sense of control (Rohe and Stegman 1994b). Home ownership is associated with reduced likelihood of nursing home admission and greater likelihood of discharge (Greene and Ondrich 1990). Owning assets is related to better health status and lower mortality, and these effects are partially independent of other socioeconomic resources (Joshi and Macran 1991; Schoenbaum and Waidmann 1997). Among older adults, liquid assets especially are associated with health more than with income and other measures of socioeconomic status (Robert and House 1996).[9] Owning financial assets as a young adult is associated positively with employment and mental health ten years later, although causality is unclear (Bynner and Paxton 2001). In part, those who own assets may engage in more prudent behaviors (Yadama and Sherraden 1996).

Regarding efficacy and control, participants in the Savings Gateway, a matched saving program in the United Kingdom, report feeling more financially secure (60 percent) and more in control of their lives (39 percent) as a result of participation (Kempson, McKay, and Collard 2003; Lister 2006). People saving in an IDA program express more confidence about the future and greater control over their lives that they attribute to holding an IDA savings account (Moore et al. 2001). Studies on the effects of home ownership suggest greater association with life satisfaction, but the associations with self-esteem, self-efficacy, and health are weaker and may vary depending on demographic, neighborhood characteristics, and other factors (Potter and Coshall 1987; Rohe and Stegman 1994a; Rossi and Weber 1996; Rohe and Basolo 1997; Rohe et al. 2001).

Future Orientation. Savings and other assets may increase people's ability to envision and have confidence about the future (Miller and Roby 1970; Sherraden 1991; Shobe and Page-Adams 2001). This confidence and outlook for the future may operate through increased self-efficacy (Bandura 1986, 1997). Assets may be one of the key factors that, in combination with other resources and a person's internal capabilities, lead people to perceive and act on a broader array of future opportunities and possibilities (Nussbaum 2000). In other words, owning assets may be one of the key elements that boost a person's life chances and ability to invest in developing long-term capabilities (Weber 1958; Dahrendorf 1979; Blanchflower and Oswald 1998; Sen 1999; Swedberg 2001; Nussbaum 2002; Glennerster 2006). For instance, when families own assets, children may grow up with a cognitive perception that such things as higher education, a career, and a house are normal and attainable (Sherraden 1991; Elliott 2008). Thus, assets may increase a person's life chances directly through what the family can afford, but also indirectly through a person's perceptions of what is possible. As Sherraden writes, "in a sense, assets are the future. . . . They are hope in concrete form" (1991, 155–56).

Limited empirical evidence suggests that savers appear more optimistic about their financial future and the economy, more satisfied with their standard of living, and more likely to believe that they manage money better than their parents (Lunt and Livingstone 1991b). Controlling for other social and economic factors, assets appear to have modest positive effects on people's expectations and confidence about the future and on their future plans (Yadama and Sherraden 1996). Self-reports among IDA participants in ADD find an increase in orientation and confidence about the future, including increased ability to plan for children's education and retirement (McBride, Lombe, and Beverly 2003).

Household and Residential Stability. Certain types of assets, such as owning a house, may also increase marital and residential stability. Controlling for other economic factors, studies find a link between family assets and family stability: home ownership is associated with marriage (Lloyd and South 1996), and home ownership and financial assets are associated with marital stability (Galligan and Bahr 1978; South and Spitze 1986; Bracher et al. 1993). Causality is difficult to determine in these studies, however, and a different study found no correlation between savings and stress levels among women who relocated in the prior year (Berger, Powell, and Cook 1988).

Some scholars suggest that home ownership may contribute to improved school performance among children by reducing family strain and residential mobility, especially in less affluent families (Rohe and Stewart 1996). These dynamics may be attenuated in distressed communities, however (Varady 1986), and some have argued that the benefits of home ownership may accrue more to wealthier families than to poor ones (Burbidge 2000). Home ownership may also bind residents to neighborhoods of declining value (Luria 1976; Burkhauser, Butrica, and Wasylenko 1995; Scanlon 1998). While home ownership and owning other assets may protect women from intimate partner violence (Bangdiwala et al. 2004), they could also have the opposite effect if assets make it more difficult for women to leave abusive relationships (Page-Adams and Vosler 1996; Sanders 2007).

Enhanced Child Welfare. Conceptually, if assets increase future orientation, then parents with assets may have a brighter view and higher expectations for their children (Shobe and Page-Adams 2001). A number of studies have examined associations between parental assets and child outcomes. Parental assets are associated with increased self-esteem among adolescents (Whitbeck et al. 1991), and parents' saving for children's college beginning in infancy is associated with child self-esteem in early adulthood (Axinn, Duncan, and Thornton 1997). One study reports later marriages and fewer teen pregnancies in families of property owners, controlling for other factors (Green and White 1997).

The bulk of studies has looked at educational outcomes for children. Financial assets and home ownership, along with higher income, are associated with school completion for children (Axinn, Duncan, and Thornton 1997). Studies also suggest that, controlling for other factors, children of home owners have higher educational outcomes than renters or public housing tenants, including fewer behavior problems, higher educational attainment overall, higher test scores, lower drop-out rates, and higher college matriculation (Essen, Fogelman, and Head 1977; Kane 1994; Haurin, Parcel, and Haurin 2001; Harkness and Newman 2003). Higher secondary school graduation rates among children of home owners may be due to greater residential stability (Aaronson 2000). When parents have income from assets, their children attain more schooling, although they do not necessarily earn higher wages (Hill and Duncan 1987). Parent wealth has an independent effect on enrollment in, and perhaps completion of, postsecondary education (Conley 2001). Another possible reason for academic achievement is higher parental expectations, which many studies suggest is a key factor in higher academic performance (Reynolds and Gill 1994; Axinn, Duncan, and Thornton 1997; Fan and Chen 2001; Elliott 2008; Grinstein-Weiss, et al. 2009; Williams Shanks and Destin 2009). Single mothers' assets are associated with their children's educational achievement, and the relationship seems to be partially mediated through parent expectations (Zhan and Sherraden 2003).

Civic Engagement. Theoretically, asset effects may extend beyond those described thus far because other people in society tend to treat owners differently than nonowners, and in response, people may change their own attitudes and behaviors. Wealth and assets confer social status and economic influence and power in society (Veblen 1899). People use assets to exert influence on politics and decision making, and often receive better treatment in society because they have the potential to reciprocate with a broad range of people (Schreiner and Sherraden 2007). In other words, wealth gives people a "superior position in social interactions" (Sherraden 1991, 164).

With status and power that accompany assets, people may gain greater access to social networks and institutions that provide avenues for mobility (Granovetter 1983), and greater influence within social institutions (Elliott 2008). Home owners, for example, participate in broader social networks than renters do (Fischer 1982; Saunders 1990). While widespread social networks may not provide much tangible assistance, they may supply "access to information and resources beyond those available in their own social circle," and these may provide avenues for mobility (Granovetter 1983, 209).

Also, because they have assets to protect and grow and because they often have strong ties to a community, home and business owners may be more likely to be involved in social and political life. For example, home and business owners are probably more apt to join neighborhood associations, parent-teacher organizations, or local service clubs. This investment in local organizations often improves the social context, their businesses, and/or their property values (Rohe and Stewart 1996).

There is some evidence that home ownership is associated with civic engagement. Overall, home owners are more likely to be involved in local organizations and to be politically active at the local level, perhaps in part because they remain longer in and identify with the community (Steinberger 1981; Baum and Kingston 1984; Ditkovsky and Van Vliet 1984; Perkins et al. 1990; Rohe and Stegman 1994a; Rossi and Weber 1996; DiPasquale and Glaeser 1999; Rohe et al. 2001).[10] People who own savings and a house are also more likely to feel social connectedness (Yadama and Sherraden 1996). Costs associated with moving may encourage residential stability as well as neighborhood activism (Cox 1982). Length of residence may be a factor in higher civic engagement, especially in formal organizations (Rohe and Basolo 1997; DiPasquale and Glaeser 1999). Some researchers find that net worth (including home equity) is associated with the propensity of Black households to give to charity, particularly religious giving, although it does not predict donation amounts (Nembhard and Blasingame 2006).

Concerning political effects, research is limited and findings are mixed. One study finds a strong positive relationship between owning a house and voting, controlling for other social and economic factors (Gilderbloom and Markham 1995). Other studies suggest that political involvement may increase with home ownership (Guest and Oropesa 1986; Rohe and Basolo 1997). However, another study finds that home and business ownership are only weakly associated with or are not associated with sociopolitical attitudes and involvement (Kingston and Fries 1994).

Feedback Effects

Some research suggests that asset ownership may result in what some call a "virtuous circle" of household development (Yadama and Sherraden 1996). In other words, in addition to the direct effects of owning assets (increases in positive options and greater likelihood of success), and the indirect effects on the asset owner (through changes in their outlook on the future and the way others react to and treat the person), there may be additional positive effects (Schreiner and Sherraden 2007, 25). If assets improve a person's opportunity structure by providing access to more information and choices, and also generate more optimism and knowledge about future outcomes, a cognitive shift may occur that has further positive effects. To take an example, if a single mother with a low income enters a well-designed savings program, begins to save money, and believes that she can save enough for a down payment on a house, this sense of future possibility may also decrease the psychological cost of saving in the present. Or when a person gains greater respect from owning assets, such as a house, this may lead to increased social interactions that reinforce and strengthen other social relationships, thus broadening the person's social network. By improving opportunities and changing worldviews about what is possible, feedback effects may further enable a poor saver to respond constructively to future possibilities. As Mark Schreiner and Michael Sherraden write, "Assets affect choices not only through their effects on the chances of realizing different consequences but also through their effects on people's perceptions of choices, chances, and consequences" (2007, 25).

Despite these largely positive findings, assets may not always be "goods." Managing assets requires knowledge, and an accompanying sense of care and responsibility (e.g., house, education). Some assets, like houses, can be costly to maintain. Home ownership could keep some people, such as older adults, in unsafe neighborhoods and hamper mobility for employment. Women who own their homes may have more difficulty escaping from abusive relationships (Scanlon and Page-Adams 2001; Sanders 2007). Home owners could *lose* money on their homes as we have observed in the recent economic crisis. In these ways, equity investments can be more or less productive, placing at risk people with less knowledge or those channeled into badly performing portfolios (Choi et al. 2005). Therefore, researchers and policymakers should keep in mind varying and potentially detrimental impacts.

A final note: research on asset effects is lacking. As this brief summary suggests, most research focuses on home ownership, which may have different effects than other forms of assets. Evidence often points to contradictory effects, suggesting conceptual and measurement problems. Most research focuses on the nonpoor. Moreover, little research examines possible negative impacts of owning property and other assets, and the possibly large debt load that may undermine the financial stability of the poor (Rohe et al. 2001). Much of the research does not address the mechanisms through which assets may affect well-being. For example, do the various hypothesized effects result from the process of saving, or from owning a certain level of savings? Are there other factors that explain these relationships? Does wealth in different forms benefit groups and individuals differently, depending on factors such as life stage or institutional context? Finally, although research increasingly controls for other possible explanations (especially income), relatively few studies sort out causation, because few use comparison or control groups and longitudinal designs (Rossi and Weber 1996; Shlay 2006). Too often, we cannot be sure that causation does not go the other way, or both ways. Stable families with an orientation toward the future, for instance, may tend to own assets, and their assets may encourage greater future orientation.

RESEARCH QUESTIONS

As Laurence Kotlikoff points out, more empirical research is necessary to narrow down the long list of factors that may explain savings (1989, 2). Further, although research suggests the possibility of multiple positive asset effects, more research, especially rigorous research that establishes causality, is required. In this volume, as we examine the saving experiences of 84 respondents in ADD, we aim to contribute to theoretical understanding and empirical evidence about saving and the effects of saving and owning savings.

In the chapters that follow, we examine several questions raised in the preceding discussion. We ask what influenced respondents' interest and ability to save. Did their economic socialization as children matter? Outside the IDA program, have they saved for short-term precautionary purposes or for long-term investment purposes? Are they, as suggested by economic theory, too income-constrained to set aside money for the future? How do low-income families think about the benefits and drawbacks of saving?

According to behavioral economics, the way that people frame and account for their money influences how they manage their money and save. Do low-income families allocate income sources to different informal or formal "accounts," and, if so, does this behavior help them to resist spending temptations and to save? How do low-income families deal with the challenges of saving, especially problems of self-control and lack of willpower? Do they do anything to counteract the human tendency to procrastinate? Do individuals with low incomes try to constrain their future behavior in ways that help them save?

Finally, if low-income families try to save, how do they assess their success? What do they perceive as barriers and facilitators of saving? What makes it easier (or more difficult) to commit to and follow through on a decision to save? If respondents say they want to save, what are their motives and goals and do these affect their success in saving? From IDA participants' perspectives, do particular program features help them save, and what do these suggest about the role of various institutional constructs in saving in low-income households? For example, how do a saving incentive, financial education, penalties on withdrawals, or a monthly savings goal affect their ability to save? What are the barriers to saving in an IDA, and are these barriers the same or different from saving outside the IDA program? Are there situations that force respondents to dissave?

Finally, we ask how IDA participants perceive the importance and meaning of their IDA savings and whether IDAs have any effects. Comparing their experiences to the experiences of control respondents, is it possible to clarify whether these effects are a result of participating in an IDA program (with its multiple plan features) or owning savings? If IDA participants fail to save, do they experience negative social or psychological effects? Among those in the IDA program, are there differences in outcomes across different levels of savings in the IDAs?

CHAPTER 3

Setting the Stage: Economic Socialization and Coming-of-Age in a Working-Poor Family

Respondents discuss their economic socialization and preparation for adult financial responsibilities in this chapter. They describe what it
was like growing up in low-income, and occasionally troubled, families. While
most did not live in extreme poverty and felt cared-for as children, they reported becoming increasingly aware of financial stress as they reached adolescence. They described coming-of-age, schooling, and preparation for the world
of work. There is little evidence that public policy provided substantial support
to their families as they did their best to prepare their offspring for the adult
world.

In many ways, the stories we will hear reflect recent chronicles of working
poverty and provide additional evidence of the possible long-term costs of
growing up poor (Edin and Lein 1997; Newman 1999, 2006; Beverly 2001;
Ehrenreich 2001; Shipler 2004). Confronting economic challenges of their own,
families sent their daughters and sons into the world with few tangible resources and little direction to help them gain an economic toehold. There were
exceptions: some families were able to provide more economic resources and
continued to guide their offspring as they made their way in a sometimes per-
ilous adult world. These families provide a vivid counterpoint to the majority
in this study who reached adulthood with few familial resources to draw upon.
Families of origin by and large were unable to muster and pass along economic
advantages to their children. Without these resources, children faced an uphill
battle to accumulate wealth in adulthood.

Camille's story is typical of the majority of respondents who began adulthood without the benefit of family resources. Her story also suggests how racial discrimination can challenge a family's ability to make financial progress. Later, we introduce Anne, one of few people in this study who grew up with financial backing. Although she rebelled against her conservative parents, they nonetheless supported her financially throughout her youth including paying for her education. Her case contrasts with the more familiar story of financial struggles in Camille's and other respondents' lives.

Camille

Camille, whom we met in the introduction, grew up in Greenwood, a part of Tulsa, Oklahoma. Greenwood had been known in the early twentieth century as the "Black Wall Street" (Satterwhite 2000). In 1921, armed White mobs, joined by local and state law enforcement, invaded Greenwood, killing at least 25 residents, detaining thousands of others, confiscating property, and burning 35 city blocks, including the means for livelihood among many residents (Ellsworth 1982; Madigan 2001; Brophy 2002; Hirsch 2002).

Greenwood and Tulsa's African American community continued to be the target of White racism and discrimination (Hirsch 2002).[1] According to Camille, this had significant impact on her family. Camille's father worked a physically strenuous and dirty job as a steel mill furnace helper, and although providing a steady income for the family, he died early from a cancer that Camille believed was work-related. Camille's mother was a domestic worker. "The only jobs [Black] women could get, you know, when I was small was to go clean the White people's homes. They called it 'day work' . . . because you went to a different home every day. And the work was scrubbing, vacuuming, cleaning, washing, whatever it was that the lady wanted you to do, ironing, whatever, you did it."

Neither of Camille's parents had much schooling, but they worked hard and long hours to provide for their seven children. Camille and her brothers and sisters didn't know their father well because he was working most of the time. "When he left in the mornings, we were asleep. And when he came in, in the evenings, we were asleep. . . . I guess the only time we really socialized with him was on Sundays." Even on Sundays, his day off, the children spent the morning in Sunday school, and their father rested most of the afternoon.

Anne

In contrast to Camille, Anne grew up in relative comfort. She was born in Nebraska, the middle sister of three girls. Although her parents had dropped out of high school in the eighth or ninth grade, they had become moderately successful. Her father completed a GED after he was married and took some college classes. When Anne was a baby, he took a job with a major airline and the family moved to Oklahoma. He "moved up in the company" over the more than 30 years that he worked there. When he retired in the late 1990s, he had reached the level of systems analyst. Anne recognizes that "he was really fortunate for someone with no education to end up with as high paying job as he had."

Anne's mother also completed a GED and attended beauty school. While Anne was growing up, she operated a small home-based hairdresser business. She worked "when she wanted," according to Anne, to cover extra expenses, like Christmas gifts. Her earnings provided "money above what the normal budget would be."

Even though Anne knew relatively few details about her family's economic situation, she had no reason to believe that there were tough financial times. She couldn't remember a time when her father took a second job to cover expenses, when they didn't take a vacation, when they didn't have clothes, or when they didn't have "more than plenty of food." "I'm quite sure at times [my parents] did struggle, because . . . I'm learning as I get older, that's a normal part of life, but . . . we weren't aware of it."

Even though they were reasonably well off, the children didn't get everything they wanted. Her parents were careful money managers and didn't approve of buying things just "because everyone else has them." Anne recalled when she was about 10 years old, "Everybody had a pair of Nike tennis shoes and I wanted a pair so bad. And they wouldn't buy me a pair and it wasn't because of the money."

> I think they tried to teach us that we didn't have to have what everybody else had in order to survive. You know, that we could learn to be yourself, not to be, you know, what you wear, what you are . . . . We didn't like it at the time, but they taught us some pretty good lessons.

Back then, Anne had no idea that some kids were poor. "It was not until after I got into college . . . [that I] even realized that there was such a thing as poverty. . . . Those are things that wasn't a reality when I was growing up." Looking back, Anne was grateful for her family's security. "I was very blessed in the fact that I never recall a time where we faced a hardship."

Neither Camille nor Anne grew up wealthy and advantaged, yet their experiences differ markedly. Poverty and racial discrimination took a toll on Camille and hampered her family's ability to provide tangible resources as Camille came of age. In contrast, Anne grew up in a family with greater resources that enabled them to support her until she matured and assumed adult responsibilities. We continue their stories, and stories of the other respondents, as we examine families' resources and ability to prepare their children for future economic success.

GROWING UP IN A WORKING-POOR HOUSEHOLD

Overall, few of the respondents' parents had much formal education. In many cases, their parents came of age during an era when a high school or college education was not as necessary for economic success as it is today. Although 50 respondents had at least one parent who completed high school or a GED and 22 had a parent who attended some college (including an associate's degree), only 11 had a parent who earned a college degree or more. At least a fourth of their parents did not complete high school. In a few cases, parents did not reach high school at all (table 3.1). With relatively little formal education, parents were limited in their ability to offer guidance and connections that would help their children obtain schooling and good jobs.

As respondents grew up, their mothers tended to work in service industry jobs (28), as waitresses, bartenders, beauticians, bank tellers, retail clerks, housekeepers, cafeteria cooks, school bus drivers, and Laundromat attendants (see table 3.2). Some mothers held semiprofessional or professional positions

TABLE 3.1. Parents' Education during Respondents' Childhoods ($N = 84$)

	Mothers n (%)	Fathers n (%)
Less than high school	23 (27)	21 (25)
GED only	1 (1)	2 (2)
High school degree	20 (24)	14 (17)
GED or high school plus technical training	4 (5)	9 (11)
Some college	11 (13)	9 (11)
Associate's degree	2 (2)	0 (0)
Four-year degree	5 (6)	4 (5)
More than four-year degree	1 (1)	1 (1)
Unknown	17 (20)	24 (29)

Source: Center for Social Development, in-depth interviews.

(19), such as bookkeepers, interior decorators, human service workers, and teachers. Some were self-employed (10), in domestic work, baking, crafts, and farming. A few mothers (5) worked in agricultural and labor positions. Others were homemakers (16), especially those with several young children.

Some respondents' fathers held professional or semiprofessional positions (13), as policemen, missionaries, teachers, and engineers. Some worked in skilled positions (13), in construction, plumbing, machinist, and oil rig jobs. Others were self-employed full-time (12), in landscaping, running a gas station, selling real estate, office cleaning, construction and contracting, and driving taxis. Some (7) were self-employed part-time or intermittently, in landscaping, handyman work, and property rental management. Others (15) worked in manufacturing or held some kind of manual labor job.

Only three parents, including Anne's father, held stable, relatively well-paid jobs with benefits and a career path. The best jobs were clustered in the airline and military-related industries.

But this educational and occupational snapshot obscures the day-to-day reality of work for respondents' parents. Respondents described low earnings, dead-end jobs, poor working conditions, discrimination, and multiple jobs held to make ends meet. Their parents' jobs seldom led to stable or more lucra-

TABLE 3.2. Parents' Occupations during Respondents' Childhoods ($N = 84$)[a]

	Mothers n (%)	Fathers n (%)
Service jobs	28 (33)	6 (7)
Self-employment	10 (12)	19 (23)
Semiprofessional	10 (12)	8 (10)
Homemaker	16 (19)	0 (0)
Agriculture/Labor	5 (6)	10 (12)
Professional	9 (11)	5 (6)
Skilled jobs	0 (0)	13 (15)
Manual labor	0 (0)	13 (15)
Military service	0 (0)	7 (8)
Manufacturing	1 (1)	2 (2)
Unknown	5 (6)	14 (17)

Source: Center for Social Development, in-depth interviews.

[a]These are categories we created based on respondents' descriptions of their parents' work during respondents' childhoods. "Semiprofessional" refers to white collar jobs, such as bookkeeping, that may not have required professional training.

tive employment, and full-time employment was uncertain. Respondents described frequent layoffs. As one respondent recalled, "My father and my mother both worked in a factory and so, you know, [were] kind of just always looking for a different job. And they weren't long-term [jobs]—they were, you know, laid-off a lot." It was frequently difficult to find the time to care for their children. One respondent, whose story was echoed by several others, said her mother worked as a waitress and her father held three jobs, making it a daily struggle to synchronize work schedules to care for their three children.

Racial discrimination trapped many African American parents in strenuous, dangerous, and dead-end jobs. They worked jobs that others would spurn (Light and Rosenstein 1995). As Camille recalled, her father's steel mill job took the ultimate toll—his life. "Back then, you know, they did not wear masks . . . and he would have to stir . . . metal and steel and things of that nature . . . so he was probably breathing all that stuff. . . . I really think that that's probably what took his life, because he died from triple myeloma, which is a bone disease."

With low pay and frequent unemployment spells, many families likely qualified for public assistance programs, yet only two families relied on public assistance for long-term support. There was a general feeling among respondents that their families considered public assistance shameful. While they turned to public assistance for temporary assistance after divorces and job losses, they avoided relying on it for long.

Some families did not even seek temporary public support. Cynthia, for example, grew up in a poor household with 11 children, yet her family never turned to the state for support.

> Never! They wouldn't even ask for it. I think people back then had so much pride. And I don't mean the wrong kind of pride like you're proud and pompous. You [just] wouldn't go to an office or a state agency to ask for something if they had it. They had pride in working at whatever level they were at to earn what they needed to provide and not out stealing or trying to get over on the government.

Cynthia's parents had never known a life without work. Each had lost a parent in childhood, and neither had reached high school. Cynthia grew up watching her parents struggle financially. "It was a miracle if we had enough food through the week. See, that was the blessing, you survived." Her parents were cautious with their money.

They never was squanderers. I mean they always measured everything out and made sure. Their sole thing was, you know, you pay bills first and from there you do the next thing and the next thing. But they never were extravagant or squandered it because they knew how hard it was to make it.

Cynthia learned this herself when her father died and she, at age 16, had to step in to help support the family. From an early age, Cynthia learned how to manage on few resources.

In other cases, family breakup exacerbated economic strain. Many respondents (30) described growing up with their mothers—some with little or no contact or financial support from their fathers. Divorce, separation, and imprisonment or death of a parent frequently led to a decline in the family's standard of living. Several were sent to live with relatives or stepparents.

Family Savings and Other Assets

Thirty-four respondents (41 percent) reported that their family saved some money. Many were unsure how much their parents saved, although about one-half of these believed their families saved regularly. Among those, one respondent expressed admiration for her mother, who despite only a seventh-grade education, was able to save because she was a "smart" money manager. She remembered that her mother saved in a credit union at her father's job for big-ticket items and kept "stash money" at home for emergencies.

Another respondent remembered that his parents saved for a down payment on a house. "They just opened a savings account. They put back so much every paycheck. My mom put so much back from hers and my stepfather put so much back from his. . . . I know they had enough for a down payment on the property and stuff like that, but I don't know how much it was. So they were saving some."

Another said she learned how to save from her mother, who was a committed saver. Although they did not openly discuss money management, she remembered helping her mother count her tips from waitressing. Earmarking different accounts for different purposes, her mother kept money in a checking account for household consumption, "cash money" ($700 to $1,000) in a small box in her dresser for special purposes, and savings in her savings account for emergencies. She remembered her mother acted "broke" if the checking account was low, even when she had plenty stashed away at home or in her savings account.

Anne's parents saved regularly. Her father's employer offered savings options. In addition to a retirement fund, he signed up to have part of his paycheck automatically deposited into savings (although Anne wasn't sure what kind of account). She couldn't remember a time when her father didn't have savings: "He did that his whole life." When they dipped into their savings, they would immediately replace it. Even in retirement, Anne said her father "still puts back savings."

Although few parents had saving arrangements through an employer like Anne's father, about half of those whose families saved said their parents saved in some type of financial institution. Others saved informally. They kept "stash money," hiding it under a carpet "for a rainy day" or "putting money up" under a mattress or in a closet. Respondents did not think these informal savings generally amounted to much; their families saved until the next emergency claimed it.

Although 19 respondents said they did not know if their families saved any money, 31 respondents said their families did not save anything. This included 17 who said their families were too poor to save any amount of money. One respondent recalled that her grandmother, with whom she lived after her mother was sent to prison, had no money to save, not even small amounts of change. "She was just barely getting by." Another respondent observed, "When you ain't got no money, you can't save no money. If you have five kids, and you make minimum wage, you ain't gonna save no money unless you get some other income besides that to save." Although respondents believed that low incomes and high expenses prevented saving, a few also thought that poor money management and wasteful spending contributed to lack of savings.

A few families tried to save some money for their children, but most used these savings before passing them on to their children. For example, a respondent's father left her some stock in a utility company to help pay for college, but when she was 15, her mother spent it. Another parent used his children's savings bonds for moving expenses. In both cases, the children did not learn about the savings in their names until they were adults.

Respondents had greater recollections about other assets. Few families accumulated significant assets other than a car, a house, and household durables. The most common was a car. But they frequently were worth little; they were used vehicles that often broke down, costing dearly in time and expenses. As one respondent recalled, her father typically paid "$500 or $600 for . . . something that was running."

Most families owned a home at some point when respondents were young. (The Midwest location, with its low home prices, made home ownership possible, and housing was often low quality, including trailers.) Most of the fifty-eight families who owned a home were two-parent families. Only seven respondents who grew up in single-parent families ever owned a home. Thirteen respondents said their families owned a farm or land, and several remembered tractors and other farm equipment, as well as animals.

Families who never owned a house tended to move a good deal when respondents were young. One respondent described moving in and out of public housing many times. Every time her mother lost her job, they would move into public housing, but when she got another job the rent would go up and they would move out.

Some respondents recalled lost assets. Four respondents mentioned their families lost their homes as a result of divorce, as part of a divorce decree or because a single parent was unable to keep up the mortgage payments. Some remembered losing a home or land through foreclosure. After her father's death, for example, Camille's family lost a plot of land in which her father had invested. Camille believed the family lost the land because they didn't understand the terms of ownership, something that she took to heart.

> My sister and her husband were going to take up the payments on [the land], but I think the lady that had it kind of beat us out of it. Because—see this is what I'm saying—we didn't know. This is why I don't think it's good for just one person to know everything and not share [the information]. But that's the way my dad was and [at the time] we didn't even know about this property.

Growing Perceptions of Poverty in Adolescence

Even though most of the families were income- and asset-poor, most respondents did not feel poor when they were young because everyone around them also lived in poverty, and for the most part, their families provided the necessities of life. Respondents recalled that their families took pride in providing for their children as best they could.

The oldest respondents were most likely to describe growing up in absolute poverty, although they, too, were unlikely to say they felt deprived as young children. Camille's memories were fairly typical. The financial situation in Camille's home was tough, but she was unaware of feeling disadvantaged as a youngster. "It took every dime they had to keep everybody in the family going, looking good, fed good," Camille recalled. "[But] we always ate good. I can't ever remember wearing shoes with cardboard in the bottom of them like some people had to do. . . . I can't ever remember being raggedy."

Rosalyn, one of eight siblings, grew up with even less than Camille, and yet she was also unaware of the extent of her poverty. When Rosalyn was five, her mother was killed and the children were separated into different households. Rosalyn moved in with her father for a while but ended up in foster care. Moving "from foster home to foster home" until she was nine, she finally settled in with a widow until age fifteen. At the foster home, Rosalyn supplemented the household income picking cotton: "to school in the morning—go to pick cotton in the evening." Like others, Rosalyn was unaware of her poverty. "I didn't know nothing about not having." Her foster mother "did all she could for me" with a small income from cleaning houses and picking cotton.

As children, respondents measured well-being as having enough food and clothing. Even if they did not get everything they wanted, they did not feel poor. As a respondent put it, "We always had enough food, plenty of food. We always had nice clothes. But nothing more."

As the respondents grew up, however, they became more sensitive to deprivation. With the pressure to conform, to wear the same clothes as other children, and to participate in school events, several respondents remembered feeling poor. One respondent's mother, for example, could not afford to buy her new clothes even for special occasions.

> It was hard. . . . I never had like a new party dress at Christmas like all the other little girls. And always got a lot of heckling from them . . . 'cause I always wore the same dress to church every Sunday. . . . [I] quit church after the second grade 'cause I just couldn't stand the persecution from the other kids.

Another, who did not feel deprived as a young child, recalled the growing stress of poverty when she was a teenager. "We didn't have any money. If you don't have money, the kids aren't very nice to you. We didn't have the best clothes or, you know, we had what we had and that was it. We were fine with it but nobody else was."

Over time, respondents gained greater understanding about the implications of want and scarcity. They also became more aware of how hard their parents had to work to provide for their families. Denise, for example, recalled her growing frustration being the oldest child but too young to work. She watched her mother struggle. "I would always tell the Lord, 'When I get a job, I'm gonna . . . help Mama.' . . . She'd just do the best she could and I couldn't help her."

LaVonne grew increasingly aware of the ravages of poverty combined with racial discrimination. LaVonne saw that her mother tried to protect her six small children from the effects of poverty and racism but was able to provide little more than food, a roof over their heads, and a loving home. She recalled an incident when, as a child, she stepped behind their old gas heating stove. "It was gas and the flames would leap over the back of the stove. And I don't know for what reason but I went back behind that stove. . . . [I] came back around and I was standing there and realized I was on fire." At the emergency room they "sprayed some cold stuff" on her leg and sent her home with third-degree burns, where she recuperated without further medical care. Looking back, she knew they did not send her for specialized care at the burn center because she was a Black child.

Growing up in a poor neighborhood posed other hazards. Fred recalled his mother as a loving and capable provider, but her low wages as a school bus driver relegated them to an impoverished neighborhood. This was Fred's biggest challenge. "The only difficult times I [had] growing up was the pull to get into drugs versus the pull to stay away from drugs. . . . The whole thing was not to get drawn into drugs like so many of the young kids. They . . . end up incarcerated." Unlike his three brothers, Fred avoided drugs by aiming for college and immersing himself in youth groups at church and athletics. "The neighborhood was into drugs and alcohol and I was trying to go to college myself. And that was tough."

While most of the respondents grew up in households where parents tried to protect them from the vicissitudes of poverty and racism, a few respondents remembered childhood as a time of emotional stress, which added to financial strain (Elder et al. 1992). Some described psychological costs associated with growing up poor with only one parent. Single parents' absences during long hours at work often left children alone for many hours each day. Some respondents, however, experienced more serious trauma—such as a parent in prison or addicted to drugs—and suffered psychological repercussions.

Learning about Household Finances

Most respondents recalled caring families who told their children to be careful with their money. Respondents said they learned how to make ends meet from observing their mothers—and sometimes their fathers—manage households on a tight budget. But most said financial matters were not discussed openly. Some parents believed that household finances were the province of adults only; others wanted to shield their children from financial worries. As Anne pointed out, "If my parents did face some hardship it was strictly kept from us kids. . . . it was definitely kept a secret." However, parents' efforts to keep financial matters away from their children did not mean that children were unaware of money problems. LaVonne's mother, for example, did not share her financial concerns with her children, but they knew when their mother was worried.

> You know, she never really laid that burden on us about when she needed money or anything like that. . . . We knew that she was worried about something when she would start singing old gospel hymns, you know. And then we knew there was a problem. But yeah, she didn't ever let us know that she was having problems financially. . . . She never, you know, burdened us with, "Oh, I can't pay this, I can't pay that."

Other parents were from an older generation who believed it was not proper for children to participate in adult conversation about money and savings. As Theresa, age 48, remembered, "I was brought up in the age of 'You will speak when you are spoken to. . . . You don't question where, why.'"

Learning about Saving

Although respondents recalled few lessons about money management, they remember being told to save. This usually came in the form of an admonition, with few details about how to save. However, there were exceptions. Anne's parents, for example, taught her to save. As a "big believer in savings," Anne's father told her to keep a minimum amount of savings in case of emergency and to avoid borrowing. "My father will tell you that you better keep a minimum of $5,000 in savings at all times. He will tell you that $5,000 can pay for anything. If you have an emergency, $5,000 will cover it. So, that's his philosophy on savings. . . . So, he lectures my husband and I all the time about putting money in savings. That was a big belief in our family."

Another respondent's parents set up a savings account for her. "I remember that I wanted to make money and save lots of money, you know, when I was little like that." The account made her feel grown-up. "I just remember, this is my first savings account and maybe it was an adult thing, you know. . . . I'm grown up enough to have my own accounts."

One of the oldest respondents we interviewed benefited from one of the early school-based savings programs that proliferated across the country in the first half of the twentieth century (Cruce 2001, 2002). This respondent opened a savings account through her grade school when she was six years old. She remembered the excitement of saving: "We used to have bank day every Monday. I think when I graduated from high school I had $300, 'cause I started saving money when I was in grade school." She earned the money she deposited by babysitting for her younger brothers and sisters. When the program ended after grade school, her father took her to open a bank savings account. Hazel spent her $300 in savings on "store-bought clothes" when she was in high school.

According to another respondent, her mother told her that saving was a matter of self-protection; it was important for a woman to have some savings of her own because men were undependable. "She would always tell me, don't ever trust a man. . . . She would always say that men are dogs. . . . Just make sure that you have your own because they can change on you. . . . There is nothing you can do about the changing, but you are still going to need your income or finances to make it."

However, even as they told their children they *should* save, there is little evidence that most parents facilitated or supported saving. Camille recalled that her father saved money and admonished the children to do the same, but he did not teach them how to save. She remembered trying on her own to save some money in a jar, but her parents did not set up a savings account or help her save in other ways.

Fred's mother, who never used a bank, told her children they should watch their money carefully and save. But Fred paid little heed.

She never did teach me about banking or financing. See, that stuff trickles down. I had to teach myself. She always used to say, "Boy, you better learn to save your money." That's telling me, but I didn't listen. She was always saying, "You gotta have something to save. . . . Fred, when you get grown, you gotta learn how to save your money."

Circumstances in other households made it impossible to even try to save. For example, one respondent believed saving was futile. Whenever she had anything of value, her uncle literally would steal it.

See, my family was really messed up. This is kind of embarrassing to tell you, but I'll tell you. . . . My uncle, he's like really a drunk and he steals everything, I mean just to go and drink. And if I did have a [piggy] bank, it would have gotten stolen. If you had a bike, it would've gotten stolen. I mean it was just like that.

Some parents—perhaps unknowingly—discouraged their children from saving. For example, whenever one respondent and her sister tried to save a little of their babysitting money, their mother always took the money. Finally, they gave up trying to save. "We figured, why work when she takes the money?" She understood that her family "needed the money," but she couldn't understand why she and her sister couldn't keep at least some of it for saving. Later, she got a job in high school, but she couldn't save any of her earnings then either because she had to pay for her school clothes, lunches, and supplies.

COMING-OF-AGE

Coming-of-age in these households was typically abrupt. Most families simply were not in a position to provide substantial financial and other support during their children's transition to adulthood. Families seldom could provide connections to good jobs, help pay for college, or provide a down payment on a house. Precarious financial—and sometimes familial—situations led families to encourage their children to enter the labor market, often at very young ages. Although respondents learned that higher education was a desirable goal, an aspiration, it was not really expected.

As we see below, Camille's and Anne's stories of coming-of-age play out quite differently, illustrating the effects of familial resources.

Camille

Camille became pregnant at age 15 and in those days, a shotgun marriage followed. Remaining in school was not an option. Until the baby was born, Camille and her husband lived with his mother. After the baby was old enough she took a job as a waitress. "Like most marriages when you marry young like that, they don't last. And we separated. . . . So, I waited tables and things of that nature, worked in cafés, served food, served drinks, and stuff like that." But Camille had dreams of going to college.

After saving and investing his whole life, Camille's father died leaving the family with a few assets, including land, a house, and a little savings. They lost the land in the dispute mentioned earlier, and despite her mother's thrifty ways, there were no resources to pass along to the children. Only the last child received any help paying for college. Camille remembered that college "was never even discussed": "When we growing up, it was just like 'Well, now, we're too poor for you guys to go to college.'" Camille wanted to continue her education, but with a baby and no financial help from her parents, college had to wait.

Many people follow in their parents' occupations, but this was not an option for Camille. Her father's work was dangerous, and by the second half of the twentieth century, these types of jobs (even if they had been open to women) were headed overseas. Her mother's backbreaking domestic work generated little income and offered no benefits.

Looking back, Camille believed that the biggest challenge was not the lack of resources but "the color of their skin." "[It was] very, very prejudiced here in Tulsa, and it still is. It's hidden, it's shielded, and it's better [now], but there's still some Ku Klux Klan around with white sheets on their heads, and this type thing. But they keep it under cover now." The situation encouraged Camille's peers to move away.

> Most kids left here.... If they stayed here, they would have had absolutely nothing because they weren't going to hire us, and you know, we refused to go clean houses and do what our moms did, you know. We wanted a better life, so most of the kids left and went to California, Atlanta, Dallas, different places where they could better themselves.

When she remarried, Camille, her new husband, and her daughter also left Oklahoma. Determined to get some education, Camille then completed a GED and attended secretarial school.

Anne

In contrast, Anne's parents' savings made it possible for Anne to go away to college (she was one of only four respondents whose parents helped pay for college). At the time, she was unappreciative. "I was acting opposite of how my parents felt that I should act. You know, they thought I should be a good, upstanding citizen, and I would do just the opposite, you know." So, although she was going to college as her parents wished, she wasn't interested in getting an education. She admitted that her immaturity contributed to her getting "mixed up in a sorority and drinking," but she also thought it was because her parents did not permit any independence in high school. "I wasn't very mature at all because my parents kept me sheltered." She handled her newfound independence poorly.

Things didn't improve when Anne returned from college after a year. "I went through several years of rebellion." Nonetheless, her parents continued to support her. They paid the first and last months' rent and deposits for her while she attended a local college. "They paid everything." By Anne's own admission, she didn't assume responsibility for her own financial life for many years.

> I worked, but I blew a lot of money. I didn't save. I lived paycheck-to-paycheck. Didn't budget. Didn't do any of that. So . . . it was kind of like throwing a ten-year-old out there and saying, "Okay, you know, pay your bills," and you know. They have a big paycheck and they don't know what to do. It's okay, well, let's go buy some here. Let's go feed all your friends. So, I didn't do very well, didn't do very well for a number of years. . . . I probably didn't grow up until I was 26 years old and had to suffer many years. By suffering . . . [I mean] I learned a lot about what it is like to be poor. What it is like not to have anything. What it is like to not eat. . . . I never knew anything about [poverty] growing up so it was a totally new experience for me.

After a long stretch of not taking responsibility, Anne was finally determined to make it on her own, and "not to take anything off my parents anymore."

WORK AND SCHOOL

For many respondents leaving home for the first time, getting a good job was the practical and expected thing to do. Earning money was a priority. This made sense when respondents came of age at a time when higher education was not essential for a good job or a successful career. For example, one older respondent said that by age six or seven he understood that he would have to work. "I started seeing that my parents weren't going to be able to provide for me the things that I wanted. So I started going out on my own. I used to go on the corner and shine shoes, and do whatever had to be done to bring in a little money." Another older respondent dropped out of high school to help his parents support their large family.

> My parents, they used to do a lot of field work. . . . We moved to California during the '40s, during the Depression when things were really hard out there. But we managed to survive. . . . We used to follow the migrational crop in the summertime. And then in those days, I dropped out of school at the age of 16. You were allowed to do that in order to help your parents out.

Rosalyn and LaVonne, as we already heard, learned early about hard work. Rosalyn went "to school in the morning . . . picked cotton in the evening." LaVonne "started picking cotton" in seventh grade even though it was physically hard on her.

> My feet were flat and so walking on those dirt clods and stuff like that, my arch would fall and I got to the place where I couldn't hardly walk. I mean, I was on my knees at one point because my feet were so sore I couldn't, so I had to stay home. I couldn't do that [work] for long periods of time at all.

However, we also found that younger respondents—who need more education to get ahead—also felt an intense pull toward work. To the detriment of future opportunity, many entered the labor market at young ages, dropping out of high school or forgoing higher education and training.

Seven respondents began working at age 14 or younger. One person got a job at a steakhouse restaurant. "I applied for a job and you had to be 15. So I lied and said that I was 15, and I got a job." Another, the eldest of three girls raised by her mother, also began working at age 14. She worked in restaurants, supermarkets, and nursing homes, "trying to help my family out as much as I could." Some worked to help pay household bills. Some worked in their parents' business. Some worked to buy school items, clothes, cars, and things their parents would not or could not afford. Working offered a greater sense of independence and control, and their own money gave them independence from sometimes problematic family situations.

Sometimes families insisted, against their children's wishes, that they work. One respondent recounted her grandmother's insistence that she get a part-time job. "She was real adamant about me going to work when I was 16" to pay for "things I needed."

By age 16, at least 26 respondents were working; many moved from informal to formal jobs, working as waitresses, servers, retail clerks, stockers, and manual laborers. They worked in fast food joints and restaurants (14), grocery and discount stores such as Wal-Mart and K-Mart (11), and unskilled labor sites (10). A few joined the military, and one joined AmeriCorps following high school.

Only a few parents objected. Anne's mother was one of them. She wanted Anne to focus on school and opposed her daughter's decision to work part-time in high school. They compromised; the money Anne earned would go into savings. But Anne spent it anyway. "I was actually pretty irresponsible. I think a lot of it again was this rebellion that I felt."

A few also made poor decisions along the way or found themselves in difficult circumstances. Five women, including Camille, quit school because of an unplanned pregnancy. Some dropped out to care for family. One young woman left high school to care for her baby niece who had just been diagnosed with a serious illness. The baby's mother had been recently divorced and had no one else to help her. Our respondent believed she was needed more at home with her niece. Moreover, she admitted that she was less than enthusiastic about high school.

A few got in trouble with the law. Some got mixed up with drugs and alcohol. One of the youngest respondents explained that by the time she was 14 she "really started getting into a delinquent lifestyle." Even though she was working, she was "consuming" her earnings "instead of thinking wisely about what to do with the money." She left home at 17 and moved from job to job. Sharing an apartment with a relative and his girlfriend, she recalled that her "main goal and objective" was "to party." After a while, she grew weary of getting nowhere, moved out, and began to get her life together.

High School

The pull of work was often accompanied by the push from a tenuous, conflicted relationship with school. Even though they recognized the value of schooling for getting a better job, respondents often lacked the self-confidence and preparation to succeed in school or to find school rewarding. Moreover, the quality of the schooling they received was questionable (Shapiro 2004). Several respondents dropped out or were expelled because they missed too much school or ran into trouble at school.

Some respondents lacked sustained support and encouragement to complete school or to continue on to higher education. Although many parents told their children that education was important, many had little schooling themselves and were often ill-equipped to support their children's education and insist on attendance. Theresa's parents, for example, were high school dropouts and did not know how to support her desire to finish school. When she did graduate, her parents were proud of her accomplishment, but Theresa felt little support along the way.

In interviews, at least 22 respondents said they quit regular high school for various reasons. Many regretted this decision. Most eventually returned to complete their high school degree or a GED, but they said it was far more costly than if they had stayed in school in the first place.[2] A respondent recalled the decision to drop out in the tenth grade. "I don't know why I quit school. I guess

I just got to where I just missed so much school I'd got to where I just got further behind and then I decided just to go to work and . . . . I thought I was too smart to go to school, I guess." She earned her GED when she was 32 years old.

Postsecondary Education: "The Future Was Never an Option"

Eventually, Camille completed a GED and attended secretarial school, and Anne finished an associate's degree in accounting. Overall, respondents attained more formal schooling than their parents, although they did not go far by today's standards (see table 1.1). Three-quarters of the respondents took at least some college classes, but only one-third of respondents completed a postsecondary degree. Many pursued technical training rather than an associate's or bachelor's degree.

Respondents often struggled for years to complete education and training programs. Some succeeded and some did not. Some pursued alternative strategies, such as vocational certificates, military training, or secretarial and business diplomas, in an effort to acquire credentials quickly and less expensively.

Families continued to emphasize the importance of work over school. As Camille pointed out, her parents' attitude was that they couldn't afford college, "so you better be good at something." As another respondent put it, "The future was never an option." Only four respondents said they ever received financial support for higher education from their families. They paid their way through school with the assistance of financial aid and other resources they assembled on their own.

But most, facing high costs for education, lack of financial support from family, increasing family responsibilities, and the draw of employment and earnings, chose work over school. It's not that they didn't try. As one respondent recalled, "I went back to school three or four different times, but something always stands in my way. I got nine months of accounting that there's no record of because I didn't finish."

Some also had to help support their families of origin. One person quit college in his sophomore year "to help with the family business" after his stepfather got cancer. Similarly, another completed high school but did not go on to college because her family needed her at home. "My dad was very sick at that time and I had to kind of help out in that situation at home 'cause it was just my mom." After her father became very ill, she did not return to school and instead worked cleaning houses.

Others had to support their own families. As one respondent said, she found it tough to go to school and also support her child: "I did that for about four months. Then finances and everything just kind of buckled under me. So, things just didn't work out anymore, so I quit, and I didn't really try any other schools after that." Another described how she weighed the benefits of education, cost of forgone earnings, and her day-to-day expenses. "It was a hard decision to make because I really would like to have stayed in school. But at that time I had bills, and so I had to make a choice. And that was my choice, to actually go ahead and stop school and continue to work full-time."

Some were prevented from further education. Cynthia married at age 16. She attended trade school, working evenings at a department store, while her husband attended school and worked two jobs on nights and weekends. The couple lived with his parents for a few years but otherwise received no financial support from either set of parents. Cynthia dreamed about a career in nursing or theology. Unfortunately, this bright young woman's dreams were thwarted by her husband who would not let his wife pursue either degree, although she qualified for both. "So that was biting the bullet many times, because there was things that I was capable of doing and wanting to do, but there again, I couldn't do it."

In sum, respondents faced greater pressure to work than to attend school. Lack of role models, financial insecurity, and family instability and dissolution contributed to their disengagement from school, which often began in childhood. Few had any hope that there would be financial support for school, so in the end it seemed that focusing on work and having a family made more sense.

DISCUSSION

Looking back on childhood, most respondents recalled that parents did their best to provide for them, but poverty and other problems presented significant obstacles for personal development. The poorest families, including Rosalyn's, LaVonne's, and Cynthia's, could afford little more than the basics—shelter, food, and clothing—while others, like Anne's family, provided more. For many, unstable incomes and financial hardship posed a constant challenge. Parents' low levels of education led to low-wage employment, so parents often worked long hours holding down two or more jobs. For African American respondents, in particular, racial discrimination formed a backdrop, constraining economic and educational opportunity, and threatening family well-being (Oliver and Shapiro 1995; Conley 1999; Shapiro 2004; Nembhard and Chiteji 2006). Relatively few families received outside assistance, such as welfare support, although some recalled receiving housing subsidies and occasional support during periods of crisis. In some cases, emotional turmoil and family instability exacerbated the lack of economic resources (Elder et al. 1992).

Most families did not accumulate much in savings and other assets. They kept small amounts at home for emergencies, and in some cases, they held bank accounts, bonds, IRAs, and the like. In at least some instances, families saved or inherited small wealth in order to be able to invest in a house or land, although the evidence suggests that most relied heavily on credit to purchase vehicles and durables.

As respondents grew up, their families' financial demands led parents to emphasize the importance of work over education. For some, the money from jobs provided cash to buy things they wanted, but for some (and especially as they got older) earnings covered costs of school clothing, supplies, and other activities (Pritchard, Myers, and Cassidy 1989).

Few respondents learned much about the details of financially managing a household and saving. Children learned how to manage a household on relatively little money from their parents' example. Families emphasized the importance of frugality and thrift to make ends meet, and they set aside small amounts for emergencies. Respondents said their parents did not discuss money matters openly with the children (Shobe and Christy-McMullin 2005), because parents believed that family finances were not a concern for children, or because they were reluctant to provoke anxiety in their children.

Relatively few respondents had savings as children. Respondents mostly learned from observation, and through trial and error, about how to manage their finances, arrange for financial services, and sometimes set aside what was left over in savings. They did not benefit from early experiences that, in Kotlikoff and Bernheim's words, would "habituate savings" (2001, 453; Webley et al. 2001). In a different era, this might not have been true. In the late nineteenth to middle twentieth century, saving was encouraged, and opportunities to save through school-based savings programs were more widespread (Zelizer 1989; Cruce 2001, 2002; Wadhwani 2006). We should ask if the absence of savings opportunities today ignores an important factor in a successful transition to adulthood.

Like young people from every walk of life, some respondents made youthful missteps. Poor performance in school, dropping out before graduation, early pregnancy, and drug and alcohol dependency were not uncommon. Some left home at a young age to escape family strife or to seek autonomy. Though sometimes understandable, these actions often had serious consequences. As we saw, Camille and several others became mothers at a very young age. Without familial and school support to continue their education, they dropped out and forged their way in the adult world with small children.

Most families were in no position to do what wealthier families do when children get into trouble: move to a safer neighborhood with good schools and after-school programs; hire a competent lawyer to get a wayward child off a drug charge; pay for enrichment experiences that develop a child's interests and keep him or her off the street; take out a second mortgage to help pay for college; or pay for health care and possibly an abortion.

Those with family support suffered fewer negative consequences, like Anne whose parents continued to support her, pay for her schooling, and generally pick up the pieces until she matured enough to assume adult responsibilities. The few respondents who benefited from familial resources as they left home, like Anne, illustrate the potential impact of what Thomas Shapiro has termed "transformative" or "head-start" assets (2004). According to Shapiro, family wealth lifts people beyond "where their own achievements, jobs, and earnings would place them" (2004, 2–3). Most respondents in this study were not as lucky and paid for their mistakes in lost time, money, and opportunity.

After their children left home, families were too stretched financially to provide tangible resources. Although parents lent a hand when they could, only a few families could afford to subsidize or underwrite postsecondary education, or help their children buy a house that would provide stability for a young family. Families were generally unable to line up resources to keep children on the right track and shape a more hopeful vision of their future (Conley 2001; Shapiro 2004). This financial instability often led to years of respondents' trying to catch up, often with children and spouses in tow.

Although many respondents sought additional education and training beyond the high school level, most did not complete a four-year degree. As a result, even though they obtained more schooling than their parents, education levels remained fairly low and did not prepare respondents for a new economy that requires higher degrees.

In sum, given families' limited ability to push, guide, and sometimes rescue them during late adolescence and early adulthood, respondents' efforts to gain an economic foothold were more difficult than those of young people who grew up with more resources and support. For a large number of the respondents in this study, the transition to adulthood was quite abrupt, with economic independence raising particularly difficult challenges (Webley et al. 2001, 73). If respondents' recollections are accurate, they learned little about how to manage their lives financially. This does not bode well for a successful transition to economic adulthood; as Shlomo Maital suggests, "we march along the milestones of our economic lives carrying mental baggage dating back to childhood" (1982, 49–50). Compared to wealthier young people, whose long tenure in college and sometimes graduate school, civic service, and internships prepares them for adulthood, respondents in this study were typically thrust into a world of adult responsibilities at a young age.

It was a hard landing. Many made their way with educational deficits, family responsibilities, and no savings. A few were dealing with thorny problems, such as drug and alcohol addiction or a prison record. Not only was there no one to help with living expenses or college tuition, no one was there to pick up an extra expense for dental work or help buy a car to get to school and work. Moreover, there is little evidence that educational, financial, employment, or social welfare institutions stepped in to assist families to get ahead (Finnegan 1998; Venkatesh 2006). Even for those respondents whose parents taught them about saving, their life situations made it difficult for them to accumulate much. In all of these ways, growing up in a working-poor household provided a weak foundation for respondents' future saving.

In the next two chapters, we follow the respondents out of their youth and learn how they make ends meet and make financial decisions in their own households.

CHAPTER 4

Managing Household Finances
and Making Ends Meet on a Low Income

The financial lives of these low-income families reflect findings of recent social science accounts that describe the conditions of working poverty and the challenges of financial survival, especially among single parent families with children (Edin and Lein 1997; Newman 1999; Ehrenreich 2001; Shipler 2004; Rank 2005). Respondents discuss major consumption pressures, including medical expenses, child care, and transportation, as well as the temptation to spend on "extras." They talk about costs associated with choosing to live in safe neighborhoods with decent schools.

As active managers of their financial lives, the respondents and their families adopt rules to help them make financial decisions (Davis 1992; Edin and Lein 1997; Romich and Weisner 2000). If they must, they borrow or negotiate bill payments, take on additional employment, or use savings. Most of the families use mainstream financial services to pay bills and save, although many use them inconsistently or inefficiently. They also use alternative financial services that are costly but accessible. Faced with low incomes and high expenses, families typically adopt a perspective that they will make it through hard times with faith and hard work.

In this chapter, we describe the ways these low-income families generate income and handle their basic monthly expenses. We then chronicle the ways they manage their bills and make financial decisions, choose their financial priorities, minimize consumption, and deal with unplanned expenses, while attempting to keep options open for the future. We explore strategies and behaviors in the context of respondents' values, priorities, and constraints, asking,

How do families track expenses and budget? Do they combine all income sources and allocate to expenses depending on priorities, as economic theory would suggest? Where do they get the money to cover large intermittent or unexpected expenses? How do they use financial services as they try to make ends meet? Finally, do these patterns of financial management shed light on respondents' ability to save?

We begin with Tonya and Ella in their efforts to manage household finances on small and frequently fluctuating incomes. Differing in age, gender, race, and family status, they, like the other respondents in this study, have to work hard to make ends meet while striving to generate enough financial security to ensure stability, and with any luck, to shape a positive future for themselves and their children.

Tonya

Tonya is raising three young children on her own and going to school. Managing the household finances is a balancing act, as it is for 41 others in this study with children at home. Tonya's life has not been easy. She broke up with her youngest child's father after she and her doctor concluded that he might have injured their baby.

As a single parent with one child, Tonya managed with her small income, but when she had a second child, it became increasingly difficult to cover her growing family's expenses. "[The baby] was really eating me out of house and home!" She had to be very careful, allotting her two paychecks each month to certain expenses, but nonetheless falling short.

> We really lived from paycheck-to-paycheck and I paid the daycare out of one check—or it may have been half the daycare out of one check and half out of the other—and the rent out of one. There was one check that always seemed to not have enough money.

Although she likely would have qualified for public assistance, Tonya did not apply at the time. "I didn't know how to apply for welfare, and nobody told me that 'you're really poor.' I didn't think I was poor. . . . Or I didn't have that mindset that I was poor."

Even though they struggled financially, Tonya made a strategic decision to return to school so she could qualify for a better job. This meant she was always busy and stressed, although she believed it was worthwhile. It helped that when she was in school she qualified for public assistance and medical coverage. She used the AmeriCorps stipend that she earned from her one year of civic service, and the college awarded Tonya a tuition waiver and a small scholarship. She took out some student loans to cover household expenses. Tonya recently landed a new job in the school system, with better health insurance and a pension.

Ella

As long as she can remember, Ella searched for ways to get ahead, and money has been a central part of her strategy. Ella learned over her 50 years how to stretch a dollar, a knack that she says she inherited from her mother. Even though the family was very poor, Ella can remember the family turning to public assistance only once in her childhood: in the period after her father was hurt on the job and before he qualified for disability benefits. Public assistance at that time meant commodities, such as milk and cheese. The children helped during hard times by bringing in extra cash that Ella's mother used to buy school clothes. Ella worked for an elderly woman, earning $15 a week.

Since she's been married, Ella, like her mother, makes all of the household financial decisions: rent, food, and utilities come first, then other expenses. "If it is something that I know that I need and we got to have, that's how they are prioritized. We have to have food. We have to have electricity. We have to have water."

> And then other things come later, you know, even if I have this credit card and even if it gets to the point where the credit card might not look like it's going to be paid this month, I'll still go ahead and take care of what I need and maybe not have all the money to send in on my card, but [I'll] try and send some.

Although her family faces financial pressures, it is important to Ella that she also help others. She stays involved in her children's sports programs, church, and local politics. Ella's job involves reaching out to young pregnant women. She helps them obtain health care, baby supplies, emergency services, and counseling. Ella said the young girls she works with never learned what they could accomplish in life. "That's the only way they can do anything is have someone else come in and say, 'If you can't do this, then I'll help you out.'"

HOUSEHOLD ECONOMIC RESOURCES

Most families in this study have low incomes, although there is variation. Mean monthly earned income from employment and self-employment is $1,103.

Combined with "other" unearned income, respondents' mean monthly income is $1,359 and ranges from $270 to $3,350.[1] Calculated on an annual basis, household income averages $16,308 (assuming similar income in all months) and ranges from $3,240 to $40,200.

Employment

Jobs are the main source of income for most families (table 4.1). Reflecting a now common portrait of working poverty, respondents' jobs tend to lack benefits and avenues for advancement (Levitan and Shapiro 1987; Swartz and Weigert 1995; Kempson 1996; Ehrenreich 2001; Heymann, with Cohen and Rogers 2002; Shipler 2004).

The largest group of respondents work in service occupations, closely followed by administrative support jobs and other semiprofessional jobs like teacher's aides, sales, and social services (table 4.2).

A small group of respondents have stable employment and earn a living wage or better. A few have jobs in the professional or service sectors. For exam-

TABLE 4.1. Respondents' Household Income Sources (N = 84)

	Total n (%)
Earned income	
Employment	74 (88)
Self-employment	14 (17)
Doing work for others	9 (11)
Taking people to places	2 (2)
Selling things you make	1 (1)
Other income	
Family/friends	22 (26)
Housing subsidies	19 (23)
Child support	16 (19)
Food stamps	13 (15)
Social Security	11 (13)
Family support	10 (12)
TANF	5 (6)
Investment income	3 (4)
Supplemental Security Income	4 (5)
Unemployment benefits	3 (4)
Veteran benefits	1 (1)
Unspecified sources	4 (5)

Source: Abt Associates, baseline survey.

TABLE 4.2. Respondents' Occupations (N = 84)

	Total n (%)
Service	16 (19)
Administrative support	12 (14)
Teachers and aides	8 (10)
Sales	6 (7)
Social and human services	6 (7)
Construction	5 (6)
Technicians	5 (6)
Administrative and managerial	4 (5)
Child and elder care	3 (4)
Nurses and aides	3 (4)
Machine operators	2 (2)
Security	2 (2)
Mechanics	1 (1)
Transportation	1 (1)
Other	10 (12)

Source: Abt Associates 2004.

ple, one person has a good job with benefits in a medical center, while another works at a computer company, and another has been a registered nurse for 18 years. A father of three went "from dishwasher to general manager to opening restaurants for people." His current employer is even helping him pay for classes toward a degree in business.

However, most respondents, like their parents, face significant employment and income challenges. With unstable job histories, most move from job to job because of low pay, layoffs, or lack of advancement opportunities. As one woman pointed out, she has held many different low-wage jobs over more than two decades. "I have been a nanny. I've been a senior companion. I've been a cook. And I've been cleaning."

Irregular and volatile job income makes it difficult for families to plan (Davis and Weber 1990; Hills, Smithies, and McKnight 2006). A participant who works as a waitress said that her fluctuating earnings, which she described as "drastically up-and-down," challenged her ability to plan and budget until she learned to anticipate the pattern. "After a few years, I figured it out. Okay, this is going to happen again this year. You know when you're doing real good for a while, and then all of a sudden it cuts back, it leaves you kind of financially in trouble."

Like Ella, who has worked two jobs most of her life, many respondents (60) work multiple jobs or overtime to boost household income. One respondent, divorced with two small children, works 50 to 60 hours a week at $10 per hour to keep up with household expenses. "You just start working yourself to death, because you never make any money unless you are making overtime. Or, at least, I haven't!" Another respondent, an older woman in her 70s, supplements her small social security check with a $7.55-an-hour nursing home job.

Self-employment provides supplementary income in several households. Respondents do jobs like hauling, yard work, hair and nails, and domestic work. They manage rental properties, hold garage sales, and provide day care. One mother opened her own home-based business so she can stay home with three children. A father works in maintenance but also does "a little barbering on the side" to help support his family of three. Another man's monthly flea market business brings in a little extra. "On the weekends you can rent a space at a flea market or something and just sell odds and ends. Like I may buy some goods from a wholesale company, just little odds and ends, and then you go to a flea market and you sell them."

Working so much places a strain on families, especially those with children at home. Torn between hours at work and time at home, mothers and fathers lament the lack of time with their children.

Some respondents are underemployed, working part-time but prefer full-time work. One mother, for example, works part-time in order to have time to care for a child with a serious chronic illness. The man with the flea market business explained that he had been involuntarily "downsized" because the business where he works was doing poorly. A woman living with a chronic health condition whose steady income comes from disability benefits works only "a few hours a day" because the regulations "allow [you] to work so much, not much, before they start snatching your benefits." She supplements her monthly disability check by caring for the elderly and performing odd jobs like cleaning houses. "I'm always doing something for somebody—it's like, 'Would you come and do this and I'll pay you?' Naturally I'm gonna say 'Okay' 'cause I can put it in my gas tank or whatever."

Six respondents were unemployed at the time of the interview. Unemployment, or the threat of unemployment, is unsettling and creates anxiety. As this 40-year-old explained, "It is just the part of being without work and not knowing where my future is going is the hardest part."

Means-Tested Public Assistance

More than a third of families receive some form of public assistance (34). According to respondents, housing subsidies (19), including Section 8 housing (11) and public housing (8), are particularly helpful, even though conditions are not necessarily safe or pleasant. One mother explained that the public housing where she lives is so dangerous that she does not let her "kids play out in the front yard." Nonetheless, she said that it is very helpful to have this resource when her income dips. "It's good when you get laid off and your income stops, because if it would have been any other house I would have had to move out."

Some families receive means-tested cash assistance, including food stamps (13), Temporary Assistance for Needy Families (5), and Supplemental Security Income (4). Even though incomes are low, respondents do not qualify for public assistance in general because they are working (a requirement for selection into the IDA program). In the past, many more of these families had received some form of assistance for periods of time.

Like their parents, respondents express reluctance to turn to means-tested cash assistance programs. Cynthia, for example, would not consider applying for "welfare." "I never was on welfare and I refuse. Because I knew as long as I have breath in my body and I could work, I will make a living and I will be a productive citizen." Another respondent, age 38 with two young children, described her dismay when a friend talked her into applying for assistance after she left her abusive husband. "I was screaming and crying over the concept of it because it was something I really wanted to avoid, but I didn't have much choice. I ended up doing it. I went on food stamps." Respondents are more likely to consider public assistance when they are in school because it is time-limited and they think they will not have to apply again once they receive credentials and better-paying jobs.

Support from Family and Friends

The majority of respondents (49) reported that they receive some financial support from family members and friends. The largest and most regular financial contributions come from former spouses or partners including paying for things like diapers or children's school clothes and supplies.

Among the 18 divorced respondents with children, only 7 receive child support. Therefore, it is not surprising to hear frustration and sometimes anger from mothers who cannot count on the father's support check. For example, one woman recounted 13 years of legal battles to get child support. "You marry somebody and, you know, things go wrong when you are young, but for them to not be responsible for a child they brought into the world!" In another case, the court awarded a mother back child support, but she never collected because her former husband was laid off work.

> He was ordered by a judge to pay back child support and current child support and then $19,000 to the State of Oklahoma for the support they lent me to get through school and to get daycare and those kinds of things. And he paid for— I don't know—a couple of months, and then he got laid off.

Tonya recounted a similar situation. After years of trying to get her children's father to provide financial support, she realized he would never make regular contributions.

> I've had to learn to let a lot of things go. Like the child support money. Everybody says you should keep fighting, but that just really tears you up on the inside and you're still not getting it, and you're spending all that energy getting upset and hounding people and calling and making him mad and then he starts in and he's still not going to give any money. And he said that if they tried to garnish his checks that he would just quit. . . . I mean that's a no-win situation.

Although Tonya knew she had to "let it go," she said, "That much money is hard to learn to let go."

Other respondents (22) receive small and irregular financial help from parents and other family members, and occasionally friends. Sometimes this support comes as a cash gift during the holidays or for birthdays. Typically, these contributions are earmarked for specific purposes. Depending on the size of the gift, respondents use it to pay for a meal, to pay for school supplies, to purchase a vehicle, to help with college tuition, or to make a down payment for a house. For example, when one woman's husband abandoned her with the children, his grandparents helped her finish paying for a car. Another respondent's parents made the down payment on a house for him and his family.

Reciprocal obligations and expectations often accompany gifts and contributions from family and friends, as Carol Stack observes in her classic study of support networks in a low-income community (1974). When a respondent comes into money (e.g., an insurance settlement or a tax refund), others may expect generosity in return. When Tonya received her tuition grant and loan money for college, for example, her mother expected Tonya to lend some of it to her for living expenses.

> When I was in school [my mom] would know when I was getting like my grants and stuff, so she would ask for money around those times. So I helped her out for quite a few semesters that way and then her bill that she owed me got way up and then what she ended up paying me in the end wasn't nearly what [she owed].

Other Resources

Some respondents receive social insurance benefits, including Social Security (11), unemployment benefits (3), and veteran's benefits (1) (table 4.1). Even though there are 11 respondents over 55 years of age, including three over 65 years, only four report any investment income. Many also rely on religious institutions for tangible assistance during hard times (more on this later).

The Family Village. Some women, including Tonya, lived for a time in the Family Village, a nonprofit that provides free rent and utilities for single women and their children. The Family Village is one of the few sources of non-family support that respondents believed helped them get ahead. Tonya lived in the Village with her mother and brother after her mother's divorce when Tonya was 13. "They have these little houses, duplexes, and you have to provide your own like stove and refrigerator, and that kind of stuff. And you have to make one improvement each year on the house and that's it."[2]

Being accepted to live in the Village is a relief. One woman described receiving the news that there was a place for her in the Village after her divorce. "When they called me, the lady got tickled at me 'cause I was like whoopin' and hollerin'. . . . You'd have thought I'd won a million bucks!" Another respondent with three teenagers similarly was thankful to have been selected to move into the Village: "I was to the point—I couldn't pay my rent. Rent was coming due. All my bills were coming due."

Attitudes toward the Village contrast sharply with those toward public assistance. The environment is pleasant and safe; respondents feel they are making economic and personal progress while there; and they understand they must make sacrifices for the privilege of staying there. As one respondent explained, families can live in the Village for many years as long as they qualify and make progress toward their goals. She spelled out the conditions: "To live there you have to be either going to school and working a part-time job or working a full-time job . . . and you have to have at least two children." Another chuckled softly as she described her life there: earning a GED, taking classes while cleaning people's houses, babysitting, mowing yards, and "anything to make a dollar." She was able to save some money and, while there, met many other women with children who "had a lot of things in common . . . women who are wanting to better themselves."

PAYING THE BILLS AND COVERING EXPENSES

In the face of low, fluctuating, and undependable income, how do respondents make financial decisions and make ends meet? Tonya recalled that when her children were smaller, managing finances was a balancing act. She brought in as much income as possible by working a full-time job and moonlighting. She kept expenses low. The cost of housing was low, and she cut back on meals as much as possible. She shopped carefully, buying things on sale. "We ate at home a lot or . . . we could get like two Happy Meals and split [them] between the three of us." She paid attention to prices. "I also went through all the sale ads that we would get and I would pick out what I was going to buy from each store and sometimes you could get a lot of groceries for like $10 doing it that way."

Like Tonya, almost all of the families employ similar strategies, actively managing their financial lives (Davis 1992; Edin and Lein 1997; Romich and Weisner 2000; Lister 2006). In households where expenses regularly threaten to exceed income, respondents "juggle" their finances to make ends meet month to month. More than half (49) reported they are managing, but they have to be very careful. The father of two small children explained that even though they pay their bills and have a decent quality of life, "there's always [financial] juggling going on."

Each respondent has a slightly different definition of "making ends meet," but most understand this to mean that they can afford the most basic things such as food, clothing, housing, and utilities on their limited incomes. Thirty-one respondents said they sometimes do not meet this standard. At the time of the interview, for example, one respondent said she was doing better, but she remembered navigating difficult financial times.

> So I was just juggling my bills just trying to . . . pay enough to keep them on, you know, and having a really hard time. I mean, we ate Ramen noodles, cereal, and hot dogs. That's all I bought and we ate those for I don't know how long. [After a while] I didn't even care if I ate, I was so sick of eating those.

Making ends meet does not necessarily include being able to cover all contingencies. Making ends meet means not having to "beg or borrow," according to one person. Another said making ends meet means avoiding problems with lenders.

> I've never had anything repossessed. I have always been able to make our car payments. . . . We don't have creditors knocking on our door or calling on our telephone. We have food. We have shelter. We have clothes. They may not be the best clothes. Our children don't have all the latest designer clothes, but they have clothes and they do well.

In a theme that emerged throughout the interviews, respondents said that unexpected expenses, such as health problems, vehicle repairs, or school fees, are particularly difficult to accommodate in a family budget. Problems with a vehicle, for example, can throw a household into financial chaos. In a typical scenario, an older respondent with a teenage son recounted what happened when his car broke down. Because he needed a car to get to work, he paid more than he should have for a new car that he bought in a hurry. "I hated I needed that car like that . . . . And now I got a $240 car payment that I really didn't want." As David Caplovitz points out in his 1967 groundbreaking study, *The*

Poor Pay More, the poor frequently pay more than their higher-income counterparts because they must act immediately to avoid even worse consequences.

Tracking Income and Expenses

In order to know where they can cut corners and where they must spend, families track their expenses and budget, especially during times when money is particularly tight, although few use formal budgeting techniques (Godwin 1990; Godwin and Koonce 1992). Theresa "had to learn how to budget" because she and the children live on a public assistance budget. "I got real good at budgeting 'cause you only get a check once a month here and that has to last you the entire month." Rosalyn mentally tracks her money.

> I know where every dime of my money goes. . . . I don't have to write down nothing for where my money is going. Right off my head I can tell you where my money went. 'Cause I remember what I spend my money on. My money is valuable to me.

One respondent stores her earnings from a temporary job in a file box with tabs for each month. She uses this file system to cover phone, cable, and gas expenses for the better part of a year. Others use an envelope system to track and control income and expenses. These systems are reminiscent of the "tin can economy" described by Lee Rainwater, Richard P. Coleman, and Gerald Handel (1959), in which families earmark and set aside money in various containers for particular purposes. They quote a woman describing her "silly little system" of setting aside grocery money in a kitchen drawer, cash in a tin can, and a checking account that receives the monthly surplus from the tin can.

> For those who practice a "tin can" or "envelope" economy, the greatest advantage in the procedure seems to be the vivid statement of their current spending power provided by an "empty" or "full" can. An empty can more dramatically commands, "thou shalt not spend," than does a nearly red bank balance. (155)

Most respondents could estimate their regular household expenses. Table 4.3 summarizes how they reported spending their money in a typical month.[3] These data, presented as median monthly expenditures, offer insight into household spending priorities among the families. The highest expenses include mortgage or rent, utilities, food, childcare, transportation, and loans. Clothing and household items are also regular and important expenses. While only six respondents pay monthly debt consolidation bills, many others pay credit card debt, car loans, school loans, and business or personal loans. We will return to this topic in the next chapter.

Some respondents employ sophisticated calculations to cover bills. For ex-

TABLE 4.3. Median Monthly Household Expenses

	Median Expenses (in dollars)	Number in Sample Providing Data
Mortgage or rent	348	83
Food	233	81
Child care	160	16
Gas or public transportation	75	81
Household utilities		
Electric	60	64
Telephone	48	80
Gas	30	58
Water/sewer	30	54
Cable TV	11	45
Miscellaneous household items	30	72
Clothing	40	71
Medical and dental	30	39
Entertainment	20	68
Insurance[a]		
Life/burial insurance	23	36
Loans and credit		
Credit cards	43	53
Vehicle loan	195	51
Business/personal loan	150	23
School loans	70	16
Debt consolidation	161	6

Source: Center for Social Development, in-depth interviews.

[a]We omit vehicle insurance from this table because only 46 respondents included vehicle insurance, whereas most talked about owning a car. It is likely that many pay for vehicle insurance semiannually and forgot to mention the expense. Among those who have vehicle insurance, premiums range in cost from $40 to $175 per month, with an average monthly premium of $97. Because not all respondents discussed paying for car insurance or specified how much they paid, this average payment should be interpreted with caution. Seventy respondents reported having health insurance, but some did not have to pay for coverage or did not know the cost. For example, some had government insurance or received coverage on a spouse's policy.

ample, one young college student uses a budget to oblige herself to set aside money to pay larger bills. She puts money in a container each week. Although she calls it a "buffer," she uses it to pay her largest bill, a student loan. "I would set money aside and I'd mark a date that I wanted to have that paid off." She has a simple rule of thumb to calculate how much she should spend each day. On days that she does not spend that much money, she considers that she has a surplus that can be spent on an extra or saved for her student loan.

Economizing

One-third of respondents focus whenever possible on being frugal and cutting corners (table 4.4). Many respondents learned about frugality from their parents, and plan their spending carefully, "looking for bargains" and "for deals" (see chap. 3). They shop with care, buy less expensive brands, shop "off-season" for clothing, and purchase food and clothing on sale. Tonya, for example, is an economizer and regularly shops sales for the children's school supplies and clothes. Knowing that buying on the "spur of the moment" is unwise she, like others, avoids shopping as much as possible.

A few people economize by cooking from scratch, growing some of their own food, and sewing or buying used clothing. One respondent, who lives in the Family Village, said her family switches to cheaper food and shops at garage sales when they need to reduce expenditures. "It doesn't bother me to eat, you know, beans and sandwiches for two weeks if that's what we gotta eat. Or just cook from scratch. Just, that's usually where I cut back." Although generally they prefer not to buy used merchandise, she and eight others said they regularly buy some "really good stuff" at garage sales and used clothing stores. Others receive hand-me-downs from family and close friends.

TABLE 4.4. Strategies for Making Ends Meet (*N* = 84)

	Total *n* (%)
Economize	28 (33)
Juggling and negotiating	22 (26)
Work more or sell things	21 (25)
Reduce the cost of debt	13 (15)
Spend tax refunds and savings	13 (15)

Source: Center for Social Development, in-depth interviews.
Note: Respondents could report multiple strategies.

Cutting back requires distinguishing among purchases based on whether or not they can get along without them. Just as they can delay some bills, but not others, they evaluate purchases. They translate this idea into rules about purchases as well. Ella, like many other respondents, establishes rules about "needs" versus "wants." As she explained, "If your car quits, that's something you've got to have because you've got to have transportation to get back and forth to work." However, if it is not necessary, it can wait. "Something that you want is totally different, you know. We can wait on this." She observes, though, that what constitutes a "need" has changed over time. "I mean I didn't have hot water growing up unless we heated it, but once I moved to Tulsa and found out, 'Man, I can just turn some hot water on,' you know, I thought that was really living! I don't want that taken away." A father of three young children asks himself, "Is it really gonna help us? Do we really need it? Can we wait another month before we can get it? Sometimes that's what we have to do." Another woman uses a list when she shops. Starting at the top, she works her way down the list until the money is gone. She delays purchasing the rest.

Part of what distinguishes a need from a want has to do with gauging the benefits of a particular purchase. In this way, money management includes important nonfinancial factors that take into consideration a family's overall quality of life. For example, a mother of two school-age children uses paper plates so that she will have more time to spend with her children instead of washing dishes. These decisions vary depending on the person's values, according to another respondent: "People just want to do different things with their money."

There are ways that respondents cut back on necessities. Tonya, for example, recalled eating less during hard times. "A few times when we were stretching until the next paycheck . . . then I gave [the children] their regular portions and I just ate a little bit." When another woman's income decreased from $1,400 to $1,000 a month, she had to say "no" to her three teenagers more often. For example, they cut back on going out to eat.

A few respondents mentioned reducing their utility bills. One person explained to the interviewer how she is keeping her air conditioning bills to a minimum. "If you look around before you leave, I got all my windows covered with like dark—maybe a towel or a dark curtain or something. Keep the lights out, keep the doors closed. . . . My bills go down so much, so much." Others admonish their children to turn out the lights, or use budget billing for light and gas bills.

Juggling and Negotiating

Like Ella, who discussed her financial decision making at the beginning of this chapter, most respondents adopt rules of thumb about the order in which they pay their bills. Their rules seem to reflect three criteria: the bill's importance, its due date in relation to the pattern of household income flows, and the cost of delaying bill payment.

First, respondents pay bills that cover basic needs or "necessities" (e.g., rent or mortgage payments, food, transportation, and child care) and typically pay them from a more or less dependable and regular income source, such as job earnings. They leave less important bills for later, using other—often less reliable—sources of income. As one mother described her choices: "If I don't feed my family, they gonna go hungry. If I don't pay the rent, we ain't gonna have a roof over our heads. If I don't make those car note payments, we ain't gonna have none of that."

Second, the bill's due date and pattern of household income flow influences when they pay a bill. Because the families often live very close to the edge, they need a backup plan if they cannot cover their bills every month. Tonya, for instance, said the rent and other basics "go straight off the top," but the calculus becomes more complicated when it comes to intermittent expenses, like tuition bills, insurance, clothing, or eating out.

> I would just guesstimate how much would need to come out of each paycheck to go towards [school]. When insurance comes due—that's around going back to school time—then I just see how much is needed to come out of each paycheck. Or, the other way I would do it is to take all the money that would be coming in throughout that time, and then take out everything that needed to go and then that was what was left over and so that would be what you got to eat out on or what you got to spend for clothes or something like that.

Another respondent recalled the panic in her mother's house when the end of the month came and there was no money left to cover the remaining bills. As a result, she is careful to pay all of the bills when her monthly paycheck arrives. "I just didn't want to come to the end of the month and not have what it is that you needed and be all freaked out like my mom was, and that kind of thing. I just hate that."

Finally, when they cannot cover the bills, families must turn to extreme methods. They weigh the cost of delaying bill payment. Tonya, for example, scrambling to come up with money to pay bills, occasionally pawns something to cover a bill. She also figures how long a bill can go unpaid before service is disconnected. Another respondent pays bills based on which is "gonna hurt . . . the worst" if she does not pay and which she can let "slide." Another develops elaborate guidelines, paying particular attention to the payment rules of various vendors, importance, due dates, and penalties. In this way, he juggles the order for paying bills and simultaneously avoids late fees (Chattoe and Gilbert 1999). He is aware how each might affect his credit rating.

> I understand the fact that on certain bills you have a 30-day window. So, if it's due on the first, you have 'til the first, or actually up to the 31st of next month to pay it before you get a 30-day charge on your credit report. So on certain bills like that I kind of "work the system." Other bills that have high fees if you're late, like credit card bills or stuff like that, I pay those to make sure, because if you miss it by a day or two—sometimes one day—I can, you know, talk to them and they'll give me a break. But if you miss it by a few days, they charge you with a $29 late fee, which totally cancels out your payment almost. So those bills, I make sure that those get paid right away. On utilities, I know that those don't go on your credit report, so if I have to skip a bill, I'm going to skip a water bill, you know. And so, I've just learned the system, and I work it to my advantage when necessary.

Many respondents (22) negotiate with service providers, especially on utility bills, but also student loans, car payments, and rent. LaVonne, who faces serious financial problems, described the kinds of bills she negotiates when she has to "pinch some money to put somewhere else." Some bills are easier to negotiate than others. "The water bill—they'll work with you." "The light bill is on a fixed thing, so they never work with you, you've gotta pay it. My phone bill, there is the same way, I can say, 'Well look, I'm gonna pay a certain amount, I'm not gonna pay all this.'"

Work More or Sell Things

For Cynthia, and 20 others, the choice is plain: either work more or go without. "You [either] do without it or you go out and find more work to be able to pay for it." One of the ways that Tonya makes ends meet is to work extra jobs. She especially likes to take on extra work that accommodates her children. When the kids were small, for instance, she worked in day care so they could stay with her. When they grew up a little, she took on a part-time job at the Boys and Girls Club "so that the kids could have a membership there."

Some work more because they have to in order to cover the bills, but some work more when they need or want to make a special purchase. For example, a mother takes on a part-time job when she has to make a large purchase, or she gets a "Christmas job" to pay for presents for the kids.

A big problem with working more hours, especially for single parents, is the time spent away from children. One mother said she works hard to keep ahead of the bills, but feels guilty leaving her children for so long.

> I realized that my focus was so much on keeping up with bills, and having good credit and all this stuff that I was neglecting time with my kids. Most of the things that would bring me money would take me away from my kids, and then my son would stand at my door and go, "Mommy, don't go to work," and, you know, I had to go anyway.

Finally, a few people (3) mentioned selling things. For example, one respondent "hocks" things at a pawnshop to raise money to cover household expenses. Another said there are many things a person can sell.

> I mean, you can go give plasma and get $30. You can go pawn off a tool that you don't need and get $10. You can go collect tin cans. You can sell a vehicle. You know, a lot of people don't do that or realize it or are just flat-out too lazy. But you do what you have to do. That's what we do.

Reduce the Cost of Debt

Thirteen respondents said they pay more than the minimum on their credit cards, pay on time in order to avoid finance charges, and avoid other charges on debt. One person explained that she divides her bills into three groups according to when they are due to make sure she avoids late payments. She also pays particular attention to paying back loans. "If we've had, for any reason, to get a loan or something like that, I always try to make sure that like if it asks for $25 or $30, I always try to at least give $100 on it, trying to get it back down."

A few people also consolidated their debt or worked hard to reduce it to avoid high interest on their credit card debt. As one person said, "I'm paying those off and just getting them wiped out instead of just paying, you know, monthly minimums."

Nonetheless, many consider interest payments an inevitable aspect, however undesirable, of their financial lives. As a respondent explained, this is how credit card companies make money.

> You pay the minimum amount, balance, and then you just paying interest on the card all the time. You just don't pay it off. . . . You know, I'm okay with that. They got to make money too. They're in the business to make money, so I understand I got to pay interest. Sometimes I just need that. Sometimes, you get where you need gas for the car, you need something. It's always something, you know. Nobody never has enough money, I don't suppose.

Spend Tax Refunds and Savings

Other respondents (13) discussed using tax refunds or savings to cover expenses. Tonya uses her tax refund to cover her car note. Another described regularly falling behind on her bills during the year. Just as she catches up, she falls behind again. "It's not until taxes come back in that I will get caught back up."

Some plan ahead using their tax refunds to pay for larger or intermittent expenses, or to pay some bills in advance. One described using his tax refund to catch up on home repairs and make purchases. In this manner, he avoids adding to household debt. "I'd have this fixed and I'd have that fixed. I had some plumbing fixed in my house. I bought a new refrigerator. I bought me a stove. Paid cash, paid cash for all that, you know. It was used, you know, but I paid cash and that was a debt that I didn't have."

Some people use savings to pay bills. An older woman with grown children recalled using savings from a 401(k) to pay bills. "When I left [my job] the money that was in my 401(k)—Well, since I didn't go directly to another job, I withdrew it . . . and that's what helped me survive for a long time."

PSYCHOLOGICAL AND ECONOMIC COSTS OF FRUGALITY

Most respondents have struggled financially for so long that these strategies for making ends meet are almost second nature. Families survive when they use these strategies, as other researchers observe, but there are psychological and economic costs. Families may feel stressed, powerless, and hopeless (Voydanoff and Donnelly 1988; Kempson 1996). There are also economic costs associated with frugality (Caplovitz 1979).

The methods that families use to stay within budget collide with lack of time. While an individual might be able to find items at a lower price, there are other financial and time costs (e.g., transportation), not to mention the emotional costs (e.g., frustration) to comparison shopping and other economizing strategies (Newton 1977, 59). Despite Tonya's careful financial rules, for instance, she recognizes that as long as she is in school, it will be difficult to make economical and appetizing food purchases. She explains to her children that despite her efforts to find the "best deals" on food they like, they have to "eat whatever I put on the table," at least as long as she is still in school. Tonya also admitted that although she tries to buy "on sale," it is not always possible because she does not always have time.

Being accustomed to economizing does not mean it is easy. Some respondents reported it is difficult to resist overindulging or buying more than they can afford. Spending a little extra on something special is enjoyable. As a respondent explained: "We do spend a little excessive money here and there and stuff but you kind of need to do that, you know, to feel un-deprived, you know." He and his wife "made a dedication to go out every week," spending approximately $50 on a nice meal and a movie. This is the only family who reported spending extra without feeling guilty. Guilty feelings contribute to even greater emotional stress.

Frugality may also lead to significant transaction costs, including victimization by unscrupulous venders and lenders (Caplovitz 1967, 180). There are many examples in the interviews that illustrate the high cost of buying cheap but untrustworthy cars or appliances that quickly require maintenance or must be replaced; making do without a car but having to make complicated arrangements to get to work, grocery shopping, or the bank; or living in less expensive but higher crime areas that add to concerns about children's well being and safety.

THE CONTEXT FOR FINANCIAL DECISIONS:
FAMILY, FAITH, AND GENDER

Researchers suggest that household financial decision making is complex and understandable only within a larger context (Buss and Schaninger 1983; Lackman and Lanasa 1993; Chattoe and Gilbert 1999; Kirchler 1999). In this study, three underlying principles guide many of the often-difficult financial decisions respondents must make. First, they frame financial decisions in terms of their obligations to their children. Second, their faith guides and supports their financial decisions. Finally, household relationships affect patterns of financial decision-making.

Putting Children First

To begin, obligations to their children underlie families' strategies for financial survival. Families place their children first, providing for their basic needs and ameliorating the children's sense of relative deprivation as much as they can. Parents talked about their responsibility and financial sacrifices for their children. As one father explained, "Everything changes with children. Lifestyle changes . . . no more going out to eat, you know, that type of entertainment kind of stops." Respondents underscore the importance of making their children feel cared for and adequate in others' eyes. Rosalyn, who grew up very poor, does not want her children to suffer the kind of deprivation she experienced as a child. "[When] I was coming up and there was so much I desired and never got. So [I] give them something in their childhood to enjoy." Likewise, another respondent explained he is willing to spend money on nice clothes for his children so their peers will not consider them poor. "We don't want our kids to be labeled, you know, 'cause, you know how peer pressure is for children, okay?" He understands that this means he and his wife have to "shop smarter." Similarly, another parent feels the pressure to buy things for her children so they can keep up with their friends. "I always struggle against the pressure to buy because [the kids] always want or need things. They have a whole lot of rich, rich friends and so it's always pressure to buy for them."

Families also consider it important to pay for opportunities for their children. They consider it a priority to attempt to respond to their children's requests to participate in sports, excursions, and other events. Tonya, for example, not only pays $300 for her son to play football but also estimates she spends $2,000 to $3,000 on summer camp for her children. She views this as an investment.

> This summer I paid for all of them to go to camp because I thought my daughters, my oldest [especially], needed to be out doing stuff instead of just [being] cooped up in the house watching the kids . . . not that that's a bad thing, but I think she needs more experiences than that. . . . So, she's been a CIT, a coun-

selor-in-training, and it cost me for her to do that. But she got to go on field trips and things like that that she wouldn't have gotten to do. . . . And then my son, I put him in more expensive camps just because I knew he would get bored going to the one that they were going to.

Religious Faith

Families also take into account their religious faith when making financial decisions. They link faith and finances in several ways. In addition to tangible support, religious institutions provide guidance and support during times of need, and ease the challenges of poverty. Some respondents seek advice and counsel from church leaders and from God through prayer. Rosalyn, for example, reflects on the notion that God will somehow provide. "We've never had a problem financially, paying bills. It's kind of, 'Now Lord, now, how should I go?' You know, the Lord just blesses us with the money. Somebody may give us something or something like that. We never had a financial problem." Another respondent recalled that her mother, who is deeply religious, believes in the power of her faith. "She always knew that the Lord will provide. . . . And she had a way of making us feel that we had everything. . . . I would say her religion helped her to cope in her hard times."

Some described how God provides in unexpected ways, enhancing a belief that the families' needs will be met if they remain faithful. As a respondent observed: "I used to worry about everything but once I put my faith in God, little things happen that come together when you don't expect it. You might not have any money to go out and get any food and when you pull your clothes out of the clothes dryer there's a $20 bill laying there." He concluded, "When I put God first, He takes care of everything." Other respondents described examples of their own initiative working in tandem with God's support. For example, another deeply religious respondent said that although her debt is a large burden, she believes that God will handle it.

You just keep, you just keep going towards your goal, and coming out of it, and I did. I'm a church woman. And I do believe highly in debt cancellation, when you do it right, with God's will, you plant the seed, it will come out. And I believe that's working. It started two years ago. And things have started breaking open. . . . They call it mountain-moving. They say, "Speak to your mountain." And if it's debt, or lack, anywhere, wherever it's at, you speak in the name of Jesus, this is gonna move and I'm going to make a difference. I'm going to see it move. And then you start taking the natural steps, which is what I'm trying to do with this [debt].

Moreover, she explained, the church is helping in concrete ways. She described taking a course at church, "a wisdom course," that "teaches you how to handle credit cards and real estate and [stock] portfolio."

Religion implies a financial obligation as well. Some respondents (17) mentioned that they tithe to their church, some consistently. For example, Camille said that she includes tithing among her top financial priorities.

> But the first, the very first thing I do when I get paid is pay my tithes. . . . I do that off the top before, because I feel like God blesses me, you know, and you can't beat him giving—I'm pretty religious, you know, and I know that that's a requirement. You should pay your tithes to the Lord. You really should, because if it wasn't for Him you wouldn't have your health and strength. And he only asks for 10 percent. That's all He asks for. And the rest He leaves with you to do whatever you want to do.

The Role of Gender

A significant issue in household financial management is how families allocate financial responsibilities. Control over spending sometimes depends on a person's status within the family. For example, in some households, the male partner retains control over how his earnings are spent. Adolescents living at home often earn money, but with few exceptions, they manage their own finances, spending for their own needs instead of for the household. Viviana Zelizer (1989, 1994) suggests that families earmark different pots of money depending on its uses and who controls it. In other words, household financial decision making involves social arrangements and roles, as well as rational economic logic (Buss and Schaninger 1983; Lackman and Lanasa 1993; Kirchler 1999; Webley et al. 2001).

Generally, respondents distinguish between day-to-day financial decision making (e.g., buying groceries, paying the bills) and larger financial decisions (e.g., purchasing a car). For larger expenditures, decision making often involves both partners. In the 34 married households, half said that they make large financial decisions jointly. As one person explained, mutuality and communication in financial decision making are essential if a family wants to get ahead. "Simply because we do sit down and talk about it, I think we are better off. We are not wealthy or anything. But I think we are on a path that can go somewhere. . . .You can't go together when you are not agreeing or talking."

Consistent with other research, the women respondents are the most likely to be responsible for mundane day-to-day financial decision making, such as handling bank accounts, paying bills, and giving family members their spending money (Pahl 1980; Wilson 1987; Lassarre and Roland-Levy 1988; Godwin 1990; Webley et al. 2001).[4] There is relatively little evidence in the interviews that decision making is contentious in their current families, perhaps because in most cases both adults in partnered households are working (Pahl 1980; Wilson 1987). In contrast, many women cited instances of power struggles and conflict over finances in prior domestic relationships (Vogler and Pahl 1994).[5]

Four out of 14 married male respondents reported making most financial decisions, including what to buy. Asked who makes the financial decisions, one respondent said, "You're looking at him." He acknowledged that he and his wife discuss everything and make decisions together, but he has the "final say-so." When asked if he makes smaller financial decisions, he replied,

> Yeah, I'm a man. She knows her position, she's the woman. I'm the man. But I don't abuse that, you see. You've got to learn how to work together. Manage a partnership. If her decision is better than mine . . . we use hers. She got a mind of her own, she can think, and if she got a better plan, why not use hers? 'Cause it's all for the same purpose, to better this family. So we work together.

Sometimes male partners use finances to control their wives and girlfriends (Pahl 1980; Sanders 2007). Tonya's story is a case in point. From the time Tonya moved in with her boyfriend at age 17, he made it clear he would handle all of the couple's finances. She complied for a while, handing all of her earnings over to him, but she was increasingly "uncomfortable" with this arrangement. "That was real difficult for me to do because none of [the money] ever came back towards me." At one point, she secretly took out a loan to cover the cost of baby diapers and food, but her boyfriend found out about the loan.

> I took out a loan under my own name and didn't put him on it and didn't tell him where it was. . . . I would go buy enough diapers and food to last. But then my car broke down and he was going to get it fixed and he figured out then that I had some place I was getting money from. So he told me the car was costing more than it actually was to get fixed and then I turned over the money to him.

Like so many victims of domestic violence, Tonya left her boyfriend several times only to return; each return was followed by another pregnancy. Her boyfriend's failure to contribute financially, his desire for control, his temper, and, finally, his physical abuse of one of their children finally convinced Tonya that she had to leave him permanently. She began to refuse his requests for money. "He was threatening to kill me then because of the protective order and stuff against him and it was just a really scary time." Eventually, however, he quit asking her for money.

> He still would show up and ask me for $5 or $10 here and there, or he would say, "Well I can't come to see the kids unless you give me gas money." Or he would show up and say he needed to go somewhere and be right back, but could I go up to QuikTrip and get him some gasoline? . . . I mean it was very stressful. Because I know how he can go off . . . I thought, really giving him the $10 isn't so bad if it's not going to cause a confrontation. But other people kept telling me that I needed to learn how to say no. So, it took a few times, but now he doesn't ask.

Tonya now understands her former boyfriend's limitations and accepts the fact that he will likely never provide financially for his children. She also tries to help her children understand and cope with their father's shortcomings as he continues to disappoint them.

Only two married women handle major as well as minor financial decisions, including Anne. "I pay all the bills, and I handle the stress of that. My husband has no concern. He knows it is going to get paid. He gives me his paycheck." Her husband reports all purchases over $20 to her. "It doesn't sound like much, but it can affect my budget either way. So, over $20 you kind of need to tell me, and tell me how important it is. And if we have it I'll tell you go ahead, and if we don't have it, I'll ask you, can we wait till next week?" Anne includes her husband in decisions about large expenditures. "If it was a big thing, I would never go out and spend a hundred bucks without telling him. So, yeah, if it's a big thing we go together to buy it."

Fifty respondents (mostly women) are single, divorced, or widowed, and therefore make most financial decisions alone. This does not necessarily make financial decision making a smooth or easy process. They often lack knowledge to manage household finances. As we saw in chapter 3, few learned much in childhood about financial management; almost no one received any financial education of any kind. Older women are most likely to have been in traditional marriages where the husband made most financial decisions (Burgoyne 1990). If they divorced or were widowed, they frequently found themselves responsible for financial decisions for the first time in their lives. One respondent described the challenge that confronted her after a divorce. "It was very difficult for me when I moved out on my own again. I'd been with somebody for 22 years. . . . I didn't really have to worry about managing money. . . . When I moved out again I had to learn all over again how to do things."

PAYING THE BILLS: FINANCIAL SERVICES AND INSTRUMENTS

Finally, families with low levels of resources often manage without secure and time-saving financial services. For example, many respondent families keep money at home, like the "tin can economy" of Rainwater, Coleman, and Handel (1959). However, respondents and their families also tend to use some form of banking services, especially checking accounts and credit cards (table 4.5) (Hogarth and O'Donnell 1999). These services often are used in combination with alternative financial services, which operate outside the regulatory structure and are not federally insured (Rhine and Toussaint-Comeau 1999; Barr 2004; Berry 2005; Karger 2005).

TABLE 4.5. Financial Instruments and Financial Services Used by Respondents

	IDA Participants ($n = 59$) n (%)	Nonparticipants ($n = 25$) n (%)	Total ($N = 84$) n (%)
Financial instruments			
Checking account	40 (68)	18 (72)	58 (69)
Savings account[a]	28 (47)	10 (40)	38 (45)
Credit cards	31 (53)	12 (48)	43 (51)
Electronic financial services			
Direct deposit	6 (10)	3 (12)	9 (11)
ATM/debit card	7 (12)	2 (8)	9 (11)
Auto-debit or online bill payment	1 (2)	3 (12)	4 (5)
Alternative financial services[b]	17 (29)	6 (24)	23 (27)

Source: Center for Social Development, in-depth interviews.

[a]This does not include the IDA savings account.

[b]Alternative financial services include money orders, check-cashing facilities, payday loans, pawn shops, and so forth.

Checking and Savings Accounts

Fifty-eight people reported owning a checking account. According to respondents, checking accounts are useful for depositing paychecks and are less expensive and more convenient than other ways of managing money. One respondent pointed out, "I can just sit at home once a month . . . stick it in an envelope, put a stamp on it, and mail it. It's so much easier to do it that way."

But one-quarter of respondents do not use a checking account, including seven who owned a checking account in the past but not at the time of the interview. Some said that checking accounts make them apprehensive. For many years, for example, an older woman in her 60s never owned an account and was "scared" because her husband managed the finances and she did not know how to use one. After her husband died, she finally learned how to manage an account. "Now, I just love it! But, at first, I didn't want nothing to do with it." Tonya remembered that it took time to feel competent and comfortable after bouncing a check when she first opened her account. She closed the account and did not open another one for at least a year.

Some avoid checking accounts because of transaction fees and penalties for low balances and overdrafts. A young mother of three closed her checking account when the bank charged overdraft fees on bill payments because her husband's paycheck arrived late. "I was just devastated at just how much—$20! $20 per check! . . . We paid hundreds of dollars in check charges that just killed me. And I thought, 'No more!'"

Even fewer own a savings account (38) (this does not include the IDA). A substantial number of these accounts are not active; many respondents bank at a credit union and maintain a small minimum savings in order to qualify for a checking account. A few others use their savings accounts as transaction accounts. A respondent explained, "At different times instead of a checking account, we would use a savings account for a checking account."

Credit Cards

Many respondents (43) own credit cards, mostly for the convenience, when they lack cash on hand, and sometimes, to build a credit record. One respondent explained that she uses credit cards with great care. "I've got two credit cards now and I pay them every month before the due dates so I don't have any interest. . . . Believe me . . . I know what it does if you're late, or over the limit. You can get yourself in trouble."

Ten refuse to own a credit card, including one man who remembered watching his father struggle to pay accumulated credit card bills. "[He] just worried about money all the time." As a police officer, it had been easy for his father to get credit, and he became chronically overextended. He remembers bill paying with consternation "Once a month he'd close his door and, boy, you didn't want to go in there!"

Electronic Financial Services

Relatively few families use electronic financial services. Only nine use direct deposit. Although not widely available to the poor, direct deposit is convenient, secure, and requires little individual effort after enrollment (Dunham 2001; Beverly, McBride, and Schreiner 2003; Barr 2004). Moreover, having money automatically deposited in the bank helps them resist spending it. Ella had recently signed up to direct-deposit her paycheck. She observed that direct deposit makes life easier and prevents overdrawing her checking account. "I know exactly when it's going to be there and that's the only time I'll write my checks out to pay my bills." Before she had direct deposit, she forgot to deposit her check right away (in part because she dreaded the long lines at the bank) and she would bounce checks. She concluded that she is better off if the money does not pass directly through her hands: "I just have a problem as far as putting that in my hand."

Nine also use an automatic teller machine (ATM) and/or a debit card. As one said, it is more convenient to withdraw money from an ATM card to pay bills than to write checks. She tracks her withdrawals using "a 24-hour thing where I call every week and make sure that what I have is what they have." Debit cards, according to another, are more convenient than writing checks because many businesses in her community refuse checks or credit cards (Rhine, Toussaint-Comeau, and Hogarth 2001; Barr 2004).

Only four respondents use automatic bill paying or Internet banking; those that do find that it is convenient and helps them pay bills on time. According to one respondent, in the past, bills that were due every few months would get her "all crossed up," but with automatic payments, she does not have to think about it. One tracks her bank balance on the Internet and says it helps her manage her money better.

> I look and I can see what's taken out, and if I think I ought to have more money than that, I can go in and check and realize that, yes, I did spend that much

money, and there is where it went. And it has helped me kind of realize where I spend money . . . because I actually look at my account, where I didn't before.

Alternative Financial Services

Research suggests that people may turn to alternative financial services for a variety of reasons, including language and identity requirements (especially for immigrants), lack of knowledge, anticipated use of an account, terms and conditions, bank charges, location, fear of overdrafts, and psychological reactions to banks (Caskey 1994, 1997, 2005; Hogarth and O'Donnell 1999; Dunham 2001; Aizcorbe, Kennickell, and Moore 2003; Barr 2004; Kempson 2006).

Even though most families in this study (75) use mainstream financial services, and therefore are not part of the so-called unbanked population, there is evidence in the interviews that they use both mainstream and alternative financial sectors simultaneously, depending on the circumstances. In other words, respondents use checking or savings accounts, but also pay bills with money orders, borrow using postdated checks and payday loans, pawn items for cash, or buy on layaway.[6]

At least 23 respondents talked about using alternative financial services, most to pay bills. As one person pointed out, "the cash saving place" provides a way to pay a bill, including a postage stamp—"and we have it right across the street!"

Some respondents said that money orders, the most common alternative to writing checks, are relatively cheap. As one person (who does not own a checking account) asserted, money orders are less expensive than a bank cashier's check for paying bills. Another person thinks money orders are safer because they prevent identity theft. Money orders help others "keep track" of expenditures and avoid overdrawing a checking account. For example, one person pays her bills in person with cash or with money orders because she is "not good with checks."

> I don't like checks at all 'cause it seems like the bank just takes your money. You know, with the charges and this and that and, I don't know, I just don't like banks. Not at all. I'm not good with that. I go around town and pay all my bills, you know, or get a money order and pay it off.

Another person got into "trouble" using checks, so he prefers money orders. "I'm not that good on the paperwork, you know. As long as I get a money order, I know that's paid. . . . I don't have to go back and look at no balance."

Others, however, believed that money orders are expensive and time consuming, and had switched to checking. One respondent said, "Buying money orders for everything . . . is just a waste of money. I mean, what you spend on money orders is the same as what a checking account would cost you monthly."

Several use payday loans and other small renewable loans. Respondents use these to pay bills due before the next paycheck arrives. For example, one person recalled using payday loans on occasion "to carry me over to the next payday"; another uses them on occasion to make a mortgage payment. LaVonne uses postdated checks. She explained, "You go in, you post date a check for a certain amount, and then they put the interest on." The problem is that "you can't ever just pay a portion of the check. . . . You pay the check off, but you've got to rewrite it because you need that money." As we learn later, she became terribly indebted in this way (Stegman and Faris 2003).

Many respondents used layaway and rent-to-own to purchase durables. For example, one person said it was convenient to arrange payments for the furniture she purchased at a rent-to-own place: "I got my living room set, my TV, my dining room set, my bedroom set, and my friends' bedroom set. So I just made one monthly payment for all the furniture."

Some pawn items when they need money. One respondent thinks that pawning stuff is helpful because it provides money to cover bills. Tonya observed, however, that she had learned from using a pawn shop that it is not a very good deal, "by the time you got that little bit of money and then what you had to pay back to get it back."

DISCUSSION

These families have low and volatile incomes. They rely primarily on jobs, sometimes multiple jobs, to cover household consumption needs. Some also benefit from social security and disability insurance, and public assistance. Over the years, the Family Village has provided a few of the single mothers and their children with a transitional home and a fresh start.

Respondents tend to have one foot in mainstream financial services and the other in alternative financial services. Many families harbor distrust of banks as they find themselves in and out of trouble depending on their financial circumstances. Some financial instruments, including credit cards, are ambiguous goods, helpful for their convenience and accessibility, but dangerous because they make it easy to accumulate debt (Prelec and Loewenstein 1998). Few respondents are in a position to take advantage of some of the most helpful and beneficial financial instruments, such as direct deposit and electronic banking, that would facilitate household financial management. At times, they also turn to alternative financial services, such as paying bills with money orders, or using check-cashing services or payday loans for their convenience and accessibility. As scholars suggest, low-income families choose financial services based on price, convenience, necessity, and safety considerations (Squires and O'Connor 1998; Dunham 2001; Caskey 2005).

Faced with low incomes and high expenses, families adopt a perspective that they will make it through hard times with faith and hard work. Respondents identify a variety of strategies to help them manage: they track expenses, economize and cut back, work more, sell things, reduce the cost of debt, and use savings and tax refunds to make ends meet. Although lacking sophisticated financial management techniques or computer software, respondents recounted sometimes-intricate financial management strategies in detail.

Other research documents similar strategies for managing on a low income, including efforts to increase income, decrease expenditures, and increase efficiency (Caplovitz 1979; Danes and Rettig 1995; Edin and Lein 1997). As researchers in the United Kingdom conclude in a review of poverty and household financial management, "In general, poor people manage their finances with care, skill, and resourcefulness. There is no evidence to suggest that there are two types of poor families—those who can cope and those who can't" (ESRC 2002, 4). Another scholar, Ruth Lister, suggests that the poor marshal their resources and trust in their resilience to cope with poverty (2006).

The poor, compared with wealthy families, are more likely to use strict budgets, often using mental accounting methods for keeping careful track of their finances (Heath and Soll 1996; Thaler 1999). This is certainly the case in this study. Families follow rules of thumb and patterns of financial management that work most of the time, although volatile income flows and fluctuating expenses constantly test these routines. They have priorities, they have budgets, and they plan (Godwin and Koonce 1992). In addition to the basics (e.g., housing, food, child care, transportation), they, like their parents, try to make sure their children do not *feel* poor, even if this only means making sure they have nice clothes and shoes for school.

Families tend to assign certain income sources to particular expenses, thus limiting the free flow of money (or fungibility, as economists refer to its interchangeability) within households. Regular job income, for instance, tends to be assigned to cover regular monthly bills, while families use savings and tax refunds for larger debts, intermittent bills (like car insurance), or major expenses. In this way, respondents do not think about or treat income sources the same (e.g., they do not deposit all income into a checking account and use this to pay all the bills). Families develop rules of thumb that they use to decide which sources of income will pay for which bills. Sometimes rules of thumb are imposed externally. For example, public assistance money is earmarked for food, housing, or medical care. Typically, family and friends also earmark contributions, explicitly or inexplicitly, for particular expenses, such as baby diapers or a vehicle.

Behavioral researchers observe that people use rules of thumb as a frame of reference for evaluating spending and borrowing decisions (Thaler 1985; Webley 1995). Although these techniques have limits, overall they help people organize their finances, and they provide shortcuts for financial decision making (e.g., decisions do not have to be made each month; decisions follow an established pattern). Rules of thumb streamline and may reduce anxiety or uncertainty about financial decisions.

Respondents make financial decisions in a social context that shapes priorities and behaviors. Respondents' devotion to their children and their faith play a key role in helping them maintain perspective about what is important in the face of economic and other life stresses. For most families, their first obligation is to their children, a pattern learned in childhood by observing how their parents made financial decisions. They also seek financial guidance and support from their church, which, in turn, imposes financial duties on them. In this way, participation in religious institutions may be both a significant financial obligation (through tithing) but also an important way to put their beliefs into practice and to ensure well-being during their lifetimes and beyond. There is also evidence in this study that gender relations shape financial behaviors, hampering free flow of information and decision-making options. This lack of transparency is unmistakable in women's descriptions of former spouses preventing them from knowing about and managing finances.

Despite respondents' efforts to keep expenditures low, income is often insufficient to cover basic expenses. When this happens, families must borrow, and sometimes they accumulate problem debt. In the next chapter, we look at ways that families get into and attempt to manage problem debt. We also explore credit and reveal how families attempt to establish or reestablish creditworthiness.

Low income and problem debt also have implications for respondents' ability to save. Although the findings in this chapter suggest that families have the financial know-how and capacity to save, it is unclear whether or not they have enough money to do so after paying basic living expenses and debt obligations. We explore saving in chapters 6, 7, and 8.

CHAPTER 5

Problem Debt and Creditworthiness

Families easily get behind as they struggle to pay for basics and to cover emergencies (Waldron, Roberts, and Reamer 2004). Falling into debt, even for the middle class, is a constant worry and often a reality (Warren and Tyagi 2003; Himmelstein, Warren, Thorne, and Woolhandler 2005). In the United States, there were over one million non-business bankruptcy filings in 2008, even after a major bankruptcy reform law in 2005 made it more difficult for many people to file (American Bankruptcy Institute 2009). Medical expenses are a major factor in half of bankruptcies (Himmelstein et al. 2009). Poor credit ratings that result from bankruptcy cost families dearly in higher interest rates and other penalties.

By debt, we mean unsecured debt like credit card balances and money owed to family members—money that families do not have. (This is different than secured debt, which is linked to assets that can be sold to cover the liability, such as a house.) As Adam Carasso and Signe-Mary McKernan (2008) point out, low-income families are not more likely to carry debt, but their debt is more likely to be unsecured, and, overall, they may be in greater financial distress than middle-income families.[1]

As we observed in the last chapter, respondents' household consumption needs exceed resources some of the time and, in a few households, much of the time. Families use a variety of strategies to address financial shortfalls, including careful planning, economizing, or earning more money. When these strategies fail, they must turn to borrowing (Huston and Chang 1997).

Most of the time, families meet their debt obligations. Unfortunately, some find themselves at some point sinking into problem debt—debt that cannot be covered in the foreseeable future. Others encounter crises that throw them into problem debt all at once. Either way, problem debt requires more vigorous responses than those they use to make ends meet.

Once in debt, families rely on financial management approaches that have worked in the past, yet they are on alert for better alternatives. Concern about creditworthiness is common because a low credit score is a "nightmare" and constrains all manner of future opportunities. Although most manage to keep afloat, there are times when they feel mired down by the enormity of their financial problems, and they despair at the seemingly impossible task of paying their debts and rebuilding a good credit record.

This chapter further develops the idea of the working poor as active financial managers. To begin, we highlight three respondents' problems with debt. We continue Ella's account, as she deals with unusually high expenses associated with her husband's workplace injury and her lack of understanding about key financial issues. We also introduce Becky, whose story of debt, while atypical, underscores the financial vulnerability that many women face following divorce. Finally, Fred's story illustrates how a couple, working together, managed to overcome problem debt.

Ella

We begin with Ella, who faced mounting credit card bills, especially after her husband was injured at work. "Well, as of right now I'm trying to pay them off because I want to get rid of those [multiple credit card bills] and maybe just have one. I have four [right now] and so that's my goal this year." She and her daughters plan to take on a new cleaning job at night to help pay the bills. "I plan on trying to find a building that the girls and I can clean at night so they will be able to save Christmas money for themselves and then that would be my savings to pay off the credit cards."

Ella also has a problem with taxes that she does not fully understand. The IRS said she owed back taxes because they claimed she illegally claimed her sister and mother on her taxes when they were living with her. A tax adviser recommended claiming the deductions.

> I have had to pay the IRS back. Why I don't know. They just didn't like me for awhile. . . . I took my mother and my sister on my income taxes one year . . . and so when I went to have [my taxes] filed and then the guy asked me and I told him, he said, "Oh, well we can use them." So I had to pay every penny of that back and from that point on it seemed like, you know, about five years

they would send me a letter that I owed this and I owed that. . . . Nope, they don't like me.

Becky

Becky had escaped an unhappy family by marrying at age 16 and became pregnant shortly thereafter. Becky found a place in subsidized housing, and after the baby was born, she signed up for day-care assistance so she could work. For five years, Becky worked in a restaurant, covering all of her expenses other than day care. "We didn't really have too much, but we got by."

Unfortunately, from the start she and her husband did not get along. He did not hold down a job for long, nor did he help with the household finances. When they separated, her husband harassed her, and at one point, Becky sought refuge at her grandmother's house. When she returned to her apartment, her husband had destroyed everything. "I opened the door and the entire house was trashed. . . . The furniture was cut up, the dressers were destroyed, and every article of clothing I had was cut into pieces: my shoes, my socks, my underwear, everything. I mean he destroyed everything." Unsure what to do, she contemplated suing the apartment manager for letting her estranged husband into the apartment but later decided against it. The police told her that her belongings were "community property." They explained, "You're married. He can cut up all your [things]." Becky was very upset. "That was the worst time in my life. I didn't have a car. I didn't have a job. . . . I didn't have any clothes. I didn't have nothing. Anything else he didn't destroy, he sold."

Slowly, she began to replace her things. She took on another job, and her financial situation improved somewhat because she worked many overtime hours. She also returned to school and earned her GED. She settled into a small house next to her grandmother. Her great-grandmother had once owned it, and her grandmother had used it as a studio. Becky took out a small loan to refurbish the place. "I only got like $6,000 so I got the house rewired, got walls put in, and got, you know, basically enough so that it could be lived in."

Several years later, Becky's financial woes from her marriage followed her. When she and her husband separated, Becky had returned the car they bought back to the dealer. She had not heard anything about the car in over five years, so she was surprised when the creditor called and demanded repayment.

I said, "I took that car back a long time ago. I ain't heard nothing about it in all these years. . . . I'm not paying it." And he said, "Well you have to." And I said,

"Well [my husband's] name is on there, too. Why not jump on after him?" And they said, "Because he doesn't work."

Unfortunately, by that time, her ex-husband was in prison. The creditor sued Becky. Soon they began to garnish her paychecks. "That was like the beginning of my financial problems." Becky's financial problems continued, as we will see.

Fred

Fred now has emotional and financial support from his wife, but he went through many rough years after leaving the housing projects and heading off to college when he was 19. Although he successfully avoided getting involved with drugs during high school, by the time he was 20 years old Fred was using. "I was a drug addict, alcoholic. I was spending all my money on drugs and alcohol." It took 10 years, but he finally kicked the addictions. He attributed his success to God. "I started serving Jesus. It changed my whole life, just like that. . . . I quit just like that. Never looked back."

Fred did not graduate from college, but he obtained two trade school credentials. Both Fred and his wife have jobs, and Fred fixes appliances on the side. One of his wife's children from a previous marriage draws Social Security Survivor's Benefits. Moreover, their daughter works, and she pays a little for room and board.

The road to stability was not easy, however. Fred kicked the drug habit by the time he was 30 years old, but by the time he was 34, he and his wife had accumulated $9,000 in debt and had a poor credit rating. They decided to get their finances in order. Just before they joined the IDA program, they paid their debt in eight months by living on Fred's paycheck and using his wife's salary to pay down their debt. As Fred described this period: "Tough, tough times for eight months."

Nonetheless, they managed to work their way out of debt. "My house is paid for. Everything in it is paid for. All my cars is paid for. I don't owe nobody nothing. I'm debt free." After learning that they could live on less money, Fred's financial goal was to consume only one of their paychecks. "If you can't—if you married—and you can't pay all your bills off one check, you're in trouble."

With a steady job and benefits, especially health insurance, Fred and his wife feel they can care for the family. "I'm doing real fine. I got a decent paying job. Make pretty good money, my wife got a decent job." Everyone in the family is healthy and his children are doing well. "None of my kids smoke, drink, or nothing. They are active in the church. They sing in the choir. My son play the drums." To top it off, Fred said, they have "bicycles to ride, fishing poles to go fishing. I mean, it's going real good."

FALLING INTO PROBLEM DEBT

When financial management strategies fail to reduce families' expenses, when families cannot earn more money, or when they deplete their small savings, they must borrow, thereby increasing debt (Huston and Chang 1997). Table 5.1 describes the types of debt that respondents reported as difficult to manage.

Much of this debt is *problem debt,* or debt that families cannot meet in the near or foreseeable future (Berthoud and Kempson 1992; Lea, Webley, and Levine 1993; Lea, Webley, and Walker 1995; Lea 1999). Of the 48 respondents who talked about household debt, 37 said they had what they consider problem debt.[2] Although problem debt looks like a straightforward problem of financial flows from an accounting perspective, when viewed from the perspective of a person's life, it is more complex (Lunt and Livingston 1991a). Next we discuss the two principal ways that respondents said they acquired problem debt: sinking slowly and capsizing.

Sinking Slowly into Debt

Borrowing too much money, getting behind in paying bills, or being responsible for someone else's debt are a recurring part of life in respondents' households, often leading to problem debt. More than half of the respondents (49)

TABLE 5.1. Respondent Problem Debt (*N* = 84)

	Total *n* (%)
Credit card debt	28 (33)
Car loan	15 (18)
Student loan	14 (17)
Medical debt	13 (15)
Personal loan	7 (8)
Loans for household goods	5 (6)
Back taxes owed	5 (6)
Home mortgage and home improvement loans	4 (5)

Source: Center for Social Development, in-depth interviews
Note: Respondents could report multiple types of debt.

said they borrowed money recently in order to be able to keep up with regular bills or to cover unbudgeted expenses. Credit cards provide a flexible source of cash for respondents when money is tight but 28 said it had become increasingly difficult to pay these bills. Most of these families are paying less than the minimum amount due each month and therefore incur high interest charges and other fees.

Tonya, for example, recently paid off her credit card bills but used the cards again when the children needed supplies and clothes for school. "I knew that would only be like $10 or $20 a month as opposed to spending out the whole thing and then maybe trying to figure out how to buy food." Another respondent accumulated $13,000 in credit card bills. "This is the thing that really saps our finances the most. Credit cards are a real snare, you know."

It is difficult to pinpoint when respondents recognize they are in serious financial trouble because they often sink slowly into problem debt. Many described a cumulative process of indebtedness, resulting largely from having too little income combined with access to ready sources of credit. Careless spending, poor decision making, and financial mismanagement contribute to the problem. Sometimes debt accumulates because people do not fully understand the impact of interest and fee structures. For example, one mother with several young children used to charge everything, thinking that she only had to pay the monthly minimum payment. "I didn't know that it worked like that. . . . I didn't read the fine print on some of them. So, we wound up ruining the credit [record] that we had."

Other respondents fall behind because they are trying to improve their lives, making an investment in education, buying a car to get to work, or buying a house. One young mother, for example, enrolled in classes, hoping to complete her college degree to qualify for a better job. In the meantime, she accumulated student loans and high credit card balances. Another was behind on school loan payments, credit cards, and car payments. "I just can't get caught up. And when I do get caught up, something seems to happen and I get behind again." Almost one-fifth of respondents were paying on school loans.

In some cases, respondents reported overindulgence as the main reason for debt. This spending is frequently associated with credit cards because they make it easy to buy things without feeling the pain of paying (Prelec and Loewenstein 1998). For example, one respondent recalled owning 14 credit cards at one time, making it very easy to spend too much but difficult to pay. "I maxed them all out. . . . I don't know what I was buying. I was buying gifts . . . and it just started adding up and accumulating and I started looking at it, and I was like, 'Where's all this?' And I was, like, so stressed out." (By the time we talked to her, she had reduced the number of credit cards she owns to two, but she continues to fight the urge to spend more than she has.)

Some respondents turn to lenders, including high-cost alternative lenders. Unfortunately, these loans often worsen problem debt. For example, although one respondent is aware that it is unwise to borrow money from "little small loan companies" that she sometimes must renew, she believes she has no other option. "I know it's dumb on my part 'cause I didn't want to get in debt again, in a loan, but [the children] needed school items and I went and I got that . . . loan for them for $300 . . . I just had to do that." LaVonne sometimes turns to using postdated checks. "I had gotten involved with these people; they are just total crooks!" She described how she got in over her head: "What happens is, it just keeps building and building until you just got a whole big bill here. I had about four or five post-dated check people that I dealt with. And I could never pay them off. I could never get those checks covered because I had to have the money right back." In addition, she owes money on a couple of credit cards and to several loan companies.

Capsizing into Debt

Sometimes respondents run up debt all at once, as they encounter unplanned expenses impossible to accommodate in the family budget. When crisis strikes, people living on the edge easily capsize into problem debt. The most troublesome and expensive crises include illness (25), divorce (16), and job loss (11) (also see Sullivan, Warren, and Westbrook 2000; Warren and Tyagi 2003; Himmelstein et al. 2005). Low-income families are more likely than those with higher incomes to borrow from high-cost alternative financial lenders when faced with a financial emergency (Rawlings and Gentsch 2008).

Medical Expenses. The most serious financial problems for these families occur when they lack health insurance. A health emergency often sends uninsured families into problem debt overnight. Fully 34 households hold no health insurance whatsoever and are paying for health care on their own. This includes some people who are already deep in medical debt (see chap. 4). And although most respondents (49) said they have health insurance coverage, there are problems with the coverage. First, many pay a great deal out-of-pocket for coverage, even with government or employer issued health insurance.[3] The high cost of health insurance can have important implications for people's lives. For example, one respondent switched jobs because of the cost of health insurance.

> It was actually like $580 a month coming out of my paycheck through [one job]. But it's going to go down in September to about $300 a month [in my new job] . . . Yeah, I mean it was like a third of my check was being taken out. But for a family of four, I mean I had to have [health insurance], you know.

Second, many health care expenses are not covered by insurance. Medications often are not covered by insurance, or the beneficiary has to pay copayments or high deductibles.

Third, health insurance does not always cover everyone in the household. Government health insurance (Medicare, Medicaid) covers at least one member in only thirteen families in this study. Four respondents have access to free services offered by Indian Health Service clinics. In several cases, children are covered under Medicaid, but their parents are not. In another case, a mother can barely afford to cover herself: "It's like—almost $100 would be my portion to pay for family coverage. So I just have the single, which is like $12. . . . I can't even afford that!"

Seventeen of the twenty-five respondents who discussed medical debt think about it as problem debt. Three have medical debt of $20,000 or more. Within three months, for example, a mother of three grown children accumulated approximately $60,000 in hospital debt for three hospital stays and additional bills. She was thinking about filing for bankruptcy because there is "no way I can pay them." Another woman owes on a hysterectomy that her work insurance would not cover. "So, I mean, that's about, almost $9,000 that I have to come up with that I don't have."

While health crises like these are impossible to absorb in a low-income budget, chronic conditions are also taxing and may lead to problem debt. One respondent has insurance, but she is responsible for a $600 annual deductible and 10 percent of ongoing costs. "[My family goes] to the doctor's a lot. Since my little girl has a lot of problems, she goes to a specialist. . . . Every visit to them is like $200 to a couple of thousand dollars." "I paid almost $3,000 for medical last year." This is a large amount of money that can set a family living on a low income behind over the long term.

Cynthia also has health insurance, but with two health conditions that require three medications, she has trouble covering the cost of her medications.

One costs $190 a month, another $60, and the third $43. "When I go to Mr. Wal-Mart to get my medication, I gotta have big money that I don't make." Like many people who are working but poor, Cynthia is not eligible for public coverage because she earns too much: "The system works against you because if you make too much, you can't get health care." Another respondent regularly goes without taking her prescription medicine. "I can't afford my medication so I don't take it. . . . I don't have insurance so I have to do without."

Finally, families sometimes turn to high-cost loans to cover their health expenses, incurring fees and high interest payments that make debt less and less manageable over time.

Divorce. Divorce also contributed to debt in 16 households, including 11 who reported problem debt. Creditors, who go after both partners, sometimes find it easier to locate women, especially when they have custody of the couple's children. One respondent reported that creditors expected her to pay all of her former husband's debt in addition to her own. "My ex-husband stuck me with everything. . . . When the divorce was over, he didn't pay anything. He just quit paying." Many years later, creditors are still pursuing her. She is considering bankruptcy in order to wipe out approximately $6,000 of her husband's credit card debt.

Similarly, another woman recalled that she and her husband "maxed out" their credit cards on their wedding, honeymoon, and "high lifestyle" expenses during their seven months of marriage. Before her marriage, she had "a pretty firm grip" on her credit cards. But her husband asked her to quit her job a month after they were married because he did not want her away from home at night. "Five months later he was gone and I was living on maybe $200 a month that I was gaining from cleaning houses. . . . My built-up credit just went to pot." It took her many years to pay the debt. "I'm finally at the point now where I can write the credit bureau and ask them to take it all off, 'cause it's been seven, almost eight years."

Job Loss. Another crisis that throws families into problem debt is a job loss. All 11 respondents who accumulated large debt because of a job loss said it became problem debt. This occurred for several reasons. Large debts accumulated because their family's income fell at the same time as their expenses continued to mount. One respondent explained how debt snowballs out of control when an income stream shuts down: "I lost my job. . . . I hurt my back and I couldn't work anymore. So, the car was repossessed, and I had all these huge payments to make." Moreover, there is sometimes a link with medical problems. For example, some job losses result from medical problems, further compounding debt because less income and higher expenses occur at the same time. Further, when families experience a job loss, they sometimes lose medical coverage. Sometimes job losses outside the immediate household also have significant impact, such as when an unemployed ex-spouse can no longer provide child support.

DEBT MANAGEMENT

Respondents use most of the same financial management techniques discussed earlier to deal with problem debt, including delaying bill payments, generating extra income, using tax refunds, and extracting a little more out of their household budgets. Some mentioned additional measures, however, including limiting their use of credit cards, declaring bankruptcy, debt consolidation, working more, and seeking help from family. Some pursue these strategies with the assistance of credit counselors.

The most common strategy, mentioned by 23 respondents, is to limit the number and use of credit cards, including 5 people who decided not to own a credit card.[4] One woman observed, "I believe that credit is a huge trap, and just puts people under bondage. I won't carry one again. . . . I just tear them up and throw them away." But she noted that credit card offers keep coming, making it difficult to resist.[5]

> And once Shell Oil gave me a card, then boom, boom, boom, boom, boom! I had 10 more within two months. 'Cause once you get on one credit thing, they all want you. And that's probably one of the hardest lessons I ever learned in my life. I have made a quality decision that I will never again carry a credit card.

Some respondents adopt strict budgets to help them pay their debt. As Fred explained in the beginning of the chapter, he and his wife dealt with their accumulated debt by assigning one paycheck to household expenses and one to their $9,000 debt, they paid in eight months. Another man gave himself more time, budgeting debt payments over a period of 10 years. He used the process to teach his children about financial management. "Well, we just figured out how much money we had to have. And then divided it by the number of years that we were willing to push that hard for it. Now that's done. That's behind us. And that's one thing I've tried to teach the children—compounding interest is an amazing thing. It can work against you or it can work for you."

In addition to budgeting carefully and economizing, others try to generate more income to pay their loans at a faster pace. They take extra jobs or work overtime. Others use their tax refunds to catch up. As one respondent said, "With the big lump sum [I] pay off everything."

Some people resort to more extreme measures. Twelve respondents had filed for bankruptcy at some point in the past.[6] (Five more considered but decided not to file for bankruptcy as a way to alleviate their debt problem.) One respondent's path to bankruptcy was typical of those who filed. By age 46, he had worked full-time for 18 years as a salesman for a hair care manufacturer. Recently, the company had downsized and cut his hours. Working only part-time, he earns less than $12,000 a year. For a while, he made ends meet using credit cards, but he accumulated so much credit card debt that he finally turned to bankruptcy.

Through bankruptcy, he wiped out his prior debt. He also severely reduced consumption and learned how to live on a very low income. Now he has only one credit card. When he cannot afford something, he avoids thinking about it. "I immediately just put it out of my mind. And just say, 'This is something I can get at a later time.'" He developed what he calls a "simple lifestyle." However, he has no children to support. Unfortunately, Becky and other parents with children at home have a more difficult time following the bankruptcy.

Bankruptcy is a tempting solution to large problem debt, but respondents also described negative repercussions. A bankruptcy record leads to expensive loans in the future. In the wake of bankruptcy, Becky fully expects to be penalized with higher interest rates if she tries to borrow money. "I don't want to even think about trying to get a loan right now because they'll try to give me some high interest rate."

Some respondents work with a credit bureau or consumer credit counseling to assist with filing bankruptcy or consolidating debt into one payment as a means to manage and/or reduce liability. One respondent, with four of her six children still living at home, said that consumer credit counseling is very helpful. "[The counselor] told me about how I could make an offer of a certain amount. They helped me with the 'legalese' of the letters that I had to write to these people. In fact, they wrote them for me. They taught me how to read my credit report and how to dispute it." Another observed that although consumer credit counseling is helpful, he is "not with them anymore" because he does not have any money to pay on the debt. "You can't go to credit counseling unless you have money to pay for these credit cards every month."

Only a few respondents (4) turn to family members for help with problem debt. Most families are unable to help, although a few families with substantial savings of their own had helped to bail out their grown children.

ESTABLISHING (OR REESTABLISHING) CREDITWORTHINESS

In contrast to the widespread belief that low-income families have a short-term financial outlook (Varcoe 1990; Muske and Winter 1999), respondents in this study are acutely concerned about establishing credit and improving bad credit records.[7] Credit is important to families because they may need to finance a purchase that they cannot pay for today (Lea 1999). Respondents understand that having "good credit" is important for their family's current and future well-being. Nonetheless, only 14 respondents reported having a good credit record, including a few who successfully rebuilt a bad credit record.

Thirteen respondents discussed concerns about their credit rating, including Fred. Despite paying off all of his loans, Fred's profligate spending when he was addicted to drugs and his wife's prior bankruptcy continue to plague them. Fred described how difficult it is to escape a bad credit history.

> Once your credit gets messed up in America, you're through. They won't let you back in no more. Only way they let you in is on them high interest terms where they rip me off. That's the way America is. So when a person's credit ever gets messed up in America, I feel sorry for them 'cause I'm a living witness. Ain't nothing you can do to straighten it out. It's a bunch of lies. So I tell my kids, don't mess up your credit, 'cause I guarantee you, it's easy to mess up but it is five times as hard to straighten it out. Now if you done paid everybody that you owe, then they call and get a credit report from Texas and everything on there is zero and you have established credit in other areas and you have paid people and you go to the bank and your house is paid for, you trying to borrow a measly $10,000 and they don't loan it to you. Okay, now tell me what does that do? A $45,000 home and you can't get a $10,000 [loan] . . . 'cause of your payment history. [The loan officer] said, "You right on the borderline." That's what they always say.

Another respondent is still fighting a poor credit rating after filing for bankruptcy ten years earlier. Her husband lost his job soon after they bought a home. They defaulted on the house payments. They filed for bankruptcy. "That was a nightmare. . . . I'm still fighting that on my credit." Similarly, seven years after declaring bankruptcy, another person, the father of three teenagers, still feels the stigma of bad credit. "So we've learned to live without credit."

Eight people described efforts to build credit. One strategy is to pay credit card bills before the due date to avoid late payments that will mar their credit history. But many expressed frustration. One person applied for credit cards in order to build up a good credit record. Unfortunately, she cannot always cover the payments and is likely adding to her debt instead of improving her credit.

Young respondents, in particular, complained that it is difficult to establish credit. One 20-year-old discovered that no credit is like bad credit. "With me being young, I have to establish credit. I don't have any credit right now. So that's like bad credit." Another couple built a little credit making payments on their truck, but it is not enough to meet the standards for a home loan. "We just needed more. And I don't have any credit cards. I don't believe in them. I'd rather pay cash." They were hoping that their faithful payments to the utility companies might help them qualify for a home loan.

Another group that lacks credit records is immigrants. They may not have been in the United States long enough or participated sufficiently in mainstream financial services to build a record. This latter challenge affects even the children of immigrants, who may conduct their financial business in much the same way as their parents. For example, one couple, both second-generation immigrants, always paid for everything in cash (like their parents). Without establishing a good credit record, they could not qualify for loans. As a result, when they borrowed to buy a car, they had a lien put on their savings account.

DISCUSSION

Falling into problem debt is a constant fear, and families try to avoid it (Maital 1982; Lunt and Livingstone 1992). Nonetheless, despite efforts to economize, families frequently generate debt they cannot cover out of regular household income.[8] Sometimes this grows into problem debt, which they cannot pay now or in the near future. Finally, with little margin for error, a crisis, such as a health emergency, a divorce, or a job loss, can throw families into overwhelming debt.

Overindulgence, addictions, poor decisions, and miscalculations may generate or contribute to debt problems. As Lea, Webley, and Levine (1993) observe, there is a group of "feckless debtors" that arise from a "culture of indebtedness." Are respondents downplaying their own lapses in good financial decisions? Perhaps, yet we find that lack of income and events over which families have little control—such as episodes of illness without health insurance coverage, a death in the family, or the loss of a job—are the foundation of problem debt. Therefore, a focus on the poor and their money management skills must be balanced with the view that, as Stephen Lea writes, "few people would be able to overcome" the financial problems most poor people face (1999, 142; see also Lea, Tarpy, and Webley 1987; Lunt and Livingston 1991a; Berthoud and Kempson 1992; Walker 1996). Researchers Teresa Sullivan and her colleagues (1989) and Elizabeth Warren and Amelia Tyagi (2003) find that even middle-class Americans fall behind because consumption costs are fast outpacing income. As Ella, a respondent in the current study, observed, jobs pay very little, usually "seven or eight dollars an hour, nine or ten if it is a good job." As we know, such income levels are below those that can sustain families (Economic Policy Institute 2007).

When they do generate problem debt, families try to economize and avoid further borrowing. They cut back on using their credit cards. They try to climb out of debt by taking jobs that pay more or offer overtime hours, or they moonlight. But it is difficult to recover. When they are unable to climb out of debt and it begins to interfere with their ability to care for their family, they act more decisively. Some cut up all their credit cards, some seek debt counseling, and some file for bankruptcy. These actions are not easy and are not without significant economic, social, and emotional consequences. Moreover, these actions are not usually the end of their financial struggles. They continue to face shortfalls in income and limited opportunities, and they carry the burden of a poor credit record.

At the end of the day, we have to ask why these families are interested in saving if they live on the financial edge so much of the time. This chapter and the previous one provide some clues. While families are trying to make ends meet month-to-month, survive crises, cover unplanned expenses, and cope with debt, they are also trying to remain true to their faith, protect their children, and, when possible, build a better future. Children are the immediate reason for choosing one course of action over another. Faith helps them persevere and gives them hope. They believe that a solid economic foundation is important. These values and goals form a foundation for their financial strategies and behaviors.

For the most part, their hopes remain in the background until a time when they perceive an opportunity and when they can gather the personal determination to begin a long arduous road to making real improvements. We see evidence in Rosalyn who wants her children to feel respected, in Fred who strives to improve his credit, in Tonya and Becky who are trying to finish college degrees so they will have more resources to raise their children, and in Ella, whose dreams include instilling hope for the future among the young women in her community. Despite high demands on limited incomes, respondents are looking to the future (Lister 2006). In the next two chapters, we focus on savings and the role that saving plays in helping families achieve their hopes and dreams. In chapter 6, we look at respondents' savings goals and efforts to save. We highlight the experiences of nonparticipants who were not selected to participate in the IDA program. Then, in chapter 7, we focus on IDA participants' experiences saving in an individual account program.

CHAPTER 6

Striving to Save

At one time or another everyone in this study tried to set some money aside in savings. Most saved at home or in a bank account, while a few others saved in retirement and other types of accounts. This chapter recounts these efforts. Although some achieved considerable success, most respondents described frustration in trying to accumulate savings. As researchers observed long ago, saving in poor households is often an unrealized goal (Rainwater, Coleman, and Handel 1959, 172; Caplovitz 1967, 110).

This chapter highlights the experiences of nonparticipants and their families. Although the focus is on nonparticipants, at times we include examples and evidence from interviews with IDA participants about saving prior to their joining the IDA program.[1] (The focus of the next chapter turns to participants' efforts to save in an IDA.)

After introducing the saving experiences of several individuals, we discuss why respondents think savings are important and what they hope to achieve through saving. We turn to types of saving next. We use George Katona's (1975) typology of saving: including residual saving, or inadvertent accumulations of surplus money in an account because revenues exceed expenditures; contractual saving, or saving through precommitting certain sources of money for saving; and discretionary saving, or money deliberately and actively accumulated. There is evidence of all three types of saving among respondents in this study, although residual savings are relatively rare.

Next, respondents discuss strategies for saving. According to Sondra Beverly, Amanda McBride, and Mark Schreiner (2003), there are three stages of saving. Savers first have to identify a surplus for saving (reallocation). Then, they may convert surpluses from liquid to illiquid forms (conversion); finally, they have to resist the temptation to spend, or dissave (maintenance). Based on a review of existing research and earlier ADD findings, respondents propose different strategies that characterize each stage (Sherraden, Moore, and Hong 2000; Moore et al. 2001). Here, we examine how these strategies for saving match those used by respondents in this study, modifying and highlighting those that seem to correspond best. The last part of the chapter focuses on obstacles to saving encountered by respondents.

We continue Ella's narrative, as well as those of three other nonparticipants, LaVonne, Debra, and Cynthia, as they describe their successes and disappointments trying to save on low incomes.

Ella

When Ella was growing up, saving money was out of the question. Her parents owned little except for their farm, house, and a car. There were no appliances. They used a washboard for laundry and a horse-drawn plow for farming. Even as a young adult, she remembered turning to relatives to help collect enough money for her father's burial. "What we didn't have, we had to go to his nieces and nephews, and his sisters and brothers [to get]. . . . So that was the way he was buried."

Ella began her adult life with two babies and few belongings. Little by little, she began to accumulate a few things. She entrusted her savings to her mother for safekeeping (she did not own a savings account at that time), and with this money she hoped eventually to buy a car.

> I had saved up—I think it was five or six hundred dollars to put down on a car, which was a lot of money for me—and then [my mother] called me and said, "We are going to have use your money to get the kids some school clothes." So that's what my money went for.

Later an older brother helped her buy a little car. "I'll never forget that. . . . I bought it used from a car lot and it ran two months, and I had to pay every dime of it . . . about 17 or 18 hundred dollars." She went back to using the bus to get to and from work.

Even though it was difficult to accumulate much, Ella always believed in the importance of saving and stashed away money in various ways (although she did not necessarily think of them as "savings"). First, she saved change at home for emergencies and incidentals. "Normally, you know, I have about $200 in change. . . . I have $90 in new quarters. . . . I have a jar about this big and then after it gets so full, then I just take it in and put it in the bank." Ella also carries life insurance. "Naturally I do have insurance on everyone. And my daughter, when she was two, I bought a $1,000 worth of savings bonds for her, and so she still got those."

Ella saved enough to buy a condemned house and fix it up. She came up with the money by cutting back on expenses, including quitting smoking. "I saved up $2,500. . . . The house they were getting ready to tear it up, and so I bought it for $2,500 and fixed it up." She invested financially—and in sweat equity—to rehab the place.

> I didn't borrow any money, you know. What I had was $60 dollars a month . . . to buy a—what do you call that stuff? Sheet rock or whatever. That's what I did. You know? And the boys helped me out. And it's a fairly decent looking home. It would probably sell now for $35,000 or $40,000.

Looking back, Ella is proud that she was able to save enough for her small home.

Unfortunately, Ella's husband has become disabled, her mother has fallen ill, and she has had to purchase a car unexpectedly. Despite these recent setbacks, she has confidence in her ability to once again set aside money for the future. She has a new job with health insurance coverage that costs $200 a month less than what she paid in her former position. "I might be able to start attempting to save some money again." She remains optimistic. "I think once we weather this storm, we'll be okay."

LaVonne

LaVonne learned little about saving as she was growing up, as we saw in chapter 3. Her mother talked to her and her siblings about the importance of work and paying the bills but never taught them how. "By the time we got to high school she started saying, 'You all need to know how to pay a bill,' or something like that. . . . But we never really knew how she did stuff."

LaVonne's husband had some savings when she married him. They bought a small house. "He'd apparently . . . saved up all the money." After that, her husband entrusted LaVonne with their savings. She kept it in the closet. She liked this system of saving. "It was easy access. If I really needed it, I would just go in there and get it. Nobody knew and I only had a little kid, you know, in the house that I had to worry about." Eventually, though, she decided it would be safer to open a checking account. "I started thinking I might get robbed."

After she and her husband separated, LaVonne found it difficult to set money aside on her small teaching salary. "We are living, like I said, from paycheck to paycheck. And a lot of times we just don't have enough to go make it over and so, you know, something is left short." Nonetheless, LaVonne tries to save. Through her job she has a retirement account that requires no action on her part. "Once you signed the contract, that's just automatically taken out of your check." The retirement account offers LaVonne some peace of mind.

In addition, LaVonne has invested in annuities. "And they were deducting it without my having to deal with it and . . . it was tax-free!" Without this automatic deduction feature, it would take a lot of effort to save, as LaVonne explained.

> If it's too accessible, it's too much temptation. And so a lot of times that's why people do not save. Anything that is automatic I don't worry about it, I don't have to deal with it. It's like, it's over there somewhere and I don't have to deal with it so, therefore, it's done and it's taken care of.

Unfortunately, unlike her retirement account, annuities are within reach, and when the family was short on funds, she withdrew it. "I just needed the money and I drew it out. And that's the only catch there, see, it's more available if you really needed it." Without her annuity, LaVonne said, "I don't have anything saved."

Sadly, it turned out that she did not really need the money, but once in hand, it was spent. "Basically I took it out around Christmas and you know how that went . . . . You sent your momma something, your kids, and they went shopping, and you pay some bills, and before you know, you looked up and you didn't have any money."

From experience, LaVonne concluded that the only way she can save successfully is to have the money automatically deposited in a savings instrument just like her annuity.

> I like the automatic deduction. That's easiest for me. . . . anything that you have to physically go and do yourself is just very difficult to keep up, you know. You may do it for a few months and then you just feel the temptation to say, well, maybe you just won't do it. But if somebody else is doing [the deduction for you] and it's not something that you have to deal with . . . and if you have to try and stop [the deduction] it's extra work for you, so you just don't do it. It just

keeps going and so . . . that's really the best thing. The best way to save is to have someone automatically deduct it from your check.

In contrast, going to the bank to make deposits would not work for her. "If you've got to go down and physically go put it in that bank, it's just not gonna happen, not too often. Or go pay something over here." She drew a parallel with her car insurance. "Now, my car insurance is automatic deduction. I know it is always gonna be taken care of because it is automatically done. But if I had to do it myself, I'd be late. I'd lose my car insurance. I've been through that. . . . I think that's the key, automatic deduction."

Debra

Debra is a more successful saver than most, despite a very tough start in life. The child welfare authorities removed Debra from her family's home when she was 15. Shortly after, she dropped out of high school, moved with her boyfriend to another state, and soon became pregnant. Debra found herself in an abusive relationship and with a growing drug addiction. Despite her drug habit, which "made it difficult to save," Debra generated a small savings, which she kept stashed in a book so her boyfriend would not find it. She explained that on more than one occasion, she wanted to spend it on drugs. "Sometimes I would take a little out and sometimes I'd put more in. It's just a matter of self-control." She used the $1,000 savings to leave her boyfriend and return to Tulsa with her child.

By the time we talked to Debra, she had kicked the drug habit and was engaged to be married. Debra and her fiancé are both savers. They earmark her second semimonthly paycheck and his "overtime money" for saving. Debra calculated that they save about $50 a month, after keeping a little out for enjoyment. She keeps at least $1,000 in the savings account. Nonetheless, it is difficult to keep money in savings. Expenses crop up. "Whenever we'd have car problems we'd have to get money out of the savings to fix it." Other times, temptation beckons. "Sometimes we want to go and spend some of it. But we usually don't unless we know that we'd be able to compensate it in a week or two. . . . But it does tempt you sometimes."

As a result, their savings fluctuate. Recently they accumulated quite a lot of money but spent most of it on car payments and tuition.

I have [had] up to $3,000 in savings and right now we only have about, a little under $1,000, which is the minimum that I will let it go to. I have to have that much in there. But with school starting and everything, I've already pulled out

the money for school and that's just all the emergency money. So, it fluctuates
. . . a lot.

As Debra put it, she has to exert "self-control" in order to save. She earmarks
money for saving, copes with extra expenditures, and relies on a pattern of
spending and saving (with a rule of thumb for how much should be deposited)
that she has now maintained over some time. Although she exhibits greater
willpower and is a more successful saver than most, we see this general strategy
in other people's saving as well.

Cynthia

Cynthia, who is 52, has always worked and spent her money carefully. She is a
bit scornful of the younger generation, who appear to have so much money to
spend. "The world has offered so much they don't think they have to work hard
anymore to earn a decent living to be able to save that money. They say the average child goes to the mall—11 to 16 years old—and spends $90. Ninety dollars
in the mall on a Saturday! I never did that in my life!"

If she has extra money, it goes into savings. She and her husband saved for
and bought the house they moved into when they were married. Even after she
and her husband divorced in 1995, Cynthia managed to save. In 1998, for example, she began setting aside $10 a week for her son's college education. She ex-
pects him to graduate in three years. "It's number one." She deposits regularly,
every Friday. "That ends my week . . . . The mentality has to be, 'I'm a saver. I'm
gonna save. I'm gonna pay myself first.' So, off the top."

> Well, to me saving is almost a "have-to"—just like your bills are almost a
> "have-to." Because if you gonna eventually improve out of your situation
> where you are now, you almost have to save. And even if it's $5 or $10, what-
> ever, I think it's very important to do something. You don't always have some-
> thing to do something with, but I really believe in savings because I know it
> works. Because you know, in my marriage time we saved. We had to do what
> we needed to do.

Since her divorce when her youngest child was 12 years old, Cynthia has built a
housecleaning business, working in a different home each day. Her finances are
tight but "stable," although she is often discouraged. She continues to save, but
medical expenses are high. Her son qualifies for Medicaid, but it does not cover

her own medications. During weeks when she has to buy medicine, she cannot cover her $10 a week savings goal. "But if I have to buy my medicine, guess what? I'm gonna buy my medicine because if I have a heart attack I can't work. And that's facts."

Although Cynthia believes "you have to have goals if you're going somewhere," she nonetheless does not feel she is getting ahead. She knows that having savings is the way to reach her goals. "In order to support our goals, the fact of the matter is you will need money." But the money is not accumulating fast enough. She is anxious to figure out ways to make her money work for her. "You have to get into the big arena in investing and stuff like that, even if you start off small, your money can work more for you. And I'm just now finding that out."

With varying degrees of success, Ella, LaVonne, Debra, and Cynthia have saved some money during their lifetimes. Like them, other respondents in the study believe saving is necessary in order to reach short- and long-term goals. Like Ella, they save at home for emergencies and try to accumulate surpluses to save for a goal. Like LaVonne, they struggle to put aside money, and they sometimes have to turn to that money in hard times. Like Debra, they try to maintain self-control in the face of adversity and personal shortcomings, but most people lack Debra's willpower. And finally, like Cynthia, a lifetime saver, they search for ways to save on more favorable terms. It takes enormous willpower to set aside money and keep it in savings, especially when income is low, there are large consumption demands, and there are few savings alternatives. Respondents say it is easier to save when they are forced to, and if the money does not pass through their hands. When they have to make the deposit themselves, most say it is more difficult. Before we turn to the strategies and challenges of saving, we explore why saving is important.

SAVING: A MATTER OF RESPONSIBILITY AND FAITH

Respondents articulate a value for saving that is deeply rooted in American culture. As one person said, "That is the American way. Save money." For another, saving is "just like the right thing to do." Saving is considered a sign of being a responsible person, according to another respondent. "[I'm] just a person being responsible and mapping out some things."

Where did they learn the value of saving? Some said they learned from their families. Camille, for example, said that her father's admonition to save made a lasting impression ("his voice never left me alone"). But she said that working for a while in a company where saving was encouraged made it easier to save. Anne recalled that her father told her to always keep $5,000 on hand. Even though she and her husband have not achieved this level of savings, she agreed it is an important goal.

> You never know when that tire is gonna blow . . . so, it's good to have money that you know is put back somewhere that is kept untouched to fall back on so you don't have to fall back on anyone else. You don't have to contact anyone else to say, "Can I borrow a hundred bucks?" Which eventually just gets you back in a bind again because you are borrowing, you know.

As we have seen, respondents in the study live in the U.S. heartland where religious faith provides important context for financial decisions (chap. 4) and also shapes many respondents' attitudes toward saving (Keister 2003; Boddie 2006). One particularly religious respondent said the leader of her church suggests that parishioners save and ensure their own stability—after first giving to the church.

> Because Proverbs says that "A wise man saves up an inheritance for his children's children." I believe that the situation that I am in my life right now is only a temporary one. I have an ultimate goal of not only being self-sufficient and financially independent, but also to be able to take care of my parents . . . my nieces and nephews and hopefully one day children of my own. My pastor's been preaching a lot about after you tithe, to tithe to yourself, and put ten percent in savings for yourself.

Tithing shapes saving patterns for some respondents. As one respondent explained, "I think that, for a lot of people the very first form of savings they encounter is in their church. And [in] their church, you know, they teach the children, you know, tithe what you need, that's how the church is run." In this way, in some families tithing may model for children that saving on a regular basis is not only possible, but desirable.

Tithing could be viewed as a substitute for saving (Keister 2003). In other words, if the assumption is that the Lord provides for those who tithe fully and regularly, there may be little need to put additional money away for one's future. Some respondents appear to believe that there is less need to save because God will provide for the devout who tithe faithfully. Yet, it appears that for people in this study, religious beliefs and tithing exist alongside their efforts to save. For example, the following excerpt from an interview with an IDA participant suggests her belief in God's protection might negatively influence her attempts to save. Yet, she includes any blessing—whether the IDA program or her social security benefit—as evidence of God's presence.

> I trust Him and He provides, you know. But a lot of people think you have to have this or you have to have that. I don't worry about it. Even though people will tell me, "See what's going to happen—you're not building up any Social Security." I say, "So? I'm not really worried about it, you guys, just relax." . . . God will provide.

WHY AND HOW DO PEOPLE SAVE?

Evidence from the in-depth interviews shows that respondents save for many different reasons. Table 6.1 presents primary and secondary savings goals extracted from interviews with nonparticipants. (IDA participants' goals are presented in the chapter that follows.) Nonparticipants saved mainly to cover emergencies or to make a particular purchase.

TABLE 6.1. Primary and Secondary Savings Goals of Nonparticipants
($N = 25$)

	Nonparticipants N (%)		
	Primary Goal	Secondary Goal	Total
Buy a house/real estate	7 (28)	3 (12)	10 (40)
Emergencies	8 (32)	1 (4)	9 (36)
Savings/investment	4 (16)	3 (12)	7 (28)
Children's education or training	3 (12)	3 (12)	6 (24)
Retirement	4 (16)	1 (4)	5 (20)
House repair	1 (4)	1 (4)	2 (8)
Spouse/own education or training	0 (0)	1 (4)	1 (4)
Business	1 (4)	0 (0)	1 (4)
Other	3 (12)	4 (16)	7 (28)
Don't know			5 (20)

Source: Center for Social Development, in-depth interviews.
Note: Some nonparticipants discussed more than one savings goal. We identified primary and secondary goals based on their emphasis in interviews.

We next discuss the kinds of saving identified by George Katona (1975), including residual saving, contractual saving, and discretionary saving. We describe these types, their purposes, and the strategies nonparticipants used to deposit funds and maintain them in savings (Beverly, McBride, and Schreiner 2003).

Residual Saving

Residual saving is the inadvertent accumulation of surplus money in an account because revenues exceed expenditures for at least a temporary period of time (Katona 1975). Respondents sometimes generate residual savings in an account without making a conscious plan to save. One of the few respondents who reported residual savings pointed out that she accumulates money in her checking account because her employer no longer has an ATM machine that would make it easy to withdraw. "So, I'd have to drive to my bank to get it free . . . . So it's just easier not to do it."

However, residual savings typically are quite small and temporary. In financially stretched households, surpluses are discovered quickly and allocated either to consumption or in some cases to discretionary savings. As one respondent said, "If I've got a certain amount of money in my checking account that is left over then I try to save that. I write that check to the savings account."

Contractual Saving

A more common form of saving is through a contractual arrangement. These contracts include defined benefit and defined contribution plans, other workplace savings plans, life and burial insurance, and home ownership. Contractual saving typically involves external actors. People enroll through a workplace, government, or financial program that precommits them to an automatic deposit to a savings instrument (Strotz 1956). Contractual saving usually incorporates features that reward, structure, and obligate saving. Many contractual savings arrangements also restrict withdrawals; however, this is not an essential feature. Restrictions often take the form of financial penalties for early withdrawals, such as taxes withheld in the case of 401(k) accounts. In our sample of low-income individuals, it is more common to find contractual saving through insurance or home ownership than through structured savings plans. Another contractual saving arrangement, discussed earlier, is to overpay income taxes and use the lump-sum refund each spring for saving, although we have only limited evidence of this in our sample (Lewis, Webley, and Furnham 1995).

Defined Contribution Accounts. At the time of the interview, relatively few respondents were saving in a defined contribution retirement plan, such as an annuity or a 401(k). However, several had done so in the past. Respondents discussed the benefits and drawbacks to these plans. Ella, for example, who was always searching for a better way to save, said that when her employer offered a 401(k) retirement savings plan, she immediately signed up. "As a matter of fact, this month I think we are supposed to have a meeting, and what they are going to do is [match] up to $50, so if I'm putting in $50 a month, then they will give me $50." This would "be a big help." Ella is particularly concerned about retirement savings; she is anxious to avoid privation in old age.

> Yesterday this old lady—she had to be 85—she was walking and picking up cans to try and supplement her income. I just think that is so wrong for anybody that's worked all of their lives to draw $400 a month [Social Security], because you know that you can't live off of that. That just gets to my heart, and I just say, "Lord I just can't do this."

Ella's goal is to buy some land and a used trailer and spend her older years in the rural community where she grew up, taking care of grandchildren. In the meantime, she plans to work and accumulate savings for "at least ten more years."

Many respondents expressed similar thoughts about saving in a 401(k) or other defined contribution plan. They like the feature that allows the automatic transfer of pay into savings. One person explained how this feature of her 401(k) makes it easier to save: "I just figured that was a way to save money and it didn't go through my hands so . . . it was out of there when I got my check." She does not miss the money when she saves this way. "'Cause what you haven't had in your hand, you don't miss." Another likes her 401(k) "'cause they take it out before I get my money." Although she refers to it as "forced savings," that is okay with her. "Besides the 401(k), the forced saving, that's basically the only type of saving that I would do besides leaving a little money in maybe a checking account."

For another respondent, the idea of deducting money from her paycheck for saving was anathema at first. By the time we talked to her, though, she was full of praise for the arrangement.

They took some out of my wages, and I said, "Ay! How can they take this? . . . But now I have about $4,000 in savings there that is growing. I haven't touched it. . . . without [my] noticing they had been taking [it] out of my wages. I think this was a good method because if you have money to save, sometimes you say, "I have $50." But [instead of saving] you are more likely to say "I'm going to buy something." And you say "I'll save next month." But if they take it out of your wages [before you see it], you don't really notice.

Another respondent who participates in a 401(k) plan at work believes it has helped her save. Her employer automatically transfers $20 of her salary every month to savings. After a year of service, the company provides a 50 percent match on employee savings. "I'll have some money in there so I can retire and have something except Social Security." At the time of the interview, she had accumulated almost $1,000. On her own, she had been unable to accumulate any discretionary savings whatsoever. "My checking would get, like, overdrawn, you know, so they would take the money out of my savings, which would close it out. Every time. I never had a savings [account] that lasted."

Another benefit of defined contribution savings plans is the ability to build credit and to borrow on the savings. This respondent pointed out that after she accumulates $2,000, she has the right to a loan. Further, she mentioned that her father has good credit in part because of his 401(k) savings. He had used his good credit to help her purchase a vehicle and a trailer. "He has so much money in his 401(k) that he took money out of [it] and they only charge him like 7 percent interest—like some places will charge you like 12 percent interest for a loan."

Defined Benefit Retirement Plans. Relatively few respondents talked about defined benefit retirement plans. (These are employment-based retirement plans, such as pension plans, in which employees receive a specific amount based on their salary history and years of work. Contributions are made by the employee, the employer, or both.) It is not clear whether respondents did not mention these plans because they do not participate—smaller numbers of low-income households participate in these plans (Paladino and Helman 2003)—or whether participants did not view these plans as savings because they are not separate accounts that belong to the individual.

LaVonne has a defined benefit retirement plan. She has mixed opinions about it. On one hand, she is grateful that she has it and cannot use it ("That's a guaranteed savings for you"). When income is low, she noted, it is always tempting to use available savings. "When you get really stressed [and] you really need some money, then you go and take that money that you were saving in some of these other plans. 'Cause it's easy to get. [But] this plan is better in that sense because you can't get it." In this way, according to LaVonne, it provides "peace of mind" because there will be money at retirement or an inheritance for the children.

On the other hand, LaVonne resents not having control over the money. If it were not deducted for retirement, she would get a "bigger paycheck. . . . It would help me pay my bills." But she is also dissatisfied with the plan because she has no voice in how the money is invested and does not trust the fund managers to be good stewards of her money. "I wish we could invest it where we would like to invest it ourselves. Though it would be mandatory that we couldn't touch it, but we would be able to invest it the way we would like to invest it." She believes she can get a better return on her money. "I can do better with the money that they have been taking out of my check, I could have had an annuity and . . . made more out of it."

Other Workplace Saving Plans. Respondents have experience with various other types of contractual saving programs. Camille's employer deducts money from her paycheck to purchase small amounts of company stock. She is not fully aware of how much money she has in this account. It's easier to save, she says, because this money comes directly out of her paycheck before she even sees it. As soon as she has the financial flexibility to save more regularly, she wants to set up another saving instrument.

> And it will be . . . direct deposit, or something like that where I won't even miss it like it is with the stocks, and the annuity, and the retirement. It's just a matter of doing it, you know, because I'm not going to sit down and write out a check and say this is going to savings. I'm not going to go to the bank and say, put that in savings.

She does not think it will be difficult. "I'm in the senior citizens account, and you don't pay any service charges. You don't pay for your checks. You don't pay for your statements. . . . I can very easily have them to deduct a certain amount of money out of that checking account and put it in a savings account every month. . . . If they just take it automatically, like I have my car insurance [paid], I think it will work."

Employers sometimes offer other types of savings plans. For example, one respondent, who also has a 401(k) plan available through work, participates in an employer profit-sharing plan. It requires no action on his part whatsoever.

The company makes all of the contributions. "Once you've been employed there a year, they sign you up and you're in. And they put money into that for your savings." According to him, this is "the first time I saved anything in any amount that I knew it was going towards something."

Another respondent had participated in a savings program through the armed forces. This had been his only successful savings attempt (prior to the IDA, discussed in the next chapter).

> I remember being in some kind of little savings program then where they would take out so much a month and buy you a savings bond. And I can remember a time for maybe six or eight months where I was sending a savings bond home every month. . . . So they take $50 from your paycheck once a month and they purchase a $75 bond for you. Now the bond may not mature for five years, so it wouldn't be worth $75 until five years later. Now you can cash them in any time, but of course it would be for just what you paid for it, maybe just a couple dollars over that.

He did just that, participating for a short time and using the money before the bonds matured. "All the bonds that I had accumulated I think I ended up cashing them in. So they never matured." Looking back, he said he did not fully understand the importance of saving at that time.

Automatic Transfer to Savings. Respondents also set up mechanisms that convert money into savings automatically, compelling them to save. These might be viewed as self-initiated savings contracts. Ella explained why individuals might choose to do this. Although more successful at saving than many other respondents, Ella admitted that she still finds it difficult. She said it would be easier to save in a program where money is automatically deposited in savings, explaining, "I can really save if I don't see it." She has plans to contact her bank to see about "taking out so much to put in my savings each month, and not let me see it at all." Arrangements like these are a sort of informal type of contractual savings, where people use a savings instrument to structure deposits.

Several people have had jobs that offered a direct deposit option. As one respondent said, "When I seriously started saving money was when I started working full-time. . . . I had direct-deposit. . . . I had a certain portion go towards savings—directly deposited as soon as my check would come in." Another respondent recalled a previous job that permitted her to automatically transfer five dollars to her savings account from her eighty-dollar weekly paycheck. "They would take five dollars out of my check before I even got it, you know, and put it automatically into my savings account."

Another respondent uses a different approach. He and his wife set up different types of savings accounts for different purposes. At their credit union, funds are automatically transferred from his paycheck to their savings account. They use this money to pay for car insurance and bills over the summer months when he is not working. Although this is only short-term saving, it makes it possible for them to afford their large annual insurance premium.

Another saves for the long term through an automatic deposit of $20 into his savings account every two weeks. Even when he and his wife withdraw their savings for consumption (e.g., to cover gas until payday), they try to leave a little in the account so the fund will grow over time.

Life and Burial Insurance. We also include commitments to life and burial insurance in contractual saving (Katona 1975; Lea, Tarpy, and Webley 1987; Kennickell, Starr-McCluer, and Surrette 2000). These are not always considered saving, but because they build wealth and are often the only assets held by families in this study, we include them here. Respondents did not initially talk about insurance as a form of savings either. However, their reasons for having some types of insurance are often linked to long-term security.[2]

Respondents talk about life and burial insurance as ways to secure the future for themselves and their families. Ella, for example, has life insurance for herself and each of her children. She believes it provides protection, security, and savings. This perspective has been noted in other research. David Caplovitz (1967) points out that by the 1960s, life insurance had become a pillar of security in low-income communities, although it had not always been viewed in this way.[3]

In the current study, 51 respondents (61 percent) talked about owning some form of life or burial insurance, a number similar to the proportion of low-income families who reported owning life insurance policies in a 1995 survey (Hogarth and O'Donnell 1999).[4] Only 20 respondents receive life insurance benefits from their job. The remaining respondents presumably have made a deliberate choice to purchase life or burial insurance, suggesting that this type of insurance is a priority. One respondent who owns a life insurance policy, for example, is reassured by the fact that if he dies, he will leave his wife and two children enough money to survive.

> I got life insurance when I was 20 when I really started getting into the work force. I went ahead and got life insurance and the type of insurance policy I got

builds a retirement plan. . . . If I die . . . my wife or whoever gets a certain amount, but if I keep on paying it like I'm supposed to, when I'm 65, I get like $250,000 or half a million or something like that. It just combines with itself.

Life and burial insurance are seen as ways to honor the dead, to prevent dishonor, and to avoid dissaving (Banks 1998; Drakeford 1998). Many respondents are mindful of possible embarrassment when a loved one dies, and they want to ensure that person a dignified burial. As one respondent declared,

I won't be an embarrassment on them when I die. Because that's the most embarrassing time in [a] family when a person dies. Because those people [funeral home staff] aren't gonna do anything to touch that body, move that body, drop that body in the ground—until they have their money. And I'm not fixing to get cremated. I'm not gonna burn on earth.

They are particularly concerned not to burden their family with burial costs. They have seen or experienced situations where death created financial problems for families. One respondent and her husband, for example, found themselves deep in debt after paying for a son's funeral. She recalled, "I had to work for a whole year paying $100 a month from what he didn't have to pay for his funeral." It was a real "hardship" for the family. "Oh Lord, I really did without a few meals trying to pay that." Determined that their other children not suffer the same predicament, she and her husband make sure that they have life insurance. She is especially concerned that the children not have to sell the house that she and her husband worked so hard to buy. They want this bit of wealth to pass along to the next generation.

African Americans were slightly more likely to carry life or burial insurance (18, or 75 percent) than whites (25, or 69 percent). Life and burial insurance may be particularly important when families lack discretionary savings. As Theresa observed, African Americans commonly hold life or burial insurance because they lack other savings.

Black people in general, I found out, they may not have anything, but they will have some life insurance. They will pay for life insurance before they pay for anything else. Or burial insurance is what they call it. That's how I buried my mother. That's how I buried my grandmother. That's how I buried my brother. That's how I buried my father. See, so those, there was nothing to say that I inherited. . . . There's nothing they left me financially. But they did make sure that when they died I didn't have to come up with a lot of money to bury them.

Life and burial insurance are culturally accepted and relatively easy methods of planning for the future. Nonetheless, many families in the study do not have life or burial insurance. Eight talked about being unable to afford it, including one respondent who is deeply concerned about what would happen to her family if she were to die. "Being a single mother and not having any family support at all from [my son's] father. . . It's just, I really need a cushion for [my son], if something was to happen to me. . . . But it's just so hard to get that started." Her concern is not unfounded. Researchers have found that lack of life insurance contributes to the impoverishment of up to 35 percent of widows (Kotlikoff with Bernheim 2001).

Home Ownership. Some respondents save through home ownership, another form of contractual saving.[5] A significant number of home owners in our study had saved successfully for a down payment in the past, but not all. In a few cases, they inherited houses or land from parents. In other instances, they received part of a down payment from their parents. More often, respondents bought homes using subsidized home purchase programs that required very small down payments, and in a couple of cases, respondents own very low value houses or mobile homes (including Ella, who participated in an urban homesteading program). Even though they may not have saved for a down payment, these respondents and their families are making monthly mortgage payments, effectively building equity over time, although not all view this as "savings."

Discretionary Saving

Discretionary saving is money deliberately and actively accumulated. At some point in their lives, almost all respondents had attempted to accumulate discretionary savings. They store these savings at home or in an account of some kind, usually a savings account.

Their decision about how much to save depends on a number of factors, including how much is left over after paying the bills, how much extra they think they might need at any given time, or how much the bank requires in an account. Therefore, savings can be somewhat arbitrary (what is left over), a specific amount (a rule of thumb about a wise amount to set aside, such as the person who keeps "at least a month of bill money in the bank"), or a minimum balance required by the credit union or bank. In addition, most families keep some small savings at home for day-to-day needs. The most common types of discretionary savings are rainy-day savings and target savings (saving for a specific goal).

Rainy-Day Savings. About one-third of respondents put aside savings as a precaution against bad times.[6] They save as a form of "backup," "buffer," or "reserve." They describe this kind of savings as money to "fall back on," "safe money," and money "on hand"; it is money "put aside for a rainy day," "for security." As one respondent put it, "The only motivation you have is that you know it's there if you need it." Economists refer to this saving motive as precautionary (Deaton 1992, 191; Lister 2006).

Respondents frequently keep rainy day money in a savings account or a checking account. One respondent, for example, tries to keep extra money in her checking account for unplanned expenses: "That's usually how we get the things that pop up on you."

Some hope rainy-day savings accumulate over time. As one reasoned, if she can manage to stay within her budget of $10 spending money per day, her savings will eventually amount to something. "That would be my buffer and then that builds up." Unfortunately, this seldom occurs. Most respondents have to dip into these savings for some reason before they amount to much.

A key feature of rainy-day savings is flexibility. Rainy-day savings are "for anything," for "whatever we need," or "for a hard time." As one person pointed out, "It always pays to save for a rainy day 'cause you don't never know when the storm is coming." Among the most common emergencies that can be covered by rainy-day or precautionary savings are illness, vehicle repairs, house repairs, and other life events. For example, one respondent commented that precautionary savings could cover him for a while if his car broke down. Without a small stock of savings, he would lose his job. With precautionary savings on hand, he "felt safer" because "I always knew I had the extra $200 in there just in case."

Most families will need their rainy-day savings sooner or later, and thus, these savings do not accumulate for long. One respondent observed, "I don't care if you put it for car repairs, then your air conditioner is going to break. I mean you always, *always,* spend it." On reflection, this person does not consider her rainy-day money as real savings. "I don't really consider that savings. I just consider that having money when I am going to need it. Because I know I am gonna need it." Another observed, "It always gets raided if there's a need."

The idea of having no backup funds, of "going broke" and getting into debt, is a scary prospect. As one person said, "Nobody wants to be broke." Another person keeps some savings in a drawer at home to avoid having to turn to a "loan company or a pawn shop" when she needs cash. She does not want to lose face if she happens to be turned down for a loan and does not want to find herself "out on a limb." As Anne reflected earlier, precautionary savings can help a person avoid borrowing that could lead to a downward spiral of problem debt.

Rainy-day savings are especially important for people who have no one to turn to in an emergency. An immigrant explained that when she came to the United States "it was important for me to save because I didn't have anybody here to give me money, I didn't have anybody to help me. Nobody." Similarly, another immigrant, concerned about day-to-day financial security, prefers to "have a little bit of money . . . because I am alone. If I get sick, nobody is here to help me."

Target Savings. Others aim to accumulate savings out of regular income flows to invest in something they cannot cover without accumulating some savings. Sometimes savings are referred to by the goal itself, such as "wedding money," "Christmas money," "house money," "car money," or "college money."

The most common goal is a house. Although several express a desire to own a house, and claim they are saving for one, they admit that it will be difficult to save enough. Camille, for instance, saved for a house but had to spend her savings before reaching her goal: "It just seems like there's always something that the kids need."

Several respondents are saving for their children's or their own schooling. For example, a mother is setting up what she called a "trust fund" for her children. Whenever she does not need her children's $200 child support check for household consumption, she deposits it into the fund. She calculates that her children "should have something pretty decent" by the time they are old enough to go to college. In this way, she is trying to help her children gain a financial foothold and also learn about setting financial priorities. She also believes that college savings will relieve financial pressure on her.

> It won't be as stressful for me, 'cause I'll be older. I don't want to get into financial debt when they get older, like some parents do. . . . You always want the best for them and you want them to be this or that. You know what I'm saying? . . . It's just there for them. I'm getting the money for them now. Why not utilize it like that?

She believes that sacrifice now will pay off over the long run. "Why should I go in and buy them the nicest of clothes that they gonna grow out of? You know, than to put that money so when they are grown that they can have something that's meaningful for them?"

A few people said they are saving to make an investment or for retirement.[7] Anne, for instance, considers retirement a "future goal." "At one point in life you have to begin looking for when you get old and don't have an income coming in. . . . I don't think it is anything that is gonna happen within the next year, but, [it's a] future goal."

Several respondents saved for durables or a vehicle, although further discussion suggests that most of these purchases are made with loans from family or expensive forms of consumer credit, such as consumer loans, layaway, and rent-to-own.[8]

Discretionary Saving Strategies

Accumulating discretionary savings requires considerable effort and willpower on the part of the saver, as several respondents pointed out in the introduction to this chapter. They described using several strategies to help them reallocate money for saving, and to keep it in savings (Beverly, McBride, and Schreiner 2003). In many ways, these strategies mirror those they use to manage household finances (see chap. 4).

Set and Focus on a Savings Goal. Respondents often set a savings goal to focus their energy and attention on reallocating money for saving. One person said she will not save unless she has a goal. "If I've got a goal to buy something, then I can put back and save for a car or a house or something like that." Similarly, another respondent said that she has to have a good reason to save. It is easier to save when she has a goal in mind: "[When you] really want something, then you'll be determined to save money."

One person voiced a strong desire to make "everything better" for his children and give them more than he had as a child. "I want them to have a better education and better toys, clothes, better food, better nutrition than what we used to have in the old days." This yearning and determination makes it easier to save, he said. Similarly, an immigrant started saving for her daughter when they lived in the old country. Thinking about her children continues to help her saving. "So whenever I start accumulating . . . I'll try to psych myself into saving, 'This is intended to buy something' [for my children]." She observed, "I don't know where I got that notion or where I got that idea, but it was like my gift to them." Another respondent, a father of three, is also motivated by long-term saving goals. He saves about $40 a month. "The most important thing that can help me save is just thinking about . . . where will I be in five years? Where will I be in two years?" He acknowledges the difficulty of maintaining savings. "It's just hard staying focused, you know, and sacrificing some things and just not indulging in stuff—just not spending money."

Monitor Resource Flows. Following a weekly or monthly budget helps some people set aside savings. Anne developed an accounting system and framework for thinking about where her money should go. As she observed, "being on a budget makes it easier to save." As long as she has enough income, Anne said it is easier to save when her budget tells her where the money should come from and what it should be used for. Monitoring flows is a prerequisite for other strategies, such as earmarking sources for saving.

Earmark Sources of Savings. A key way that respondents avoid consuming all of their money is by keeping track of where surpluses are, framing different pots of money in different ways, and earmarking some for saving (Kahneman and Tversky 1979; Thaler 1985). Although mental accounting is a cognitive process, respondents usually discuss this in the form of an action (earmarking) for reallocating money to savings. The following examples illustrate approaches to mental accounting and earmarking, some simple and some complex.

Respondents sometimes earmark certain sources of money for saving, such as regular income streams and windfall income (Romich and Weisner 2000). The main source of discretionary savings is income, including job earnings, public assistance, social insurance, and child support. Some earmark a particular flow for saving. For example, Debra earmarks a portion of one of her semimonthly paychecks for saving. Some earmark earnings outside a regular job for saving, including Cynthia, who uses earnings from her extra house cleaning jobs, and Fred, who sets aside money he earns doing side jobs.

> Starting January of this year, I took every side job I done, I put in the . . . [lock] box and I guarantee you in five months I had $1,700. I didn't know I was making that much money on the side! $100 job here, $50 job here, $75 job here, $65 job here, sell a washer here for $250. . . . Man, I had $1,700!

One couple, both of whom are self-employed, uses a more complex system of earmarking. They save in separate accounts for each business and the household, according to the savings goal.

> In my one bank account I have the money set aside just for my photography business basically. Then, in my other savings account . . . just the other things

that I need. . . . [My checking account is] where I pay my bills and buy groceries, you know, that's my primary usage account. Then my husband has an account which I also am on. And that's primarily for his . . . business. . . . So, you know, in other words, I kind of have one account for each specific reason as to what I want that money to go for. That way the money stays separated.

Another respondent developed a simpler yet effective system for saving. She opened a checking and savings account, and deposits one source of income into her checking account, and the other source into savings. As a member of the National Guard, she works one weekend a month and two weeks once a year. "My weekend money I would put in checking, and then once a year I would do two weeks on active duty—and that would be a bigger check. I would put that into the savings." She does not have a goal in mind for her savings. "Well, basically I would just put my extra money in the savings. . . . I'd need the extra money in the future. So I would just put it away just for the future."

Some respondents use windfall income (a lump sum) for saving. Anita, a 30-year-old single mother with a son in fourth grade recently deposited some of her tax refund in a mutual fund for herself and some in a savings bond for her son.

Having a big lump sum at one time helps me. . . . I told the banker man, I said, "I'm gonna be back here once a year and make investments." I said, "Once a year. I don't know about that $50 a month. That looks like a bill to me." Just one lump sum. I never would have thought, I never really thought about that 10 years ago.

Another person reported saving some of her deceased husband's life insurance benefits. Several respondents save tax refunds, including one who considers her refund as a "form of savings" because she overwithholds all year, receiving it all at once at tax time (Neumark 1995). Then she puts "aside a certain amount" of her refund in savings.

In addition to tax refunds, windfall sources also include job bonuses, insurance settlements, and back rent due. As one respondent put it, "We don't really set aside a portion of our paycheck; we just wait until we have extra income." Those who save from windfall income tend to be irregular savers, but the amounts are often larger. One couple recalled using an insurance settlement from a car wreck to pay off the balance on their home mortgage. Another person, who said she is bad at saving, plans to use her tax refund and back rent that her tenant owes her for savings. This is an easier way for her to save, and besides, she observed that the money would disappear if she didn't set it aside. "It would just be absorbed somewhere."

Build a Checking Account Surplus. A few respondents overdeposit in their checking account or overpay bills, building a savings cushion. For example, Camille keeps an extra $100 cushion in her checking account for security, even though she knows she could be "drawing a little bit of interest" if it was in a savings account. "I like to see a big number in my checkbook!" Extra money stored in a checking account does double duty; in addition to providing a source of emergency money, they also protect an account owner from overdraft charges and bank fees. One respondent accumulated a $500 surplus in his checking account. He knew he would need it sooner or later, but it also turned out to be a good way to avoid bank charges. "So that way I don't ever bounce any checks." Another keeps a similar cushion "in order to not pay any fees on the account."

Camille not only likes to see a big balance in her checkbook, she also pays extra on her credit card balance every month, generating a cushion in that account for times when her bill is higher than normal. "I always believe in paying over," she explained. For example, she might pay $100 when she only owes "maybe $50 or $40."

Others consciously deposit money and try to ignore the balance, hoping that there will be surpluses that inadvertently accumulate. A retiree laughed as she told the interviewer about the cushion in her checking account. "I've got, I think, $700 in checking and I try my best not to bother much of it." When she works a job here and there, she deposits it into her checking account instead of "throwing the money away" by carrying it around. "I'm good about getting it there fast. I don't know why, I just got to be fast."

Another respondent uses a mental technique to reallocate to savings. Like setting a clock ahead to avoid being late, he rounds up check amounts in his check register so the recorded balance is lower than the actual balance.

> Like if I wrote a check for like $14.50, I'd always write it down as $15 in my book. That way I was always ahead. If I ever wrote a check over, or if I didn't think I had the money in there, I actually knew I had it because I always kept a little bit more in the bank than what I thought I would use. Like now, if I can, I always try to keep like a month's worth of bill money ahead in the bank.

"That way," he said, "I knew no checks would ever bounce."

Reduce Consumption. Some people reduce consumption in order to set aside money for saving. Ella, for example, finds money to save by purchasing less expensive food and buying clothes at secondhand stores and garage sales. As noted earlier, she also quit smoking. With perhaps an unusual level of willpower, Ella quit "cold turkey." "I was smoking two packs a day. So you know—that's a big savings for me."

By spending less, a young respondent finds $50 a month to set aside in savings. "I have to keep myself from buying things that I don't really need. . . . I keep to the very simple things that I need." In order to know where to cut back, another said she tracks her expenses in order to identify possible surpluses that can be set aside in savings.

> When I didn't budget, I didn't know where I was putting my money. And so I didn't have money a lot of the times and I didn't always know where it was going to. So when I started back to having a permanent job again, I decided that I was definitely gonna make sure that I always had a budget. And that way I would always know, well, how much am I spending for this? And then over the few years that I have been doing it, gradually I've just weeded out things that I didn't really need and included things I did need. You know, I kind of whittled it around until I got it the way that I want it.

Some also increase spending efficiency in an effort to free up money for saving. Similar to strategies used to make ends meet, they can free up a little money for saving by using coupons, shopping for bargains, buying in bulk, fixing their own cars and appliances, or growing a garden. A single father saves 10 percent of his weekly salary by keeping expenses low and not spending the extra money he received after he got a raise.

> I mean, I live the same now making what I make now than I did when I was making $6.50 an hour. I mean . . . I buy stuff at garage sales. If it wasn't for garage sales, this boy would grow out of so many britches it wouldn't be funny! I just wear my overalls, is what I wear to work, and I got a couple nice pair of jeans I wear . . . to church.

Increase Income. Like the father who saves the amount of his raise, others also increase the money coming in (and resist spending the gain) in order to have money to save. Some take on extra jobs or sell goods. The following respondent, for example, took a job, not to increase the family's level of consumption but to have money to save. Previously, she thought she might start working when they needed the extra money for consumption, but she decided differently.

> Maybe I could work just to kind of get ahead of the game, you know? And so I applied for a job and I got a wonderful job that I just love. And since that time, we've . . . been saving $500 every month. . . . We paid off a [car] loan that should have taken three years and we paid it off in three months.

Store Money at Home. Some convert extra money into savings by setting it aside at home. These savings are often designated for emergencies, and sometimes respondents keep this money to protect other discretionary savings. Savings stored at home are more susceptible to being spent because of easy access (Beverly, McBride, and Schreiner 2003). Anita stores $20 to $25 a week under her bed or in socks. "I got all kind of socks around here. . . . I have little stashes here and little stashes there. I don't keep it all in one place." "They aren't big piles . . . they're little piles." This money is for emergencies. "I was just saving for bad days or something. Like if I get sick or something and couldn't go to work, I'd have something to pay my bills with." But the money tends to quickly disappear. "Something always comes up, though, and I end up spending it. And then I get started back over again and then something always comes up and I end up spending it."

She has tried other methods of saving. At times, she has given money to her sister for safekeeping. "I knew I'd get it and get up into it. . . . I used to tell her, 'If I need it, just give it to me if I need it for an emergency. *Emergency only!*'" She has also tried to deposit into her savings account from each monthly child support check. But saving in this way feels "like a bill" and has not worked for her. She has had more success saving her tax refund.

Another respondent employs a backup system for saving. Like Anita, she stores money in socks at home for short-term needs, but she also deposits money into a saving account. The emergency "sock" savings prevents her from dipping into the bank savings. Thus, her sock system provides rainy-day savings, but it is also a method of ensuring against her raiding her longer-term savings in the bank.

Define Savings as Off Limits. In an effort to maintain their savings, savers frequently adopt simple rules of thumb about when they can use savings. One method is to put the savings out of sight and out of mind. Like Ella, who recalled saving for a car by giving the money to her mother for safekeeping, another respondent said that her savings, which she deposits intermittently in her bank account, is off limits. She earmarks it as unavailable. Once set aside in savings, she uses a mental trick to avoid the temptation to consume it. "It's kind of a mental thing," she explained. "Once you put it into savings, it's not yours anymore. . . . You know, it's savings, it's not mine anymore, so—it keeps me from blowing excess money, just spending it frivolously."

Another respondent owns several different types of savings, including a certificate of deposit (CD) that she intends to keep for the long term. She is also "working on" a 401(k) for retirement. She mentioned insurance that she has "in case something happens to me, all my debt will be paid off, and I won't stick my kids with all that." She asserted that they are not "real savings," suggesting that "real savings" for her is money not earmarked for a specific purpose. Like the others, she ignores her savings, in order to avoid spending it. "Savings is, you know, something you are gonna keep. You know, like if I have a CD that I'm not ever gonna touch. I mean, it's like I don't even have it, I don't even pay attention to it. It renews automatically, you know."

A small business owner accumulated $6,000 in a money market account that she treats as untouchable unless she absolutely needs it for her business. She acknowledged that she likes to watch the interest payments accumulate. "I don't use it unless it's an emergency or something that I really, really need." She has been saving since her husband died. "When I think of money that I have to spend, I just don't consider [my savings]. . . . Basically it's for an emergency. It's something that keeps me from getting frantic when I'm not making any sales." LaVonne expressed a determination not to touch her savings at all until she has enough for a house. "I will not touch it. I don't care. I'm just gonna have to have that frame of mind that it is not going to be touched this time. And let it build so I can have some money . . . for a house."

Choose Accounts with Restrictions. Some choose a method of saving that discourages withdrawals and maintains savings. There may also be a penalty for early withdrawal from some instruments (e.g., a certificate of deposit). In one case, instead of giving her children an allowance, a respondent buys savings bonds for her children through her place of employment. Some people purchase certificates of deposit. Another invests surplus money in his budget to purchase CDs, which "come in real handy" because interest accumulates. "After a certain maturity date then you can get that money and the interest grows so fast in there." Another person bought CDs with money that his mother gave him and his wife. He believes they are less likely to withdraw the money this way. "You can't take the money out. . . . If you take it out there is a penalty."

In the past, one respondent and his wife tried to save. They set up a savings account but never accumulated anything more than "the five dollar minimum balance you have to have to keep it open." However, when they were about to have their first baby, they became more anxious to save. "We decided we've got to buy some savings bonds for college." They deposited into the account on the day he was paid so they would not be tempted to spend it. "The only way I could save it was when I got paid. . . . That day I would go to the bank." They knew that savings bonds would appreciate in value over time, and if they cashed them in early, they would forgo the incentive (return). "I would buy, say, a $100 savings bond that would mature in . . . 15 years, and it would double in value." In this way, they have accumulated $700 or $800. Unfortunately, in their case, they sold the savings bonds to cover debt. "We ended up having to cash them all in."

OBSTACLES TO SAVING

A variety of factors make it challenging for respondents to have and maintain residual, discretionary, and contractual savings. Most prominent are low incomes and financial need, lack of financial knowledge and access to financial instruments, financial scams, family conflict, and lack of willpower.

Low Incomes

Low incomes make it difficult to set aside and maintain any kind of savings. Because respondents give priority to household bills, there is often little left for saving. As one respondent said simply, "there is no money to save."

Almost all respondents save some money some of the time, but they frequently turn to their savings to cover unexpected bills and emergencies. Savings stored at home are particularly vulnerable because the money is so accessible. According to one respondent, "When I got it under the rug [or] I got it stuck someplace, it's too easy to get to. You know what I mean? And so it is easy to spend it. That makes it harder to save it."

Savings accounts are raided also. The respondent just quoted accumulated money over time in a credit union account by having $25 of each paycheck automatically transferred to the account. Although he believes that "it's better to have it somewhere in a bank," he finds it difficult to maintain his credit union savings. "I would get to thinking over the weekend. . . . 'Well, I can spend this 'cause I got that already in the savings account.' I'd go back Monday, Tuesday, and Wednesday. And I'd get that back. . . . I just never could keep any money in there like that."

Ella, a successful saver by most measures, also says that it is difficult to cover all contingencies using regular income. At times she turns to her savings. "Something goes wrong, and I've got to pull it out and spend it." Most recently, she had to withdraw savings when her husband was in a construction accident. After the accident (a year and a half before we met her), she worked 16-hour days in two jobs. When her mother fell ill, she quit the second job to care for her mother also. Always optimistic, Ella looked forward to her husband receiving disability payments, and resuming her saving regimen.

Contractual savings are somewhat less vulnerable to depletion than residual and discretionary savings. Nonetheless, despite barriers and penalties, respondents sometimes cash in their 401(k) savings and other contractual savings. One couple, who is relatively savvy about investing compared to other respondents, turned to their retirement savings to support the family during a job transition. "I've been using that money because there's been things coming up since then—because I was out of my job." Similarly, another person had to withdraw her 401(k) savings when she left her job because she did not have another job to roll it over to. She used the "$3,000 or $4,000" savings to live on while she looked for a new job. "That's what helped me survive for a long time." Although she needed the money, she might not have spent all of it if she could have easily rolled it over into another savings plan.

Lack of Financial Knowledge

Respondents are often uninformed and uneasy about making decisions about saving. Some do not understand the value of savings. Looking back, for example, one respondent admitted that he did not fully understand the implications of withdrawing the money from his savings bonds before they matured. "I just didn't have knowledge of the importance of savings." Another respondent cashed out her 401(k) savings. "I made a foolish mistake and took it out, you know. I guess it's gotten me in a financial bind." Fortunately, she also has a defined benefit retirement account. "It will be there for me when I retire."

Others lack knowledge about how to invest their savings. Some people's savings are susceptible even as they sit in a bank account. For example, one individual closed her savings account after fees on the account exceeded her savings. Originally, she opened the account to build her credit record but was unable to make deposits for a long period of time. One of her creditors also took half of the savings. "Some company I owed money to went into it and took half of it out. So I've got like a whopping $25 or something." She did not know creditors could do that. For people in debt—including many in this study—this makes saving in the bank impractical.

Lack of understanding may be particularly common in contractual savings arrangements because of plan rules. Respondents frequently do not grasp the full implications of their investment and withdrawal decisions. In the introduction to this chapter, we described LaVonne's decisions regarding her annuity investments. She was unhappy because taxes would be assessed upon withdrawal: "It was really was gonna cause me a lot of problems as far as taxes if I wanted to pull it out." Not understanding that most annuities are set up for retirement, LaVonne had originally planned to withdraw her savings after accumulating enough for a house down payment. "I hoped that I would be able to save up money for a house. . . . I had almost gotten it there, I mean, I figured $3,000 down payment, but it wasn't what I thought it was. So I figured I better get it out of there before it got too far, so I closed it."

Many respondents seek ways to save and invest their money that will be more productive. In the process, they become potential victims of poor decisions or unscrupulous practices (see next section). One participant, an immigrant, searched for a promising savings plan and contemplated a "fabulous program" a friend had told her about over dinner one evening. In this plan, her friend told her, a company would automatically deduct $50 a month from her wages for the investment. She was vague about the details, and although the program may indeed be "fabulous," it is unclear that she understood the terms and types of investments the company would make in her name.

Another respondent owns an IRA that he opened about 10 years earlier. He acknowledged that having saved very little "was just negligence" on his part. "There's only like maybe a few hundred dollars in there after all that time. Just putting a little in here and there, and going for long periods not putting anything in." Unfortunately, the account was also losing money because of fees. "They have the fee like once a month or once a year they take out—so what little bit I had there they're still taking a fee out of it and there's just—what can I say?" On the lookout for good investment options, he also tried something that turned out to be a poor investment.

> I invested in some penny stocks at the time, and a lot of them, the companies didn't make it. So they just kind of went out. . . . These transactions were in my retirement account. So that's one reason now why my account is just sitting idle. It only has a few hundred dollars.

This experience made him realize that there is widespread lack of knowledge about investing, particularly among African American families.

> All my friends, even my family—we don't have the knowledge. I mean, how many of your friends have stocks in Texaco, Exxon Oil? . . . I have a lot of white counterparts, colleagues [who] know about that stuff. I mean, their parents, they tell them about that stuff. You know, and they do some of that stuff for them and it's there.

This quote underscores respondents' descriptions in chapter 3 about the lack of financial training they received as children.

After her husband died, Rose collected $5,000 of insurance money. She decided to save the money and try living off her Social Security check. In order to resist spending the insurance money, she invested it in an IRA. "I barely touched it. I really did." Unfortunately, she needed the money, and when she withdrew it from the IRA, she incurred a steep penalty. Clearly, with greater knowledge, or some good advice, she might have invested in a financial instrument better suited to her circumstances.

At 60 years of age, another respondent owns a 401(k). Although he acknowledges that he did not fully understand how it worked, he believes that the 401(k) was a bad investment because he was required to pay taxes when he withdrew $1,200 of his $1,500 savings.

> I don't understand that . . . account either. The way they tax you, you know. I drew like $1,200 and I only got $800, which is, well it's not an early withdrawal 'cause I was 59 and a half, but they still penalized me for it. . . . If I was 65 years old they'd a still took out 20 percent for federal taxes and then another 10 percent for state taxes. What's the advantage in that? I'm not understanding that. I needed to talk to someone about that. . . . I thought that was tax free. . . . I thought that if it was a 401(k) plan, that they didn't tax you like that if you put that money in.

He has concluded that there is little advantage for older workers to save in a 401(k). "What's the advantage? I could be putting that money somewhere else drawing some kind of interest." When the interviewer asked what he was told by his employer, he admitted he did not inquire further. "No, I never did ask anyone about it. . . . No one knew. You know, whenever you ask that kind of question, 'Oh, I didn't know that, you know.' No one seems to know why that is."

In another case, it is unclear if a respondent misunderstood the terms of the account or if her employer deliberately misrepresented the plan. After accumulating approximately $1,000 in a 401(k) account, she planned to withdraw the money because she said her employer would not match her deposits as promised.

> I've got a 401(k) that I just stopped because they had promised when this new company took over that in a year's time they would match dollar-for-dollar. Well, they are not doing it so I stopped it. . . . I shouldn't have listened to them . . . . They didn't do what they said they were gonna do.

She is disillusioned. "I think it stinks . . . because they lied. . . . Corporations are for corporations, it's all about money for them." She added, "The 401(k) would have been a fine program if when the period was up they had kept their word." She planned to invest her money elsewhere. "I intend to get my money out of there and put it in the credit union. They have mutual funds."

Inferior Financial Services and Scams

The poor are especially vulnerable to bad advice and financial scams, leading to poor financial decisions and creating hazards for the poor investor (Hudson 1996).[9] Lacking easy access to secure investment options, they are also susceptible to being swindled because they lack financial knowledge and legal protections (Caplovitz 1967; Belsky and Calder 2005; Karger 2005; Hogarth 2006; Silver and Williams 2006).

Some respondents save fairly large sums of money at home or in other ways when they could be saving in more productive ways. Anita, for example, is looking for a better way to invest her money. She owns a savings account, mutual funds, and savings bonds. She is considering still more. "I didn't know quite what I was doing when I got a mutual fund. . . . That was kind of higher, a higher risk. And I didn't know what I was doing with it." Anita considered an education savings account for her son. But when she consulted with a banker, she decided this would not be the best option.

> I wasn't too sure about that educational IRA because the banker tells me, "What if your son decides he doesn't want to go to college?" And I was like, "He's gonna go." And he was like, "Well, what if he doesn't want to go? If he doesn't want to go, you can't make him go. And then the money that you have for college

. . ." I mean, you can only use an IRA for college. See? What if he gets a scholarship? What if he gets a full 4-year scholarship? He can't use that IRA for the tuition because the tuition is already paid for.

Finally, when the banker said educational savings accounts are not FDIC-insured, Anita settled on a savings bond for her son. "Then once I have quite a bit of those saved up, then I kind of want to go off into some stocks and stuff like that." Anita's investment decisions might have been far worse, as suggested by recent research on financial services in poor communities (Belsky and Calder 2005; Berry 2005; Silver and Williams 2006). Nonetheless, even in Anita's case, it would have been helpful to have better savings options and advice.

The interviews provide insights into how people sometimes get caught up in scams. A respondent recalled investing in what she called a "money market thing." "My dad took us all to this seminar thing and we bought into that. It was like $30 a month for the rest of your life kind of thing. But it went under." Luckily, they got their money back, but she observed that "it wasn't the investment opportunity that we hoped it would be."

As a result of people's suspicions that they might be fleeced, even beneficial programs encounter skepticism. Cynthia captures the concern that many people feel about financial deals.

But see, a lot of us don't want to venture out because I've been scammed. There's people that scam you. And you wind up losing out. People want a legitimate way. Something that's secure. . . . What's the secure system?

Means-Tested Programs and Asset Limits

Asset limits for receiving public assistance not only inhibit saving but also may deplete what little savings low-income households have. As a result, some respondents are very careful about how they report what they own. One respondent, who was determined to save, was very careful about where she keeps her money because of welfare rules. "My idea of savings is putting cash in a box. Because you can't have a paper trail that says you have money somewhere, 'cause if you have $30, it darn well [will] be counted against your food stamps . . . You know, I go to college and I have five kids and I can't have them counting." She sometimes keeps thousands of dollars at home, thinking it too risky to deposit them in a bank because it would make her ineligible for public assistance. The rules shape her saving behavior. Asset limits make her savings more vulnerable to spending and less secure.

Asset limits are an issue for many respondents. As one person observed, "My concern is that the welfare doesn't have anything to help you take steps to do better. Really, I mean, once you start doing better they kick you down by cutting your funds." The welfare department required Camille to spend her life savings before they would provide monthly stipends for Camille's young grandchildren (see Introduction). As a single person with a low income, she had little choice but to turn to public assistance. Once she spent down her savings, Camille had a difficult time regenerating any significant savings.

> And so since that time, just like I said, it's chipped off here, and it's chipped off there, and it's chipped off here. So at the beginning of this year, I got "X" number of dollars, and I set it up in . . . something. Anyway, and it lasted—and I tried my best not to touch that money, I really did. But something happened and I had to—I think my car broke down and I needed some work done on it. . . . Well, as a result, it got totaled out. A girl ran into me and she didn't have insurance, and whatever, and so my insurance went up.

Hardworking and responsible, Camille is discouraged but not about to give up. "I mean it's just always something, you know? So now [the savings are] virtually gone. And so I said, 'Well, I'm not giving up.' I said when I file my income tax this time, I'm going to try to already have it set up where I can go buy me a house. And then if I could take the money and hurry and put it down, you know. But those type things—but I do want a home, I really do, you know. I really do."

Referring to problems with asset limits, the IRS, and banking practices, Ella summed up people's reluctance to save in a bank or other financial institution: "We have so many tales in the community . . . and they're afraid."

Family Discord and Divorce

Saving is also difficult when there is family discord and disagreement about financial goals. Maintaining savings is especially difficult in cases of divorce. As we saw in the previous chapter, some women learn little about financial management when they are married, or in some cases, partners exclude them from financial decision making (Sanders 2007). When a divorce occurs, women often face serious challenges managing the household finances, especially when they have little financial knowledge and experience (Grable and Joo 1999). In addition, they are sometimes left with financial liabilities and other problems.

For example, a twice-divorced woman was saddled with bills from her first marriage. Although the judge awarded her the couple's house from the first marriage, she sold it to pay bills. "I was paying bills that I got stuck with in my first divorce with my house money. So, really it was real hard for me. A lot of my money, most of everything from my first divorce kind of dwindled—trying to survive on my own." She does not have any assets from the second marriage. "My name wasn't on the house. . . . I couldn't really touch his 401(k) 'cause it was his. So, that was it, I started over again. I've started over a lot."

However, she did retain a 401(k) account she had accumulated prior to marrying the first time. In this way, contractual savings have features that may help to protect individuals from family discord. As another person pointed out, it is good that money cannot easily be withdrawn from retirement accounts, "'Cause if my wife could get a hold of my 401(k), she would probably find a way to get it." He is relieved that "the government won't let you take that."

Lack of Self-Control and Willpower

As Debra pointed out in the introduction to this chapter, self-control is important in saving. Exerting self-control or willpower (or self-regulation) suggests that people alter their own actions (Baumeister, Heatherton, and Tice 1994). Saving requires that people set aside and resist the temptation to spend money that is available. Most respondents said it is a challenge to maintain self-control in order to save. One respondent thinks she is unable to save because she lacks willpower. About those who save, she says, "I think they are probably more wise with their money . . . where I'm not. . . . Maybe they have goals. You know, certain people have goals for themselves and some [are] just stronger than others when it comes to saving money."

Anne also admitted that she and her family are not yet willing to cut back on consumption and make the sacrifice to save more.

There's money that we have that I could put back in savings rather than eating out so much. . . . And there is a lot of things that we spend money on that aren't necessities in life that could be put in savings, but at this time we are young and we still choose to do the fun things in life. So, in that aspect, I think . . . that I could put a lot more back in savings than I do if I had my mind set on it. But at this time in life, it is not as big of a priority as it might be in five years to come.

Another respondent wants to save but finds it difficult. Her income disappears quickly: "I spend it as fast as I get it. . . . What I'm putting in, I'm taking it out as soon I put it in." She believes that if she could resist buying things, eating junk food, and going to restaurants and Quik-Trip, she would be able to save. She recognizes, however, that these are difficult habits to break. "We kind of got ourselves in a habit." She knows that it would take "a lot of discipline" to reach her goal of having a down payment on a house.

> I am just gonna have to just discipline myself to tell myself "No!" Get what you need. Only what you need and not extras. . . . See, that is my problem, it's just because I want it or if it is something that I want my kids to have, then I say, "Well, I've got the money, I can go ahead and get it," you know. It will be a just-on-need basis and not a just-want.

Impulsiveness and addiction also pose serious problems for saving. Impulsive behavior is a strong desire to act in certain ways, while addiction is a dependency on a substance (Baumeister, Heatherton, and Tice 1994, 132–33). Not only does impulsivity—especially in acute forms like addictions to drugs, alcohol, and gambling—often cost considerable sums of money, but it also has intense influence over behavior, making it difficult for individuals to exert the self-control required to set money aside. Impulsive people and addicts, therefore, have trouble saving.

Debra and Fred are two respondents who have been able to overcome their addiction problems, making it possible to save. Fred, for instance, said that it was "impossible" to save when he was in his twenties and was addicted to drugs and alcohol.

> Man, you want to get high, you want a drink. You go to the club and buy beer and whiskey, chase women, you know what I am saying? . . . It's where your mind is. See, immaturity. At that age in your life, a lot, not everybody, but a lot of young people, from 20 to 30, in America, they drink their life away and drug away . . . and some of them never come out of it.

Another respondent, a middle-aged woman with an adolescent son, grew up in fairly comfortable circumstances, earned a junior college degree, and worked and saved until she had a baby. She and her husband relied on his salary, and they saved much of hers, mostly for short-term purposes. However, her husband died when their child was quite young, and after that the woman struggled emotionally and financially. At some point she began to gamble and before long found herself in debt. By the time of the interview, she had cashed out all of her savings and a retirement plan at work to support her growing gambling addiction.

> Gambling is what messed me up. When I started going to, you know, they have these machines that will pay great money if you can hit. It's not exactly like this, it's not the casino machines, but it's another kind of machine. But it is still all about gambling, you know. That's what really put me in a rut. 'Cause before I was introduced to the game, I had money. So it was a choice I made. It was a bad choice. I'm suffering the consequences of it but I won't do it no more, you know. 'Cause once I get myself back in a good position, I know I won't do it any more, you know. I've learned.

Another respondent who struggled with drug addiction spent much of his lifetime earnings, as well as work bonuses, on drugs. He knew he should be saving. "But I just ruined it, spent it, you know, [on] entertainment. You know, I can say it easily now because, you know, I'm 45 years old now, so I can be honest with myself and everything else, but that's where it went, you know, lot of money." Nonetheless, he and his wife have accumulated savings because his wife is a determined saver. He has learned to leave the family's financial management in her hands. "Believe me, everything we had ever saved was her, 'cause I would spend it in a minute." When his wife decided they should buy a house, for example, she organized their saving routine. "My wife was the one that made, that has any decent 'spenditure that we've had. [It] was always my wife's idea and abilities, not mine. I cannot save money." She told him nothing about their savings. "She basically saved [money] by not telling me she had money."

But there was also another reason why they are able to save. Both he and his wife worked full-time. She received a good salary and employee benefits, including a 401(k) plan. "So she was able to save money through work." He explained, "She always took out the maximum for any type of like matched funds-type things. I don't know what they call it, 501(k) or something like that. She always saved money in there." Even when their expenses increased and they had less surplus, his wife kept saving in the 401(k). "My wife always had her savings through work. So that always stayed the same. That money would always go in there off the top, so we didn't ever—we never touched that."

Finally, he entered drug rehab and counseling. Along with increasing age and maturity (mostly as a result of having children, he said), he overcame the drug dependency. "Drugs was the first thing to go probably." It was difficult, but he observed, "You can only fool yourself for so long." Nonetheless, he admitted that without his wife to manage his finances and without her 401(k), it is very unlikely that he would have ever been able to save any money.

DISCUSSION

The idea of saving held by families in this study corresponds to normative values of thrift and financial responsibility. In fact, their notions about saving conform to George Katona's observation from more than three decades ago.

> Savings are associated with important values and are seen as a goal for which it is worthwhile to strive. Not saving is regretted and sometimes considered morally wrong. The high value attached to thrift has puritan undertones that persist among many people despite the much-lamented "thing-mindedness" of our age. (1975, 234–35; see also Maital 1982)

In contrast to the common assumption that the poor do not value saving because they lack a future orientation, there is evidence that respondents in this study want to save and, in many cases, do save. Most families save small amounts for precautionary purposes, aiming to have a financial buffer for times when income cannot cover consumption needs. Others save to reach a goal—to pay for a durable, for education, for a car, a house, retirement, or a burial—all investments that cannot be made out of regular earnings.

How do they save? Although some have residual savings, it is more common for respondents to accumulate contractual savings or discretionary savings. Savings in a checking account provide backup and a cushion against bank penalties for low balances and overdrafts. Savings stored at home offer a small reserve. At some point, many also have accumulated target savings, although this is more difficult.

They use a variety of strategies to deposit money and to keep it in savings (Beverly, McBride, and Schreiner 2003). They use reallocation strategies such as focusing on a savings goal, monitoring their finances, and earmarking particular income flows for savings. They bring in more income and spend carefully, trying to generate surpluses for saving. Some enter contractual savings agreements to regularize and make depositing automatic, including ways to deposit income directly into a savings account, without it passing through their hands. To prevent spending their savings, they use rules of thumb for when to use them. Others purchase savings bonds or CDs to make withdrawals less convenient—or at least to give themselves time to reconsider a withdrawal—and to keep their savings out of sight or in instruments that penalize withdrawals.

Despite the will and effort to save, total savings tend to be low, according to respondents. In the face of financial pressures, they find that making regular deposits and resisting spending requires great initiative, determination, motivation, and self-control. A few are successful, like Ella, who as a single mother saved enough to buy a house, purchase insurance for her children, and help her sons through college, or Cynthia, who bought a house and is saving for her son's college education. But the majority are less successful, like one respondent, who simply stated, "Most I ever saved was $5!"

Thus, saving—especially long-term saving—is more often a desire and a dream than a reality. One respondent articulated the challenge. This person saved throughout his life, withdrawing for specific goals. Then he would begin saving again.

> I always managed to save a little bit for a goal, you know, like a down payment on a car or something. I could save that and then when I reached that goal, then I would draw the money out, and I'd go buy whatever I need to buy, and that would clear out the savings account, you know? . . . I just couldn't leave it in there a long time.

This kind of saving is valuable; after all, he successfully saved for important goals. However, he was disappointed that he was not able to accumulate savings for longer periods of time, for purposes such as retirement savings and an inheritance for his children.

In other words, although short- and medium-term savings are important, families also need long-term savings to meet large goals. Few of the families are successful at this kind of saving. Some even hesitate to begin saving for such purposes unless they can identify significant sources of potential savings—amounts that can realistically help them reach their goals. As other research finds, tax refunds are one source that might help someone reach a long-term goal (Barrow and McGranahan 2000; Romich and Weisner 2000; Smeeding, Phillips, and O'Connor 2000; Beverly, Schneider, and Tufano 2005). As one respondent in the study explained, "I get a big check back at one time and I can use that to buy things."

This suggests that saving motives—at least for long-term, target saving—may be driven in large measure by the availability of a saving opportunity, such as the receipt of a lump sum of cash. In other words, when respondents can identify reliable sources of money, they might be more likely to articulate a saving goal and make an effort to reach it.

Another part of the problem that the poor face in saving is that accumulated savings are often within fairly easy reach. Some keep their money at home, for example, and although this is convenient and prevents overdrawing a checking account, it is also readily available for consumption. Self-imposed rules of thumb about using savings help them resist temptation, but in low-income households where the demand for money is often acute, observing these rules consistently is very difficult.

Respondents believe automatic transfers into savings make it easier to save. However, these arrangements require employers and financial institutions to offer direct deposit and automatic transfers, services that are frequently unavailable to low-wage workers and in low-income communities (Dunham 2001; Barr 2004). Some people also have lost savings as a result of poor investment decisions or financial scams. For most respondents in this sample, discretionary savings remain vulnerable to depletion because there is little incentive to continue saving other than the accumulation itself; interest rates are low and there are few or no tax advantages.

Contractual plans structure saving in such a way that setting aside money and maintaining savings may be easier, even for low-income individuals. Some contractual savings, especially in work-based savings plans, burial and life insurance, and home ownership, may offer better terms and greater saving incentives. Work-based savings plans implemented by employers require little action by savers other than enrolling in the program (Maital and Maital 1994). Respondents treat other types of contractual savings as priority bills. Home mortgage and insurance, for example, promise future security and may prevent financial disaster and humiliation. Burial and life insurance policies may not pay for much (e.g., a funeral), but they suggest that the poor do think about the future—in ways that are feasible given their financial position (Newberger and Coussens 2008).

Respondents who are unsuccessful discretionary savers appear to be able to save more successfully in contractual savings plans. At first Rosalyn said she could not save anything. "I didn't have enough to save for nothing. No, ma'am. I didn't have nothing left." However, later she revealed that her husband saved some money during a time when he held a job with a direct deposit option. "The Lord blessed us to save that way. But it wasn't a whole bunch that we saved. But at least we were saving something." Although it was this structure that helped them save, she nonetheless attributed it to her husband's motivation: "He has a mind to want to save." These findings suggest that there is more to successful saving than ability and desire; people need structure and incentives (Sherraden, Schreiner, and Beverly 2003). Moreover, the stated desire to have automatic saving mechanisms—and the tendency to procrastinate in enrolling in these mechanisms (Akerlof 1991)—suggests that a more formalized and universal method of enrolling people in contractual savings plans might increase participation in saving programs.

Contractual savings are also less likely to be subject to depletion because they require action and inflict penalties for early withdrawal. Paperwork required for early withdrawal of retirement funds, for example, discourages withdrawals. Like other savings held in financial institutions (as opposed to saving at home), contractual savings are less likely to be spent, given away, or stolen. The proprietary nature of contractual savings protects an individual's savings in cases of economic abuse or divorce.

Nonetheless, interviews suggest two fundamental problems with contractual savings in these low-income households. First, respondents have limited access to such plans, especially to those that offer a financial incentive that benefits the poor, such as a savings match. (Tax incentives do not help the poor because their tax liability is low or negative. A relatively small number of respondents have ever participated in such tax-favored plans.)

Second, although contractual savings are less vulnerable to depletion than other savings, there are several examples of families who withdrew these savings, sometimes paying significant penalties for early withdrawal. It is difficult for poor families going through troubled times to avoid turning to accumulated savings, despite penalties. Respondents gave many examples of withdrawing money from contractual savings, suggesting that poorer families may be treating these assets as liquid, perhaps more so than less financially constrained families. But as one researcher suggests, once families withdraw funds from contractual savings, the temptation to spend may intensify because the poor have "already broken the mental barrier" and "behavioral rule" against spending out of illiquid assets (Levin 1998, 79). This poses an additional challenge for saving in poor households, and for policy, suggesting the need for policy instruments that prevent use of contractual savings for consumption.

Despite the significant challenges, respondents stressed the normative and practical importance of savings. They offered many examples of how even small amounts of savings can be helpful, including helping a woman and her children weather a period of divorce, helping a family survive a shift in jobs, or helping a young woman leave an abusive relationship. These outcomes will be explored further in chapter 9.

Finally, we observe that many respondents are discouraged by their inability to accumulate savings. Older respondents in particular believe that at this point in their lives, they should be doing better. An older immigrant lamented that she has been unable to accumulate any savings. "I feel a little tired because I have worked for 40 years without letup. I was born in '42. I am 58 years old and I've worked 34 years—34 years without stopping. I don't have a pension, I have nothing. . . . I have nothing."

Reflecting on her financial situation and ability to save, LaVonne echoed these comments. "I'm 46 years old and I am not living the abundant life. And I feel that I should be living a lot more prosperous at this point in my lifetime." For LaVonne this includes owning savings.

> I should have money saved and in the bank. . . . I shouldn't be strained up every month. I shouldn't have to live from paycheck to paycheck. So this is not just it for me, there has got to be another way to make money. I've devoted my years to this here and . . . it's keeping me in poverty really. It's keeping me on the lowest edge, just living from paycheck to paycheck. . . . You know, 'cause like I said, life, things come up and there you are strained up and stressed out.

A long-term saver, Cynthia, said that saving has not always been difficult for her, especially during the time when she and her husband were earning money.

> It really wasn't difficult because we were young, we were energetic, we worked, we wanted to save. And we did accomplish [that goal]. We bought all our furniture, practically just about all of it in cash. We saved and my husband believed in paying it off right then and there. And then eventually we bought a home. We've owned—when I was married—we had businesses and cars, you know.

With the drive to improve her situation, Cynthia is constantly searching for a way to make her money work for her and her family.

> I'm a product of people that never saved but there was something in me. I guess the way my dad was. It made me know that, you know, I can look at you and see there's something more. And you might look at another person and say, "There's nothing there." But I'm always that person that's trying to find some-

thing more. I want that next hand to get me where I'm going. And I am going somewhere. But it's a process, and knowledge is power, and I'm just now finding out institutions and places where I can get the information I need to start investing.

But she believes there has to be a better way than saving her $10 a month in a savings account. "You don't get much off of the money that you put in. It took years to learn that one. A lot of times people tell you to save and do this and do that. They don't always tell you the keys of making your money worth more for you. And I'm just now starting to find that out." She cleans houses for wealthy people and knows there has to be a better way.

'Cause you know even people with money will tell you—people with lots of money, I work for people with lots of money—and they say, "Oh, you need to save. You need to invest." But nobody takes the time to say, "Let me give you a little information how you get on that track, that running track to start doing that."

When these women heard about the IDA program, they thought it might offer such a "running track." In the next chapter we hear about the program and saving experiences of those who joined the program.

CHAPTER 7

Saving in Individual Development Accounts

When respondents signed up for an Individual Development Account (IDA), they joined a program that structured their saving. The program matched savings for home ownership (primary residence only), home repair, business start-up or expansion, postsecondary education or training, and retirement savings.

The IDA program included a bundle of features designed to help low-income families save. What stood out most in respondents' minds is the savings match (incentive). There are two different match rates. For home purchases, the program matched participants' savings at $2 for every dollar saved, and for all other purposes, it matched $1 for every participant dollar saved. Participants had to deposit a minimum of $10 per month in 9 of every 12 months that the accounts were open. The program matched participants' savings up to $750 per year over a three-year period.

Other IDA program features include financial education, annual and lifetime match caps, time caps, minimum monthly deposits, IDA account statements, saving reminders, and limits on savings withdrawals. Each is described below in greater detail and discussed from the perspectives of participants.

The chapter focuses on participants' perspectives about features of the IDA program. We begin with Heather, Becky, Denise, and Theresa, who describe why they decided to sign up for the IDA program.

Heather

Although Heather was reticent about discussing her upbringing, she opened up when talking about the IDA program. After a difficult childhood and an early transition to adulthood, Heather had worked hard to improve her life. She married as a teenager and had a baby. She and her husband struggled to pay the bills; her mother helped pay for a few things like diapers. "We didn't save money. We had just enough to pay bills and then we'd go out to eat and waste the rest. I guess saving wasn't important then."

After her divorce, Heather began training as a hairstylist and moved into a small house near her mother's. She supported herself with the help of food stamps and public assistance, along with a monthly $200 child support check. Not long ago, she purchased a small house with advice from a staff member in the IDA program; her boyfriend helped her with the down payment. She also worked her way up in the hairstyling business.

Her first impression of the IDA program was that it was a "good deal." Although she believes that saving money is the right thing to do, she'd never saved much money previously. Her goal is to invest in home repairs. She believes that having "goals for yourself" makes it easier to save.

Heather is hopeful that she will soon receive a promotion to manager of a new salon. This, along with the opportunity provided by her IDA, makes Heather believe that her life is going in a positive direction.

Becky

In Becky's hardscrabble life, she never observed anyone saving. Prior to saving in the IDA, she had only owned a checking account and saved change in baby formula tins at home. "We have those all over the house that we're always throwing change in." At one time, she opened a savings account but never accumulated any savings. "I ended up withdrawing the money for something. I don't even remember what I withdrew it for."

Some time after filing for bankruptcy, Becky learned about the IDA at her son's day-care center. The savings match caught her attention. "Just the fact that that they would match money that you put into a savings account! And all you really have to do is go to these classes, you know. I just thought that that was really neat."

Without the promise of a match, Becky would not likely have joined the IDA program. "I don't think that I would have really put money into a savings account."

The only aspect of the IDA program she is not enthusiastic about is financial education. Although she attended the first three classes, she is concerned that the IDA staff will oust her from the program because with two jobs and two children, she has been too busy to complete the other three required classes. But staff reassure her that they will not do that. Although she sees the value of evaluating her finances in "black and white" ("I thought about it, you know, and I even started writing down everything I would spend my money on for a while"), she has not adopted a household budget to help her figure out how and when to make IDA deposits.

Denise

Denise, whom we met in chapter 3, grew up very poor. By age 17, she was pregnant and married. Ten years later, Denise and her husband finally divorced, and Denise was raising their four children on her own. A year later, she joined the IDA program.

Other than saving $20 under the mattress for emergencies, Denise's past efforts to save were unsuccessful. She tried to focus her mind on setting aside the little extra money she had, but something usually got in the way.

> I didn't used to spend it wisely. . . . Well, I would buy—if my kids needed something extra like for school or if they needed a pair of shoes, you know, I'll go do that. . . . I'll put it in the savings account until something come up. . . . I'll focus my mind, "I'm gonna put this in there and I'm gonna save this money," but it seems like something always comes up to where I have to go and get it out. And there won't be nothing in the savings.

Denise joined the IDA program because of the savings match and the financial education. She believes that "saving takes discipline." The classes have taught her how to focus on her goals. Determined not to touch her IDA savings for anything other than a home, for the first time she thinks she can save if she puts her mind to it. At the suggestion of one of the IDA instructors, she encourages her children to save, and as a result, they share Denise's excitement about owning a home some day. Denise appreciates the staff's support and encouragement. Having staff tell her she can save has helped jump-start her saving. She feels free to contact them with any concerns or questions, and they always make her feel confident in her saving ability.

> I've never seen a program like this before. I mean this is my first time ever— where they'll take you through step-by-step and show you how to reach that goal. I mean, 'cause a lot of people don't know how. They say they got a goal but [they] don't know how to get to it.

Theresa

Theresa did not grow up saving, nor was saving discussed at home. "If you're not raised with that in your household, you know, you don't do it. You don't think about it." She learned little about financial management, and when she married, her husband took over most aspects of their financial lives. Later, after they divorced, Theresa encountered one financial challenge after another. She left the marriage without claiming any of the couple's assets. Moving from job to job, she sometimes covered her expenses, sometimes not. She withdrew and spent the savings in her only retirement account, a 401(k). With a poor record with the bank, she could not open a checking account, and she had accumulated debt from credit card purchases and from a household finance loan.

When Theresa learned about the IDA program, she thought perhaps her luck had changed. "I thought, 'Okay. Maybe something good is starting to come my way.' So I took being accepted in the IDA as a positive boost for me." She knows that saving is important and she has a saving goal.

> Everybody has a dream of something that they want. And you know, the system makes it very, very, very, difficult—and I'm not just gonna say for black people—for lower-income people to achieve what they're set out to do. There's all kind of programs out there that are supposed to help you do this . . . help you, say, for instance buy a house. But then you go to them (I don't know this from experience, it's just been from what I've heard people tell me) . . . either your credit's not good enough or you don't have enough money for a down payment.

Expressing a shared feeling among respondents, Theresa described why saving is important to her: "Everybody—I don't care what they say—everybody wants to own something that is theirs. You know?"

None of these respondents saved prior to the IDA program. Heather said the program, especially the savings match, was a "good deal" and would boost her saving. Becky was drawn to the match, although she was not excited about the idea of financial education. In contrast, Denise joined the program to learn how to manage better financially and to save for her dream home. Theresa hoped that her knotty financial life finally had turned a corner.

What about other IDA participants? What is the process of saving in the IDA? What aspects of the IDA program help participants save? What impedes their saving? This chapter addresses these questions, beginning with participants' perceptions of the program and the reasons they signed up.

THE IDA PROGRAM AS OPPORTUNITY

Charles views the IDA program as an opportunity that he never had before. He described its significance this way.

> [The IDA program is] long overdue. Specifically for the underprivileged people who may not have had a start in their life, may not have had a goal, an object, because no one took the time to teach them this. Some of these people may have been so underprivileged that they never foresaw an opportunity.

Two-thirds of participants described the IDA program as an opportunity. They believe the program is a "blessing," "luck," "headstart," "steppingstone," "help," "privilege," "chance," "deal," and "positive boost." As Fred put it, "God is sending me a blessing, He sent it right to the doorstep." (Seven others also referred to the IDA as a "blessing.") It is different from other programs for the poor, according to Fred. "[The IDA] is developed to get you back on the track. You know, get you back going up the ladder. . . . the IDA program is developed to get you back to saving, to accomplish some of your goals."

What is it about the program that led participants to describe the program in such positive terms?

IDA PROGRAM FEATURES

When people join the IDA program, they enroll in a plan with a variety of features that facilitate and encourage saving. Like other contractual savings plans, these features reinforce and sometimes create automatic mechanisms, rules, and guidelines for individual actions. For example, participants are compelled to save a minimum monthly deposit of $10 to remain in the program. They are discouraged from withdrawing their savings because they would forfeit the savings match. Individual actions are still required, but the program makes some choices clearly beneficial and others a poor choice. The program also leaves fewer decisions and choices in the hands of individual savers, shaping their actions in favor of saving. In the sections that follow, we discuss program features that encourage deposits and those that impose rules to discourage withdrawals.

The Savings Match

The savings match caught Fred's attention: "Other accounts don't match you penny for penny. The IDA account is the only one matching like that in all America that I know of." The promise of a savings match ("free money" as several participants called it) captured people's imagination about a better future. As we learned, many participants had goals before joining the program, but most learned to set these aspirations aside, focusing instead on the daily reality of making ends meet and hoping they could encourage their children to get enough education to obtain a good job and escape poverty. The IDA program, however, presented an opportunity about which few ever dreamed. The promised savings match was literally unbelievable to some, who were suspicious that the program was yet another financial scam targeted at poor people.

The promise of a match increases the reward of saving, increases total accumulations, and encourages participants to visualize a different future, one in which they have resources, often for the first time in their lives, with which to pursue goals that were previously out of reach.[1] They may plan to buy a home or a business of their own. They may pursue a long-hoped-for education. They may invest in repairs to their house. Or they may anticipate a financially secure retirement. The match makes the possibility of saving seem attainable (Davis 1992). As Theresa said, her IDA savings will help her reach her dream: "Everybody that's in the program has a goal—not a goal—has a *dream* of something." Saving in the IDA allows Theresa to dream, and to aim for a better future.

Rarely do the poor have this kind of opportunity, according to Theresa. "Nobody matches your money in a regular savings!" A savings match can make it possible to reach a savings target more quickly and encourage further saving.[2] Theresa continued, "They're gonna match you, either two-for-one or one-for-one. So, that was incentive enough. That's incentive enough for anybody! I mean, I have to put one dollar and you're gonna put two dollars in? Oh, yeah, that'll work for me." It helps her overcome her doubts about her ability to save enough.

> You know, I mean, it's amazing. That just makes you want to save it faster so you can get to that point and say, "Oh. Look. I got to $1,500 and all this extra stuff I put in there just adds to it." So that's what made me do it. The $50 and the $100—that's what made me get way up there real quick.

Another participant, Dawn, also talked about the importance of the match. Dawn had managed to save small amounts of money at home, even though her parents never saved and never encouraged her to save. Since joining the IDA program, however, Dawn has saved more.[3] She attributes this to the savings match incentive. "I have $500 in my account, but because, there is an incentive there. . . . If I can put it in and they'll match what I make, that's free money. That's help." The incentive also makes her more aware of how she manages her financial life. "And in doing that, that action with that knowledge, it makes you think about it. . . . It kind of just brings your awareness."

Many participants talked about the unusual "returns" implied by the match. One participant, for instance, views this as a rare opportunity.

> Anytime you are getting that kind of return—I mean, you couldn't get that interest, you know, no other way. Savings bonds, or some kind of stock, I mean, nowhere that you could get a dollar for a dollar. Some jobs give you 50 cents on a dollar to a certain percentage. . . . If you're planning to buy a home or something. You know . . . you put a dollar away and they give you two dollars toward your down payment. That's hard to beat. So if you've got that type of a goal, that'd be a real encouragement to someone to save. . . . Instead of having $80 in the bank, I'll have $160. And I only put in $80! So that encourages me to keep this going and I am gonna try to do, I just wish I had more to put in there.

In fact, this participant and several others said they were unlikely to be saving without the match. The match provides motivation for saving, and without it the money that is going into the IDA would probably be spent on household consumption. As another participant noted, "How long would I save without getting that matched? Um, I don't know. . . . If there wasn't some motivation for getting it matched, I probably wouldn't save at all. I mean, there has to be some goal, some reason why you are doing it."

Legitimacy and Trust

Although it was the match that attracted participants to the IDA program, most respondents were initially skeptical. They worried it was one of many financial scams. One participant explained that people "couldn't believe that you were gonna get something for nothing. . . . They couldn't believe free money. . . . They're thinking it's a catch."

Several factors finally allayed participants' skepticism, including the program's affiliation with CAP, where many receive help with their tax returns. Others received reassurances from friends and family, or felt more comfortable after hearing a staff member or other participants talk about the program at church. Still others found reassurance in the program's affiliation with a well-known Oklahoma bank.

The program's reciprocal obligations further alleviated people's concerns. They believe it is important for individuals to have to exert effort. It makes them feel like they are doing their part. As one participant explained, "[The IDA] makes you work for it a little bit. And that's the way it should be." The interviewer observed that it seems he has a strong work ethic. He replied, "I don't believe in giving stuff away. God helps those who help themselves."

Another participant signed up when she learned that the money was not entirely free. They would be required to attend classes and talk about their experiences in the program.

> You have to answer all these questions and you're going to be interviewed in two years, in five years. So, that made it seem more legit. I was like "Okay." So it's not just free money. I mean I am going to have to go to these classes, and I'm going to have to answer questions, and they're going to keep tabs on me for the next two years. . . . And I thought "Okay, I can buy that."

Nonetheless, many people hesitated before making inquiries. One participant drove around with the flyer he picked up at the community college for a few days before calling for more information: "I threw it in my car and I drove around with it for a day or two and then I picked it up again and I read it some more and I think I called a 1-800 number on there." Based on these reactions, it is likely that some potential participants never got around to applying for the program because of doubts about its legitimacy.

A Savings Goal

Many participants said that the program pushed them to articulate their goals. As one participant recalled, "Well, for one thing, it helped me . . . determine what I wanted. I knew what I wanted in kind of a general idea. This gave me specific information that I needed to plan, to go for that goal. And that was the main thing. It wasn't any one thing. It was a lot of things, that would help you attain what you decide you want to do."

Psychologically, setting a goal—and having a tangible way to reach it through savings—may allow participants to dream of a better future. IDA participants discussed their goals, linking their current saving to long-term plans.

Thinking about the time she would be in the program, for example, Theresa focused on improving her credit record and saving for a down payment on a house. "I mean, that kind of structured my whole goal setting for everything else that I'm doing. . . . It helped me to start setting my goals again."

Staff Encouragement

Participants reported that the staff encourage, expect, and structure saving. Respondents said IDA program staff are "very sweet," "very encouraging," and "helpful." In contrast to being treated as incompetent, bothersome, or even worthless in other social assistance programs, participants generally find IDA staff to be down-to-earth and responsive. Participants are grateful for returned phone calls, kind voices, encouraging words, and help. As a participant pointed out, "They didn't make you feel like you were stupid or too dumb to save. They just tried to help." People with low incomes are often in some kind of trouble, observed another, so it is constructive for staff to be sympathetic and sensitive. She confessed, "I was in crisis. I needed the support of the staff." In fact, sensitivity on the part of staff is a thread woven through interviews. "[IDA staff] are ordinary people," said another participant. "They strike me as common people, if that makes sense, everyday people. They are not uppity. . . . They never made you feel like a low-life or anything like that, like you are irresponsible." Another concurred, "I feel treated, you know, as a human being."

As Theresa said, encouragement is crucial because she worries about her financial abilities. "So it's not like something you just start and then you never hear from them again until you mess up. . . . They keep in contact with you." She reflected on how much she has to learn. "If you come from a background like me where you've never been around savings. . . . Your family didn't do that kind of stuff. So you have a lot more to learn than somebody who's used to saving. You know? It takes discipline. It takes change. It takes time." As we saw in chapter 3, Theresa is not alone; many other respondents also grew up lacking financial support and training.

Feedback

Participants receive feedback in several ways. Participants receive monthly IDA account statements from the financial institution, along with quarterly account statements from the program showing both their savings deposited and the match dollars accrued. Program staff send monthly deposit reminder postcards to IDA participants. Staff answer questions, provide feedback on participants' saving activity, offer information in money management and asset management classes, and provide referrals for other assistance.

Monthly statements help people visualize their saving progress. Statements itemize deposits, accumulations, and eligible match.[4] Participants reported that seeing their savings accumulate encourages continued saving and discourages unmatched withdrawals. As one person said, the savings statements keep her mind focused on saving. "It makes me remember to save every month. This is how much you have, how much more do I need? . . . Because you can actually see how much you have and what your activity has actually been."

The bank statement helps them feel they are making tangible progress toward their savings target. As Heather observed, her statements help her see how much she is "really putting in there." Watching the savings accumulate (through the bank statements) helps another participant have patience.

> [The] IDA has helped me to learn patience in saving. Does that make sense? . . . Savings doesn't happen overnight, you know. . . . You set a goal [what we refer to as a target], and you save it. . . . I can see when we reach the $750 every year, not spending it and saving for another year. . . . I can see that easily happening because you are getting used to watching it build, to not touch it, just let it continue to grow.

Theresa said the IDA statements prevent her from getting "discouraged" when she falls behind in her reaching her savings target. They give her hope. "It's still a joy to get my bank statement, you know, and look at it and say, 'Look, you got almost $1,000 in here!'"

When participants are late making deposits they also receive reminders. Theresa was impressed that the staff make a special effort to encourage her to make her deposit. "You don't just sign up and they accept you and that's it. . . . Even after you finish the classes, you know, I still get stuff all the time from them." Another believes that the reminders help her develop a saving "habit." "I would have forgot it completely if they hadn't sent those notices because it just wasn't an established thing yet."

Information on Managing Money and Investing

The IDA program also included financial education classes. All participants were required to attend six two-hour money management classes over the course of the three-year program and to attend a seminar with specific information related to participants' saving goals. Courses followed an adult learner model (Hogarth and Swanson 1995). Instructors made the material as accessible as possible, avoiding tests and penalties in favor of positive reinforcement, informality, and applied learning. Overall, participants said they learned the most from experiential activities.

Money management classes incorporated budgeting, credit and debt management, credit repair, financial planning, and saving. Although about a third of participants (19) who had attended all of the money management classes said they merely reinforced what they already knew, most said they learned something new. As one participant explained, classes underscore the importance of saving. "It just makes me appreciate that it's important to save. When you get older you should have something saved up for yourself, you know, retirement and whatnot."

Although Heather did not anticipate getting anything out of the classes, she was pleasantly surprised. "At first I thought it was, you know, 'Just go through these stupid classes.' But you really do get something out of them." She observed that the classes fill a void in her financial upbringing: "For those who didn't have that training, they never know [about the importance of saving]. I mean, they know they should, but it never clicks . . . until you're sitting there and having to put it on paper." She said classes reinforce her desire to save. "They make you realize—or they did me anyway—why you were there, why you wanted to save money instead of spend it."

Asset-specific training included seminars on home ownership, business development, entry to postsecondary education, and retirement. Almost all of the participants who had taken the asset-specific classes found the topics on home buying, retirement investing, or saving for education and business ownership useful (Sherraden et al. 2004). This information was more likely to be new, as one participant observed about saving in an Individual Retirement Account (IRA).

It was foreign and hard for me to understand, and I wanted to go through the class again with my husband with me so that maybe the two of us would understand better. For instance, like, an IRA, I didn't realize when you open an IRA that you need to decide how you want your money invested. You know, I thought when you put it in the IRA that was the investment. But you decide if you want to buy, you know, use a certain percentage to buy this or to buy that to make a bigger investment and I didn't realize that. And I don't understand the stock market or these things that determine the rates and all that kind of thing.

Finally, money management classes are encouraging to a few people because of the peer support. Denise observed that the group spirit helps her focus on saving: "When you've got people around you, you know, just excited about what they're doing . . . it gives you a little bit more confidence about what you're doing."

Required Deposits

The program requires a minimum $10 monthly deposit. As Dawn pointed out, the savings incentive helps her want to save, but the required monthly deposit helps her actually deposit it.

> Everybody wants to save. It's easy for anybody to say, "Well, gosh, I should start saving," or, "Well, I've got a savings account, I should put something in it." But when you *have* to put something and you're doing it regularly, it puts it on your mind. You know what I mean? It makes you start thinking of saving. It's not something you can put off. It's not just the IDA account, but you're saving for the IDA account.

Although program staff allow for exceptions, participants take the $10 a month deposit rule seriously. Many participants (28 of the 59 IDA participants) talked about the required monthly deposit and said that it provides a reason to make deposits, even when their financial situation is tight. Internalizing the program requirements and expectations helps participants stay focused on sustaining a monthly savings pattern. As one participant observed, "It's made the savings account an obligation first of all. It's not something optional, because if you don't make the payment to savings every month, I mean after a while they'll kick you out of the program."

Participants believe that the required $10 monthly deposit seems "reasonable" ("we can all come up with ten bucks a month," said one person), even those who previously could not save regularly.

The saving requirement helps people overcome procrastination. One participant admitted to a tendency to procrastination. However, the requirement to save, along with the impetus provided by the savings match, encouraged him to procrastinate less. He reported, "I've been making deposits every month."

Several commented that they liked the fact that the requirement makes the

IDA like a bill. Some even "pay" their IDA account at the beginning of the month along with other important bills. As one person said, "It's just like a regular bill that has to be paid." Another observed that it is useful to think about the deposit as a bill because otherwise it might "slip your mind." Another participant—a single father who had never saved any money in the past—said that the requirement structures his deposits.

> To save money . . . it has to be like a bill. It has to be like if you don't pay your rent, you're gonna get put out. It has to be like if you're buying a car, if you don't make your car payment, they're gonna take your car. That makes it easy to save.

Not everyone likes the idea that the IDA is like a bill; for example, Anita, a nonparticipant, commented that monthly savings requirements feel unpleasant "like a bill" and prefers saving her annual tax refund as a lump sum (chap. 6). Another participant also finds a once-a-month commitment inconvenient. Though she understands the logic, she prefers to deposit her annual savings all at once "and then not have to bother with it again."

Savings Target

While a few participants calibrate their deposits to a self-determined savings target, most participants seem to turn the annual match cap into their savings target. As one participant noted, he wants to "make full use" of the possible match. As one person explained, "My goal was to meet *their* goal. . . . I decided to shoot for the max." Thus, the idea of the match cap is not lost on participants. The fact that so many participants are trying to reach an externally imposed savings goal suggests that their preferences are malleable and that they "anchor" on the match cap as a savings target (Tversky and Kahneman 1974). Further, it suggests that loss aversion may play a role as well. Participants seem to perceive forfeiting the total match to be a significant loss (Tversky and Kahneman 1981). One participant plans to meet the maximum match; not doing so would be "crazy" and "stupid."

> It would be stupid if we didn't save $750, which is the maximum a year. It would be stupid. We would lose out on 150 free dollars if we save $600, you know. So . . . we are gonna make sure we have the $750 in there at the end of the year. . . . I mean, it's crazy, it's a wonderful craziness . . . and the first time we cash in, it's just gonna be incredible.

Halfway through the year, Becky already had accumulated $650 in her account. She aimed for the maximum or more. "Right now all I'm doing is putting in enough just to meet the $750 a year." Another participant stressed, "I don't want to blow *one dollar* of that money. . . . It's just an opportunity that is laid before me that is unbelievable that I would be a fool to screw it up!"

Those who were unclear about the exact amount nonetheless were aiming to save the maximum. Rosalyn, for example, was not quite certain about the maximum that the program will match: "I try to put at least $50 a month. Nothing less than that—$50 a month. Because anything less, I feel like it's a waste. Because if I put $50, then they gonna match me and that's $50. So that's $100 right there. So I'm trying to make it to, I think it's $700, I believe it is."

Few participants plan to save more than the matchable amount. As one participant points out, there is not much of an incentive to deposit more because the bank savings account "interest rate is not too high."

Adopting the match cap as an annual savings target, participants described their plan for reaching it. Several people deposit the required ten dollars per month, topping it off with their annual tax refund to meet the annual savings target. As one participant calculated, "I'm looking at all three years as one lump sum. So I put in all of the money that I would need minus ten [dollars a month]. . . . I just calculated how much would be above ten dollars every month and I put that whole amount in there."

Even participants who did not finish the program calculated the amount they would need to deposit monthly in order to meet the match cap. For example, this participant, who did not draw an IDA savings match in the end, had worked out the math: "To get the maximum amount—you are allowed $750 a year that they will match—and that would cost, that would be like, you'd have to put like $67 or something like that, in there a month to reach the maximum amount that they will match."

A Formal Savings Account

Many respondents, both participants and controls, observed that storing savings in a formal savings account discourages withdrawals. Simply having their savings out of sight and held separately seems to help people resist the temptation to spend it. As one person simply explained, "It's not so easy to take out." For her, owning a separate account and keeping her goal in mind helps her resist spending her savings. "The separate savings account has helped me save.

And not wanting to withdraw it unless it is for education or [for an] IRA. I mean, I haven't wanted to withdraw it for anything but what that's for, for some reason . . . it affects you somehow."

Another mentioned that she is happy that her IDA is out of sight in a bank account. She seems reassured that the money will be available in an emergency, but she is happy that it is not *too* accessible.

> I'm glad I'm in this IDA thing where I can't go get it. You know what I mean? . . . If something happens, I'm going to leave it. So, that's the best thing, I can't bother it. I won't even think about it. That's it. It's just kind of like it's not even there really, 'cause I can't go get it when I want to go get it. So, that's the best thing they can do for people who are trying to save.

Consequences of Unmatched Savings Withdrawals

There are three key features that discourage unmatched withdrawals. First, the program permits participants to make up to three withdrawals per year from their IDAs for nonasset uses, but when they withdraw their savings, they forfeit the match on withdrawn savings. We refer to these as unmatched withdrawals. (Withdrawals for asset purchases can be made after participants' accounts have been open for a minimum of six months and participants complete all required financial education.)

IDA program rules that limit participants to three unauthorized withdrawals per year discourage some people from making withdrawals and help them resist the temptation to spend their savings. They believe it is a good idea to have the withdrawal rule, generally in agreement with one participant who said, "You've got to have those rules."

Some claimed they had never been able to maintain a savings account until they started the IDA program where these restrictions are in place. As one participant with an admittedly "real bad track record" in saving said,

> I believe that the rules are necessary because otherwise people would be raiding it every other week, and they would never accomplish any of the saving, you know? I mean, that's definitely something I take into consideration before I even think about going and touching that account, "Well, I've only got one more withdrawal this year, and I really want to stay in this program." And so, it's a deterrent to go raid the account for money all the time.

Although it is unclear that the program actually terminated anyone for making too many withdrawals, participants seemed quite concerned that too many withdrawals could result in being asked to leave.

Second, the program discourages withdrawals by requiring paperwork that forces people to jump a hurdle and perhaps reconsider withdrawing their money. The process for withdrawing money reminded one participant about the implications. "I found even the paperwork that I had to go through to withdraw—it made me realize—I don't know—it made me take it seriously."

Third, and perhaps the most effective at discouraging withdrawals, is the program rule that an unmatched withdrawal is not accompanied by a savings match. Everyone in the IDA program agrees to put their savings in an account that when withdrawn for unapproved uses will not come with a savings match. In other words, participants forfeit a 100 or 200 percent match (depending on their saving goal). Even people who successfully saved in the past believe they are more likely to keep their money in savings because of the match rule. As one participant pointed out, "If you take money out you are losing twice as much money." He gave an example: "Say if I decide to buy a new pair of pants and I don't have the money, then I certainly wouldn't take it out of my IDA account!" In the past, this person said, he was always "taking it out" of savings when he wanted money to pay for something. In the IDA program, however, he said he would only withdraw it "for purposes that it is designed for." Another participant withdrew money from his account, and as he thought about it afterward, he realized, "Instead of $30, I took out $60. . . . I felt like I was ripping myself off!"

DISCUSSION

One of the simplest and most important findings from this study is that respondents saw the IDA program as a real opportunity and tried hard to save. Although these respondents may have been more motivated or more able to save than the average low-income individual, the evidence challenges a common assumption that the poor cannot or will not save. The idea of saving appealed to respondents; it corresponded with normative views about responsibility and social status. Even though the program targeted low- and moderate-income families, they felt they could participate and still hold their heads high. After all, saving required individual effort, and through their involvement in the program, they believed they were investing in their family's future. In their life experiences, such opportunities were unusual.

Positive reactions to the savings match show that participants responded to economic incentives, as suggested by most economic theorists. For participants, the promise of a savings match (the incentive) is the single most important feature of IDAs. It initially attracted them and is a major factor in their motivation to save and to remain in the program. However, interviews also suggest that a savings match by itself is not enough.

Once participants joined the IDA program, they learned that the savings match was part of a larger program that structured, encouraged, and compelled saving. In these ways, the IDA program included contractual savings features. From their vantage point, the whole bundle of IDA program features helped them save. In this way, evidence from in-depth interviews supports the idea that people may desire to participate in economically attractive saving plans, but they are more likely to be successful if their desire to save is supported by appropriate plan design. Design features of an IDA, at least to some degree, take into account the lives of the poor, making the accounts accessible and facilitating participation among low-income individuals and families.

One way that the IDA program reinforces participants' desire to save is by providing access to a trustworthy and formal savings plan. Although some participants had saved in savings accounts in the past, not all had. Bad experiences and fears about financial scams made many participants initially wary of signing up for the IDA program. However, a respected nonprofit agency that offered the IDA program and a well-known bank that held the savings helped to confer legitimacy and to overcome initial skepticism (at least for these participants).

Program staff support and facilitate participant saving. Staff provide words of encouragement and resources to help participants and their families. They also offer regular feedback about participants' saving efforts through savings statements and deposit reminders. Further, some participants said that information on money management and specific assets was helpful. They received this information through classes and in individual interactions with staff.

Program expectations help participants focus their saving effort. For example, the requirement to save a minimum amount each month establishes a base, but it is the match cap (the maximum that the program will match) that participants turn into a savings target and toward which they focus their saving effort. For most participants, the $750 annual match cap becomes the de facto savings target, or "anchor" (Tversky and Kahneman 1974).[5]

Restrictions also shape saving and encourage participants to keep their savings in the IDA. Approved uses for IDA savings coincide with participants' goals. In other words, saving for a home, education, a business, or retirement are goals that resonate with participants, reinforcing the idea of saving. The restrictions on withdrawals, including limits and loss of match, make sense to participants and further discourage (but do not prevent) unmatched withdrawals.

In short, while the generous incentive is especially important, participants believe that the *bundle* of IDA program features help them save. In other words, people may desire to participate in economically attractive saving plans but are more likely to be successful if their desire to save is supported by other appropriate design features. The in-depth interviews thus provide evidence in support of institutional theory and behavioral economic theory: Appropriately designed programs—that is, programs that take into account barriers to saving faced by "real" people—can encourage participation and make saving easier.

This chapter suggests that IDA program features are attractive to participants and make it easier for participants to save. However, there are aspects of the program that do not address the challenges of saving in a low-income household. The next chapter examines the strategies participants used and the challenges they encountered trying to save.

CHAPTER 8

Saving Strategies in Individual Development Accounts

Although the IDA program encourages and obliges saving, and imposes rules about withdrawing savings, participants must play an active role in saving. They have to find money to save and figure out how to cover household necessities and emergencies without raiding their IDA savings. In low-income families where money is in great demand, finding the money to save is not simple. As one father pointed out, "There's a lot of people that want my paycheck when it comes in!"

Overall, the strategies IDA participants use to save are similar to strategies used by nonparticipants, although participants are more conscious and consistent about applying a range of saving strategies. In this chapter, we again organize saving strategies according to the schema provided by Beverly, McBride, and Schreiner (2003). We explore the range of strategies that people in the program believed helped them find the money to save, make deposits, and maintain their savings. Does the IDA provide support for saving compared to regular discretionary saving? What obstacles do participants encounter in saving in an IDA? What are their successes and failures in depositing and maintaining savings? In the end, how different is the IDA saving experience from the mostly self-initiated saving described in chapter 6?

We begin by continuing the IDA saving narratives of Heather, Denise, Becky, and Theresa. These participants used a variety of strategies for saving that reflect the diversity of saving approaches of the other 56 participants.

Heather

Heather, who deposits her waitress tips into the account, finds it easier to save in the IDA program than on her own. She believes that IDA program rules (or "boundaries" as she calls them), including classes and monthly savings requirements, are there not only to help people but also to teach them how to save.

> You have to put something in to get something out of it. And if you don't go to the classes and if you don't spend the time and aren't actually sitting there—whether you're bored or not—you're not gonna get anything out of it. . . . The monthly [savings deposit]—you know, you can't just get your income taxes and go deposit it all at once and then expect someone to go in "halfsies" with you. . . . This is a program that they're teaching, you know, for the future—and without having to go every month, you're not learning to put money back every month.

Without these requirements, she believes, "you're not getting into that habit" of saving every month.

Denise

Denise is motivated to save because she very much wants to purchase a house. She thinks it will improve life for her family. At the same time she makes it clear that her children's needs come before saving. The choice between saving and spending her small income tears at her constantly.

> That really frustrates me, because I say, "I've got to put this $10 in my account but I really do need this $10." But then I look and I think that I really do desire a house. . . . So, when I think about that, it makes me go ahead and just say, "Okay. I'm gonna do this." But it'd be hard because I'd be needing that money to do other things for my kids. . . . I got to make sure those four kids' needs are met.

Denise's small savings provide a tangible glimpse of progress, encouraging her to want to save even more. "We have to put everything in a notebook and you can look at that and you say, 'Okay, gosh, I came from here to here.' I think I'm doing okay. But I want to do just a little bit better." She also concentrates on her goal of buying a house as a way to convince herself to leave the money in the IDA.

I just think about my goal when I think about that account. . . . And that's to buy a house. So, I just think about that. And when I think about that, it make me not want to touch it. Because I know if I keep saving and keep that in there, then one day I'll get to that point to where I can purchase. So I just think about that.

So far Denise has not deposited much in her IDA. However, she is determined to save more in the coming year. She hopes that what she learned in the money management classes, along with greater focus on saving, will help her stay on course.

It's gonna be a lot different for me this year because last year I didn't really deposit it into my IDA like I should have. . . . The money management classes and all of that . . . sort of enlightened [me] a little bit, you know. I said, "Okay, I'm gonna do it different this year. I'm gonna make sure I save."

Denise understands that saving requires "sacrifice," but despite her yearning for a house, she is clear that caring for her children must come first.

Becky

With her part-time postal service job, Becky thought she could manage the required monthly deposit of $10. Soon she added another job working full-time at night. "I was like so happy. Everything seemed like it was going better in our life." "Because of working nights I got an eight percent shift differential, and on working weekends I got 50 cents more an hour." The new job also provided health coverage for her and the children. She can afford a phone for the first time in years.

Just right now I'm better off financially than I've ever been in my life. And I've put at least $50 in that IDA savings program each month. Sometimes I put more, but most of the time it was an accident. I'd think I hadn't made a deposit for that month so I deposited more. And one month I ended up putting three $50 deposits in. I was working so much and I didn't know what I did or what I hadn't.

Becky makes IDA deposits in person at the bank. "I'll go by the bank and then write a $100 check, and I'll put $50 in that account. . . . So I put $50 in there and then $50 back to me." She prefers this to using the bank's automatic teller machine because of the 75 cent ATM fee. Her sister says she is "the cheapest person there is today."

At the end of the year Becky plans to deposit whatever is needed to reach the match cap of $750. When she takes on extra jobs, she increases her monthly deposits. She has missed only one month's deposit in the past year, and that was because she was busy at work and forgot.

Theresa

Theresa figures she has the three years that she is in the IDA program to get on a solid financial footing, clean up her credit record, and save enough for a down payment on a house. Unfortunately, she recently had lost a stable and relatively well-paying job (due to a conflict among the proprietors of the business). She dipped into her IDA savings to cover an expensive car repair because her small stash at home was not enough. "I withdrew $250 that I have not put back in there. My understanding was that if you took something out you had to replace it, plus your regular minimum $10 [monthly] deposit. I haven't done that. That was in May. This is July. So I'm figuring . . . I'm not even in the program no more."

But so far no one has called to terminate her from the program. She hopes they will allow her to continue. "I'm just sidetracked for the minute. But, it'll get back on track." She believes that the IDA program is the only way she will be able to save. It helps that she has a savings goal. She believes that the savings match and the monthly statement make saving in an IDA easier than regular saving.

> And nobody matches your money in a regular savings! You know? You don't get anything for it. And it just really keeps you going when you look at your statement and say, "Okay. I put in $500, they've matched $500, so I've got $1,000. Even though I can't touch it. I still got it." You know what I mean? That makes a big difference. . . . It's something to keep you going.

Heather, Denise, Becky, and Theresa believe they can save more in the IDA program than they have in the past. The IDA match inspires Heather to earmark her tips from work for saving. Denise's small savings accumulations give her hope that she will be able to save more in the future, although her family's household consumption demands threaten to overwhelm her desire to set money aside. Becky deposits much more than the minimum required deposit each month thanks to her extra job, health coverage, and no debt (because of her recent bankruptcy). Despite the unmatched withdrawals from her IDA for car repairs, Theresa is optimistic that she will "get back on track" to saving again.

STRATEGIES FOR SAVING IN AN IDA

Like these four women, other IDA participants have adopted strategies for setting money aside in their IDAs (see table 8.1). These strategies, addressed in the following section, help participants contend with low incomes, emergencies, and other barriers to saving in an IDA. We turn to a discussion of barriers in the second half of the chapter.

Reduce Consumption and Spend More Efficiently

One of the most common strategies for saving is to reduce consumption and/or spend more efficiently. Fred summed up the importance of being conscious of his spending in order to have money to save. "You just gotta do some belt tightening. . . . You gotta do some belt tightening." As we have seen, participants learned the importance of careful spending long before entering the program. After all, most had lived on low incomes for a very long time. (As Steven said, "I've scraped money to survive so many times, there wasn't very many

TABLE 8.1. IDA Participants' Strategies for Saving in IDAs
($N = 59$)

Saving Strategies	IDA Participants *n* (%)
Reduce consumption and spend more efficiently	42 (71)
Focus on savings goal	34 (58)
Use mental accounting and earmark sources of saving	27 (46)
Increase income	16 (27)
Develop a saving habit	13 (22)
Monitor resource flows	12 (20)
Pay savings account first	12 (20)
Adopt "rules of thumb" for when savings may be spent	11 (19)
Pretend IDA savings are not there	5 (8)
Move assets	5 (8)

Source: Center for Social Development, in-depth interviews.
Note: Participants could report multiple strategies.

ways they could tell me how to save money.") Nonetheless, some participants find that the IDA program provides information and encouragement about how to economize.

Participants try to distinguish between "wants and needs." IDA participants (42) reported gaining additional insight into how to do this. The program taught Theresa to reflect before making a purchase. "I've changed the way I spend. Like I said, I think about now, 'Do I really need this?'" Denise also said that the classes encouraged her to set her goals, track resource flows, and distinguish between needs and wants.

> I mean, set your goals and how to work toward those goals and how to save and track your money. . . . How we spend money that we really don't need to spend on things that we . . . really don't need. "Wants" can wait but "needs" are important. We did a little thing to where we number them and put them in order as far as our "wants" and our "needs." And I found out a lot of stuff that I thought I needed was a want, really. It really could wait.

Another participant said that by thinking through her household expenditures, she gradually "weeded out" things she does not need. "I kind of whittled it around until I got it the way that I want it." This helped her save in the IDA program. Another explained how classes help.

> The classes, the way they told us how to go about saving, budgeting. You know, to set up those things, you look at your income, you figure your bills and you see what you got left. And you know, just kind of be careful about extra spending and realize some of the things that you can really do without. . . . You know, be conscious of what you spend. I think that was the most helpful thing.

For example, "food is a need" and "clothing is a need," but a "Polo shirt is a want" and "Air Jordans is a want." In other words, this participant explained, "You just don't buy everything you see. . . . You keep your wants under control."

Participants identify ways to cut back that will not endanger well-being or diminish a family's quality of life. Occasionally, they must make a real "sacrifice," according to one participant, but most of the time, economizing means cutting back on little things that add up over time. Classes provide insights into how even these small expenditures add up. Another father of two young children observed that many people in the class are "astounded" by how much they spend on small things.

You can talk about it all day, but when you see it on paper, with the numbers added up, then you really realize how much is going out and how much is coming in. . . . Some of the numbers kind of astounded me when they started adding up . . . it's just amazing how much you're wasting. I know it astounded a lot of people that were in the class.

Participants said that knowing there is an incentive in the form of a savings match and knowing they have to come up with a ten-dollar-a-month deposit gives people compelling reasons to spend with greater caution. As a participant noted, every $150 she spends on jewelry "is now $300 if I was saving it in my IDA account!"

Participants spend their money more carefully in order to free up money for saving. They clip coupons, buy in bulk, and substitute less expensive items. Becky thinks carefully and shops around before buying things. "I don't just buy things on a spur [of the moment] or on a whim." Another participant learned in classes that he qualifies for the local food bank. He figures he can save a little money in this way. "I think we qualify for like $30 worth of food . . . that helps us save an extra $30."

Some efficiencies are simply not possible. One participant, a busy mother with two young children, observed that although they taught her in class that cooking at home reduces food expenses, she often does not have time to cook. "Before the IDA program, when I wasn't working two jobs, I did cook a lot at home. You know, I cooked all the time. Now, I hardly ever cook." She is a little disappointed that she had not learned other ways to manage her financial life better.

In contrast, and much to her surprise, Heather believes the financial education classes helped her learn how to resist spending and make better financial choices. Before joining the program, she, like many others, lived "paycheck to paycheck." As we learned in the introduction, at first she had a low opinion of the classes, but in the end she acknowledged that she learned how to avoid spending money on "junk," to shop for groceries weekly, and to be a more careful consumer. Perhaps most important, she figured out for herself the importance and role of saving in her life. "They make you realize—or they did me anyway—why you were there, why you wanted to save money instead of spend it." She sometimes compares herself to her coworkers, who "freak out" because their "checks are gonna bounce." She asks herself, "Why would you write checks when you don't have money in the bank?" but laughed as she recalled acting the same way.

I was just like them. And now I wouldn't dare spend money that [I] don't have. I wouldn't dare run up a credit card—and I'm freaking out because, "Gosh, they're gonna charge me interest!"

When the interviewer asked if the family has less money for other things since she has been saving in an IDA, Heather observed that she does not see it quite that way.

Less money to waste, I guess. . . . It's not like I'm having to take money out, to take away from something else. 'Cause I just re-did my spending habits. It's not like I have less money because I'm having to put some back, because you just re-cycle the way that you're spending it.

Focus on Savings Goal

Another very common strategy for saving in IDAs was to focus on the savings goal. Participants joined the program aiming to save, but the savings goal helped them articulate their goals and think through what would be required to meet them. For Fred, having a savings goal is fundamental to successful saving. He explained, "[Saving] depends on the purpose. . . . See that's the key to saving. It's what you want. If you want something bad enough, you'll save for it."

Focusing on a goal helps participants (34) resist spending temptations and set money aside. One participant said the goal puts "your focus on the ability to save." "It puts your focus on the ability to control money." Another said she needs a goal to help her focus on why she is saving and to help her resist the temptation to spend. "I know you have to have your goal. I always have to have something in my head. . . . If I don't have a reason not to, then I'll spend it. You know, I'm not impulsive, but that's because, I think, because I have a goal."

Similarly, Charles believes goals are a key to saving; they give people the "initiative" to save and to resist impulsive spending. "The IDA has given me a sense of direction. It has given me a sense to restrain myself before I go on the spur of the moment and do something." When asked how he would advise a friend who wanted to join the IDA program, Charles replied, "Well, first I would ask them some questions. . . . What are your goals in life? What would you like to happen to you? What would you like to achieve? How far do you want to go? What sacrifices do you intend to make?"

Focusing on an attainable goal seems to make it easier for participants to practice self-control. This may be true in the most unlikely cases. For example, in chapter 6 we described one participant's gambling problem. Despite her problem addiction, she had some experience saving prior to her husband's death. Although she has not saved in years, she finds the program boosts her willpower and helps her concentrate on saving. "It's easier because I'm focusing a little bit more." Although she still owes gambling debts, she reports that she has stopped gambling and is trying to keep her focus and change the direction of her life (Walker 1999).

Use Mental Accounting and Earmark Sources of Savings

As discretionary saving, participants saving in an IDA must identify possible sources of money for saving. The majority of participants (54) draw on earned income as their primary source (table 8.2). Theresa, for example, decided she would deposit $50 from her wages into the IDA each month. Like putting aside discretionary savings, a vow to set aside a certain amount of wages for the IDA is difficult because it seems like yet another difficult bill.

Many participants (27) said it is easier to make deposits if they earmark a particular income flow—such as a second income, tips, babysitting money, child support payments, or income from odd jobs—for saving. They often refer to these income sources as "extra" money. Saving is at the "top" of Fred's list; he deposits all income from side jobs into his IDA.

TABLE 8.2. Sources of IDA Deposits for
IDA Participants ($N = 59$)

	IDA Participants n (%)
Employment	54 (92)
Tax refund	18 (31)
Child support	7 (12)
Social Security/Disability	3 (5)
Welfare payments	1 (2)
Loose change	1 (2)
School loans	1 (2)
Insurance settlement	1 (2)
Unknown	1 (2)

Source: Center for Social Development, in-depth interviews.

Note: Participants could report multiple sources.

God mapped me out a savings. See, between September first when I get back from vacation . . . to December, the night before Christmas, I map me out a savings program to get that money back in there. What I do is take all my side jobs and put that money back. I got to have that $750 in there at the end of the year. Which will give me 1,500 bucks for two years.

Seven women said they save part of their child support payments in their IDAs. One couple sets aside the wife's small income for the IDA, leaving the husband's income to cover living expenses. His wife's income is "just like extra money, hidden money. I don't even think about it as money." Heather and others save their tips. As one participant described, "I mainly count on my tips . . . which isn't a whole lot, but it is extra cash that I wouldn't normally have" for saving.

Nonetheless, even setting aside extra sources of income can be very difficult, as Heather pointed out: "I'll try not to spend [my tips]. It's really hard. That's gas and milk and stuff like that." She resolves this by putting money in the IDA every other day or so.

Some participants explained that they find it easier to mentally assign their tax refunds to savings than to set aside smaller amounts each month. As one participant pointed out, it is difficult to save from her regular income stream. She only manages to save when she has "extra money coming in . . . like when I got my tax return." Most often, participants turn to tax refunds to meet the annual $750 match cap. This includes some people who have never saved their refund money in the past. When one man joined the IDA program he despaired at not being able to save to the match cap ("I've never had $750 in the last ten years!"). "Then I took that tax class. . . . And instead of paying off on the bills like I usually do . . . I'll take that money from income tax and put it in [the IDA]." Another person saves some of her tax refund. "As a rule, if I have tax money, I'm going shopping for something I need, or think I need anyway." This time she put it into her IDA. "That's the first time that I ever done that."

Others use different windfall sources. For example, a middle-aged man saved $3,000 in his IDA from an auto insurance settlement. He reported that it is easier to save an unexpected lump sum than regular income, especially since he has a large monthly child support obligation.

Increase Income

Some participants (16) find ways to add to income in order to make IDA deposits. They work overtime and take on odd jobs, like babysitting and appliance repair. When participants earmark these funds (in whole or in part) for saving, they are less apt to miss the money. One participant recalled taking on a job that brought in about $25 a week. She earmarked it for the IDA. The benefit is that she did not miss it. "Because, about the time we got in the [IDA] program is when I started receiving [these extra earnings], so I wasn't used to getting the money anyway."

Another respondent plans to use his tax refund to meet the IDA match cap, but if the refund is insufficient, he plans to take on another job because getting the match is so important to him. "If I wasn't getting my income tax back . . . I would work extra hours at work or pick up a part-time job to get that $750. That's like free money." If he did not make the effort, "that'd be just like throwing $750 down the drain!"

Develop a Saving Habit

Some participants (13) said that the program helped them develop a "saving habit," a psychological condition where saving is normal and a part of everyday life (Camic 1986). As one participant said, saving had become "a lifetime thing" that she would "always" do. Another described it as "like a compulsion." One participant described her new saving habit: "You get in the habit, you know, keep at it. I got these good habits, so I believe it will be a lifetime thing. No matter what, even if my income gets worse, I will probably still put five or six dollars away because it's a habit. That's my basic thing I think I really learned is that you can save." As if saying that she no longer has to think as hard about saving, she said, when it's a habit, "You don't have to worry about it." Some associated the habit with developing a routine; others equated habit with discipline. Several also said that because saving had become a habit, they anticipated continuing to save in the future beyond their participation in the IDA program.

Becky, for example, predicted that after being in the program for three years and watching her savings accumulate, she would develop a savings habit.

> I think I will [continue saving], because I think after three years it's going to become a habit. You know, and I could see that I'm making progress by doing that. I mean I see that already, because $50 a month, I mean that's really not that much money. . . . And then I see, I ain't even been in there a year and just putting in a little bit which really hasn't even been an inconvenience to me at all. I've already got like $650 in there.

Of the thirteen who said they have developed a saving habit, six described it primarily as internalizing the required monthly IDA deposit. Heather, for example, linked obligatory saving to developing a saving habit: "There has to be rules set. . . . Without having to go every month [to deposit], you're not learning to put money back every month. You're not getting into that habit." Theresa credits the program requirement with teaching her to be consistent in her saving pattern: "The [IDA] makes it ingrained that you *have to,* okay?" It is difficult to know if participants deposit savings because of the program requirement, or whether they have indeed developed a "lifetime" habit of saving.

Monitor Resource Flows

Many IDA participants (12) said they have increased their vigilance over the household budget, identifying and tracking money they might be able to deposit in the IDA. Financial management classes encourage them and offer them additional tools for budgeting savings. Fred believes that tracking the flow of household money (being "conscious of what you spend") is a key to figuring out where to find the money to save, and the budgeting class is useful in helping to learn how. "So you can see exactly what you got left." "You know where your money is going. Almost to the penny." He thinks this is fundamental.

> That was the most important thing. You gotta know where your money is. How, see, you gotta know how much money you got first of all. First is how much bills you got, so you can cut back in some area to make available to put in there. So it's gotta be the budgeting. The budget thing was the key. That was the key.

Many participants recalled learning techniques to track and budget in class. Heather, for example, began to track her spending more carefully after attending the classes. She can visualize more clearly the money she has to save.

> So it's plain black and white. You know where your money is going, what, how many times [you bought] lunch this week. . . . That's two days tips right there. So, just little things like that, that you don't know you're spending money on. And actually getting on a budget, to where before I didn't know how much I made or how much I had going out. No wonder I had so many money problems! And now I actually have in my mind how much spending money I have in a month. You know, how much I should be putting back, how much extra I can use to fix this or to get a new washing machine.

Others tracked their money flows before joining the program but said the program increases vigilance. Prior to the program, a participant in her early 30s kept track of her household financial flows "mentally." However, she found that once she began using a computer program to budget, she gained a better understanding of where she can spend less.

> I got a computer program and I keep track of my money in my checking account and what I spend it on and things like that. So that's something I do differently. . . . I didn't know I was spending that much money. . . . It's like, "Wow!" . . . Like going to a movie here and there or getting an ice cream cone, you know, those little things end up adding up.

For another participant, saving seems more feasible now that she has a better understanding of her household finances and knows how small amounts can accumulate. "My mind [is] set on saving. Like I said, you can put $10 or $20 or whatever away, instead of having to wait until you get $100 or $200 to put in there."

Although few actually began to use formal paper budgets, in the words of one participant, "it at least made us talk about it, and sort of evaluate some things, and make some priorities."

Pay Savings Account First

Some participants (12) make a focused effort to deposit money in their savings account before spending the rest of their paychecks, a strategy that demonstrates the financial priority of IDA savings. When they deposit into their savings first, participants said they overcome a desire to spend, and they do not worry the rest of the month about making the required IDA deposit. As this participant explained, he does not miss the money if he deposits it immediately.

> I really don't miss it that much as long as I take it off the top. Most important thing, I think, is when you first get your check and when you cash it, you can put something right there, then. . . . I think you should do that off the top to make it easy.

One of the ways that participants pay their accounts first is to sign up for direct deposit, although we could only find evidence that six people signed up for this financial service.[1] Those who set up direct deposit reported that it helps them avoid procrastination[2] and the temptation to spend the money. As many respondents observed, including IDA participants and nonparticipants, it is easier to save when the saver never sees the money.

> I guess it is a little harder actually putting it aside by going to the bank. . . . What's the first thing you are going to do when you get paid? You are going to make sure all your bills are paid first . . . versus if they had taken it out before you actually got your check, then you wouldn't even miss it.

Another benefit of direct deposit is that it takes work to reverse it. For example, a participant has arranged for her paycheck to be divided into three parts: five dollars go into a credit union savings account, ten dollars into the IDA, and the rest into a credit union checking account. She observed, "It's all automatic. . . . I couldn't stop it unless I filled out a lot more paperwork." She did not miss the money "because it is gone before I get it. . . . It's just become the norm. It is something that I am used to."

The idea of setting aside savings first appears to tap into a well-known cultural adage. Theresa said she was taught always to "pay yourself first," but once she joined the IDA program she actually began to do it. Similarly, another participant said she learned from her mother to put aside something for herself. She now interprets this idea within the structure of the IDA: "I always try to put something back for myself first [into the IDA] before I even start paying the bills."

Adopt Rules of Thumb for When Savings May Be Spent

Once participants place their IDA savings in a separate mental category from other money, some (11) also adopt rules about when they can use their savings. In addition to her IDA, a young mother with one child has two other savings accounts; one for short-term and one for long-term savings. She has a rule not to touch her long-term savings "for any reason." Another participant and his wife vowed not to touch their IDA savings for any reason—even an emergency—until the program is over and they invest in their asset goal. "We have not touched the IDA. We would never touch the IDA, until it's time to get our goal met." Another participant said her IDA savings "is something that needs to stay there and be solid." Another described his IDA account as "sacred."

The IDA is like a sacred account, you know. . . . It's money that I won't touch. . . . It's money that I don't think about . . . until the time comes when I am able to spend it.

Some participants' rule of thumb is to keep the money in savings except for emergencies. Denise, for instance, pledges to use the money only when she absolutely must. "It's like, I'm not touching it. Unless it was a life and death situation—that's different."

Because friends and extended family members sometimes pressure individuals to share their savings (Stack 1974), some participants also vow not to give their savings to others, except in emergency situations. Or, for example, Fred vows not to share IDA savings with others unless the request involves children or another genuine need.

If it was something where they had children involved and they don't have groceries and they're hungry, I would take the IDA account and give it to them. That's an emergency. But to go to the movies or to go get some whiskey, it's not an emergency. Say that sewers were backing up in their house and they didn't have a way to get it repaired and they needed $65 to pay the sewage man and the house is stinking, you can't use the toilet, I would give it to them and let them pay me back. Yeah, I would give them the IDA account.

Pretend IDA Savings Are Not There

Like discretionary savers, others (5) avoid using their IDA savings by ignoring them. Rosalyn, for example, pretends her savings are not there. Before the IDA, she said she could not resist using her savings. In contrast, she never withdraws money from her IDA. "It never crossed my mind. It's just like it's not there." She said the key is to "put it there, forget it. Leave it alone." Similarly, another participant tries to ignore her IDA account.

I can be penniless and I don't even think about that money that is in there. I mean, it's not that much anyway, but I don't even think about it. So, it's helping to say, this money is for something, I'm not gonna touch it.

Nonetheless, ignoring the money is a strategy that frequently fails, especially for those with high consumption demands. For example, one participant already broke her rule to pretend the savings were not there and made "four or five" withdrawals. She is discouraged but determined to replace the withdrawn money.

> It took me probably four or five months, man, to save that $125 that I had to go draw out. So in order for me to replace that, it's gonna take another, probably three or four months before I can get that money back to where it was before I made that withdrawal. You know, I'm doing it gradually. Ten dollars at a time . . . I'll get it back.

Another rule of thumb to protect savings is to keep the IDA a secret from others as well. Theresa, for example, keeps her financial business private. She has told only three people, her two daughters and her best friend. "Nobody else knows I have it." After many years of watching her siblings misuse their money, Heather came to the same conclusion.

> No one really knows that I have any money put back. When my sister—this may be a little selfish—but my sister asked to borrow money and I said "no," just because I don't want that to become habit. . . . You know, she's single, she doesn't have any kids, she works. There's no reason for her to be borrowing money from me. That's my attitude now. They just don't spend their money wisely.

Move Assets

Sometimes savings in the IDA are not new savings but are "reshuffled" assets (Schreiner and Sherraden 2007). There are two types of reshuffling: taking money from an existing account and depositing it in the IDA; and forgoing other investments while saving in the IDA.

Five participants mentioned that they met their savings targets by moving savings from other accounts into the IDA. For example, an immigrant, one of the few people who always have saved, reported that she moved money from an old savings account to her IDA. She finds it reassuring that, from the beginning, she has deposited a substantial part of the annual savings cap.

> In my mind, [meeting the savings goal] is taken care of already by the lump sum that I [deposited]. I put that $650 in the first time I opened the account. And then this year when I got my refund, I put in another $650. . . . I just have to meet the requirement putting in some every month.

In these cases, IDA savings do not represent new savings (except for the match). In other words, their net worth increases only to the extent that the program matches their savings. Nonetheless, despite the relative ease of shifting existing savings into an IDA, there is little evidence that participants have significant existing savings that they can move into the IDA.

What appears to be a more common way to reshuffle is to redirect income into the IDA instead of depositing it into an alternative savings vehicle. As one participant said, she would be saving in an old account if she were not in the IDA program. ("I don't know [where I would have gotten the money to save]; probably it just would have went into the other savings account that I have.") There is some evidence that this may be happening with others as well, but it is difficult to ascertain how often and how much. One participant, for example, owned a credit union savings account prior to joining the IDA program. She deposited money from her paycheck and from her tax refund into this savings account. After joining the IDA program, she continued to make deposits into her credit union account and also to the IDA. Without a careful accounting of prior and current savings, we do not know if her overall savings deposits increased or remained the same. Although we do not know if her IDA savings represent new savings, her IDA savings most certainly outperformed her prior saving method in terms of total return.

In households that do not clearly earmark specific sources for saving, it is difficult to assess the extent of reshuffling into an IDA. An immigrant mother with five children, for example, described paying household bills first with her earnings and tax refund then depositing the surplus in her IDA. "I did it around income tax time. Because of the income tax, I had taken care of some things that I normally would take care of from my paycheck. So when my paycheck came I had that much there to put in." Such relaxed accounting makes it difficult to determine if she is shifting assets. Because of the savings match, she said she would give IDA deposits priority over other saving. "Yeah, because [the IDA] is like a compulsion. You have to do this if you want to see a dream realized. But the other savings is, like, I can skip and there's no penalty, you know." In this case, the amount of shifting is likely small because her income is so low.

Another participant, an independent contractor with two young children, was not explicit about where his savings come from, suggesting that some of his deposits may be transferred from another account. He described a financial management style where he had to regularly "borrow from Paul to pay Peter," although he suggested that his IDA deposits are "left over."

Sixty dollars isn't much to put into the IDA, but many times I have to go with that minimum of ten bucks, because it's just—where I end up. They always say to pay yourself first, and that is a good rule, but the IDA is always put back at the end of the month. Whatever's left over goes in there.

Another way to shift assets is to borrow (Beverly, McBride, and Schreiner 2003). In an unusual twist, one participant borrowed from her own IDA in order to make her deposit because she was worried that she might lose her "spot in the program." ("They said if you miss a deposit, you will be thrown off the program.") In the months when she has no money to deposit,

I go up there and I withdraw out of my IDA and then I just put some of it back in there and then the next two or three days, I go and put the rest back. And then that way, it's like, even though I didn't really save that much. I didn't save nothing, but I still put it in there. Do you see what I'm saying?

Acknowledging that she forfeits the match in this way, she tries to make it up later. "I try to do a little extra [later]. . . . That's what I try to do."

Other participants borrow from family to make their IDA deposits. Theresa and her children frequently give each other money. "My daughters always bring Mama some money just because I'm Mama and they know that if there is anything that they ever really need—all they have to do is call me and I'm going to do it and I'm going to get it for them." Theresa likely uses some of money borrowed from her daughters for her IDA deposits.

Borrowing for saving, however, is relatively rare. Most borrowing, as we observe in chapter 5, is for consumption. Overall, the IDA does not appear to be a sufficient reason to borrow. Most participants seemed to understand that if they borrow for their IDA deposit, they will have to withdraw it later to pay the debt (Thaler 1992a). This is difficult in the IDA program because of the restricted uses.

Although the extent of reshuffling is likely underestimated here because we did not have a detailed series of questions aimed at determining amount of reshuffling, most IDA savings are likely new. Participants reported little savings when they entered the program; therefore, there are limits to the extent to which they can engage in shifting (Schreiner and Sherraden 2007). In fact, participants say that most of their money was destined for consumption prior to the IDA program. One participant's response to a question about how she would have used her money prior to the IDA program is typical. "It probably would have just gone in our checking account and been used for a bill or to buy groceries." Similarly, when the interviewer asked where the money for her IDA deposits came from, another participant said she does "not touch" her existing CDs, but saves instead from her job income. Another has IRAs, which he said have penalties for early withdrawals. He said it would be difficult for him to borrow for his IDA. In fact, according to his wife, they opened a new savings account at a different bank at the same time as they opened the IDA.

> One of the good things about the IDA is that since we joined, my husband ac-tually opened up another account. We thought it would be wise to open up an-other account besides the IDA account. And so now we have the IDA account plus another account.

She believes that the IDA program encourages more saving. "That's a good thing, you know, I think about the IDA program. It just, it really encourages you to save."

CHALLENGES OF SAVING IN AN IDA

The IDA program features and self-initiated strategies for saving and main-taining savings in an IDA do work, but not all the time and not for everyone. In the end, like nonparticipants who are attempting to save, IDA participants also have low incomes, surrender to the temptation to spend, procrastinate or for-get to make IDA deposits, and withdraw their savings for unmatched purposes. For the 22 participants who never made a matched withdrawal (appendix A), the program simply could not offer enough support to sustain long-term sav-ings. As other researchers find, several barriers stand out (Hogan et al. 2004; Shobe and Christy-McMullin 2005; Beverly and Barton 2006).

Low and Volatile Incomes

Like Denise, those living from tiny paycheck to tiny paycheck are accustomed to spending almost every penny for daily living. They find it difficult to deposit even the $10 required monthly deposit. Denise needs that money for her chil-dren. Although she receives child support for her two eldest children, and she has a steady 30-hour-a-week job with benefits, she earns only $6.83 an hour. She tries to squeeze an IDA deposit out of her monthly budget.

> I just take all those incomes and make sure our bills are paid and [the children] have clothes and they have food and I pay my tithes and make sure I deposit into the IDA account and go from there. . . . After I do all that I don't have extras, really as far as go out and do a lot of activities with my kids or put in—I don't have. I wish I could.

Reminders from IDA staff are helpful because she is so busy, but in the end, she simply is strapped for cash. Denise and others may be able to save for short periods, but they typically need this money to cover shortfalls. This is evident in saving patterns among some participants. Over the course of the program, for example, two participants made substantial deposits but also withdrew all of the savings prior to taking a matched withdrawal. One made unmatched withdrawals in 15 different months (totaling $10,815) and the other made unmatched withdrawals in 22 different months (totaling $1,356). This pattern suggests that they were using their IDAs as a combination short-term saving instrument and transaction account (Schreiner and Sherraden 2007).

Income volatility is also a challenge to regular saving (O'Curry 1999). One participant, whose financial life—her income, expenses, and ability to save—fluctuates significantly, finds it difficult to know when she can make a savings deposit. Her income (temporary work and intermittent child support) and expenses (holidays and emergencies) are hard to predict. During an emergency, as another participant observed, the IDA account is "not exactly a priority." He understands how people sometimes have a difficult time making deposits.

> There are times when I don't care if someone threatened me—threatened my life—I could not have given them $10! I did not have it. And so, on one side, I can see how that seems like a lot of money to somebody and it would be very hard for them to do that. On the other side, if they made it mandatory that somebody put $20 or $30 a month so they were more likely to get that $750 a year, a lot of people wouldn't be able to do this.

He might have been describing this participant, who emptied her IDA account because of a series of financial problems.

> The highest balance I ever had was $200 (which with the match was $600). So that grieves you when you see it go from 600 dollars to 36 cents. . . . And then I started to build it up again and I had up to like 60-something dollars, when I

raided it three months ago for the (traffic) ticket. It's back up to $30 now, but it's not $200. And it's not what it could have been. You know?

She continued, describing a high tax bill, car problems, health problems, and a job loss. So, even though she "started out really good" depositing $50 every two weeks, she "had to turn around and yank it all back out." She believes that without these problems she would have been able to maintain her IDA savings.

Even when participants used strategies designed to safeguard their small savings from consumption, they sometimes had to violate them. For example, one participant deposited the requisite $10 a month in her IDA but, at the same time, set aside money in a separate savings account for consumption needs. Eventually, she planned to transfer this other savings (if it remained unspent) in a lump sum to her IDA. Unfortunately, in the end, she needed all of the money from both accounts for consumption and never received a matched withdrawal from the program.

Medical and Other Emergencies

Although unexpected expenses of all kinds threaten savings, medical expenses are particularly devastating. As we observed in chapter 5, many people lack health insurance, and even for those who have it, coverage often is inadequate. Therefore, when a health problem arises, families take a financial hit. In a story retold in slightly different ways by several respondents, Theresa describes the debt accrued by her family that eventually led to her leaving the IDA program.

> I don't know how we got into financial trouble. I really don't. But we got into real serious financial trouble. I think it started with medical bills. I think that's where it really started at. . . . I remember my son being real sick and almost dying and he was in the hospital for a long, long time. And I remember the bills started coming in. Even with the insurance, there was still like $20,000 or $30,000 we had to pay. And I think that's where it really started going—just downhill. We ended up taking what we had in the savings and still ended up owing balances on these bills. And it just seemed like it went from bad to worse. . . . And I'm talking about serious money—like $20,000.

Another participant accumulated $90,000 in medical debt, making it impossible to save in her IDA. Although the program staff tried to help, the participant found it too stressful to continue in the program. Another participant, with one grown child and two others still at home, is unable to work regularly because of prior surgery and illness. She has difficulty saving even the minimum ten dollars a month. None of these participants drew a savings match.

Because of medical problems, a young mother with a teenage daughter did not make deposits during eight months of her first year in the IDA program. The pressure to keep up with her IDA deposits, she believes, contributed to her ill health. She recognizes that she made the decision to participate; no one forced her. Nonetheless, the stress of saving is proving difficult. She recalled the time around her daughter's birthday when her "world fell apart."

> The whole world fell apart after that, financial-wise, I mean. She didn't get anything huge, but what she did get, you know, she just had some friends stay the night and, you know, we bought food and that kind of thing. It was just enough extra money out to get behind.

When she sought help from the IDA program staff, she told them, "I have medical problems, I've lost touch. I've lost control. Whatever you want to call it. I've not been saving. I've not been paying bills. I've not been doing anything." Although she said they got her "back on track" for a while, it was not long before she left the program.

Thus, for people experiencing illness, stress, or depression—especially when combined with low incomes—even small things can impede saving. One participant found that forgetting her account number and not having a deposit slip on hand is enough to discourage her from making savings deposits. These are, in her words, "just silly little things," but with "so much other challenges in my life, that was just one too many."

Inconvenient Financial Services

Participants noted that inconvenient financial services also may contribute to procrastination. Participants' days are busy with work and caring for children. Making an IDA deposit is one more thing they must add to their long list. One participant remarked that simply remembering to make the monthly deposits is cumbersome. "Many times, I was driving by the [bank] and I was in a hurry to get to where I needed to go and I thought, 'Okay, you have to do it,' and then [I would] procrastinate, and then you just don't have the time." Another said she is always "in the middle of doing something" or the bank is closed when she remembers to make her IDA deposit. A mother with three young children said she gets busy and forgets to make her deposits. "I have so much stuff going on." As a result, her total savings are quite low. Another mother with young children also admitted that being too busy leads to procrastination. Despite reminders, she also "forgets" to make her IDA deposits. "They send little cards, but then you misplace those cards. It's procrastination. I'm a procrastinator."

Some find the bank location inconvenient. As one person said, "It's not any-where near where I live or work." In Denise's case, the bank is not only incon-venient, but she does not own a car to get there. Friends give her rides (she pays for the gas); she economizes by taking care of other financial business at the same time. Nonetheless, the inconvenience, along with her low income, con-tributes to forgetting to make deposits. "If you're not careful—and it happens to me—I forget. They send you little reminder cards every month. Those help me out. And I normally put them on the icebox. But I forget because in my mind, I be so busy doing stuff."

The IDA account may also be held in a different bank than the one partici-pants use for financial transactions. It would be easier, said one participant, if she could take care of all of her banking at once. "I wish my bank and my check-ing account and my savings account was at the same place, because I probably could find myself doing it a lot easier versus trying to do it with me having them both separate."

Several people mentioned that direct deposit would help solve their prob-lem with procrastination. Denise plans to sign up for direct deposit as soon as she gets a new job.

> I won't even touch the money. . . . I won't have to even worry about it. I know that it's going there. So I'm gonna direct-deposit it into the IDA out of my check. 'Cause I forget. . . . My mind just be busy with the fourth baby. . . . The bank will just take it out and put it right into the account.

Nonetheless, even among those in the IDA program, only six people re-ported using direct deposit. For the most part, only participants who work full-time for large employers have this option; it is unavailable to most others (Dun-ham 2001; Barr 2004). Employers have to be willing to set up direct deposit and arrange with their payroll vendor to split the deposit among accounts.

The IDA program reminded another participant of a savings plan she once had at work. She said the only problem with the IDA, unlike the employer-based savings plan, is that savings for the IDA are not automatically transferred.

"It was just a hassle to go by the bank and try to remember to do that on the certain day before it was the end of the month." As a result, she missed many required IDA deposits. She joked that it is easier to spend the money than to save it. "It's real easy to just drive on by the bank . . . go to the Dollar Store and get ten things!" Turning serious, she said the urge to spend instead of save is too powerful, so she finally arranged for direct deposit. "It's just like everything else, you don't put it up there with your other bills, you put it over to the side and it slips your mind. Or you find another reason to spend the money on, another purpose, you know? . . . So, you don't end up putting it in savings."

DISCUSSION

Participants generated savings and stored them in their IDAs using practices learned in a lifetime of surviving and setting aside small amounts of money on a low income (chap. 6). But IDA participants used these savings strategies more consistently and successfully in the IDA because features of the IDA program structured and supported saving activity. The IDA match inspired them to save; the rules and expectations helped them focus on, plan for, and make a priority out of saving; and the classes and support from staff encouraged them and gave them hints about ways to set money aside in the account.

They adopted rules of thumb for guiding and streamlining decision making. These rules helped them distinguish between a need and a want, and decide when to deposit savings, whom to tell about their IDA savings, and what constitutes an emergency for withdrawals.

As behavioral economics suggests, participants used mental accounting to help think about savings sources and destinations. As they focused on their savings goal, they tracked resource flows, looking for places to reduce expenditures, increase efficiency, increase income, or move assets around. They earmarked particular income sources for saving. They picked a time of the month when they would make their monthly IDA deposits, although some found it easier to mentally assign their tax refund or other windfall income to saving. (Almost everyone used regular income streams, in part because of the monthly savings requirement.) Some found these strategies reinforced by classroom instruction.

There is evidence that some people moved other assets to the IDA (Engen, Gale, and Scholz 1994; Poterba, Venti, and Wise 1998), including steering some money into the IDA that they had previously deposited into other savings. Some may have deferred investing in other savings instruments, instead choosing to save in the IDA for the duration of the program. Generally, however, asset shifting is probably fairly limited among these families because most of their assets are not liquid (Carasso and McKernan 2008), and few have a record of long-term saving. The minority of families with more resources and a history of saving probably shifted assets, but we are unable to assess the extent of this practice in this study. Even if they did shift funds from other savings, the 100 to 200 percent IDA savings match almost certainly results in a substantial net gain.

Despite the savings structure and program support, IDA participants nonetheless reported difficulty saving. The amounts of money they could set aside were often quite small. Although participants articulated fewer saving challenges than nonparticipants, there were some similarities. Low incomes made it difficult for some people to save. Participants, like nonparticipants, carefully weighed their ability to save against the current consumption needs of their family. Especially in very poor families, parents provide first for their children. But because they believe that savings offer important benefits for the future, they sacrifice when possible and practical to set money aside in their IDAs.

It may be too much to ask very poor families, or families with large problem debt, to find much surplus in regular household budgets. Indeed, we find that mental accounting and earmarking techniques are insufficient in many such cases. With little margin for error, participants who deposit too much into the IDA account might have to retrieve it; if they do not deposit enough, they risk failing as savers or being asked to leave the program. An inability to accumulate savings in the program provokes feelings of failure among some, like the one participant who felt shame when she admitted she was having trouble saving. We also observed this challenge in Denise's and Theresa's cases.

Second, families frequently face pressing health, car repair, and other expenses (Varcoe 1990; Beverly and Barton 2006). Medical expenses are a particularly severe problem because of the high cost of health care and lack of health insurance coverage. These events often overwhelm respondents' ability to save. Other studies note the challenge of saving in the face of high medical costs and other emergencies (Rhine, Toussaint-Comeau, and Hogarth 2001; Hogan et al. 2004; Beverly and Barton 2006; Kempson, Atkinson, and Collard 2006). These frequently unexpected events made it difficult for even the most conscientious saver to keep savings in the IDA.

Third, the IDA requires more individual volition than typical contractual savings schemes. Participants in the IDA program must generate the funds out of low resource flows and deposit them in their IDA savings accounts themselves, which is markedly different from employer-based retirement savings programs that deduct and match earnings before they reach employee hands. Although IDA account features relieve individuals from some of the effort required in discretionary saving, other key features of contractual saving are not included, most significantly the use of electronic transfer of earned income into an account. The absence of this automatic feature means that IDA participants must take greater initiative and expend more individual effort than participants in a typical employment-based retirement plan. The onus is on the participant to generate the small savings out of typically very tight budgets and deposit these funds into the IDA.

In this way, saving in an IDA is largely discretionary saving. IDA participants must exert considerably more willpower and invest more time to save. Therefore, it is not surprising that seemingly small barriers, such as time, transportation, or bank location, stand in the way of regular depositing (Bertrand, Mullainathan, and Shafir 2004). One IDA participant concluded that she needs even more encouragement than the program can offer: "They really, really motivate you to stick to the budget that, for me, I need more motivation than once, you know, a month or so. I need it *everyday.*"

These findings suggest that low-income savers—like middle- and upper-income savers—need automatic features in order to be successful savers. Even with a large incentive and a personal (and sometimes family) commitment to saving, saving in an IDA requires substantial personal action. Behavioral economic theory suggests that despite the rationality of cashing in on a generous incentive (the savings match), people will tend to avoid making the painful step of setting money aside for the future (Kahneman and Tversky 1979). This is especially true in low-income households where there is intense demand for small surpluses for consumption.

Despite the challenges, participants in the IDA program (and nonparticipants to a lesser degree) managed to save small amounts of money. What difference did this make? The following chapter examines participant and nonparticipant views on the psychological and economic effects of saving.

CHAPTER 9

Effects of IDA Program Participation

While economic theory proposes that income and consumption shape people's well-being, asset theory proposes that what they own may have effects above and beyond the ability to pay for current and future consumption (Miller and Roby 1970; Sherraden 1991; Bourdieu 2001). Michael Sherraden proposes several key psychological and economic effects of assets, including improved household stability, greater future orientation, development of human capital and other assets, enhanced focus and specialization, more stable foundation for risk taking, improved outcomes for offspring, and increased self-efficacy, social influence, and political participation (Sherraden 1991, 148). Although research on asset effects is increasing, evidence on causality is largely missing, and we still know relatively little, especially about impacts on the poor (Page-Adams and Sherraden 1996; Scanlon and Page-Adams 2001; Schreiner and Sherraden 2007).

In this chapter, we examine the evidence on outcomes from in-depth interviews.[1] When people signed up for the IDA program, they wanted to accumulate savings. As we found in chapters 6 and 7, respondents believe that saving is the right thing to do, they hope saving will help them afford things they want but cannot purchase out of household income streams, and they think owning savings will provide security and opportunities in the future. This chapter examines IDA participants' perceptions about whether they achieved saving goals. Did saving and owning savings live up to their expectations? What difference did they make in their lives?

For an initial glimpse into these questions, we continue the savings narratives of three IDA participants, Heather, Becky, and Denise.

Heather

As a hairstylist, Heather does not make much money. But she has only two children, one receiving regular child support. Moreover, since joining the IDA program, life has improved in several ways. She is purchasing a small house through a rent-to-own arrangement, and she is in a satisfying relationship with a man she plans to marry. Although these do not help her save in the IDA, she believes they help support her plans.

When the interviewer asked Heather, "How important is [the IDA] to you?" she gave an interesting answer. Unlike others who emphasized that the match helped them afford something they could not have afforded otherwise, Heather stressed that the IDA reminded her about her life goals. She grappled to explain. It is "not because of what they're pitching in or anything." She believes that the IDA has helped her gain a new perspective. "I guess it's a way to transform your life and to quit wasting it on junk and check-to-check—to be able to get things that are meaningful." Heather sees a direct connection between saving and a better future.

> I think I'm just beginning to build goals that I wouldn't have thought about if I wasn't in the IDA program. You know, to save money. Or actually think about a savings account or something. It wasn't even important before that, until you go in and you see, "Wow. This is important." You don't want to be paying rent and you don't want to be working at McDonald's when you are 75. So I think it's easier to save money now because it's more important. Even if I'm not putting a lot back, it's something, you know.

She also thinks about her children's schooling, and, in contrast to her parents' approach, Heather tries to encourage her children's education. She has never told her eighth-grade daughter that none of her family members graduated from high school. She wants her children to believe that college is in their future. "You know . . . think that college is mandatory, you know?" although she added, "I don't know how I'll pay for it at that time."

As she talked, she returned to the idea that the IDA changed her relationship and view of money and assets. "But, everything, from, you know, our car to the house. I don't think I would ever have tried to buy our house if I wouldn't have gone through the IDA program. You know, I probably would have paid rent for another five years."

As a result of this experience, Heather, like many other participants in the program, believes that she has changed the way she spends and saves. "It's taught me how to save money so I'll be saving for their future. So I think the IDA program will have something to do with the rest of my life." She laughed, "Kind of corny."

In her three years and seven months in the program, Heather made two unmatched withdrawals totaling $25.[2] By the end of the program, she saved almost $1,400 from her tip money. She withdrew almost $2,800 to make improvements on her new house.

Becky

Saving makes Becky feel like she has accomplished something important. "I feel like really proud. You know, because I told you I put the roof on my house myself during the last few months. And whenever I do something like that, that I put money in there and it was quite a bit, it makes me feel better about myself."

Her original savings goal was to fix up her house. She already invested considerable effort and money in rehab, but because the house is, in her words, "junk," her other goal is to buy a better house. "I'd like to get myself in a better financial situation, and I would like to buy a house. I don't know when, but I would like to do that." Thus far, she has resisted taking any money out of the IDA account, hoping to accumulate enough for a down payment. At the time of the interview, however, she did not want to borrow money for a home loan because she had gone through bankruptcy proceedings not long before joining the IDA program. "I don't want to even think about trying to get a loan right now because they'll try to give me some high interest rate."

Becky believes that savings will have become a habit by the time the program ends, and she hopes to keep saving $50 a month in the same account. She has begun exploring other saving options as well. On the advice of a friend, Becky invested a small amount of money in stocks. "He got me into buying stocks at work." She is following the example of the IDA deposits by starting small. "At first I just started putting $10 in every check, because I didn't really know too much about it."

Although Becky saved a substantial amount of money, she also made at least six unmatched withdrawals, totaling $3,085. Nonetheless, she kept a positive balance. At the end of the program, she made two matched withdrawals totaling $6,500 ($2,250 was her own savings and the rest was match). The first withdrawal was for a down payment on a house, with the remainder invested in an IRA.

Denise

Despite her difficulty saving, Denise is enthusiastic about the IDA program. She compared it to other social assistance programs.

> A lot of programs, they help you, but the IDA program sort of break it down, you know . . . sort of show you—give you confidence, try to show you how to reach that goal. [They] take time to set up classes for you to come to. And they helping you, for one, by matching your funds. You know, to work toward that goal. . . . A lot of programs they don't offer that.

Denise, a child-care worker, believes that the program is helping her attain a better future. She is saving in her IDA to buy a house so she can open her own day-care center. She believes the day care will allow her to bring in more income and, at the same time, reduce her own day-care expenses because her children will stay home with her. She hopes to no longer be living "from paycheck to paycheck" so she can begin saving for her children's college education. Over the longer term, she said, "I'll have enough money saved. . . . I'll have emergency funds. . . . I know I'll have a car. Probably have two cars. . . . I'll be at my goals and probably working towards some more in five years."

Denise said that the IDA program helps people realize their goals by helping them save. "They encourage you and they give you confidence about reaching that goal." In this way, Denise has gained more confidence in her ability to reach her goals. "They make you feel confident. You know, like, 'You can do this.' They make you feel like you can do it. You can reach that goal."

Nonetheless, at times, Denise's confidence fails her, especially when she thinks about her responsibilities. "At first I [thought] 'Oh, I don't know if I can . . . save,' 'cause I got so much on my plate, you know?" As we saw in the previous chapter, she also has difficulty setting money aside in her IDA account. Her monthly savings deposits are small, and sometimes she has to skip months when expenses are too high.

Even so, Denise thinks the program has had a positive effect on her and her children's lives. For one, she is more careful with her money. "I used to splurge all the time. I don't splurge all the time any more. I mean, I used to go—you know, women like to shop. . . . But now, I don't think I really shopped for myself in about three months." She believes she has sorted out spending priorities. "I sort of look at needs now more than wants. I try to do away with wants and say, 'They'll come when you know, the time comes.' But I try to just look out for what we really need. . . . I look at it different now."

Despite Denise's goals and her hard work trying to save, she took at least 11 unmatched withdrawals from her account totaling over $1,300 during the three years and eight months she was in the program. She never was able to make a matched withdrawal and thus was unable to purchase her house and future day care with her IDA savings.

Despite significant differences in these women's saving experiences, all three said that saving and owning savings instill confidence and help them envision and plan for a more hopeful future. The IDA program helped them save, although Denise's savings had to be used for household consumption before she was able to make a matched withdrawal. This chapter explores what these and other respondents said are the economic and noneconomic effects of saving in IDAs and owning IDA savings.[3] We begin with participants' perceptions about the cognitive and psychological effects of saving and owning savings, either or both of which could have effects.[4]

COGNITIVE AND PSYCHOLOGICAL EFFECTS OF SAVING

The interviews suggest cognitive and psychological effects of saving and owning savings, such as changes in feelings and attitudes. These include feelings of greater security, lower levels of stress, greater self-confidence, greater sense of control over their lives, greater capacity to set and achieve goals, and more sense of personal responsibility and civic attitudes (and intentions to contribute to the welfare of others) (table 9.1). Some of the unsuccessful savers in the IDA program also said their small savings made them feel more secure and self-confident. This suggests possible broad psychological effects of saving, or participating in an IDA program, but it does not necessarily mean that the level of savings would offer major financial security in the future.

Security

Some IDA participants (28) and nonparticipants (9) said their savings provide a sense of security. Sometimes they referred to short-term security. As we saw in chapter 6, savings provide a backup to cover unplanned expenses and emergencies. IDA participants can choose to withdraw IDA savings in an emergency.[5] The median number of months in which unmatched withdrawals were taken by participants in this sample was 3 (range 0 to 21), suggesting that many people needed or could not resist using the money along the way.

A participant explained that it is comforting to know she can use her IDA money in an emergency (even though she only made an unmatched with-drawal in one month during her time in the program). "I mean I know it's there. I know I can use it when I need to. And if I did have an emergency and I did need to take it out, I know I can do that too."

The security that accompanies savings reduces feelings of stress. Backup funds function as a form of insurance when income flows are irregular. In one person's words, it is a "relief" knowing that her savings are there if she needs them. (Apparently, she did need them; after the interview she made at least 14 unmatched withdrawals.)

> It's just nice to know that . . . if money is going to be tight . . . you can still with-draw that money if you need it. And I haven't had to do that yet. But there has been a couple of times where that has been a relief to me to know that that money is there. So it's a little less stressful.

Some participants partition their savings, using one account for short-term security and the IDA for long-term investment. One participant keeps a sepa-rate savings account as a backup for her business ("something that keeps me from getting frantic when I'm not making any sales"). Another IDA participant has a short-term savings account that holds "security savings money."

> See, I have some savings I have set aside just for one thing and I don't touch that for any reason. Then I have savings that I set aside just in case I need money for something. So, it just depends on what it is that I have saved it for. . . . In other

TABLE 9.1. Perceived Psychological and Cognitive Effects of Saving in IDA (N = 59)

	IDA Participants n (%)
Security	28 (47)
Future orientation and hope	16 (27)
Self-confidence	16 (27)
Personal and civic responsibility	6 (10)

Source: Center for Social Development, in-depth interviews.

words, I have security savings money and then I have money that I have saved up for something specific.

Other respondents talked more about long-term security. Compared to nonparticipants, IDA participants were more likely to discuss long-term security. One IDA participant, for example, referred to her IDA as a "security blanket" that is "there and in our family." In other words, with IDA savings, participants said they would not have to worry about having money in the future, they could afford larger purchases, and they could provide financial protection or an inheritance for their children. An older participant who is saving for her retirement in the IDA said her savings (along with Social Security) provides "peace of mind" as she contemplates her future.

It gives me peace of mind to know that I will have some money whenever I'm too old to work. I mean, I don't plan to retire as long as I'm able to function, but it would be nice not having to work so hard. It's nice to know that that will be there. I mean, there's not going to be a lot because I started so late in my life, but it's better to start now than not at all. It's better to have a little bit than nothing.

Future Orientation and Hope

Many respondents expressed enthusiasm for the IDA program, but one participant, an older immigrant, was especially effusive. He believes the program provides an unusual opportunity. "It has played a most important part in my life. It has restructured a lot of things that I never thought was possible for me normally, before I entered this program. . . . [The] IDA has already set me on the road with an idea, with a goal and an achievement with a purpose in life."

These comments come close to what social psychologist C. Richard Snyder suggests are the ingredients of hope. Snyder writes, "Hope is the sum of perceived capabilities to produce routes to desired goals, along with the perceived motivation to use these routes" (2000a, 8; 2000b). The perception of opportunity, which Snyder says provides a "route" to a desired goal, may generate optimism and greater motivation to act. Hope and focus, therefore, may contribute to more saving and also to other future-oriented actions. The IDA participant continued his description of the opportunity presented by the IDA program.

It opens my intellect. It opens my eyes. It gives me an incentive to go on from where I am. It strengthens me, it strengthens me really. . . . It give everyone a sense of, of being appreciated. It gives you a sense of knowing where you are. It gives you a sense of being independent. To bring out the best in you that you had not known was there. . . . My IDA account gives me an incentive to go on from where I am.

In a sense, he believes that his savings embody hope.

Well, my IDA savings, I will tell you sweet and short, it gives me one thing, it has made me a person to persevere along these lines whether hail or storm comes. It give me the incentive that it is a must in my life. That this have to be done and no matter what, I am going to do it. I have set my goals and I am going to achieve my goals.

Sixteen IDA participants (and five nonparticipants) said their savings instilled hope and opportunity for the future. As a middle-aged widow said, "I know that there's something in there, in the bank, and that if I keep adding to it then, you know, it will help me, help improve my life very much."

Some said that generating savings encourages them to develop other goals. For example, Theresa said her participation in the program and her growing savings encourages her to think more about her goals. "I set my goals again— after I joined the IDA program, because when I joined the IDA program—just going to the classes and listening to the things and saying, 'Okay, this is what I'm saving for. This is how much time I have. This program is three years, so okay.'" As a result, Theresa began to reassess her life in relation to what might be possible with some savings. "I mean, that kind of structured my whole goal setting for everything else that I'm doing."

Similarly, another participant said, "I think it helps, helps a person set your priorities a little bit, you know. And then besides saving for the purpose and accomplishing a goal and feeling good about yourself, that you got a part in it and you got rewarded for doing it too."

For a different participant, the IDA is part of a strategy for reaching a different "level" in life. This includes a better job and income, reliable transportation, and quality housing in a neighborhood that offers greater opportunities. "I mean, [the IDA] changed [my] priorities. I know that if I can take care of the job part and take care of the vehicle part that [the IDA] is going to help out on the shelter part. . . . I couldn't have done near this [well] on my own."

The hope embedded in saving in an IDA appears to create a sense of opportunity as well. A participant saving for house repairs said that this is "the first time I saved anything in any amount that I knew it was going towards something." A single mother of one child who was also saving for house repairs said that before she joined the IDA program, she had given up hope for making any improvements on her house. "It wasn't like a husband and wife making a salary and enough money to put in. It was just me."

Self-Confidence

Accumulating savings boosts self-confidence and feelings of self-efficacy. As we observed earlier, Becky said she feels a sense of accomplishment each time she uses her savings to make improvements on her house. Another participant said he feels good just knowing he's saving: "I could say I feel better about myself—the fact that I know now that I am definitely saving—it seems like it's easy now since I'm in this program and I've started doing it. . . . I feel better about myself in that respect."

Participants may gain self-confidence for several reasons. First, saving feels like the right thing to do. Heather, for example, attributes her growing confidence to saving, as well as to maturity and living according to Scripture: "You know, growing up and learning what you're supposed to do—you know, saving money."

Second, having savings confers security. Another participant, a mother of three teenagers, said that savings give her "confidence" because her life feels more secure. She appreciates the fact that her money is accumulating into something she can invest, but that she can also draw on it in an emergency. Over three years in the program, she made seven withdrawals and eventually accumulated over $2,000 (matched by the program at 200 percent) that she used to purchase a house.

Even people who have difficulty saving say they gained self-confidence, suggesting that the act of saving itself may have some positive effects on self-esteem. Denise, for example, despite her many challenges trying to maintain her savings, asserted that the program makes her feel more confident. As one person said, she feels better about herself because she has learned she can save. "I'm saving more than I ever saved. I'm still not where I want to be or need to be but I am saving. So I feel good about that." Likewise, another asserted that this is the first time she had ever saved any money (other than her retirement fund through work); it makes her feel good about herself. Even nonparticipants feel better about themselves during times when they are able to save, further suggesting that increased confidence may be linked (at least in part) to the process of saving and owning savings, not to the IDA program per se.

Third, it is possible that participating in a program where staff encourage and support participants' efforts to save, instills greater confidence and makes participants feel more hopeful. Participants said that their interactions with IDA staff were more positive than with staff from other human services programs. At the same time, there is little evidence that participants evaluate their saving effectiveness in terms of trying to please or look good to staff.

In contrast, some people experience feelings of disappointment and failure when they cannot accumulate much in savings. Although more common among nonparticipants (see chap. 6), these feelings also occur among IDA participants. Theresa, for example, feels good when she looks at her savings statement but is discouraged by the slow pace and seemingly unattainable amount she will need for a down payment on a house. "Sometimes it can get discouraging because when you look at your balance you're thinking, 'Gosh. I got so far to go. I'm never gonna reach it.'" As a result, Theresa said, "Right now I feel kind of stuck because I haven't put it back and I don't know when I'll be able to put it back in there." In the end, she withdrew all of her savings from the IDA without drawing a savings match.

Another participant experienced even greater difficulty saving because of the financial strain in her household. She feels disheartened by her lack of savings. She described the "rut" she is in trying to make ends meet without support (especially from the children's father who does not pay any child support). But she places most of the blame on herself.

> I was very excited at the beginning ... [but] after getting started and everything ... I've been really disappointed, you know, in myself—not with the program because the program I think is wonderful—It is just, you know, just disappointment with myself, and not—just still being in that same rut, that rut that I've been in pretty much all my life.... It's like you pretty much so stuck in a rut when you are trying, just trying to make ends meet from day to day.

Personal and Civic Responsibility

Interviews reveal that accumulating savings and assets may also contribute to an increased sense of personal and civic responsibility (6). Beginning with personal responsibility, interviews suggest that people think they *should* be saving.

They believe that saving is the mature and responsible thing to do (see chaps. 6, 7). Therefore, when they are able to save, they feel they are accomplishing something beyond reaching a personal goal.

Moreover, the IDA program provides an opportunity to assume responsibility for the future. Several participants remarked that their selection into the program implied trust in their ability to save, making them feel, as one participant said, "the more responsibility you get, the more you do with it."

> [It's] kind of like a trusting . . . it just makes you want to do something good with it. You know? Like if somebody was gonna give you $500, what are you gonna do? Go out and blow it? Or do you spend it on something you know that person would want you to do with it? I think that's the main thing. . . . Just kind of putting it in your hands and saying, "Do something good."

The IDA program, according to another participant, encourages people to take responsibility for their lives. "My financial goals aren't just going to happen [by themselves]." "This is what the American Dream is all about," he said, "if you work hard enough you will eventually achieve your goals." He contrasted this to a "lottery sort of mindset" in America, in which "some people win and some people lose, and so all you can do is just sit there and hope that you win some day." The program reinforces his feeling that "it's what you do that's going to make a difference." A devoutly religious participant feels vindicated by her saving. "I think that it's maybe kind of validated myself as an individual because I have something to wave in the face of the devil when he tries to accuse me of being delinquent or irresponsible."

Some participants believe that making certain asset investments may have an effect on civic behavior. An IDA participant said, for example, that owning a house makes people feel more invested in their neighborhood. "It's like teaching people to read and write. Home ownership changes your life and that you're now invested, you know, in the neighborhood and everything and make people belong in society and their way of thinking and all of that." Similarly, another participant believes the IDA has changed his "outlook" toward others, including those in the IDA classes.

> It's made me, maybe kinder in a sense, more aware, you know. I'm serious. When I was attending these classes and I'd see these people in there who haven't owned a home and who had no chance of owning a home. But when I see them [in the program], they are talking about saving the money that they are gonna

save, you know, man, that feels good, you know. Because you want the people in the world to be able to own their own home, to have their own things and such, you know. And so I guess it's—I don't want to say it's made me kinder and stuff—but it makes you feel good for these other people, you know, that wouldn't get a house, who haven't owned a house in their whole life. And to own a home . . . after you've never owned anything . . . that kind of feels good.

A mother of two young children drew a stark comparison between IDAs and welfare. She suggests that the IDA program encourages altruism, while welfare encourages a survival mentality. "[Welfare] kills self-esteem and it makes you worry about getting by instead of trying to help others. And the best way for people to benefit is to start looking beyond ourselves, to try to help others see that they came to be a benefit to society, and then in turn they'll have their money." Despite the many barriers to civic engagement described by respondents in this study, including lacking time and transportation, these examples hint at a possible link between asset accumulation and civic engagement (McBride, Sherraden, and Pritzker 2006).

ECONOMIC EFFECTS

Nearly two-thirds of IDA participants (38) said the IDA program makes it easier to save. In fact, all IDA participants made at least some savings deposits during the course of the program. In this section, we address economic effects of saving and owning savings in an IDA, including more active participation in mainstream financial services and asset investments made possible as a result of owning an IDA.

Participation in Mainstream Financial Services

Although all IDA participants opened a savings account as part of the program, there is little evidence to suggest that these are first-time savings accounts for most participants. However, interviews suggest that it may be the first time that many actually used a formal savings account to accumulate savings. Further, some participants learned more about financial services in financial education classes. They reported learning how interest rates vary in different financial instruments, how credit scores affect interest rates, how to obtain their credit scores, and how to build or repair their credit records. For example, although this participant left the IDA program because he was having trouble saving, he cleaned up his credit record during the short time he was in the program.

> Yeah, well, the best thing they did was . . . I had someone that I could go to and get my credit report, and go over it. And me and her sat there on the phone and we called the guy up that I owed the money on the truck, you know, the $2,000. That's what they settled for. They said I owed $4,000 and with interest, it was $9,000. So I offered them $1,500 and they didn't take it, so I offered them $2,000 and they took it. That's what made a difference in my life, is going in there, and cleaning that credit report up.

Some participants opened other accounts after joining the IDA program, suggesting that they may have been more inclined to work with mainstream financial institutions as a result of being in the program. One participant opened an IRA, and two others opened new savings accounts. Another opened a checking account for the first time because, she explained, she no longer feels intimidated by the thought of managing an account. Other respondents reported that they are more watchful and careful with their bank accounts because of their participation in the IDA program.

IDA participants also learned more about how to manage and afford different kinds of assets, especially those that are the focus of saving in the program, including home ownership and home repair, retirement savings (especially IRAs), small business development, and postsecondary education.

Asset Investments

By the end of the program, 36 participants drew a savings match. We call them "matched savers." Others—"unmatched savers"—did not draw a savings match. Being an unmatched saver implies little about how long a person remained in the program because most participants remained in the program for its duration. An unmatched saver did not ever draw a match for one of the approved investment options and therefore did not qualify for the savings match.

Some IDA participants and nonparticipants saved for long-term purposes prior to the IDA program, but they reported finding it easier to save for such investments while they were in the program. In the past, many had invested in houses, vehicles, furniture, and other durables.[6] Some had owned savings accounts and retirement accounts, and some were eligible to receive pension benefits in the future. But they reported that the match, match cap, rules about deposits and withdrawals, support staff, and other IDA program features structured and encouraged their saving (chap. 7).

Unmatched Withdrawals. Almost all participants made at least one unmatched withdrawal during the course of the IDA program. That is, they withdrew savings for a purpose other than the asset investments approved by the program and therefore could not draw an IDA match on that withdrawal.

Savers who ultimately made a matched withdrawal also made unmatched savings withdrawals in an average of 2.9 months (median 1 month).[7] Their total mean unmatched withdrawals were $742 (median $82). Unmatched savers, who made more unmatched withdrawals, withdrew savings after an average of 7.7 months (median 6 months).[8] Their total unmatched withdrawals were also higher than "matched savers," averaging $1,747 (median $1,160).[9] Denise, as mentioned at the beginning of the chapter, used her IDA account much like a transaction account, saving a total of $1,300 but taking 11 unmatched withdrawals and never drawing a savings match.

Matched Withdrawals. As of March 2004, the last data point in the ADD research, 36 IDA participants had invested in one or multiple assets, and 23 made no matched withdrawals (table 9.2). The largest number of IDA participants (16) made matched withdrawals for house repairs and improvements. At the time of the interview, one participant had used his IDA savings twice for home repairs. This man and his family are careful money managers and live a thrifty existence, eating from their garden and cutting corners whenever possible. The IDA opportunity came at a time when he "needed it"; he would have had to pull

TABLE 9.2. Purposes of Matched
Withdrawals by IDA Participants (*N* = 59)

	IDA Participants *n* (%)
Matched Withdrawal	
Home repair	16 (27)
Retirement	12 (20)
Home purchase	10 (17)
Education	9 (15)
Microenterprise	2 (3)

Source: Center for Social Development, Management Information System for IDAs (MIS IDA) (2004).

Note: Nine IDA participants purchased more than one type of asset; 23 participants made no matched withdrawals.

the money to cover these repairs from somewhere else. "I'd have had to do something else that might have hurt the family at that time. I don't know what I'd have had to do. I'd had to go sell my truck or something, I don't know . . . and I've got to have that to work, to make money for them."

The match offered by the IDA helped respondents reach savings goals more quickly. In other words, having the matching money eased the family's savings burden and reduced the time they needed to save for the repairs. A participant, whose financial situation had slowly improved, said that without the IDA program, he likely would have used his financial surplus to repair his house. Without the match, his money would not have gone as far. "You know, we might have gotten a back door. Like I said, we're right in that transition period where now we have more money available. So we might have done some work on our house. It needed it but we wouldn't have done $750 worth of work on it."

In another case, when asked what she would spend her money on if she was not in the IDA program, a participant pointed out, "Probably the same thing. It's just that I wouldn't have as much to work with." Another participant explained, "It would just be harder to do the projects. . . . You'd have to wait until next year to finish it up or something, only getting half as much. . . . It would just make the projects longer." The IDA with its savings match made it possible to make improvements at a pace that is visible and encouraging.

> Now [my wife] knows that stuff will get done around the house instead of having to wait. . . . [Before] it would be, "We'll just have to wait until I get some extra money." . . . Now, where we've got the IDA money as long as it is something for the house, we can repair it. So, say if the roof leaks or something, we can get it fixed instead of having to wait on it. If somebody comes in and throws a bottle through the window or something we can get it fixed.

Some participants noted that house repairs increase family net worth. One of the participants mentioned earlier said that with the repairs they made, he believed that the family's net worth had risen significantly. "I'm probably worth $10,000. Whereas two years ago I was, you know, didn't have a net worth. I was at a zero." In other words, he said, "If I sold my house today, we could walk away with $10,000 cash, and we wouldn't owe anybody anything." Another said that her IDA gave her "extra money to use that I wouldn't have otherwise had for my home repairs," which resulted in a "better market value for my house."

Twelve IDA participants invested at least some of their accrued savings in a retirement account, mostly in Roth IRAs. Relatively few (8) owned retirement savings when they joined the IDA program. Moreover, several told stories about withdrawing money from retirement accounts when they needed money in the past. Retirement appeared to be a bigger concern for older participants, although three younger participants invested their surplus savings in a retirement account after using the bulk for a house or other asset. They reported that owning retirement funds increases their sense of financial security over the long term (see next section).

Although 25 of the 59 IDA participants originally were saving for a house, in the end only 10 withdrew money for a down payment. Some likely chose a house purchase as their initial goal because of the higher match rate (two dollars to one instead of one to one) but by the end of the program had not accumulated sufficient amounts to qualify for a down payment. Some never drew a matched withdrawal, and others switched their savings goal, despite the lower match rates.

Nine IDA participants withdrew savings for education.[10] One participant, for example, said that with her IDA savings she can afford to pay for tuition and books, and dedicate her household income to supporting her children. She suggests that without her IDA savings, she might have had to cut corners on her children's school clothing to cover her college tuition.

> [The IDA] will free up other funds that I can use. . . . And part of my school money, by having the money in an IDA account, and them matching it, my tuition is gonna be exactly covered by that money, and my books. I may end up with a couple dollars for my books . . . which means my children will have some clothes when school starts.

Only two participants invested in a business. Fred is one of them. He described the IDA as "my road map to my own business." "It's my highway to my own business. . . . That's my future business sitting up in that Bank of Oklahoma. When I get that match, it's gonna open the doors." At the end of the program, Fred withdrew $6,750 for his business.

EFFECTS ON CHILDREN AND FAMILY

As Michael Sherraden (1991) suggests, assets may have positive effects on the next generation. Of the 42 IDA participants with children at home, 17 mentioned positive effects on their children's welfare. Some noted direct welfare effects, including having savings to help pay for their children's education, improved living environment (including home purchase or home repairs), or some future need. Others noted the benefits of the IDA program and saving on attitudes and behaviors related to money and saving.[11]

Regarding direct benefits, an IDA participant observed that home improvements made possible by the IDA have had a positive effect on his children's health: "[We] got rid of the old dirty carpet, holding all that dust and stuff. So now they don't sneeze."

A middle-aged participant saves for her retirement because she wants to be able to care for her grandchildren. She considered saving for her daughter's education, but ultimately decided that work and loans should cover those costs. Instead, she decided to save for her own retirement so she will be in a position to help her daughter when she has children of her own.

> So I can keep my little grandkids.... So they can have a place to come play and see their grandma and I can feed 'em. Actually I would even like to ... if I'm in that situation where I could, watch her kid or kids ... because that is really a big thing these days with day care. It costs so much.

Others said they are better models for good financial management and saving behavior for their children. With a better understanding of household finances they attribute to their participation in the program, some respondents also try to teach their children about household financial management. One respondent thinks it is wrong that people used to keep all money matters secret from their children. Looking back, she is disappointed that she did not learn about saving earlier. "Family business was so secretive. You know sometimes they didn't find out if anybody had money until after they died, or something." She believes this is a "detriment" for children. "I wish my family would have explored those arenas. But they never came out of that little hub they were in."

Similarly, another single mother explains the family's financial situation to her three children.

> I sat down with the kids ... right after I went through one of the programs talking about showing your kids, you know, what the money situation is. And so that was when I got into doing that with the kids. And basically what I did [was] write down all the things that they would want to spend money on and then I showed them my income and what all of our bills were and how much money we had left and, you know, I said, "Okay, so if you were gonna do all these things [you want to do] ... this is what it would leave us for groceries and gas, for us

to get anywhere. So, you know, is that feasible or is that not feasible?" And they were like, "No way. That's not gonna work." So it was an eye-opener for them and an eye-opener for me, because it made it easier for me because then they really understood.

She concluded, "I don't think any of them have worried about it or anything." But many people do not share that opinion. In fact, one participant has a friend who believes that talking to children about household finances will provoke unnecessary anxiety. "He feels like that's a grown-up thing and kids shouldn't have to worry about [a family's] financial situation." Prior to the IDA program, she would have agreed. But after taking the classes, she now believes that children worry about the family finances whether or not their parents discuss them. She believes they are more likely to worry—like she did as a child—when they do not understand what is happening. They wonder, "Am I gonna have a roof over my head? Are we gonna have groceries on the table?" She continued, "I don't want them to worry, but I want them to understand when I say 'no' . . . I don't have that. You know, it's hard for them to understand. I don't want them to be worried that we're gonna starve or anything like that, but they have to know."

Some borrow ideas from IDA classes to teach the children about financial matters, including Denise who said the children are sometimes invited to participate in financial education activities.

This summer we took the kids on a field trip to the Bank of Oklahoma downtown, and they . . . talked about saving. And they taught them how to write out checks. And we went to this accounting place. And I thought it was so neat because I was going through the same thing with my money management classes and I was really learning stuff too.

Another mother is teaching her 12-year-old son how to manage his money using the "envelope system" they teach in IDA classes. She teaches him to separate money that he earns and receives as gifts into envelopes for tithing, savings, and his small business. Overall, she said, "I have no doubts that he will have a real sense of money."

She is proud that her 12-year-old son, who earns tips as a magician in a small restaurant, saved enough money to buy presents for the family for Christmas. Unfortunately, she cannot set up a savings account for him because she is afraid the "government" will find out and she will lose their welfare benefits. "If he gets a savings account—that counts against our food stamps. It actually takes food out of our mouths for him to save money. So we have to save money, cash on hand."

Another person hopes that his family's experience in the IDA program will be a catalyst for teaching his preschool children to grow up to be financially responsible. He and his wife hold out on buying expensive things for their children. "We never indulge that because, quite honestly, we didn't want them to end up like me, you know, with the sense that you should always be able to get whatever you want all the time. So we're trying to keep it pretty conservative." Unlike his own experience growing up, he wants them to understand how to make sound and productive financial decisions. "I'd like to think they see a connection between what they do and what they get, because I didn't always see that connection, you know."

He also believes that his improved ability to manage and save money has contributed to better family relations. Growing up, he learned little, but since joining the IDA program, he has learned how to save and is thinking more about the long term, something that his wife has been encouraging him to do for a long time. Before the IDA, "it was just a losing battle," but he believes that since joining the program, "it's made things less stressful for her" because he is getting "a little more serious."

> That's just something we don't argue about very often anymore. Our goals are a lot more similar. We can talk about where we want to be in three months or six months, or a year. And we're basically going in the same direction. Whereas before, it was real obvious we weren't going the same direction.

Families teach their children not only about how to manage finances but also about how those finances might be linked to other priorities. One participant, a single mother with two young children, observed that her family spends more time together as a result of reducing expenses to save money in the IDA. "Now that I'm trying to . . . stay on a budget and not spend as much money, we do a lot of things together that doesn't always cost a lot of money." At the end of the program, her $416 savings were matched and rolled into a retirement account.

A SAVING HABIT?

It is often assumed that people can develop a saving habit that, once established, will help people save in the future. In this section we explore what participants reported about their saving habits.

Half of the IDA participants (30) said they learned how to save in the program, 33 said the program makes it more likely they will save in the future, and most intended to continue saving after the program ended. One participant asserted he will have a savings account "forever." Another declared, "We're gonna save even if we're not in the program." Another planned to continue saving after the IDA ended. "When the program is over, definitely I will have a set savings plan. And I will save something every month. And it's because of the program." All of these participants successfully received a savings match in the IDA program.

Many claimed that saving has become a "habit" that will help them save in the future. Several people described their future savings plans with certainty. Becky said that saving was becoming a "habit." Another said, "I need to have that habit of saving money so that I know I can achieve those goals." A participant who never had been able to save before the program believes that saving has become a "good habit" and henceforth will be a lifetime practice. "I got these good habits, so I believe it will be a lifetime thing. No matter what, even if my income gets worse, I will probably still put five or six dollars away because it's a habit." Then she added, "You don't have to worry about it," suggesting that once saving becomes a habit, it requires less thought and planning.

Even unmatched savers said they plan to continue saving. Denise, for example, is determined to continue saving. "I'm just gonna continue [saving] for a considerable time. I mean, you know, just, I'm not going to stop. After I purchase [my asset], I'm just gonna keep saving." Another unmatched saver emphasized that the IDA has taught her to make saving a habit even when there is little surplus to set aside.

> Well, just what I can't say enough is [the IDA program] teaches you to practice to save. To make saving a habit. 'Cause I used to think, well, saving, who cares, you know? . . . That was the way my attitude was, why I never had a savings account. . . . I never had $5 to save. I mean, I really don't have the $10 to save but I save it. I make myself have that $10. And you can make yourself, like I said. . . . I just got this thought. I'm known for having a basket on my desk full of candy for people. You know, the money I spend getting that candy, you know, I could be saving it and setting that aside, you know. Little things like that, if you think about the little things like that, that you do, you know . . . it will help. But it has really helped me to get the habit.

Another unmatched saver—who similarly had not saved any money prior to joining the IDA program ("I didn't think it was possible to save anything")—said she learned how to save in the program. Although she is concerned that her poor health might interfere, she plans to continue saving when the program ends.

> I'll probably continue saving now since I've gotten in the habit of it. I'd like to, it's just—I never know how long my health is gonna hold out and I need to have something to fall back on if I get ill again—pay yourself first—so it has given me a good basis of learning how to save and why you should save.

To begin to understand the role that habit might play in saving, we turn to Fred's experience. Fred believes that IDAs get people into the "mood" to save because IDAs encourage change in spending and saving patterns.

> Once you start saving again, it is contagious. It might trickle down to your kids and everybody. It gets you back in the mood to save. Once you get out of the mood of saving the money, it's hard to start back. See what I am saying? Say you have been saving all your life, then it's easy for you to save. But when you start saving and you quit for 10 or 15 years, it's hard to get started [again].

Saving may indeed be influenced by habit (once a saver, always a saver), but, as Katona observes (1974), saving may be reinforced by the sense of achievement savers feel when they save. He notes, "Levels of aspiration may rise with accomplishment . . . so that the acquisition of some reserve funds may whet the appetite to save more instead of weakening the motives to save" (1974, 5). It may be, therefore, that saving is less about individuals developing a habit than about their feeling a sense of accomplishment that reinforces the effort to save. Greater saving leads to more saving as the act of saving becomes a rewarding pattern of behavior.

In any case, an individual must exercise willpower in order to be a successful saver. A key question regarding IDAs, however, is whether the desire to save by itself translates into adequate willpower, or if the desire to save must be coupled with a saving structure that encourages or compels saving. Katona's research suggests that a desire or intention to save may not be enough: "Many people complained that they were unable to carry out their 'good intentions' because important needs to spend came up, and the amounts saved turned out to be smaller than desired" (1974, 6).

One of the goals of the IDA program is to instill a habit of saving that may lead to a lifetime of saving among families with low incomes. If a structured program is necessary for individuals to save, however, we would expect respondents to have more trouble saving after the program ends. Participants themselves were more tentative as they discussed their future ability to save, suggesting that the promise of an incentive and other program features may be influence saving behavior.

One person, for instance, hesitated when discussing his ability to save in the future, saying he would "like to think" that he'd "still see savings as something important," but he sounded doubtful. Another participant provides further insight. She, like others, believes that saving in the IDA program has helped her figure out ways to generate more savings. The program structure, especially the saving incentive, she said, makes saving a "habit," a part of everyday life.

> I think by that time, saving with the IDA, because you're forced into $10 a month. . . . It's something you have to do in order to gain your reward every month. That creates a habit. So you know, at that point, as soon as I get a job, I think it'll be real easy to step into maybe putting something away. . . . I plan to start saving for my house and my car, [and] trying to figure out how to get out of these debts.

However, it is not enough to want to save, she said. There has to be something that compels saving. "It's easy for anybody to say, 'Well, gosh, I should start saving' or, 'Well, I've got a savings account, I should put something in it.' But when you *have* to put something in and you're doing it regularly, it puts it on your mind. You know what I mean?" Her comments suggest that the IDA program structures saving and leads to a different way of thinking and acting.

Others echoed her comments, suggesting that without the matching funds, depositing requirements, reminders, and withdrawal penalties, it may be more difficult to save. As one participant asked rhetorically, "How long would I save without getting that matched? I don't know. . . . If there wasn't some motivation for getting it matched, I probably wouldn't save at all." The importance of direct deposit (chaps. 6, 8) further suggests that participants find that a structured savings program makes it easier to save.

In sum, most of the IDA participants said they plan to continue saving when the IDA program ends because saving has become part of their routine, a "habit." Others are not quite sure and raise the very likely possibility that without the match incentive and other program features it will be more difficult to make the commitment and to follow through on saving. Other research that examines self-predictions suggests that these doubters may have a more sophisticated read on the future than the former—and more naive—optimists. People tend to be overly optimistic because they base their predictions on current intentions without taking into account possible future situations (Tversky and Kahneman 1974; Dunning et al. 1990). Although overly optimistic predictions may be understandable in the heat of the moment (Loewenstein 1996), researchers have found they are also the norm in less impulsive situations (Koehler and Poon 2006). Some (perhaps even more prescient) participants also said their asset investments had associated costs (e.g., home repair or higher monthly mortgage) that might prevent them from being able to save in the future.

MEANING OF SAVING AND OWNING IDA SAVINGS

One couple, who had difficulty saving, said that repairs to their home and car sometimes stretch their financial capacity. But, the husband emphasized, the home and the car "belong to us." What is the meaning behind the phrase "belong to us?" According to respondents, saving and having savings has a range of economic, psychological, and cognitive benefits.

We begin by exploring the idea that savings offer hope for the future. According to the evidence presented in this chapter, watching savings accumulate for a future goal appears to change the way people think about the future and may lead to more hopeful and long-term thinking. In interviews, this is especially evident among IDA participants.

Somewhat ironically, although raising children makes saving difficult, children are a major reason why parents save. More than a third of parents with children in the home link their savings directly to their children's current or future welfare. Not all of them intend to invest their savings directly in their children, but they perceive that savings, as well as present and future assets, will provide increased security and future opportunities for their children.

There is qualitative evidence that in some cases, the structure of the IDA program may contribute to a different understanding about the role of savings in the family. One couple always saved money, for example, but said it was out of a sense of responsibility instead of understanding what savings could do for the family. The husband believes that the IDA program helped him appreciate the real value of owning savings. "I was saving then just because it's something you're supposed to do. I'm saving now because I've learned the benefits of what it does. You see what I'm saying? There's a difference."

What might account for this cognitive shift? Kenneth provides some insight. With a small income from part-time work, Kenneth, like most other respondents, learned over many years how to be careful with his money. He became especially careful after filing for bankruptcy in the 1990s. After joining the IDA program, however, he shifted his focus from spending to saving, as he watched his growing retirement fund with pride.

> Since I joined the program maybe [my focus] has changed a little bit because since I've joined the program I've managed to save a little bit of money every month for going on a year now. And so of course that's made me feel a little better and it's made me know that you can save money, you know, if you just really work hard and really strive hard.

Ordinarily, Kenneth said, trying to save is a waste of time because the temptation or need to spend is always there, and nothing is forcing him to put some away. "There's always something you want if not something you need. So that $500—if you don't save it, who's gonna get you? Nobody. It's your money. Who's gonna do anything to you? Nobody. So, it's hard, you know, it's hard." In contrast, the IDA program expects people to save, and there is support to follow through. "So it has to be a program like this that will teach you or train you that it's important, but not only that, it's got to be set up to where if you don't do it—there's some kind of a penalty."

Although Kenneth did not feel bad about his prior inability to save, he reports that he feels better about himself since he began to accumulate savings. This feeling of increased self-worth may be linked to his sense that saving is valued by society, but it may also be a direct result of the greater sense of well-being, security, and future options that savings give him.

Further analysis suggests that a savings program may increase people's proclivity and ability to save for the future. Using the same savings categories we used to select participants (low, medium, and high savers),[12] we examine participant and nonparticipant perspectives on saving. The lowest savers are statistically least likely to articulate long-term savings goals (23 percent), compared to middle savers (36 percent) and high savers (41 percent) (table 9.3).[13] The finding that low savers are more likely to articulate short-term savings goals (e.g., having savings "on hand" to pay for consumption needs, emergencies, or to keep from "going broke") and higher savers are more likely to articulate long-term savings goals (e.g., having savings for asset investments or inheritance) suggests that the process of saving or greater amounts saved (or

both) encourage people to think more about future goals and to earmark saving for long-term purposes.

An IDA participant described how her thinking shifted after joining the program. Her desire to save accelerated as she visualized her savings accumulations.

> You go put your money in and they give you your deposit slip and you're sitting
> there saying, "Well, gosh. I've got $350 in there just because I didn't go to Mc-
> Donald's. Maybe I should start saving something. Maybe I should put this
> money I [earned] away for the cable bill." You know, and it just kind of brings
> it up to the front. Instead of something that you *need* to do, it's something that
> you *are* doing, and therefore it spills over to other aspects of your life.

Even respondents who accumulated savings without the assistance of the IDA
program express more hopeful feelings, suggesting a possible independent effect
of owning savings. One nonparticipant talked about how saving and returning to
school give her a different perspective on her family's future: "This had got me in
the thinking mode of saving, and getting ahead, and doing more than getting by."
When the interviewer encouraged her to talk more about this, she described how
saving, along with higher education, has changed her thinking.

> One thing that changed was thinking about our future more. Thinking that I
> could have control of something, you know, thinking, "Wow, I can really plan
> some things." I've always, we always kind of lived, whatever happened, hap-
> pened. You know, never thought, "Wow, I could save for this or plan for this or
> I better plan for this 'cause something might happen." We just never thought
> like that. And so we started thinking, "Wow, you know, this would help us in our
> future. . . ." And just on a basic level . . . if one of us was ever out of work for a
> month and you didn't get workman's comp, you know. How would we pay for

TABLE 9.3. Saving and Long-Term Goals among IDA Participants ($N = 56$)

	Short-Term Savings Goal ($n = 17$) Frequency (%)	Long-Term Savings Goal ($n = 39$) Frequency (%)
Low savers	9 (53)	9 (23)
Middle savers	6 (35)	14 (36)
High savers	2 (12)	16 (41)

$\chi^2(2, N = 56) = 6.444$ $p = .040$

Source: Center for Social Development, Management Information System for IDAs (MIS IDA)
and in-depth interviews.

these? And so to me, it's just basic, everybody should have $1,000 somewhere just in case that happened. You know, and so it was just kind of a thinking for the future. A [future of] not having to rely on my family or WIC[14] or others. You know, a feeling like, "I can do this." And more than that, I can maybe help somebody else.

Having some savings makes her feel more self-confident and optimistic about the future, perhaps resulting from feeling more control over her life (Rodin 1990, 8). This nonparticipant even suggested, like others mentioned earlier, that this may lead her to help others. Behavioral economists suggest that one reason for this outcome could be that people care more for others when they believe they are being treated fairly themselves (Etzioni 1988; Jolls, Sunstein, and Thaler 1998). Although only suggestive, saving and increased optimism about the future may lead to a greater sense of social and civic mindedness (McBride, Sherraden, and Pritzker 2006).

Second, in simple terms, if people have savings, they tend to feel they have more money and more options. In the IDA program, several people opened their first savings account in a bank. Others actually deposited savings in a bank savings account for the first time (many owned savings accounts before but had never made deposits beyond the first one). After joining the IDA program, participants reported saving more successfully than prior to the program. While only 24 percent reported saving regularly prior to the program, 71 percent said they deposit regularly in the program.

Only 12 percent of IDA participants reported being able to accumulate long-term savings prior to joining the program (Hogarth and Anguelov 2003), but once in the program, two-thirds (66 percent) are saving at a middle- or high-level of saving (as defined in this study). Participants attribute their enhanced ability to save for the long term and the change in their perspective to saving in the IDA program.[15]

Indeed, compared to nonparticipants, IDA participants are more likely to articulate a long-term perspective on saving.[16] Furthermore, they are more likely to be saving regularly for long-term purposes (69 percent) compared to nonparticipants (40 percent) (table 9.4) (Sherraden et al. 2006).[17] It is not surprising that IDA participants are more likely to have a long-term saving perspective since they are participating in a program that structures their savings for long-term uses. As a result, they talk a great deal about the investments they plan to make with their IDA savings. By the end of the program, 37 made asset investments with their IDA savings.

Denise articulated the difference between saving on her own and in the IDA program. In the past she had told herself that she was saving for a house, but "in the back of my mind I was saying I wanted a house, but I wasn't working toward that goal." Once she was in the program, she began seriously putting money aside for a house.

However, although she was depositing money in her IDA (she deposited a total of $1,315), Denise was unable to save enough in the three years permitted by the IDA program and never drew a savings match. We observe this pattern particularly among the most financially "stressed" households (Davis 1992). The fact that 22 participants did not draw a savings match suggests that future savings programs should consider several possible issues. These may include additional sources for saving, more household income, emergency backup, medical insurance, or a transaction account. It is also likely that people with low incomes (like others) will experience times when their accounts lie dormant, and a three-year program is too short.

Moreover, although saving may increase people's sense of self-efficacy, the disappointment and discouragement we observe in Denise and others raises the very real possibility that the way IDAs are currently designed may *harm* people's sense of confidence. For people who have lived difficult lives and suffered the ravages of poverty, the time-limited IDA program may become one more failed strategy they have pursued in their quest to improve their lives. It does not seem desirable that one participant said she was "almost ashamed to say" how little she saved.

The financial situation of these participants makes it nearly impossible for them to save for the long term, at least for the time being. This suggests the very real importance of income support policies, short-term precautionary or emergency savings plans, long-term investment plans, and, possibly, forms of "insurance" to protect savings. We return to these ideas in the next chapter.

TABLE 9.4. Time Horizon for Saving among IDA Participants and Nonparticipants ($N = 83$)

	IDA Participants ($n = 58$) Frequency (%)	Nonparticipants ($n = 25$) Frequency (%)
Short-term saver	18 (31)	15 (60)
Long-term saver	40 (69)	10 (40)

χ^2 (1, $N = 83$) = 6.120   Fisher's exact text = .016
Source: Center for Social Development, in-depth interviews.

CONCLUSION

Saving and owning savings appear to have a range of positive psychological, cognitive, and economic effects. First and foremost, participating in a savings program and having savings appears to confer a sense of short- and/or long-term security, a finding observed in other studies on saving (Shobe and Page-Adams 2001; Kempson, McKay, and Collard 2003). In most cases, respondents said that savings provide backup in case of emergencies or unplanned expenses. This alleviates stress because respondents believe they will not have to scrounge or borrow money, or delay paying for something else. It appears that even a small amount of savings confers a greater sense of security. A relatively small amount can make a significant difference, as we observe in Debra's story (chap. 6) of the $1,000 savings that gave her the autonomy to leave an abusive relationship.

Savings also signify future security for savers and their children. In contrast to the short-term perspective so often attributed to the poor, respondents' keen interest in long-term security suggests that low-income individuals do have a future orientation especially if and when a better future is perceived as a possibility. (The large number of respondents with life or burial insurance, observed in chapter 6, suggests a similar idea.) Money set aside alleviates people's concerns about what the future holds.

Saving for the future and accumulating savings in an account for long-term investment purposes may allow people to look toward the future in more positive and hopeful ways. The self-confidence they gain from being able to save underscores Michael Sherraden's suggestion that savings can be seen as "hope in concrete form" (1991, 155–56). Saving seems to make people feel like they are taking greater responsibility for themselves and their families. Some respondents even appear to be more likely to take greater civic responsibility, although more research is needed to understand a possible connection between saving and civic responsibility.

Saving and owning savings in an IDA also encourage more active engagement with formal financial institutions. All participants made at least some savings deposits, even if they were unable to reach their long-term investment goal. Some participants treated their IDA savings account as a transaction account more than a long-term savings account. Nonetheless, even these families who were unable to draw a savings match benefited from the IDA program. They stored their money in a less liquid form (and were less likely to spend it in unnecessary ways), their savings were more secure than at home, and they had precautionary savings on hand. Many other participants drew an IDA savings match and invested in home repair or improvements, higher education, home ownership, or business development. Participants generally commented positively on the influence of the IDA on themselves and their families. Those with young children at home discussed the positive welfare effects on their offspring.

However, there are questions that remain unanswered. First, we do not know if participants are able to continue saving once they leave a structured savings program. Second, it is difficult to know how much the cognitive, psychological, and economic effects identified in this chapter are the result of participation in a savings program and how much they result from the process of saving and/or owning savings. Moreover, we do not know the degree to which the amount of savings (size effects) explains outcomes. These are key questions for future research. Finally, interviews occurred in the first half of the program, and although we have data on savings and matched and unmatched withdrawals that span the entire program, we would learn more about the impact of program participation with data following the termination of the IDA program.

CONCLUSION

Saving Theory, Policy, and Research

Reflecting core American values, respondents in this study believe that saving is essential for survival, being responsible, and getting ahead in life. The study documents respondents' interest in savings products, sheds light on the saving process, and provides evidence of the effects of saving. For these families, having savings balances means something more than having more money. They believe that savings provide security, but they also believe that savings lead the way to a better future. Respondents welcome an opportunity to save, and although many struggle to make ends meet, they believe that setting aside money is essential to make a meaningful difference in their lives and the lives of their families.

We began in the introduction with Camille's story. The money she had accumulated for decades was almost gone because she had to spend it down before she could receive welfare assistance to help cover costs of raising her five grandchildren. She has a small retirement fund in her current job, but she does not think she'll accumulate much before she retires. "[I'm] 57, and I just started doing this, say, four years, five years ago, you know?" Although she did not think she would benefit from the money, it might help her grandchildren. "I doubt if I'll ever use it because it will never be large enough for me to use, but maybe it will benefit them." She wishes there was more. "I just feel like one day when I stop working, you know, whenever that day is, there should be something you could fall back on instead of just having absolutely nothing."

Like Camille, Cynthia is frustrated with her small savings. Although a relatively successful saver compared to other respondents, she believes that it takes more than hard work to accumulate significant savings. Without savings and investments, Cynthia believes there is little hope.

> Because when you have only what you're earning and there's none left over (which I saw a lot in my life) to not even take ten dollars out, you're looking at a very grim world. Because it spells no hope. And when you have no hope, you cannot move to the next phase of things, even if you want it.

Despite high demands on limited incomes, Camille, Cynthia, and the other respondents in this study are anxious to figure out how to live more secure and promising financial lives. Respondents believe that saving is a good idea. Most have tried to set aside savings at some point in their lives, although few believe they have been successful.

Faced with the challenges of covering household expenses, respondents are discouraged about their ability to save. Where can the money come from? What will the family have to give up in order to save? Cynthia asked these questions of herself. Would she quit taking her heart medication? Should a mother pay her utility bill or set aside $10 in saving? "That's when you're up against a big wall."

Nonetheless, Cynthia, Camille, and the other respondents try to set aside some savings by pinching here and there. As LaVonne said in the book opening, families "need some kind of savings." They use a variety of psychological and behavioral strategies, including focusing on savings goals, using mental accounting, monitoring expenditures, arranging for direct deposit into a savings account, setting aside surplus money, and adopting rules of thumb about depositing and withdrawing their savings (Shefrin and Thaler 1988, 1992; Beverly, McBride, and Schreiner 2003). They save under a mattress or in a closet, in a savings account, at a relative's house, in a savings bond, or in a retirement account. Respondents often have different rules of thumb about using these different pots of money (Zelizer 1989, 1994; Thaler 1990). Despite the desire and effort to save (some make many deposits), they often struggle to make deposits or have to make withdrawals for immediate needs. As a result, total savings tend to be low. Typically they blame themselves, family members, or lack of income for saving failures. Many describe saving on their own as an exercise in frustration.

Moreover, their savings are often within easy reach. This, according to respondents, is both an advantage and a problem. The advantage is that their savings are available when they need them to prevent overdrawing a checking account or to cover an emergency, for example. This provides security, a definite benefit in a low-income household. Respondents provided many examples when even small amounts of savings prove helpful.

The problem is that they are easily tempted to use their savings before they can accumulate the larger amounts. While a number of people manage to save successfully for things they cannot cover from regular income flows, money saved at home is especially at risk of depletion. Withdrawals of discretionary savings from a bank account or other instrument is less tempting because it requires effort and gives respondents time to reconsider, but this seldom prevents people from using the money when needs (or sometimes wants) arise. Moreover, there is little advantage, incentive, or expectation to keep this money in savings. Interest rates are low. There are no tax advantages. Accumulations grow slowly. In households where the demand for available cash is high, maintaining savings is difficult.

Some respondents invest in CDs or savings bonds. These alternatives keep savings out of sight and impose a penalty for early withdrawal, thereby making funds less liquid and less vulnerable to spending. Respondents tend to draw on certain income sources to save in these instruments, such as a tax refund or a child support payment. Nonetheless, saving in these forms requires surplus funds and considerable determination on the part of the saver.

Respondents find it easier when they precommit to saving through contractual savings plans. Paying on a home mortgage, buying life or burial insurance, or investing in a defined-contribution retirement plan, for example, have required payment schedules or require no action of the individual other than "enrolling." As George Katona suggests, contractual saving does "not result from strong motives to save." Katona continues, "Although the desire to accumulate financial reserves arises early, most younger and lower income families 'save' by buying a house for their own occupancy and buying durable goods, contributing to social security and private pensions, and not by putting money in banks or securities" (1980, 13). This is the way most people accumulate assets.

One problem is that even though contractual plans offer better terms and incentives than other forms of saving, most poor households lack access. Generous savings plans, such as retirement plans where employee savings are matched by the employer, are least likely to be available to the poor. Moreover, tax-advantaged contractual savings plans, such as 401(k)s, are not a great benefit to the poor whose tax liability is low. Only a small number of respondents had participated in contractual savings plans (other than home ownership and insurance). Another problem is that the poor, in their search for better returns, sometimes lose their money through poor investment decisions and financial scams. Finally, although contractual savings are less vulnerable to depletion than residual and discretionary savings, families sometimes withdraw contractual savings, often exacting significant penalties (McCarthy and McWhirter 2000). In the face of income constraints, even contractual savings may become vulnerable to spending (Levin 1998). These problems suggest a need for regulation that prevents exploitation, financial education for low-income consumers, and increased access to saving plans that are advantageous and practical for poor families.

Overall, the families in this study have had little opportunity to save in plans designed for their circumstances. While small precautionary savings provide crucial backup for low-income families, respondents expressed frustration about the challenge of accumulating long-term savings. Without a structure and assistance in depositing and shielding savings from withdrawal, low-income families stand little chance to accumulate significant sums.

"WE NEED MORE KEYS"

Camille thinks she has to will herself to save. She knows it is difficult. "When you're not in the habit of doing something, you know, and you've got to take that first step. It's just like a baby, you know, knowing you've got to take that first step before you can walk. . . . I just need to take that first step. Just do it."

But how? She believes it will work best if she does not see the money before it is deposited, just like the retirement savings she held in her job in Georgia before returning to Oklahoma to take over raising her grandchildren. She plans to set it up herself using a no-fee savings account available to senior citizens.

> If I set it up on direct deposit, or something like that where I won't even miss it, like it is with the stocks, and the annuity, and the retirement. It's just a matter of doing it, you know, because I'm not going to sit down and write out a check and say this is going to savings. I'm not going to go to the bank and say, "Put that in savings."

She continued, "If they just take it automatically like I have my car insurance [deducted], I think it will work." Although she does not have much money to deposit, she figures that out of the $100 of surplus she carries in her checking account, she could spend a little less and set some aside. "You know, so instead of running around with $100 in my pocket, I'll run around with $75 in my pocket, or $50 in my pocket, you know."

Other respondents are not as patient as Camille. Cynthia, a nonparticipant, believes that life requires hard work. In her 52 years, she has managed to do pretty well, though not without great effort. She believes she has been a good mother and a productive citizen. She works six days a week, saves money for her child's education, goes to church on Sunday, and passes up public assistance even in hard times. "Work's not the problem. In society, to think everybody doesn't want to work—that's a lie. People want to make it. Especially young people coming up today. But we need more information. . . . We need more answers. We need more keys. We need more tools put in our hands."

For Cynthia, an intelligent and ambitious woman, saving is her measure of ability to accomplish something. Having savings helps her envision a future, a future that she wants to create for herself and her son. She explained, "It shows me what I can do and what I have, and it gives me purpose. It shows me I have a goal ahead of me . . . something that I have to produce." What Cynthia knows is that some people have access to more favorable saving and investment opportunities. She expressed frustration as she explained that her savings and financial position do not reflect how hard she has worked her entire life.

"Savings has to go to bigger levels. Just having your money sitting in a regular bank doesn't make gross income." Although Cynthia knows better savings options exist, she feels ill equipped to choose one. "This is the kind of stuff me as a little bitty person don't know." She wants advice. She cleans the houses of wealthy people and knows they have brokers, but she wonders, "What is a broker? But you know what? I'm gonna find out. I might be a little ant in the corner or a roach on the floor, but I'm here, you know."

Cynthia understands that she is not alone. Many people lack access to the types of information and technology necessary to invest on favorable terms (Brimmer 1988).

> Saving is the only tool we have. Investment is the only tool we have. But we don't know how to get into these arenas. It's shut out to the poor and the middle class. You're very seldom around people who have that kind of influence or knowledge, depending on where you work. I mean, most people work on the street. I mean, let's be for real.

In the past, well-heeled employers, who no doubt recognized Cynthia's capabilities and motivation, had offered investment advice.

I had the advantage of going into people's homes who are very reputable people and people that's money holders in this very city. And I've learned so much from a lot of them because they would tell me things and speak about it. One man told me, he said, "You know the greatest thing you can do for your son?" (And this man was a VP. . . .) He said, "The greatest thing you can do for your son is go through the newspaper, find a good stock you want to invest in. Start minimal. Put it in your son's name. Do that for him."

But Cynthia recognizes that "little nuggets like that" are not enough. "Don't just tell me, 'You need to save.' Or, 'Are you saving?' Help me. Show me the arena. Give me the arena. Give me access to the arena. And I'm gonna go there, because this is my lifeline to the future." Cynthia and other respondents make it clear that they have few such opportunities. Other than the few with access to 401(k) plans through work, respondents know of no programs that will match savings. As Cynthia explained, it is even difficult to get information on how to invest savings.

Nobody takes the time to say, "Let me give you a little information how to get on that track," to start doing that. Because a lot of people don't know about investing. A lot of ethnic groups don't know about investing. We've never been in that arena.

SAVING IN LOW-INCOME HOUSEHOLDS

The theoretical perspectives discussed in chapter 2 make assumptions and have implications about saving in low-income households. Neoclassical economic models suggest that people rationally decide how much to spend and save. Economists expect low-income households to save small amounts for precautionary reasons, and they expect attractive incentives to encourage saving to some degree. However, because of income constraints, economists do not expect poor households to accumulate very much.

Behavioral economists identify psychological and cognitive issues that often make saving difficult. Richard Thaler and Shlomo Benartzi (2004) identify several problems that people confront in their efforts to save. Instead of being the rational optimizers proposed in neoclassical economics, people tend to be "quasi-rational"; their emotions and perceptions tend to interfere with rational thinking (Thaler 2000, 137). People tend to lack the self-control to set money aside for future benefit, and people have a tendency to procrastinate (Akerlof 1991). People overvalue the present over the future; what they are doing now is more important than what they plan to do in the future (Thaler and Benartzi 2004, S168). A bias toward the status quo leads to inaction and inertia. Finally, people feel losses more than gains; for example, the loss of disposable income weighs more heavily than an equivalent gain in savings (Thaler and Benartzi 2004, S170).

As we have seen in this study, people often recognize and can articulate these problems. They try to address them by framing or mentally assigning money to different accounts—making money less fungible (Kahneman and Tversky 1979; Thaler 1985; Shefrin and Thaler 1988). People figure out ways to precommit to future saving in an effort to resist spending in the present. Behavioral economists suggest that savings programs—if well designed—can accommodate or help people overcome lack of self-control, tendency to procrastinate, status quo bias, and lopsided perceptions of loss (Laibson, Repetto, and Tobacman 1998; Thaler and Benartzi 2004). Important features of savings programs include simplicity, automatic enrollment, financial education, automatic deposits, and precommitment to saving in the program. In addition, savings programs allow participants to time increases in saving to wage and salary raises (Stegman 1999; Beverly, McBride, and Schreiner 2003; Thaler and Benartzi 2004).

In other words, savings programs can accommodate human shortcomings. So far, however, the poor have not benefited from what we know about human behavior and saving. Savings plans help wealthier people save. Why not also the poor?

Building on economic and psychological observations about people and saving, institutional theory suggests that savings plans consist of a bundle of features that reflect access, security, incentives, information, facilitation, expectations, and restrictions (Sherraden, Schreiner, and Beverly 2003; Beverly et al. 2008). Using the lens of institutional theory, we can see how the poor are excluded from savings programs. For example, incentivized employment-based retirement savings programs cannot structure and reward saving for the many low-income workers who lack such benefits. Similarly, direct deposit into savings does not facilitate saving for low-income households that lack a bank account or lack access to this service through their workplace.

Individual Development Account programs are a deliberate effort to design a savings program that takes into account the challenges to saving faced by low-income families. IDAs are consistent in a number of ways with institutional and behavioral economic principles, so there is reason to believe they will be effective. But how well do they actually work?

Saving in Individual Development Accounts

Anticipating people's difficulty saving, IDA programs support saving efforts. They do this by urging would-be savers to commit to saving and to focus attention on a meaningful and valued savings goal (Hoch and Loewenstein 1991). They provide a generous match incentive, access to a secure account, financial education, and other encouragement.

The incentive—a large savings match in this case—catches people's attention. It attracts them to the program, encourages them to save, and helps them accumulate savings more quickly. Because of the match, participants view saving in the IDA program as an authentic opportunity and a realistic way to reach their goals.[1] Participants soon learn, however, that the match is only one program feature. The program also requires participants to identify a savings goal, attend financial management classes, and follow rules about deposits and withdrawals; it provides savings monitoring, deposit reminders, and offers of other assistance. Most participants said that each program feature helps them to save.[2]

In fact, perhaps surprisingly, participants generally appreciate program rules and restrictions. They perceive the program as offering "choice" and an "opportunity" to pursue their goals. Rather than focusing on the ways that rules constrain choice, they tend to interpret rules from a "big picture" perspective. They draw a clear distinction, for example, between the IDA program and "welfare" programs. The former they see as offering genuine opportunity, while viewing the latter as restrictive and dead-end. The IDA program empowers, they suggest, while "welfare" makes participants feel irresponsible and unworthy.

Participants said they found it easier to save in the IDA program, compared to their own prior saving. Participants also seemed to find saving easier than nonparticipants. They said it helps to be in a program that expects saving. The rules help them resist pressure to withdraw savings. In essence, IDA participants turn to the program as motivation and backup to support their saving efforts, while nonparticipants try to force themselves to save and to maintain savings as best they can. In this way, saving in the IDA program is like saying out loud, "I will save and attend financial education classes, and in return I will get a savings incentive and encouragement." As an IDA participant pointed out, IDA program requirements "make it easier" to save. Without rules, he said he would save only irregularly. In other words, individuals are willingly handing over some individual volition to a program that structures their saving actions. Respondents' reactions suggest that an attractive savings program can have rules and requirements without being perceived as heavy-handed or exploitative.

Most participants in the IDA program made savings deposits. They exert effort and willpower to set aside these savings, using a range of psychological and behavioral strategies for depositing and maintaining savings (see Beverly, McBride, and Schreiner 2003). Overall, they seem to apply these strategies more consistently and with greater enthusiasm and optimism than nonparticipants. Reflecting principles of behavioral economics, they mentally track their income and expenses in order to earmark particular flows for saving, including part of a paycheck, "extra money" earned in tips, or earnings from odd jobs. Some incorporate saving into monthly bill paying, consequently relieving the pressure to make a decision each month about when to save. Some adjust spending, economizing as needed, to come up with deposits. Some look ahead to a windfall, such as a tax refund or insurance settlement, for saving. They keep their eye on the match cap as their savings goal or "anchor" (see Kahneman and Tversky 1979). The specific path for saving varies depending on respondents' circumstances and inclinations.

Reaching a long-term savings goal is more difficult. Like other restricted saving vehicles, IDAs make savings somewhat illiquid. When participants withdraw savings for unapproved purposes, they forfeit the savings match, a whopping 100- or 200-percent penalty. They may also jeopardize their participation in the program if they make too many unmatched withdrawals. In accordance with prospect theory, they are loath to forfeit the IDA match (see Kahneman and Tversky 1979). To avoid withdrawals, and to comply with IDA program rules, participants adopt rules of thumb to discourage withdrawals. For example, they create rules about what constitutes an "emergency," and they keep their accounts secret. Others try to ignore their savings accounts (see Hoch and Loewenstein 1991; Ainslie and Haslam 1992; Schelling 1992). As Paul Webley observes in his work on saving in childhood, even children understand the value of keeping money out of sight in order to avoid the temptation to spend it (1999). With the help of bank statements, some participants visualize their savings accumulations and the progress they are making toward their goals.

Nonetheless, even with the support and structure of the IDA program, it remains difficult for some low-income families to accumulate much or avoid spending their savings (Schreiner and Sherraden 2007). Sometimes the mental accounting techniques and other strategies they use to deposit and maintain savings are insufficient. For others, small incomes cannot cover household consumption demands.

Behavior, Habit, and Institutions. A key theoretical question about saving is the degree to which saving and savings accumulations are the result of individual behaviors, saving habit, or participation in a supportive and well-designed savings plan.

To participants, saving in an IDA feels like individual behavior because personal agency remains a significant factor. After all, as the previous section underscores, each participant decided to join the IDA program, and in order to save successfully each identifies sources for saving, changes some consumption patterns, makes deposits, and maintains them for a period of time. Without a doubt, saving in an IDA requires conscious saving behavior by participants.

Some IDA participants say that because of their participation in the IDA program, saving has become semiautomatic because they have developed a "saving habit" (chap. 9). Habits streamline or remove the need for deliberate decision making because they lead an individual "to engage in a previously adopted or acquired form of action" (Camic 1986, 1044). Habits are important because they help people economize and simplify human action, minimizing conscious decision making (James 1890; Twomey 1999). John Dewey suggests that habit is more than a "fixed way of doing things," it is how actions and experience modify the individual and affect subsequent experiences (1938, 35).

Therefore, when participants say they have developed a "saving habit," they are indicating that they no longer have to exert as much effort. A saving habit is an individual-level explanation. It implies that people achieve a psychological or cognitive state that makes saving more or less automatic, and which may be reinforced by certain strategies (e.g., adopting rules of thumb).

An alternative explanation for saving is that what people perceive as a saving habit is—at least in part—the result of actions shaped by the savings program itself. In other words, participants act in certain ways because the IDA program structures their actions in ways that support and expect saving. It is difficult for people to visualize how institutional structures affect action. Nonetheless, participants' comments in chapter 7 make it clear that institutional features (e.g., saving incentive, rules about depositing and withdrawals) have a great deal to do with their increased ability to save and accumulate savings. For example, participants are more likely to discuss the $10 monthly deposit obligation in terms of meeting a program requirement (or a savings goal) than as a matter of habit (although a few did). Further, many participants plan to meet the annual match cap by capturing windfall income, such as their tax refund. Although a person could plan to save all future income tax refunds, we would probably not view this as a habit but as institutional influence that results in individual saving action.

Nonetheless, we must ask, is it possible that over time the IDA program instills a saving habit? Saving in the IDA program lasted three years. If it led to habituated saving behavior, the institutional structure and support would not be necessary to maintain the behavior. Or does saving require ongoing external reinforcement and structure? Although future research must take up this question, in-depth interviews offer some evidence.

Some participants and nonparticipants, including Camille, Cynthia, Ella, LaVonne, Theresa, and others, view their ability to save as linked to a savings structure and plan. Others, including Denise, Heather, and Becky, view their ability to save as largely a matter of habit. In the lexicon of behavioral economics, these differing perspectives may reflect more "sophisticated" or more "naive" understandings of willpower and self-control. The former (we might call them pessimists) have an intuitive understanding of the strength of their consumption preferences and the necessity for precommitment and inflexibility, while the latter group (optimists) believe that their current behavior can be sustained (Tversky and Kahneman 1974; Dunning et al. 1990; Griffin, Dunning, and Ross 1990; Lunt and Livingstone 1992; Buehler, Griffin, and Ross 1994; Koehler and Poon 2006). Optimism is understandable, given that people tend to be overconfident and underestimate the effect of visceral factors and future uncertainty (Dunning et al. 1990; Ross and Nisbett 1991; Loewenstein 1996). Notably, the pessimists tend to be among the most successful savers in this study. Perhaps they are also the most realistic.

In all likelihood, it is an interaction of individual agency (behavior) and institutional structure that induces saving actions. The IDA program assumes some—but by no means all—of the decision-making burden. As noted earlier, although the IDA program incorporates aspects of contractual saving, it is mainly a discretionary savings program. IDA participants must engage in individual action; in other words, they have to find the money and make the savings deposits and resist spending them. Based on the evidence in this study, the IDA program appears to reinforce individual saving behavior and the development of what participants perceive as a saving habit. There is little evidence, however, that individual saving behavior would result in savings accumulations without the program structure.

SAVINGS EFFECTS

Respondents' enthusiasm about joining a savings program and the economic, psychological, and cognitive outcomes documented in this book suggest that having savings is important for low-income individuals and their families.

With regard to economic effects, there are some indications that participation in the IDA program strengthens connections to mainstream financial services and results in saving and asset accumulation. Although this cannot be asserted with total confidence, interviews suggest that participants generated at least some "new" savings. Evidence in support of new savings includes participant observations that saving is easier and the fact that they identify new sources for deposits (new income, tax refunds, and economizing). However, a few participants acknowledged shifting assets from other accounts into IDAs, borrowing to make an IDA deposit, or steering money into the IDA that they previously had directed to another form of savings. Although some may have delayed investing in nonfinancial assets, such as education or a home, there is no evidence of this in the interviews. Overall, asset shifting seems less likely among families in this study, especially the poorest, who reported not being able to accumulate savings in the past (also see Thaler and Benartzi 2004, S185). In addition to any asset accumulation that results from "new" personal deposits, we expect asset levels to increase further when participants draw a 100- or 200-percent match on saving and receive help investing in a long-term asset. Having savings increases security and opportunity because funds are available to weather crises and to invest in the future.

Discussions with respondents suggest that even greater psychological and cognitive effects result from having savings (see Sherraden 1991; Baker and Jimerson 1992; Sen 1999; Wärneryd 1999). Respondents report that saving makes them feel they are doing the right thing. Owning savings also confers a sense of security and control, a finding observed in other research on saving in low-income households (Lunt and Livingstone 1991b; McBride, Lombe, and Beverly 2003). In most cases, respondents talked about short-term security effects, such as having money for an unexpected expense. For some, having savings leads to feelings of long-term security, such as retirement security. IDA participants articulated a long-term perspective more than nonparticipants.

The acts of saving and owning savings also appear to impart a longer time horizon. As Heather told the interviewer, "I'm just beginning to build goals that I wouldn't have thought about if I wasn't in the IDA program." In contrast to the short-term perspective so often attributed to poor people, the way respondents in this study talked about the effects of saving and owning savings suggests that a future orientation may emerge when people have a realistic means to reach their goals (Snyder 2000a; Newberger and Coussens 2008). Many parents, for example, believe their IDA savings will directly or indirectly benefit their children and will contribute to their future opportunities and welfare. This is important because of the role that inheritance plays in building wealth (Conley 1999; Shapiro 2001, 2004). Although it is difficult to know for sure, if parents have savings set aside for postsecondary education, for example, they may be more likely to encourage their children to choose academic pursuits over vocational ones early in life (Hossler and Vesper 1993; Zhan and Sherraden 2003; Zhan 2006; Chowa and Elliott 2007; Elliott and Wagner 2007). This would represent a significant change from respondents' own childhood experiences (chap. 3).

These findings suggest that having savings may change the way people think about their lives, their potential, and the future. Notably, all respondents with long-term savings expressed similar reactions (e.g., feeling more secure, hope for the future), suggesting the possibility that owning savings has an independent effect, although it is also possible that the act of saving itself or participation in a savings program causes the effect. Overall, the findings on savings effects refocus attention on the meaning and implications of holding wealth instead of only on resource flows and consumption levels now or in the future. As Theresa said, "Everybody wants to own something that is theirs." Moreover, interviews suggest that savings may provide much more than a safety net; they may provide a springboard for future development. As Heather explained, saving is encouraging her to develop goals for the future and to escape the poverty she experienced as a child.

In sum, the evidence from in-depth interviews suggests that respondents accumulate more short-term and long-term savings with the help of the IDA program. The process of saving and the accumulated savings appear to result in a range of positive economic, cognitive, and psychological effects.

At the same time, we have also observed that poverty and associated challenges, such as lack of health care and unstable neighborhoods, make saving difficult for some families. As LaVonne said, she is "all strained up and stressed out." Although some families blame themselves for their inability to save and maintain savings, the evidence suggests dissaving is frequently the result of circumstances beyond their direct control. These barriers to saving beg for policy solutions. Are there ways to design savings policy that accurately reflects the reality and circumstances of low- and moderate-income families and helps them accumulate savings? The next section explores possible policy directions.

TOWARD SAVINGS POLICY

With people like Cynthia, Camille, and others in mind, researchers and policy analysts have promoted various saving policies for low-income households. In addition to Individual Development Accounts (Sherraden 1988, 1991; Kempson, McKay, and Collard 2003; Schreiner and Sherraden 2007), these proposals include lump sum capital grants for youth (Tobin 1968; Haveman 1988; Sawhill 1989; Ackerman and Alstott 1999; Nissan and Le Grand 2000; Halstead and Lind 2001; Le Grand and Nissan 2003), a refundable Saver's Credit (Gale, Iwry, and Orszag 2004), progressive college savings plans (Clancy, Cramer, and Parrish 2005), children's savings accounts (Sherraden 1991; Lindsey 1994; Goldberg and Cohen 2000; Boshara 2005; Goldberg 2005), and a "super simple" low-cost retirement savings plan (Perun and Steuerle 2008).[3]

Research shows that the poor want to and can save if there are beneficial savings plans in place (Rutherford 2000; Schreiner and Sherraden 2007; Collins et al. 2009). Although it is hard to generalize from a small sample such as is described in this book, respondents' enthusiasm for saving is suggestive and reveals a need for more research, as well as more debate about savings policy for families in poverty. As the United States[4] and other nations, most notably the United Kingdom, Canada, Singapore, and Korea, move toward universal savings policies, this study offers useful insights for policy (Kingwell et al. 2005; Kempson, Atkinson, and Collard 2006; Loke and Sherraden 2006; Sodha 2006; U.K. Department of Work and Pensions 2006).

Universal Savings Policy

The first and most obvious suggestion is to ensure that savings policy deliberately and proactively includes the poor. Current policies are designed for and favor the nonpoor. Like Richard Thaler who admonishes policymakers to "design savings policies for real people," savings policy should reflect the reality of households living in poverty (1992a, 150; Sherraden, Schreiner, and Beverly 2003; Schreiner and Sherraden 2007).

The preeminent example of universal savings policy is the Child Trust Fund (CTF) in the United Kingdom (U.K.) (Prabhakar 2009). CTF provides a savings account for every child born after 2005. Types of accounts vary (e.g., equities, cash deposit accounts, bonds, alternative equity investment) and may be transferred to any financial provider anytime (Gregory and Drakeford 2006). The official goals of CTF are to help people understand the benefits of saving and investing, encourage people to develop a saving habit and engage with financial institutions, ensure that children have a financial asset in transition to adulthood, and build on financial education (Kempson, Atkinson, and Collard 2006). The U.K. government estimates that by age 18 account holders will have savings ranging (in real terms) from U.K.£911 pounds (with no additional savings) to U.K.£14,854 (assuming savings of U.K.£40 per month) (HM Treasury and Inland Revenue, cited in Gregory and Drakeford 2006).

In addition to examining universal savings programs in a wealthy country like the United Kingdom, savings programs for some of the world's poorest people may offer helpful insights. Stuart Rutherford (2005), a pioneer of savings programs in very poor countries, notes that poor families are more interested in savings plans if they offer security and flexibility. Although specific security and flexibility issues may be different in the United States, they remain important. U.S. savings plans, for example, must address a legacy of exploitation and/or discrimination against the poor and minority groups. As we saw in chapter 7, respondents were skeptical initially about the IDA incentive, suggesting that legitimacy is a key concern for savings plans for the poor (Hogan et al. 2004; Shobe and Christy-McMullin 2005). As Cynthia pointed out, saving and asset-building programs must deal with people's experiences of financial exploitation. "A lot of us don't want to venture out because [we've] been scammed. There's people that scam you . . . all kind of bogus ways of saving money. . . . And you wind up losing out. People want a legitimate way. Something that's secure." In this way, security is linked to trust and institutional legitimacy.

Regarding flexibility, savings plans must reflect the reality of living on a limited income. For example, savings plans should take into account low and volatile incomes and lack of insurance. Low-income savers in this study like contractual savings features, as do low-income families in poor countries (Collins et al. 2009); nonetheless participation should be voluntary. One way to accommodate both principles is to adopt "opt out" programs—in which people are automatically enrolled in a savings plan but can decline to participate— thus safeguarding an authentic right to choose not to participate (Sunstein and Thaler 2003). Further, low-income families may find it easier to save when they can vary the size and timing of their savings deposits, when the plan allows withdrawals for emergencies, and when good loan products are simultaneously available (Rutherford 2005, 25).

Simultaneously, policy barriers to saving by the poor, such as asset limits in social benefit programs, should be eliminated, and other factors that threaten savings in low-income households, such as lack of health insurance, must be addressed (Ifill and McPherson 2004; Chen and Lerman 2005; Beverly and Barton 2006; Nam 2008).

Finally, the IDA program was a time-limited program, while most saving occurs in plans that have a longer trajectory. Although we do not know what saving in poor households would look like in a long-term savings program, many IDA participants wished saving in the program extended beyond three years. They pointed out that there are good and bad times for saving. In the end, there may be a trade-off: a time-limited program may instill an urgency to save (and therefore, more motivation), while a long-term program might capture more periods during which a low-income family realistically can set aside savings.

The respondents in this study endorse the idea of a savings plan that is universally available and beneficial for low-income savers. The following sections highlight other key policy features that respondents said would help them save.

Beyond Behavior

Saving would be easier for the poor in plans that facilitate deposits. Observations by behavioral economists about how behavior can be channeled suggest great potential for bringing the poor into savings programs using marketing techniques to facilitate entry (Bertrand, Mullainathan, and Shafir 2004). Nonetheless, while channeling appears to increase enrollment, facilitating savings accumulations in poor households may require more. For example, some poor families may not be able to commit to a regular automatic deduction from earnings, nor do they necessarily have access through their employer and their bank to automatic deposit of pay into restricted savings accounts. In other words, savings plans for the poor and the nonpoor may reflect similar principles but should include key features that address varying income levels.

IDAs facilitate saving by encouraging monthly savings deposits. But they rely more on an incentive (a large savings match) and the desire to save than on default enrollment ("opt out") and automatic deposit features common to defined contribution retirement plans for the nonpoor. In other words, despite a savings program that encourages participation and reinforces individual willpower, participants have an unrealistic (according to behavioral economists, as well as study respondents) responsibility for allocating resources, making deposits, and maintaining IDA savings (Beverly, McBride, and Schreiner 2003).

"Opt Out" Plans. Saving would be easier for the poor if access to a savings

plan is automatic. People often lack knowledge about the benefits of various savings plans (Kempson, Atkinson, and Collard 2006); therefore, it makes sense to offer a simple and attractive savings plan to everyone routinely. They would be able to opt out, but theory and evidence suggest that most would remain in the plan (Thaler and Benartzi 2004).

In the absence of automatic enrollment in a savings plan, people may achieve a similar result by locking themselves into savings. Gerd Gigerenzer and Peter M. Todd (1999) observe that providing good but limited options does not imply that people are hopelessly muddled and irrational. It simply recognizes that people possess limited ability to "know, memorize, and compute," and that it is possible to make satisfactory choices by adopting "rationality through simplicity, and accuracy through frugality" (Gigerenzer and Todd 1999, 33–34).

Some raise concerns about defaults and so-called opt out savings plans because of the potential for manipulation or abuse of savers (Stewart 2005), although new regulations provide greater security for investors in such plans.[5] Researchers have noted that people tend to stay in default plans even when they are bad for them (Madrian and Shea 2001; Choi et al. 2002, 2004). Without a default plan, however, Eric Wanner, an economic sociologist, suggests people are susceptible to manipulation by marketing (cited in Lambert 2006, 95). Cass R. Sunstein and Richard Thaler (2003) recommend savings plans that facilitate and guide people toward beneficial plans, offer accurate and helpful information and assistance in selection, but ensure free choice and the option to opt out. Richard Thaler explains, "Our whole agenda is to create forgiving environments" (quoted in Stewart 2005, 42; Thaler and Sunstein 2008).

The potential for abuse may be even greater in savings programs for the poor. There are many examples of mismanagement and exploitation in the name of helping the poor. The choice to opt out guards against some abuses (Hirschland 2005), but additional features would also likely have to be incorporated. Plans should be fully transparent, include oversight, provide financial education to savers, and be subject to ongoing research and evaluation.

Automatic and Lump Sum Deposits. Participants have to exert willpower to resist spending and set scarce money aside for the IDA. In an IDA, the participant must mail in or hand-deliver a monthly deposit, a daunting prospect for even the most motivated saver (only a few IDA participants in this study have access to direct deposit). They must attend orientation and financial management classes that are offered in the community (not at the workplace on company time). This reality differs markedly from work-based retirement savings plans where, after initial enrollment, employers deposit an employee's savings automatically every pay period, and employees are given time off to attend optional financial seminars. It is doubtful that the typical person in an employer-based retirement plan would make as much effort as many people are required to make in an IDA. In these ways, IDAs differ from defined contribution retirement plans that require no particular "behavior" on the part of participants beyond enrollment.

Therefore, it makes sense to adopt elements of contractual savings plans in savings plans for the poor. This study and others suggest that the poor understand and like contractual savings services, as well as services that include automatic deposit (Romich and Weisner 2000; Cronqvist and Thaler 2004; Hirschland 2005). A simple modification of conventional plans could be automatic deposits of much smaller amounts of money into savings (Hirschland 2005).

Because regular automatic deposits may not be realistic for some people, another option is to offer what Hirschland (2005) calls "time deposits." Like certificates of deposit, these are lump sum deposits that individuals commit to savings for a specified period of time, but they have additional attractive features, such as a savings match. These "time deposits" may be especially well suited for capturing windfall income, such as tax refunds, although they do not provide options for withdrawal in emergencies (Hirschland 2005). Others underscore the importance of long-term contractual savings instruments, accompanied by access to convenient transaction accounts for cash flow management and general purpose loans, in the world's poorest households (Ashraf, Karlan, and Yin 2006; Collins et al. 2009). These recommendations may have to be altered to fit the U.S. context, but they offer ways to begin thinking about how to modify contractual savings plans to meet the circumstances of the low-income saver.

An alternative might build on existing savings instruments (Barr 2004; Caskey 2005; Stuhldreher and Tescher 2005). For example, researchers highlight the benefits of allowing individuals to split tax refunds, with a portion deposited into savings (Smeeding, Phillips, and O'Connor 2000; Beverly, Schneider, and Tufano 2005), or expanding college savings plans to provide financial incentives for the poor (Clancy, Orszag, and Sherraden 2004).

Toward Financial Capability

The poor should have more opportunities to build financial knowledge. In order to overcome potential challenges and risks of savings plans, consumers need better information about their financial and saving options (Bernheim

1994; Clancy, Grinstein-Weiss, and Schneider 2001; Kotlikoff with Bernheim 2001). Further, they have to know how to find resources to deposit, how to use savings instruments effectively, and how to avoid dissaving (Lusardi 2008).

However, financial literacy is not enough (Stuhldreher 2005).[6] Some argue that the case for financial literacy lacks empirical evidence, and the benefits are doubtful given the often confusing array of financial services (Willis 2008). The outcome for some consumers, posits Lauren Willis, is that "financial education appears to increase confidence without improving ability, leading to worse decisions" (2008, 3). Ultimately, an emphasis on financial literacy alone focuses blame on the consumer and may substitute for regulatory safeguards (Willis 2008). As the earlier discussion about agency and habit suggests, financial education will be more effective when paired with inclusion in financial institutions and savings plans (Sherraden and Barr 2005). We have called this "financial capability," a combination of financial knowledge and competence and, importantly, the opportunity to act in ways that benefit the consumer (Johnson and Sherraden 2007).[7] Financial capability involves linking individual functioning to institutions. Financial education is likely to play an important role in saving, but only when paired with access to beneficial savings plans. Financial education paired with a financial account, for example, can make "book learning" come to life and provide benefit to the consumer.

Participants have generally high regard for financial education in the IDA program, although we find some variation. The curriculum occurred in two parts, beginning with basic money management and followed by asset-specific training. Some participants find money management helpful; others find it too elementary. Almost everyone who had taken asset-specific training said it was useful, although at the time of the interview, most had not yet taken those courses. Moreover, there is a group of participants who lack knowledge of financial management and financial services and face serious obstacles in saving. They require more intensive training and guidance. On one hand, these observations suggest that financial education curricula should vary according to diverse student interests and needs. On the other hand, targeted curricula pose a dilemma for IDA programs because financial education is among the more expensive features of IDAs (Schreiner 2005). Providing a choice of financial education modules according to student needs would make it even more costly.

This dilemma highlights a need for a broader approach to financial education that begins in early childhood and continues throughout a person's life. Financial education in the schools could lay a foundation of financial knowledge

(U.S. Department of the Treasury 2002; Beverly and Burkhalter 2005; Greenspan 2005). Decisions about content and application can be informed by research on economic socialization (Lunt and Furnham 1996), how and when children absorb economic concepts (Berti and Bombi 1988; Sonuga-Barke and Webley 1993; Elliott and Sherraden 2007), children's economic lives (Webley and Plaisier 1998), and approaches to program delivery (Sherraden et al. 2007; U.S. Department of the Treasury, 2009).

A developmental approach to financial education could be productive. Coupled with the fundamentals taught in school, specific topics could be covered during times when people face important financial decisions: when youth begin to earn money for the first time, at high school graduation, when entering college, at enrollment for job benefits, when deciding how to handle retirement accounts during job transitions, when borrowing to purchase a house or car, or at retirement (McCarthy and McWhirter 2000). Motivation to learn may be higher and financial education may be more successful in influencing behavior during these "teachable moments" (U.S. Government Accounting Office 2004; OECD 2005). Mass public education and hotline advice can reinforce lessons in financial management but are likely insufficient by themselves (Bernheim 1991, 1994, 1995).

Finally, community organizations can be organized to provide more in-depth support, mentoring, counseling, and ancillary services for the smaller group of families who would benefit from intensive intervention. A universal savings program would not solve the difficult issues facing these families, including extreme poverty, ill health, mental illness, substance abuse, or domestic violence; nonetheless, along with support services, a savings opportunity could be a crucial element in a developmental plan for very poor, ill, or troubled families (Midgley 1995).

In sum, efforts to build financial capability may be more effective when schools teach the fundamentals, other organizations teach specific topics at key decision points, and government informs people about options through public education campaigns. Moreover, the costs of financial education would be shared across the private sector (e.g., families, employers), public sector (e.g., schools, libraries), and nonprofit sector (e.g., IDA programs, churches).

Financial Protection

Saving in low-income households requires financial protection at both the community and the household levels. In addition to increasing financial capability, low-income families and poor communities need access to improved financial products and services, and protection from policies and practices that have contributed historically to low asset levels (Oliver and Shapiro 1995; Conley 1999; Barr, Kumar, and Litan 2007).

Financial Products and Services. Poor and minority communities often lack access to mainstream financial services, despite policies such as the Community Reinvestment Act that aim to increase access (Avery and Bostic 1997; ACORN 2004; Immergluck 2004; Squires 2004). Financial protection, such as overdraft protection and "real-time" banking (consumers and merchants can check results of transactions as they occur), can also address some financial services market failures and prevent low-income families from having to turn to savings in an emergency (Caskey 1997; OECD 2003; Barr 2004; Kempson 2006).

Regulatory Policy. Better regulatory policy could protect poor people (and others) from predatory lending (Relman et al. 2004; Engel and McCoy 2007). When the poor lack access to good banking products and services, they frequently turn to available, but often costly, credit services and alternative financial services (Caskey 1997, 2005; Rhine and Toussaint-Comeau 1999; Carr and Schuetz 2001; Elliehausen and Lawrence 2001; Rhine, Toussaint-Comeau, and Hogarth 2001; Braunstein and Welch 2002; Barr 2004; Karger 2005). In the last two decades, new lending products in the consumer credit and housing markets made credit more accessible to low-income and minority families (Manning 2000; Stavins 2000; Aizcorbe, Kennickell, and Moore 2003), but some of these new products exploited vulnerable and unsophisticated borrowers.

The median credit card balance for U.S. families in 2001 was $1,900; for nonwhite and Hispanic families, who are disproportionately poor, it was $1,500 (Aizcorbe, Kennickell, and Moore 2003). By 2004, the numbers of families carrying a credit card balance increased to 46 percent, and the size of the balance also grew by 10 percent (Bucks, Kennickell, Mach, and Moore 2009) and averaged nearly $9,000 in 2008 (Morgenson 2008). By 2007, almost 26 percent of families in the lowest quintile of income and 40 percent of families in the next to lowest quintile of income carried credit card balances (Bucks et al. 2009). Although these percentages are lower than they were at the beginning of the decade, families had median credit card balances of $1,000 and $1,800 in the bottom and next-to-bottom quintiles respectively (Bucks et al. 2009). As families face the challenges of paying their credit card debt in the economic turndown (Bird, Wagstrom, and Wild 1999), we remember the words of the respondent in chapter 5 who said, "Compounding interest is an amazing thing. It can work against you or it can work for you."

In mortgage lending, many poor families have become victims of an unregulated financial industry that uses dubious practices (Morgenson and Glater 2008). Consumers with poor credit history and low credit scores often turned to the sub-prime market, where loans have higher interest rates than conventional loans. Financial institutions frequently extended these loans without proper verification of borrower income and credit, and borrowers often did not understand loan terms. During the 1990s, there was a 1,000 percent increase in sub-prime lending, much of it targeted to minorities and the poor (Jacob, Hudson, and Bush 2000; Hinnant-Bernard and Crull 2004; Belsky and Calder 2005). In the first three months of 2009, over five million home loans were delinquent or in foreclosure; almost half of these loans were subprime (Reuters 2009). As a result, millions of borrowers will lose their homes (usually the largest source of household wealth), which will have large spillover effects on surrounding neighborhoods (Schloemer et al. 2006; see also, Lyons 2003; Center for Responsible Lending, 2007, 2008). Moreover, renters, including many low-income families, make up a substantial proportion of people facing eviction due to foreclosures (Pelletierre 2008). This contributes to predictions that almost two million children and youth will be losing their homes (Lovell and Isaacs 2009).

Alternative financial services in poor communities include payday lenders, check cashing or currency exchange outlets, pawnshops, rent-to-own operations (Lacko, McKernan, and Hastak 2001; Stegman and Faris 2003), and auto title lenders. Although they provide credit to low-income consumers (Braunstein and Welch 2002), these financial operations are often exploitative, charging up to 300 percent or more on an annual basis. Moreover, consumers who use alternative financial services in a responsible way do not build a favorable credit record (Brooks 2006). The Center for Responsible Lending has estimated that predatory payday lending fees cost U.S. families $34 billion annually (Ernst, Farris, and King 2004; see also Carr and Schuetz 2001; Smith 2003; Belsky and Calder 2005). Immigrants are charged between $6 and $40 per remittance transaction (Comptroller of the Currency 2004) when most Americans can withdraw money free or for a nominal charge using an ATM.

Policy should reduce the impact of predatory lending—lending that exploits vulnerable and unsophisticated borrowers—on families (Engel and McCoy 2007). Fair lending laws and regulation, which are receiving more attention in policy circles, can further protect the savings of poor consumers (Barr 2004; Brooks 2006; Fellowes 2006).

Shielding Household Savings. The other challenge is at the household level.

Policy should help families protect their savings. Many poor families—recall Denise and others—find it nearly impossible to avoid turning to their savings for household consumption. Although the purpose of short-term savings is often to finance consumption during crises, Denise and others also yearn to reach long-term goals. Some families in the IDA program are under such constant financial pressure to cover basic living expenses and emergencies that they cannot hope to save for these purposes. This suggests the very real need for income support policies that complement asset accumulation strategies (Prabhakar and Gamble 2006). Health insurance and income support (without asset limits) would go a long way to protecting small savings accumulations from the ravages of poverty.

The number of unmatched withdrawals from IDAs described in the previous chapter speaks for itself. Low-income families need precautionary savings, especially because they lack low-cost credit options. Without emergency savings, the poor are unlikely to accumulate long-term savings. Therefore, along with access to long-term savings plans for the poor, they need short-term savings. Possible approaches include an ability to borrow from long-term savings (without penalty), a program that helps the poor maintain small backup savings, and also perhaps a program with small emergency grants for savers (that do not have to be repaid) (Lopez-Fernandini, Seidman, and Cramer 2008).

A related and even thornier issue is how policy should address situations where low-income families must decide between paying debt and saving. As we observed in chapter 5, unsecured debt is often so large that families probably could not save anything for many years, if not decades, if they were required to pay debt first. It makes sense, therefore, to support saving for future investments at the same time that families are paying their debt.

While debt may result in part from poor individual decisions, a lack of protections that other Americans take for granted (such as health insurance or a secure job) and of financial instruments that protect assets underlie low net worth in low-income households (Birnbaum 2008). Given that many families accumulate significant debt because policy does not protect them from the impacts of predatory lending, health crises, or economic downturns, it seems reasonable that policy should address the major challenges to building savings in low-income households. This could be accomplished by developing a debt and savings plan in which poor families pay debt more slowly while building savings. Depending on the nature of the debt, public assistance for debt payment may be necessary. Such plans would not absolve individual responsibility; instead, they recognize that it is to society's advantage that people invest in themselves and their children while simultaneously paying their (legitimate) debts.

FUTURE RESEARCH

This study underscores the value of qualitative research in exploring participants' experiences and perceptions of a matched savings program and the effects of the program on daily living patterns, aspirations, expectations, and achievements in asset accumulation. Participant comments shed light on saving theory and policies. Further, many of the findings in this study reinforce findings from quantitative analysis of IDA programs in the American Dream Demonstration (Schreiner and Sherraden 2007).

This study contributes to understanding how low-income families think about saving and the challenges they face in saving for long-term investments. Moreover, it offers insight into how a structured savings program may promote saving, even among families with little surplus income. It sheds light on the role of individual volition compared to program structure in saving. The study also suggests possible effects of saving for the individual saver, the family, and the next generation.

Figure C.1 is a graphic depiction of proposed theoretical relationships in IDA saving. The figure suggests that well-designed savings programs, with their bundles of institutional constructs (access, incentives, security, expectations, information, facilitation, and restrictions), create hope and focus related to saving. Hope and focus may further encourage people to engage in a variety of saving strategies, which in turn lead to saving and asset accumulation. In some cases, saving does not require conscious strategy on the part of participants other than signing up for the program; therefore, the figure also shows that saving and asset accumulation can occur without individual behavior. Saving and asset accumulation lead to a variety of possible psychological, cognitive, and economic effects. The figure shows feedback loops, with effects possibly encouraging more saving strategies and enhancing hope and focus (Sherraden 1991; Schreiner and Sherraden 2007).

In addition to recommendations for more research identified throughout this chapter, there are other potentially fruitful areas for inquiry. Families need both income and assets, yet we know little about the appropriate combinations and how income subsidies and asset-building strategies might be coordinated. Scholarship on effects of assets tests begins to address this question, but further research is needed. Respondents told us that program features matter, but, in this study, since features did not vary, we cannot measure their independent effects.[8] Do some constructs (and features of a plan) lead to changes in individual behavior (saving strategies)? Do other constructs lead directly to saving and asset accumulation with little individual action? Future research may be able to

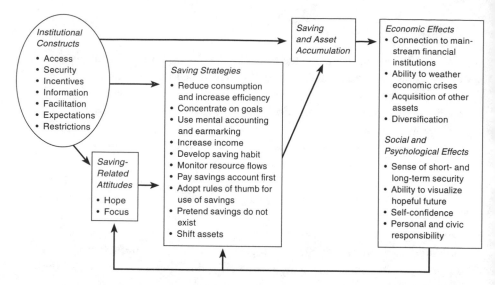

Fig. C.1. Theoretical relationships: Saving and asset accumulation in Individual Development Accounts

untangle how each aspect of a savings plan contributes indirectly to individual saving strategies and directly to saving and asset accumulation

Similarly, although many IDA participants in this study attributed a number of positive outcomes to their IDA experience, we do not know whether saving or owning savings, or whether participating in a program where staff express a belief in them, contributed more to these outcomes. Perhaps saving (or even the adoption of particular saving strategies) contributes to some outcomes, owning saving to others. Nor do we understand how, or whether, feedback effects work. These are intriguing topics for future research.

Overall, more research is needed on the relationships among social institutions, individual behaviors, and their effects. The study suggests that these may be robust, but we do not understand the specific mechanisms and roles of each. For instance, institutional features of the IDA program facilitated and increased saving in participant households. Future research should address the roles and importance of these relationships, using multiple methods of investigation and analysis (Schwartz 2006), including testing with larger representative samples.

Regarding the savers themselves, we should develop a better understanding about how families make saving decisions. Questions include how members of the household make day-to-day saving decisions, how they resolve conflicts about how much to save and how much to spend, and who in the nuclear and extended family is involved in saving decisions (Webley et al. 2001). Our findings address the experiences of a relatively small group of people who signed up for an IDA. They may differ in important ways (such as motivation to save) from other low-income people (Reutebuch 2001; Rohe, Gorham and Quercia 2005; Schreiner and Sherraden 2007). Future research should test these findings with larger representative populations that avoid possible selection bias.

This study further suggests that there are powerful barriers to saving in low-income households. Some of these barriers are addressed by this IDA savings plan, but others are not. Future research could examine different types of savings plans in order to identify effective ways to overcome these barriers. For example, how do different savings plans balance the desire of participants to precommit to saving and have restricted withdrawals with the inevitable need to spend some savings at some point in time?

Research should also explore which policy and program strategies are the most acceptable, efficient, and effective for different groups of savers. This study focuses on families with low incomes in the United States. Future research should examine these questions cross-culturally and comparatively, generating a better understanding of institutions and saving in varying social, economic, and political contexts.

A key question is whether the findings discussed here would differ if the savings period did not end in three years. This study does not address the longer-term effects of saving and asset building. While there are certainly potential benefits to asset holding, there are also reasons that savings might not be beneficial over the longer term. The subprime lending crisis suggests that low-income families with some savings could be the target of corrupt financial practices. For example, families could invest in property that depreciates instead of appreciates. They could save for education that does not result in legitimate credentials, or degrees that do not lead to good jobs. In future crises, families might tap retirement savings or default on loans secured by 401(k) plans, leading to steep penalties and long-term insecurity, or their investments could lose value in an overall decline in the market. Research should follow families for longer periods of time, to identify possible risks of asset holding for low-income families and policy and programs that address these risks.

We have little idea of the impact of lifelong accounts in households with low incomes. Would accounts help families cope with periods when they have no surpluses to save, knowing that they will be able to save in the future? Or would the program recede into the background and no longer command their attention? Related to this, what are the long-term effects of savings plans on low-income families? In other words, how do institutions shape choices that people make, affecting their economic "selves," which then "constrain whole streams of future choices" (Lea and Webley 2005, 601)?

CONCLUSIONS

Reflecting on the respondents' lives, beginning in childhood, we confront obvious serious need for access to better education, health care, and more generous income supports for children and their parents. However, we must ask, why not also savings? As we have seen, savings may offer important short- and long-term benefits, as well as access to opportunities during young adulthood and throughout life. As several cases in this book illustrate, even relatively small amounts of savings can make a difference (see also Edin 2001). Yet we have only limited policies in place that help the poor save.

During a period of near revolution in saving theory led by behavioral economists, this study illuminates the desire to save among the poor, the strategies they use to save, the institutional features that may influence their saving outcomes, and the potential effects of savings. Most important may be the insights into ways people with low incomes themselves think about saving, the strategies they use to save, effects of the IDA program on their ability to save, and ways that respondents think about themselves and their futures as a result of saving (Schwartz 2006). The study underscores enduring efforts by respondents to save. Although most had been able to save in the past for the short term, longer-term savings had largely eluded them. Income constraints and the exigencies of poverty hampered their ability to save. However, the evidence also suggests that when the opportunity came along to save in the form of an IDA—and once its credibility was established—people signed up. Reflecting American roots and values as well as religious backgrounds, respondents believe that they should save and that saving can help them reach their goals. When a legitimate and feasible opportunity to save materialized, they allowed themselves to think about constructing a better future, reaching for goals that had been sitting on a back burner. One participant's perspective on goals is instructive.

> Change isn't the right word. I would say, you know, I believe that a lot of things of who you are and what you want to do, and goals in life are all inside of you. And it's realization, coming to discover your purpose and realizing who you are and what your gifts and talents are, and what you're called to do that unfolds,

kind of like how a flower starts out like a bud, and you don't see it—a flower as a flower when you're looking at a bud. But then as it grows and matures, the petals unfold and then it becomes a beautiful rose. . . . I wouldn't say necessarily that my life goals have changed, I would say that I've discovered more of them.

This suggests that short- or long-term perspectives may be less a matter of personality, attitudes, income, or individual behavior than an outcome of viable and authentic opportunities for saving and asset building and reaching one's goals. Saving may not be a matter simply of easing income constraints and developing self-control and future-oriented preferences (Hutton and Holmes 2005) but also of increasing access to a structure for saving designed to attract and support secure saving by low-income families. Currently, saving options for low-income families are inferior. The poor, like everyone else, require a mix of savings plans that dovetail with their lives and livelihoods. Without the appropriate structures and supports for saving, many families, perhaps most, are unlikely to accumulate savings and assets.

We close with a final comment from Cynthia. Despite her discontent, Cynthia continues to dedicate herself to being a good mother and a productive citizen.

I'm in the big world and I want to advance in it. I want to be a plus to my country and my society. I never was on welfare—and I refuse. Because I knew as long as I have breath in my body and I could work, I will make a living and I will be a productive citizen. And I am.

But she wishes for more. In contrast to her parents, who had little understanding of anything other than hard work, Cynthia has higher aims. As someone who believes that savings provide "security" and "power," she also plans to increase her assets. "Now I need to go to the stage where I'm an advancer." Cynthia observed that people come to her door for taxes and for the census count, but no one is knocking on her door to help her reach the middle class.

Nobody in an institution—government or whatever—has knocked on my door and said, "You want to get [into] middle-class America?" . . . It's not fair that it's so unbalanced. The world would be a better place if we all had the same opportunities.

Cynthia and many of the 83 other respondents in this study are searching for opportunities and avenues for advancement. Most are willing to work hard to improve their situation. They believe that saving is an essential step. Of course, not everyone is as determined as Cynthia, nor would everyone take advantage of a matched savings program. Based on this study, we cannot say what would happen if structured savings products and savings plans were offered to the entire low-income population. But from this study of IDAs, research among poor populations in developing countries, and the growing body of research in behavioral economics, we can offer the following observations.

People of very low incomes save; they must save in order to survive. Few existing formal savings products serve the poor well; as a result, the poor seek informal alternatives, which are sometimes predatory. Some portion of the poor will respond positively to a savings program with an institutional structure that supports saving. A matching incentive is a powerful inducement to participate. The poor, like others, have complex financial lives, and they seek ways to "put away" resources for long-term goals. In this regard, default enrollments through a universal program, precommitments, and restricted accounts, accompanied by backup savings, may be as appealing and as likely to be successful for the poor as for the nonpoor.

The implications of these observations are that public policies that structure savings, especially savings plans such as 401(k) plans and 529 college savings plans, might be successfully extended to reach a greater portion of the population. Based on lessons from this study, such an extension might emphasize a direct saving match (for those who do not receive a tax benefit); ample use of default and automatic features; financial information; and a long-term savings plan that reaches across the life course, including savings for key asset purchases such as homes, as well as savings for retirement and higher education. Overall, the experiences of low-income IDA participants in this study suggest that existing saving policies can, and should, be restructured to serve more people, with special attention to people with low incomes. The key point is not that IDAs as presented in this study should be expanded, but that the poor should be brought into the types of savings plans and subsidies that are working well for others. As a public policy matter, the potential gains from a savings plan for the poor may be worth the investment. As Cynthia observed, no one has yet knocked on her door to ask her to join the middle class. She is trying to get there, and carefully designed and inclusive savings plans could help her succeed.

APPENDIXES

IDA Participants' Demographics
and IDA Saving Experiences

Appendix A. IDA Participants' Demographics and IDA Saving Experiences

IDA Participant Pseudonym	Race	Age[a]	Marital status	Number/ Ages of Children	Total Matched Withdrawals (including match)	Withdrawal Uses
Abel	African American	40	Divorced	Four (ages 6–21) (pays child support)	Unmatched withdrawal	
Adrienne	White	49	Divorced	Three (adult)	Unmatched withdrawal	
Amy	White	37	Single	None	Unmatched withdrawal	
Becky	White	28	Divorced	Two (ages 2, 8)	$6,490.31	Home purchase
Brad	White	43	Married	Three (all under 12)	$4,494.08	Microenterprise and home repair
Brian	White	41	Married	Two (infant, age 5)	$3,100.00	Retirement
Carlos	Latino	59	Married	Seven (adult)	Unmatched withdrawal	
Charles	African American	65+	Divorced	Six (adult)	$484.42	Retirement
Christine	Asian American	48	Separated	One (age 16)	$5,760.40	Home purchase, home repair, and education
Claire	American Indian	40	Divorced	One (age 18)	$3,959.78	Retirement and home repair

Name	Race	Age	Marital status	Children	Amount	Savings goal
David	White	45	Married	Three (3–17) (ages 13–17)	$4,500.00	Home repair
Dawn	White	32	Divorced	Five (ages 6–15)	$1,695.44	Education
Denise	African American	29	Separated	Four (ages 3–9)	Leaver	
Dorothy	White	58	Widowed	All adult	$3,463.78	Retirement
Fred	African American	36	Married	Five (ages 4–19)	$6,750.00	Home purchase
Geraldine	African American	36	Divorced	Three (ages 3–16)	Leaver	
Gina	White	49	Widowed	Two (ages 12, 13)	Leaver	
Gloria	African American	43	Married	Four (ages 5–17)	Leaver	
Grace	White	23	Single	None	$2,339.74	Education
Heather	White	30	Divorced	One (age 13)	$2,775.83	Home repair
Heidi	White	19	Single	None	$4,500.00	Retirement
Ian	White	53	Married	Three (ages 12–17)	$1,524.81	Education
Jasmine	African American	27	Single	Two (ages 4, 6)	Leaver	
Jason	White	27	Married	Two (ages 1, 2)	$4,500.00	Home repair
Jessie	White	47	Divorced	One (teen)	$6,129.39	Home purchase
Jill	White	32	Single	One (age 13)	Leaver	

Appendix A.—*Continued*

IDA Participant Pseudonym	Race	Age[a]	Marital status	Number/ Ages of Children	Total Matched Withdrawals (including match)	Withdrawal
Jocelyn	White	42	Divorced	Three (ages 10–18)	$500.00	
Joe	White	45	Married	Three (ages 9–12)	Leaver	
Kenneth	African American	46	Divorced	One (adult)	$1,355.86	Retirement
Linda	White	25	Single	One (age 8)	Leaver	
Lisa	White	38	Divorced	Two (ages 7, 9)	$3,766.53	Microenterprise, home-repair, and education
Maria	Latina	45	Divorced	One (age 11)	Leaver	
Mark	White	33	Married	Two (ages 3, 5)	$431.66	Home repair
Melissa	White	35	Long-term partner	Two (ages 9, 11)	Leaver	
Nancy	Native American	53	Divorced	Two (adult)	$1,860.00	Home repair
Natalie	African American	41	Single	Two (ages 10, 12)	Leaver	
Pam	African American	45	Widowed	Two (adult)	Leaver	
Pat	White	46	Divorced	Two (ages 17–19)	$2,656.72	Education

Name	Race/Ethnicity	Age	Marital status	Children	Amount	Goal
Rachel	White American	61	Single	None	$3,879.54	Home purchase
Reggie (and Sherna)		36	Married	One (age 3)	$2,928.49	Home repair and education
Ronald	Multiracial	60	Divorced	One (age 15)	Leaver	
Rosalyn	African American	45	Married	Six (2 teens, 4 out of home)	$3,691.76	Home repair
Rose	African American	63	Widowed	None	$1,900.00	Retirement
Roxanne	White	40	Divorced	Two (ages 8, 22)	$4,296.00	Home purchase
Scott	White	45	Married	None	Leaver	
Shanta	Multiracial	43	Single	One (age 16)	$5,036.78	Home purchase and repair
Shirley	Multiracial	45	Widowed	One (age 1 8)	$831.28	Retirement
Shondra	African American	40	Divorced	Two (ages 13, 18)	Leaver	
Sonya	White	29	Married	One (age 12)	$3,745.94	Home repair
Stephanie	White	55	Divorced	Unknown (adult)	Leaver	
Steven	White	41	Married	Three (ages 1–9)	$3,741.86	Home repair and education
Sylvia	Asian American	35	Divorced	Three (ages 12–15)	$5,207.76	Home purchase and repair
Tasha	African American	31	Divorced	Three (ages 3–10)	$1,000	Retirement

Appendix A.—*Continued*

IDA Participant Pseudonym	Race	Age[a]	Marital status	Number/ Ages of Children	Total Matched Withdrawals (including match)	Withdrawal
Terri	White	49	Divorced	Three (grade-school)	Leaver	
Theresa	African American	48	Divorced	Two (adult)	Leaver	
Tyrone	African American	25	Married	One (age 4)	$1,500.00	Retirement
Wendy	White	49	Married	Three (adult)	$4,500.00	Retirement
Yolanda	African American	31	Single	None	$3,251.86	Education and retirement
Yvonne	African American	43	Divorced	Five (all teens)	$4,199.51	Home repair and home purchase

Source: Data on race, marital status, and number and ages of children are from in-depth interviews. Data on age are from Abt Associates 2004. Data on total matched withdrawals, withdrawal uses, and reasons for exiting program are from Center for Social Development, Management Information System for IDAs (MIS IDA).

[a]Those over 65 years of age are identified as 65+.

Control Respondent Demographic Characteristics

Appendix B. Control Respondent Demographic Characteristics

Control Respondent Pseudonym	Race	Age[a]	Marital Status	Number/ Ages of Children
Anita	African American	30	Single	One (age 9)
Anne	White	33	Married	Two (infant–age 6)
Camille	African American	57	Divorced	Five (ages 8–20, grandchildren)
Carolina	Latina	57	Married	One (age 12)
Cynthia	Multiracial	52	Divorced	One (age 16)
Darlene	African American	33	Single	Three (ages 5–10)
Debra	White	23	Engaged	None
Denisha	African American	20	Single	Two (infant–age 3)
Ella	African American	50	Married	Two (ages 12, 13)
Gerald (and Hazel)	African American	65+	Married	Two (ages 10, 11, grandchildren)
Gordon	White	27	Married	Three (infant–age 4)
Jake	White	34	Single	One (age 6)
Kathleen	White	32	Divorced	Two (ages 9, 13)
LaVonne	African American	46	Divorced	Two (ages 4, 19)
Mary	White	22	Single	One (toddler)
Nicole	White	26	Single	One (age 5)
Shannon	White	39	Divorced	Two (ages 13, 15)
Sharise	African American	33	Single	Two (ages 4, 6)
Tammy	White	37	Married	Four (ages 2–11)
Terrell	African American	28	Married	Three (infant-age 5)
Tiffany	White	29	Single	None
Tonya	White	33	Single	Three (ages 7–12)
Tracy	White	38	Single	One (age 1)
Trish	American Indian	30	Married	Three (ages 4-8)
Victor (and Elvia)	Latino/a	62	Married	One (age 10, grandson)

Source: Data on race, marital status, and number and ages of children are from in-depth interviews. Data on age are from Abt Associates 2004.

[a]Those over 65 years of age are identified as 65+.

Notes

INTRODUCTION

1. Although IDA is the most common term for these accounts, they are also known as family development accounts and Individual Savings Accounts. For children, they are known as Children's Savings Accounts, and by various other names.

2. Camille is a pseudonym, like all other names used in this book. We also have changed some details of people's stories to protect their identities, but in ways that do not change the meaning of their stories. Quotation marks indicate direct quotes from respondents, unless otherwise attributed.

3. As we will see in chapter 7, not everyone signed up immediately. Many were initially skeptical about the IDA program's legitimacy.

4. We use *assets* and *wealth* interchangeably to mean what a person owns. We use *net worth* to signify what someone owns minus their liabilities.

5. Although family median net worth increased markedly between 1998 and 2007, the increase for the lowest 20 percent of families was small (Bucks, Kennickell, Mach, and Moore 2009).

6. Carney and Gale (2001) estimated lack of transaction accounts at 20 percent in all households and 45 percent in African American households in 1993. Nonetheless, there were improvements between 1989 and 1998, when financial account ownership among low-income families increased from 49 to 62 percent (Hogarth, Anguelov, and Lee 2001).

7. We define *saving* as the process of setting money aside, and *savings* as the money accumulated.

CHAPTER 1

1. Average monthly deposit (AMD) is *gross* deposits into the IDA accounts. Withdrawals from IDAs for nonapproved purposes are included in this calculation. AMND, or average monthly net deposits (gross deposits minus withdrawals for nonapproved purposes), is the emerging standard in the field; however, this calculation was not available at the time of sampling.

2. A limitation of this study is that in-depth interviewing overlapped with Abt survey interviews conducted by telephone with the larger sample, which ran longer than expected (Abt Associates 2004). As a result, some respondents may have been confused and/or may have had heightened awareness of certain issues resulting from two contacts around the same time. Further, a few nonparticipants had friends who were IDA participants, which may have influenced their behaviors and attitudes. We were cognizant of

these potential complications when coding and omitted responses that seemed unduly confused or influenced by one or the other of these factors.

3. Only one respondent declined to be taped, although a few asked to stop the tape when they discussed sensitive material.

4. Notes, tapes, and transcriptions were analyzed with case numbers only. All identifying information was stored in a separate locked cabinet, according to the human subjects protocol.

CHAPTER 2

1. We are especially indebted to Lea, Tarpy, and Webley (1987), Bernheim (1991), Browning and Lusardi (1996), Beverly and Sherraden (1999), Wärneryd (1999), Nyhus and Webley (2006), and Schreiner and Sherraden (2007) for cogent reviews of saving theory. Lea, Tarpy, and Webley (1987), Bernheim (1991), Nyhus and Webley (2006), and Wärneryd (1999) contributed to our thinking especially in the overview and discussion of behavioral economics. Overviews of institutional determinants of saving and effects of saving in Beverly and Sherraden (1999) and Schreiner and Sherraden (2007) were especially useful.

2. There even may be a biological basis for impulsive versus self-controlled and strategic behavior. According to one metaphoric view of the brain, there are two interacting parts: one part of the brain is "cool," cognitive and contemplative, and the other is "hot," emotion-ridden and impulsive (Hoch and Loewenstein 1991; Metcalfe and Mischel 1999). People's ability to plan for the future (the cool side) is affected by the emotional part of the brain (the hot side) that wants to satisfy desires now. The ability to exert self-control comes with age, education, and experience, but it requires that the cool side exert control over the hot side. Neurological research identifies possible automatic processes and affective systems that guide economic behavior and may help explain irrationality and self-control problems (McClure et al. 2004; Camerer, Loewenstein, and Prelec 2005).

3. In addition to these explanations, there is also a strain of economic psychology focusing on personality factors, although we do not address this area of work. Economic psychologists have posited possible associations of personality and self-control, including locus of control, future orientation, and ability to delay gratification (Lea, Tarpy, and Webley 1987; Maital and Maital 1993; Wärneryd 1999; Webley et al. 2001).

4. Other scholars have proposed different types of mental accounts. Adrian Winnett and Alan Lewis (1995), for example, suggest three mental accounting schemas, liquidity (asset/income), windfall/regular, and capital/labor. Their research demonstrates that families, especially those with children, often have numerous household accounts (income and expenses) that are nonfungible, designated for certain purposes, and subject to negotiation within the family. Another study identifies nine "psychological purses" or spending categories (Kojima and Hama 1982), and yet another suggests that people use two types of mental accounts (Ranyard and Craig 1995). People also appear to have different mental accounts for savings (Groenland, Bloem, and Kuylen 1996).

5. See Sondra Beverly et al. (2008) and Mark Schreiner and Michael Sherraden (2007)

for more complete discussions of these constructs, including more detailed summaries of empirical evidence.

6. Although defaults may permit social engineers to promote social goals, defaults leave open the possibility of lower earnings. New regulations provide some protection for uninformed investors and automatic enrollment programs are increasing especially among large employers (Salisbury 2008).

7. In social psychology, individual expectations are an important concept (Bandura 1997). Here we refer to *program* expectations, such as expectations associated with program rules or perhaps program staff.

8. For reviews of empirical evidence related to asset effects, see Page-Adams and Sherraden 1996; Scanlon and Page-Adams 2001, 2005; Dowding, de Wispelaere, and White 2003; Schreiner and Sherraden 2007; and Lerman and McKernan 2008).

9. Other studies suggest that causality moves in the opposite direction, that is, that health may lead to greater wealth (Lum and Lightfoot 2003; Lum 2005).

10. In many studies, however, the direction of causality is not clear: Home ownership may increase civic engagement, or civically engaged people may be more likely to purchase homes.

CHAPTER 3

1. In 1997, the Oklahoma legislature created the Tulsa Race Riot Commission to investigate and make recommendations for restitution. John Hope Franklin and Scott Ellsworth prepared the historical overview of the riots that concluded that the city and state played key roles in the community's destruction (Ellsworth 2000).

2. Abt survey data indicate that high school incompletion is relatively rare among respondents. This finding is explained by the fact that many later returned to high school or completed a GED.

CHAPTER 4

1. In the month prior to the Abt interviews, median monthly earned income was $1,100, ranging from $50 to $3,000. Mean monthly "other income" was $256 (the median was $220, ranging from 0 to $1,088). Combined, median monthly income was $1,300.

2. The Family Village (the name has been changed) was founded in the early twentieth century for the children and widows of killed oil field workers.

3. Interviewers asked respondents about their family's expenses at the end of the interview. The numbers reflect respondents' best estimates (they did not have their financial paperwork with them). Most seemed to have a fairly good idea of their regular monthly expenses, although we cannot confirm these figures. Kathryn Edin and Laura Lein's research (1997) suggests that it takes considerable effort to gain a complete perspective on household expenses. Our figures are certainly imperfect (for example, they probably underestimate miscellaneous and intermittent expenses), but they provide a rough idea about household expenses.

4. Although gender relations in financial decision making was not a focus of the interview, it emerged repeatedly, particularly in the context of divorce. This suggests that

more research on financial management and saving with gender at the center of analysis would be helpful.

5. Financial decision making in prior relationships also was not a major focus of the interview; more questions may have yielded additional data.

6. Respondents frequently talked about using alternative financial services in obscure ways, perhaps in the same way that patients often conceal from their physicians the simultaneous use of Western and alternative medicines, such as home remedies. Because we did not pursue questions about alternative financial services in depth, we cannot say how many respondents use them.

CHAPTER 5

1. These data underestimate levels of debt in poor households because they are less likely to include debt owed to alternative financial providers, a major source of cash in emergencies (Rawlings and Gentsch 2008).

2. Respondents put different kinds of debt into different categories. For example, they distinguished between "debt" and "problem debt." No respondent included home loans in either category; home loans are considered to be more like a bill or an investment, not debt. Further research is needed to understand how people think about and respond to household and personal debt.

3. Overall, health insurance was expensive, costing an average of $112 per month ($94 for IDA participants and $130 per month for nonparticipants), including those who do not pay out-of-pocket for insurance.

4. In all, ten respondents chose not to own a credit card, including four who never owned one and five who had problem debt.

5. Since that time, federal regulations and Congress have tightened the availability of credit and introduced some consumer protections, including limits on fees and penalty interest rates (Pulizzi, 2009). Nonetheless, many low- and moderate-income families with credit cards continue to pay on their credit balance and use credit cards to cover household expenses and emergencies.

6. These interviews took place prior to changes in federal bankruptcy law, which, among several new provisions, requires counseling, has stricter eligibility guidelines, and requires more debtors to repay. Therefore, bankruptcy may no longer be a viable option for some families.

7. We expected respondents in this study to be concerned about credit. The intensity of their concern, however, suggests that this issue should be examined more broadly among low-income families. IDA participants may be particularly aware of credit issues because of discussions about credit in money management classes (see chap. 7). However, greater awareness is also probably the result of more discussion about credit records in the media, and greater knowledge among the public that lenders and employers, among others, use credit records to make important decisions, such as hiring decisions and interest rates for loans.

8. Because debt was not the focus of this study, we cannot be sure about the point when people perceive they have enough "problem" debt to act. As we have observed, the definition of debt is confounding. Some debt is "good" debt, some is "bad." Families can

manage a certain amount of problem debt, but when does it get to the point when they switch into debt management mode? For example, is it a quantitative issue (e.g., a calculation of debt relative to income or other financial markers), a question of penalties for holding debt (e.g., inability to borrow, threat to an asset), or a personality issue (e.g., tolerance for uncertainty)? The answer has important conceptual and practical implications.

CHAPTER 6

1. We were cautious about using examples from IDA participants because of the influence of the program on their memories of saving. Proportionately fewer IDA participants, for example, believed that their past efforts to save were successful. We only include examples here if the interview strongly suggested they were saving prior to the IDA program.

2. Researchers also observe that owning insurance may be associated with other forms of saving (Lunt and Livingstone 1992).

3. Viviana Zelizer observes that within a hundred years, life insurance went from being considered abhorrent to being considered a provider's duty to those left behind, a way to cope with death, and a route to immortality (Zelizer 2001). In the United Kingdom, for example, coverage for a proper burial was considered so important that funeral expenses were built into social insurance provisions, although the allocations have since been significantly eroded (Drakeford 1998).

4. We combine life and burial insurance because some respondents seemed confused about the difference. Further, we did not ask everyone in the interview about forms of insurance, only those who said that their insurance payment was a regular expense. In this way, we likely missed some people who had burial insurance in particular.

5. The rate of home ownership is lower than that of low-income populations as a whole. In this study, 30 percent of respondents own a house, compared to nearly half of low-income families in a 1995 survey (Hogarth and O'Donnell 1999).

6. A few families accumulated savings in order to deal with predictable fluctuations in income; these are different from rainy-day savings. For example, one respondent is a teacher who survived the summer months with little income, so she saved every month during the school year to cover most of her family's summer expenses.

7. Our in-depth interviews may underestimate the number of respondents with some retirement savings (because some people do not think of workplace retirement plans as "savings"), but research suggests that few people living in poverty are making progress toward building retirement savings (Hogarth and Anguelov 2003; Paladino and Helman 2003; Helman and Paladino 2004; Rodriguez and Martinez 2004).

8. Some researchers consider durables as expenditures, and others consider them as savings. Durables and savings, according to Lea, Tarpy, and Webley (1987), have similarities and differences: during poor economic conditions, people stop buying durables and save, moving their "savings into a more liquid form" (516).

9. Our interviews took place prior to the economic crisis. It is quite likely that we would have heard even more from respondents about inferior financial services and scams and their consequences if we had talked to them more recently. Although low-in-

come Americans have not been the focus of media reports on the effects of the crisis, there are indications that their situation has worsened, and includes losing homes and other small amounts of wealth (Ehrenreich, 2009).

CHAPTER 7

1. How much difference did the savings match make for participants in the IDA program? In *Can the Poor Save?* Mark Schreiner and Michael Sherraden (2007) report that the 2,350 participants in ADD had net savings of $16.60 per month (approximately $200 a year) that was eligible for a savings match. The average participant saved $558, and approximately half of participants ended the program with a net savings of at least $100. Given the average match rate (1.88 to 1) and assuming all matchable savings were withdrawn, the average participant accumulated a total of $1,609 in the IDA (Schreiner and Sherraden 2007, 123).

2. Some participants said the size of the match is not as important. Some said that even 50 cents on the dollar would be sufficient incentive, although they would prefer a larger match. In addition to the match, the very basic idea that the program offered a savings account to every participant is something that should not be ignored. Although most participants had bank accounts at some point in their lives, many managed accounts ineffectively. Some continued to use expensive alternative financial services for transactions, and some lacked a transaction account. Theresa, for example, said her poor credit history prevented her from having a bank account. She said that one of the most important benefits of the program was that she opened an account.

3. Dawn had never saved in the bank because of the asset limits set by public assistance programs. The IDA program had a waiver from the state permitting savings.

4. Although participants generally find the savings statements to be useful, not everyone fully understands them. One participant commented, "Sometimes I don't understand it completely. So it would be better, you know, if somebody would even sit down with you and discuss how, why this statement is saying what it is saying and how you can improve."

5. Participants tend to consider anything less a loss (because they would forfeit a potential savings match). This suggests that loss aversion may also play a role in IDA saving (Kahneman and Tversky 1979; Kahneman, Knetsch, and Thaler 1991).

CHAPTER 8

1. Because of a certain distrust of financial institutions, not everyone agreed on the benefits of direct deposit. One participant suggested that programs may need to be flexible about how participants interact with the bank. If participants are ever going to develop greater trust in financial institutions, this participant pointed out, they need more information. "I prefer going up there and putting it in there myself. That way I can check up on it and stuff like that. That way I know they are not drawing it when I don't need it drawn. . . . It is just I prefer dealing with people than having my money just drawn out. People contact. I prefer that."

2. However, one participant even procrastinated about setting up direct deposit. "I've

talked about doing it, but I just haven't taken the time to do it," she added with a self-conscious laugh.

CHAPTER 9

1. Assets effects discussed here reflect what participants perceived at the time of the interviews, in addition to quantitative data on IDA account withdrawals (matched and unmatched) available when the program was completed.

2. All data on savings withdrawals in this chapter come from CSD (2004).

3. Increased range and use of saving strategies could also be considered a program effect, but this is discussed separately in chapter 8.

4. Saving is the act of setting aside money for saving and savings is the money. It is difficult to sort out the difference between effects of saving and effects of owning savings.

5. Officially, the IDA program allowed participants to use their savings (not the match) for emergencies up to three times a year. However, they were encouraged to redeposit the amount as quickly as possible. The newly deposited savings would then be eligible once again for the match incentive.

6. Although we do not know the debt/equity ratio, many respondents reported that they purchased assets on credit, especially vehicles and other durables. In total, 33 IDA participants (56 percent) and 13 nonparticipants (52 percent) had acquired homes. A few had inherited them, some had borrowed the money for a down payment, and others had purchased homes through a low-income home ownership program or an urban homesteading program. However, we assume that some had saved money for at least part of the down payment. Fifteen respondents (18 percent) reported they had a 401(k) or other retirement account prior to the IDA program, although some did not track their worth. The number with retirement accounts is likely an underestimate. As noted earlier, some people do not consider retirement accounts to be "savings" and so may not have reported these accounts in the interview. However, IDA participants with workplace savings are more likely than nonparticipants to consider them savings and to monitor them. This is likely because of the financial education they received in the IDA program. Several participants and nonparticipants expressed remorse at not having taken full advantage of workplace savings options over their lifetimes.

7. These numbers require clarification. On one hand, MIS IDA data indicate only the *months in which withdrawals were made.* Thus, the average *number* of withdrawals may be higher than the average months in which a withdrawal was made (because some people made more than one unmatched withdrawal in a month). On the other hand, the number of withdrawals typically includes a final withdrawal of savings left over after participants closed their accounts—after making their principal matched asset investment. Therefore, the number of matched savers who withdrew unmatched savings (and the number of times they made an unmatched withdrawal) may be slightly more or less than the reported figure (Schreiner and Sherraden 2007).

8. $[t(2,57) = 3.469, p = .001]$.

9. $[t(2,57) = 2.350, p = .022]$. These withdrawal patterns suggest that unmatched savers have financial needs that prevent them from retaining enough savings to qualify

for a matched withdrawal. Matched savers accumulate enough for a matched withdrawal, suggesting less dire financial circumstances and perhaps longer-term saving plans.

10. Several said they intended to save in the future for their children's postsecondary education, and some chose not to save for education because they believed their children would qualify for scholarships that would cover the costs.

11. This section is based in part on an analysis by Trina Williams Shanks, an interviewer on this project and now at the University of Michigan.

12. Recall from Chapter 1 that "Low savers" had an AMD ranging from $0 to $27 ($n =$ 18). "Middle savers" had an AMD ranging from $28 to $63 ($n = 22$). "High savers" had an AMD ranging from $65 to $513 ($n = 18$). Median AMD of selected participants was $54, and the mean was $60.

13. $\chi^2 (2, N = 56) = 6.444, p = .040$.

14. Women, Infants, and Children (WIC) is a special supplemental nutrition program for low-income mothers and babies.

15. The entire sample is likely biased toward long-term saving compared to the general population, but because of the experimental design, participants and controls ostensibly began the study with the same proclivity for long-term saving.

16. We interpret these results with caution, given the limitations in the methods and the sample. There are alternative explanations that beg further testing of life-cycle theory in particular. For example, nonparticipants are younger and more likely to have children at home than IDA participants. This could be a reason for less long-term perspective and less long-term saving among nonparticipants.

17. $\chi^2 (1, N = 83) = 6.120$, Fisher's Exact $= .016$. We were somewhat liberal in our determination of long-term savings for nonparticipants. We included them as "long-term savers" if they indicated that they were saving even small amounts for long-term purposes.

CONCLUSION

1. Some participants believe the match could be smaller and still act an incentive to save (e.g., a 50-cent match for a dollar saved), although others wished it was larger.

2. Participants have a range of opinions about the importance of various program features. In an effort to sort out importance, we asked participants to identify program features that could be eliminated if there were future funding cuts. They had difficulty answering this question. Many said the program might reduce the number of classes. Some, who learned basic money management skills on their own, believed that these particular classes might be optional. (Although a minority found money management very helpful, participants tended to prefer the asset-specific classes, such as those on home buying and retirement accounts.) A few suggested that the match rate could be reduced in order to cut costs, suggesting that a smaller match would remain an attractive incentive to save. Some said the program could trim the number of staff without jeopardizing program operations. However, there was little consensus; most said all features were helpful.

3. Daniel Schneider and Peter Tufano (2007) also summarize a variety of proposals for building assets.

4. See Lopez-Fernandini, Cramer and O'Brien (2008) and the Asset Building program of the New America Foundation (http://www.newamerica.net/programs/asset_building, and http://assetbuilding.org), and CFED (http://www.cfed.org) for U.S. policy proposals.

5. Researchers suggest that the worst abuses of employment-based investment plans, such as defaults into bad savings plans, can be avoided if people are required to be involved in choosing a savings plan (as distinct from day-to-day choices about how much money to set aside in savings) (Choi et al. 2005). Others note, however, that evaluating different savings plans may not be realistic for inexperienced savers (Cronqvist and Thaler 2004), suggesting that plan design must take into account diverse socioeconomic groups of savers.

6. Lois Vitt and colleagues (2000, xii) define financial literacy as "the ability to read, analyze, manage, and communicate about the personal financial conditions that affect material well-being. It includes the ability to discern financial choices, discuss money and financial issues without (or despite) discomfort, plan for the future, and respond competently to life events that affect everyday financial decisions, including events in the general economy" (see also Lyons, Chang, and Scherpf 2006).

7. We build on the idea of financial capability—introduced in the United Kingdom and Canada (SEDI 2004, 2005; U.K. Financial Service Authority 2005; Dixon 2006). The concept of financial capability draws on Amartya Sen's and Martha Nussbaum's seminal work suggesting that capabilities, or "the freedom that a person has to lead one kind of life or another" (Sen 1993, 3; 1999), are tied to opportunity.

8. Other research has similarly been unable to untangle the independent effects of program features (Thaler and Benartzi 2004).

References

Aaronson, Daniel. 2000. A note on the benefits of homeownership. *Journal of Urban Economics* 47, no. 3: 356–69.

Abramovitz, Mimi. 2001. Everyone is still on welfare: The role of redistribution in social policy. *Social Work* 46, no. 4: 297–308.

Abt Associates. 2004. *Evaluation of the American Dream Demonstration: Final evaluation report.* Cambridge, MA: Abt.

Ackerman, Bruce, and Anne Alstott. 1999. *The stakeholder society.* New Haven: Yale University Press.

ACORN (Association of Community Organizations for Reform Now). 2004. *The great divide: Home purchase mortgage lending nationally and in 120 metropolitan areas.* Washington, DC: ACORN.

Ainsley, George, and Nick Haslam. 1992. Self control. In *Choice over time,* ed. George Loewenstein and Jon Elster, 177–211. New York: Russell Sage Foundation.

Aizcorbe, Ana M., Arthur B. Kennickell, and Kevin B. Moore. 2003. Recent changes in U.S. family finances: Evidence from the 1998 and 2001 Survey of Consumer Finance. *Federal Reserve Bulletin* 89, no. 1: 1–32.

Akerlof, George A. 1991. Procrastination and obedience. *American Economic Review Papers and Proceedings* 81, no. 2: 1–19.

American Bankruptcy Institute (ABI). 2008. Annual business and non-business filings per year, Amerian Bankruptcy Institute, Alexandria, VA. Available from http://www.abiworld.org/AM/AMTemplate.cfm?section=Home/CONTENTID= 5/826+TEMPLATE=/CMContentDisplay.cfm [cited 15 October 2009].

Anderson, Steven G., Min Zhan, and Jeff Scott. 2004. Targeting financial management training at low-income audiences. *Journal of Consumer Affairs* 38, no. 1: 167–77.

Arber, Sara, and Jay Ginn. 1993. Gender and inequalities in health in later life. *Social Science and Medicine* 36, no. 1: 33–46.

Ashraf, Nava, Dean Karlan, and Wesley Yin. 2006. Tying Odysseus to the mast: Evidence from a commitment savings product in the Philippines. *Quarterly Journal of Economics* (May): 635–72.

Avery, Robert B., and Raphael W. Bostic. 1997. Changes in the distribution of banking offices. *Federal Reserve Bulletin* 83, no. 9: 707–25.

Axinn, William, Greg J. Duncan, and Arland Thornton. 1997. The effects of parents' income, wealth, and attitudes on children's completed schooling and self-esteem. In *Consequences of growing up poor,* ed. Greg Duncan and Jeanne Brooks-Gunn, 518–40. New York: Russell Sage Foundation.

Baker, Deborah, Hazel Taylor, and the Alspac Survey Team. 1997. The relationship between condition-specific morbidity, social support, and material deprivation in pregnancy and early motherhood. *Social Science and Medicine* 45, no. 9: 1325–36.

Baker, Wayne, and Jason Jimerson. 1992. The sociology of money. *American Behavioral Scientist* 35, no. 6: 678–93.

Bandura, Albert. 1986. *Social foundations of thought and action: A social cognitive theory.* Englewood Cliffs, NJ: Prentice-Hall.

Bandura, Albert. 1997. *Self-efficacy: The exercise of control.* New York: W. H. Freeman.

Bangdiwala, Shrikant I., Laurie Ramiro, Laura S. Sadowski, Isabel A. S. Bordin, Wanda Hunter, and Viswanathan Shankar. 2004. Intimate partner violence and the role of socioeconomic indicators in worldsafe communities in Chile, Egypt, India, and the Philippines. *Injury Control and Safety Promotion* 11, no. 2: 101–9.

Banks, Dwayne A. 1998. The economics of death? A descriptive study of the impact of funeral and cremation costs on US households. *Death Studies* 22:269–85.

Barr, Michael. 2004. Banking the poor. *Yale Journal on Regulation* 21:121.

Barr, Michael S., Anjali Kumar, and Robert E. Litan, eds. 2007. *Building inclusive financial systems: A framework for financial access.* Washington, DC: Brookings Institution Press.

Barrow, Lisa, and Leslie McGranahan. 2000. The effects of the Earned Income Tax Credit on the seasonality of household expenditures. *National Tax Journal* 53, no. 4: 1211–43.

Baum, T., and P. Kingston. 1984. Homeownership and social attachment. *Sociological Perspectives* 27, no. 2: 159–80.

Baumeister, Roy F., Todd F. Heatherton, and Dianne M. Tice. 1994. *Losing control: How and why people fail at self-regulation.* San Diego, CA: Academic Press.

Becker, Gary S. 1981. *A treatise on the family.* Cambridge: Harvard University Press.

Bell, Elizabeth, and Robert I. Lerman. 2005. Can financial literacy enhance asset building? Urban Institute Opportunity and Ownership Project no. 6. Washington, DC: Urban Institute.

Belsky, Eric S., and Allegra Calder. 2005. Credit matters: Building assets in a dual financial services system. In *Building assets, building credit,* ed. N. P. Retsinas and E. S. Belsky, 10–41. Cambridge, MA: Joint Center for Housing Studies; Washington, DC: Brookings Institution Press.

Berger, Peggy S., Judith Powell, and Alicia S. Cook. 1988. The relation of economic factors to perceived stress in mobile families. *Journal of Family and Economic Issues* 9, no. 14: 297–313.

Berk, Richard A., and Sarah Fenstermaker Berk. 1983. Supply-side sociology of the family: The challenge of the new home economics. *Annual Review of Sociology* 9:375–95.

Bernheim, B. Douglas. 1991. *The vanishing nest egg: Reflections on saving in America.* New York: Priority Press.

Bernheim, B. Douglas. 1994. Personal saving, information, and economic literacy: New directions for public policy. In *American Council for Capital Accumulation. Tax Policy for Economic Growth in the 1990s,* ed. American Council for Capital Formation, 53–78. Washington, DC: American Council for Capital Formation.

Bernheim, B. Douglas. 1995. *Do households appreciate their financial vulnerabilities? An analysis of actions, perceptions, and public policy. Tax Policy and Economic Growth.* Washington, DC: American Council for Capital Formation.

Bernheim, B. Douglas. 1996. Financial illiteracy, education, and retirement saving. In *Living with defined contribution plans: Remaking responsibility for retirement,* ed. Olivia S. Mitchell and Sylvester J. Scheiber, 38–68. Philadelphia: University of Pennsylvania Press.

Bernheim, B. Douglas, Daniel M. Garrett, and Dean M. Maki. 2001. Education and saving: The long-term effects of high school financial curriculum mandates. *Journal of Public Economics* 80, no. 3: 435–65.

Bernheim, B. Douglas, and John Karl Scholz. 1993. Private saving and public policy. *Tax Policy and the Economy* 7:73–110.

Berry, Christopher. 2005. To bank or not to bank? A survey of low-income households. In *Building assets, building credit: Creating wealth in low-income communities,* ed. Nicolas P. Retsinas and Eric S. Belsky, 47–70. Cambridge, MA: Joint Center for Housing Studies, and Washington, DC: Brooking Institution Press.

Berthoud, Richard B., and Elaine Kempson. 1992. *Credit and debt: The P.S.I. report.* London, Policy Studies Institute.

Berti, Anna Emilia, and Anna Silvia Bombi. 1988. *The child's construction of economics.* Cambridge: Cambridge University Press.

Bertrand, Marianne B., Sandhil M. Mullainathan, and Elder Shafir. 2004. A behavioral-economics view of poverty. *American Economic Review* 94:419–23.

Beverly, Sondra G. 2001. Material hardship in the United States: Evidence from the Survey of Income and Program Participation. *Social Work Research* 25, no. 3: 143–52.

Beverly, Sondra G., and Jared Barton. 2006. *Barriers to asset accumulation for families in the SEED pre-school demonstration and impact assessment.* SEED Research Report. Lawrence: University of Kansas, School of Social Welfare.

Beverly, Sondra G., and Emily Burkhalter. 2005. Improving the financial literacy and practices of youth. *Children and Schools* 27, no. 2: 121–24.

Beverly, Sondra G., Amanda Moore McBride, and Mark Schreiner. 2003. A framework of asset-accumulation stages and strategies. *Journal of Family and Economic Issues* 24, no. 2: 143–56.

Beverly, Sondra, Daniel J. Schneider, and Peter Tufano. 2005. Splitting tax refunds and building savings: An empirical test. Harvard Business School Working Paper No. 06-018, Harvard Business School, Boston.

Beverly, Sondra, and Michael Sherraden. 1999. Institutional determinants of saving: Implications for low-income households and public policy. *Journal of Socio-economics* 28:457–73.

Beverly, Sondra, Michael Sherraden, Reid Cramer, Trina Williams Shanks, Yunju Nam, and Min Zhan. 2008. Determinants of asset holdings. In *Asset building and low-income families,* ed. Signe-Mary McKernan and Michael Sherraden, 89–151. Washington, DC: Urban Institute Press.

Bird, Edward J., Paul A. Hagstrom, and Robert Wild. 1999. Credit card debts of the poor: High and rising. *Journal of Policy Analysis and Management* 18, no. 1: 125–33.

Birnbaum, Jane. 2008. Law makes debt relief harder for homeowners. *New York Times*, January 12.

Blanchflower, David G., and Andrew J. Oswald. 1998. What makes an entrepreneur? *Journal of Labour Economics* 16:26–30.

Blank, Rebecca M., and Michael S. Barr, eds. 2009. *Insufficient funds: Savings, assets, credit, and banking among low-income households.* New York: Russell Sage Foundation.

Boddie, Stephanie C. 2006. Way to give: Tithing practices that benefit families, congregations, and communities. Baltimore: Annie E. Casey Foundation.

Boehm, Thomas P., and Alan M. Schlottman. 1999. Does home ownership by parents have an economic impact on their children? *Journal of Housing Economics* 8, no. 3: 217–32.

Boehm, Thomas P., and Alan M. Schlottman. 2001. Housing and wealth accumulation: Intergenerational impacts. Low Income Homeownership Working Paper LIHO 01-15, Joint Center for Housing Studies, Harvard University, Cambridge.

Boshara, Ray. 2005. Individual Development Accounts: Policies to build savings and assets for the poor. Welfare Reform and Beyond Policy Brief no. 32, Brookings Institution, Washington, DC.

Botti, Simona, and Sheena S. Iyendar. 2006. The dark side of choice: When choice impairs social welfare. *Journal of Public Policy and Marketing* 25, no. 1: 24–38.

Bourdieu, Pierre. 2001. The forms of capital. In *The sociology of economic life*, 2nd ed., ed. Mark Granovetter and Richard Swedberg, 96–111. Boulder: Westview Press.

Bowles, Samuel. 2004. *Microeconomics: Behavior, institutions, and evolution.* Princeton: Princeton University Press.

Bracher, Michael, Gigi Santow, S. Philip Morgan, and James Trussell. 1993. Marriage dissolution in Australia: Models and explanations. *Population Studies* 4:403–25.

Braunstein, Sandra, and Carolyn Welch. 2002. Financial literacy: An overview of practice, research, and policy. *Federal Reserve Bulletin* 87 (November): 445–57.

Brimmer, Andrew F. 1988. Income, wealth, and investment behavior in the black community. *American Economic Review* 78:151–55.

Brooks, Richard R. W. 2006. Credit past due. *Columbia Law Review* 106, 994–1028.

Brophy, Alfred L. 2002. *Reconstructing the dreamland: The Tulsa Riot of 1921, race, preparations, and reconciliation.* Oxford: Oxford University Press.

Browning, Martin, and Annamaria Lusardi. 1996. Household saving: Micro theories and micro facts. *Journal of Economic Literature* 34, no. 4: 1797–1855.

Bucks, Brian K., Arthur B. Kennickell, and Kevin B. Moore. 2006. Recent changes in U.S. family finances: Evidence from the 2001 and 2004 Survey of Consumer Finances. *Federal Reserve Bulletin* 92 (February): A1–38. Available from http://www.federalreserve.gov/pubs/bulletin/2006/financesurvey.pdf [cited 10 August 2009].

Bucks, Brian K., Arthur B. Kennickell, Traci L. Mach, and Kevin B. Moore. 2009. Changes in U.S. family finances from 2004 to 2007: Evidence from the Survey of Consumer Finances. *Federal Reserve Bulletin* (February) A1-56. Available from http://www.federalreserve.gov/pubs/bulletin/2009/pdf/scf09.pdf [cited 15 October 2009].

Buehler, Roger, Dale Griffin, and Michael Ross. 1994. Exploring the "planning fallacy":

Why people underestimate their task completion times. *Journal of Personality and Social Psychology* 67:366–81.

Burbidge, Andrew. 2000. Capital gains, homeownership, and economic inequality. *Housing Studies* 15, no. 2: 259–80.

Burgoyne, Carole B. 1990. Money in marriage: How patterns of allocation both reflect and conceal power. *Sociological Review* 38:634–65.

Burkhauser, Richard V., Barbara A. Butrica, and Michael J. Wasylenko. 1995. Mobility patterns of older homeowners: Are older homeowners trapped in distressed neighborhoods? *Research on Aging* 17, no. 4: 363–84.

Buss, W. Christian, and Charles M. Schaninger. 1983. The influence of sex roles on family decision processes and outcomes. *Advances in Consumer Research* 10:439–44.

Bynner, John, and Will Paxton, eds. 2001. *The asset-effect*. London: Institute for Public Policy Research.

Camerer, Colin, George Loewenstein, and Drazen Prelec. 2005. Neuroeconomics: How neuroscience can inform economics. *Journal of Economic Literature* 44:9–64.

Camic, Charles. 1986. The matter of habit. *American Journal of Sociology* 91:1039–87.

Caner, Asena, and Edward N. Wolff. 2004. *Asset poverty in the United States*. Annandale-on-Hudson, NY: Levy Economics Institute of Bard College.

Caplovitz, David. 1967. *The poor pay more: The consumer practices of low-income families*. New York: Free Press.

Caplovitz, David. 1979. *Making ends meet: How families cope with inflation and recession*. Beverly Hills, CA: Sage Publications.

Carasso, Adam, and Signe-Mary McKernan. 2008. Asset holdings and liabilities. In *Asset building and low-income families*, ed. Signe-Mary McKernan and Michael Sherraden, 33–66. Washington, DC: Urban Institute Press.

Carney, Stacie, and William Gale. 2001. Asset accumulation in low-income households. In *Assets for the poor: The benefits of spreading asset ownership*, ed. Thomas M. Shapiro and Edward N. Wolff, 165–205. New York: Russell Sage Foundation.

Carr, James H., and Jenny Schuetz. 2001. Financial services in distressed communities: Framing the issues, finding solutions. Washington, DC: Fannie Mae Foundation. Available from http://www.ppionline.org/documents/bank_part2.pdf [cited 11 February 2007].

Carroll, Christopher D. 1992. The buffer-stock theory of savings: Some macroeconomic evidence. *Brookings Papers on Economic Activity* 2:61–156.

Carroll, Christopher D., Karen E. Dynan, and Spencer D. Krane. 1999. Unemployment risk and precautionary wealth: Evidence from households' balance sheets. Working Paper no. 1999–16, Board of Governors of the Federal Reserve System. Available from http://www.federalreserve.gov/pubs/feds/1999/199915/199915pap.pdf. [cited 20 January 2004].

Carruthers, Bruce G. 2005. The sociology of money and credit. In *The handbook of economic sociology*, ed. N. J. Smelser and R. Swedberg, 355–78. Princeton: Princeton University Press.

Carruthers, Bruce G., and Wendy N. Espeland. 1998. Money, meaning, and morality. *American Behavioral Scientist* 41:1384–1408.

Caskey, John P. 1994. *Fringe banking: Check-cashing outlets, pawnshops, and the poor.* New York: Russell Sage Foundation.

Caskey, John P. 1997. *Lower income American, higher cost financial services.* Madison, WI: Filene Research Institute.

Caskey, John P. 2005. Reaching out to the unbanked. In *Inclusion in asset building: Assets, poverty, and public policy,* ed. Michael Sherraden, 149–66. New York: Oxford University Press.

Center for Responsible Lending. 2007. Subprime lending: A net drain on homeownership. CRL Issue Paper no. 14, March 27. Available from http://www.responsiblelend ing.org/mortgage-lending/research-analysis/Net-drain-in-home-Ownership.pdf [cited 18 May 2008].

Center for Responsible Lending. 2009. Soaring spillover: Accelerating foreclosures cost neighbors $502 billion in 2009 alone; 69.5 million homes lose $7,200 on average. CRL report, May 2009. Available from http://www.responsiblelending.org/mortgage lending/research-analysis/soaring-spillover-3-09.pdf. [cited June 15, 2009].

Center for Social Development. (2004). Savings account monitoring data from Tulsa CAPTC Management Information System for Individual Development Accounts (MIS IDA). Unpublished raw data.

CFED. 2007. American Dream Demonstration: Participating communities. Available from http://add.cfed.org/communities.html. [cited 15 May 2007].

Chang, Mariko Lin. 2006. Women and wealth. In *Wealth accumulation and communities of color in the United States,* ed. J. Gordon Nembhard and N. Chiteji, 112–32. Ann Arbor: University of Michigan Press.

Chattoe, Edmund, and Nigel Gilbert. 1999. Talking about budgets: Time and uncertainty in household decision making. *Sociology* 33:85–103.

Chen, Henry, and Robert I. Lerman. 2005. Do asset limits in social programs affect the accumulation of wealth? Opportunity and Ownership Project no. 4, The Urban Institute, Washington, DC.

Chen, Martha Alter, and Elizabeth Dunn. 1996. Household economic portfolios. Microenterprise Impact Project (MIP), USAID Office of Microenterprise Development, Washington, DC.

Cheng, Li-Chen, and Deborah Page-Adams. 1996. Education, assets, and intergenerational well-being: The case of female headed families. CSD Working Paper 96-3, Center for Social Development, Washington University, St. Louis.

Cho, Esther Yin-Nei. 1999. The effects of assets on the economic well-being of women after marital disruption. CSD Working Paper 99-6, Center for Social Development, Washington University, St. Louis.

Choi, James J., David Laibson, and Brigitte C. Madrian. 2004. Plan design and 401(k) savings outcomes. *National Tax Journal* 57, no. 2: 275–99.

Choi, James J., David Laibson, and Brigitte C. Madrian. 2005. $100 bills on the sidewalk: Suboptimal saving in 401(k) plans. NBER Working Paper No. 11554, National Bureau of Economic Research, Cambridge, MA. Available from http://www.nber.org/ papers/w11554. [cited 17 July 2007].

Choi, James J., David Laibson, Brigitte C. Madrian, and Andrew Metrick. 2002. Defined contribution pensions: Plan rules, participant decisions, and the path of least resistance. In *Tax policy and the economy*, Volume 16, ed. James M. Poterba, 67–114. Cambridge: MIT Press.

Choi, James J., David Laibson, Brigitte C. Madrian, and Andrew Metrick. 2004. For better or for worse: Default effects and 401(k) savings behavior. In *Perspectives on the economics of aging*, ed. David A. Wise, 81–121. Chicago: University of Chicago Press.

Choi, James J., David Laibson, Brigitte C. Madrian, and Andrew Metrick. 2005. Optimal defaults and active decisions. NBER Working Paper no. 11074, National Bureau of Economic Research, Cambridge, MA. Available from http://www.nber.org/papers/w11074. [cited 17 July 2007].

Choi, James J., David Laibson, Brigitte C. Madrian, and Andrew Metrick. 2006. Saving for retirement on the path of least resistance. In *Behavioral public finance: Toward a new agenda*, ed. E. McCaffery and J. Slemrod, 304–51. New York: Russell Sage Foundation.

Chowa, Gina, and William Elliott III. 2007. Increasing parent educational expectations for children in sub-Saharan Africa: The potential role of assets. CSD Working Paper 07-18, Center for Social Development, Washington University, St. Louis.

Clancy, Margaret, Reid Cramer, and Leslie Parrish. 2005. Section 529 savings plans, access to post-secondary education, and universal asset building. Washington DC: New America Foundation. Available from: http://www.newamerica.net/publications/pol icy/section_529_savings_plans_access_to_post_secondary_education_and_universal_asset_building [cited 10 July 2008].

Clancy, Margaret, Michal Grinstein-Weiss, and Mark Schreiner. 2001. Financial education and savings outcomes in Individual Development Accounts. CSD Working Paper No. 01-2, Center for Social Development, Washington University, St. Louis.

Clancy, Margaret M., Peter Orszag, and Michael Sherraden 2004. State college savings plans: A platform for inclusive policy? CSD Perspective, Center for Social Development, Washington University, St. Louis.

Collins, Daryl, Jonathan Morduch, Stuart Rutherford, and Orlanda Ruthven. 2009. *Portfolios of the poor: How the world's poor live on $2 a day*. Princeton and Oxford: Princeton University Press.

Comptroller of the Currency. 2004. Remittances: A gateway to banking for unbanked immigrants. *Community Development Insights*, Community Affairs Department, 1–17, September.

Conley, Dalton. 1999. *Being black, living in the red: Race, wealth, and social policy in America*. Berkeley: University of California Press.

Conley, Dalton. 2001. Capital for college: Parent assets and postsecondary schooling. *Sociology of Education* 74, no. 1: 59–72.

Conley, Dalton, and Miriam Ryvicker. 2005. The price of female headship: Gender, inheritance, and wealth accumulation in the United States. *Journal of Income Distribution* 13, no. 3: 41–56.

Cox, Kevin R. 1982. Housing tenure and neighborhood activism. *Urban Affairs Quarterly* 18, no. 1: 107–29.

Cramer, Reid, Rourke O'Brien, and Alejandra Lopez-Fernandini. 2008. The assets agenda: Policy options to promote savings and asset ownership by low- and moderate-income Americans. New America Foundation, Washington, DC. Available from http://www.newamerica.net/files/Assets%20Agenda%202008%20Final.pdf [cited 15 June, 2009].

Cronqvist, Henrik, and Richard H. Thaler. 2004. Design choices in privatized social-security systems: Learning from the Swedish experience. *American Economic Review* 94, no. 2: 424–28.

Cruce, Ashley. 2001. A history of progressive-era school savings banking, 1870–1930. CSD Working Paper 01-3, Center for Social Development, Washington University, St. Louis.

Cruce, Ashley. 2002. School-based savings programs, 1930–2002. CSD Working Paper 02-7, Center for Social Development, Washington University, St. Louis.

Curtis, Richard F. 1986. Household and family in theory on equality. *American Sociological Review* 51:168–83.

Dahrendorf, Ralf. 1979. *Life chances: Approaches to social and political theory.* Chicago: University of Chicago Press.

Danes, Sharon M., and Kathryn D. Rettig. 1995. Economic adjustment strategies of farm men and women experiencing economic stress. *Financial Counseling and Planning* 6:59–74.

Davis, Elizabeth P. 1992. Financial management practices among households with differing resource constraints. *Journal of Consumer Education* 10:27–31.

Davis, Elizabeth P., and Judith A. Weber. 1990. Patterns and obstacles to financial management. *Financial Counseling and Planning* 1:41–51.

Deaton, Angus. 1992. *Understanding consumption.* Oxford: Clarendon Press.

Denton, Nancy. 2001. Housing as means of asset accumulation: A good strategy for the poor? In *Assets for the poor: The benefits of spreading asset ownership,* ed. Thomas M. Shapiro and Edward N. Wolff, 232–66. New York: Russell Sage Foundation.

Destin, Mesmin, and Daphne Oyserman. 2008. From assets to school outcomes: How finances shape children's perceived possibilities and intentions. *Psychological Science* 20, no. 4: 414–18.

DeVaney, Sharon A., Elizabeth E. Gorham, Janet C. Bechman, and Virginia Haldeman. 1996. Cash flow management and credit use: Effect of a financial information program. *Financial Counseling and Planning* 7:71–80.

Dew, Jeffrey. 2007. Two sides of the same coin? The differing roles of assets and consumer debt in marriage. *Journal of Family Economic Issues* 28:89–104.

Dewey, John. 1938. *Experience and education.* New York: Macmillan.

DiPasquale, Denise, and Edward Glaeser. 1999. Incentives and social capital: Are homeowners better citizens? *Journal of Urban Economics* 45:354–84.

Ditkovsky, Orit, and Willem Van Vleit. 1984. Housing tenure and community participation. *Ekistics* 307 (July–August): 345–48.

Dixon, Mike. 2006. Rethinking financial capability: Lessons from economic psychology and behavioural finance. London: Institute for Public Policy Research. Available from https://www.ippr.org/publicationsandreports/publications.asp?id=471. [cited 27 November 2006].

Domowitz, Ian, and Robert L. Sartain. 1999. Determinants of the consumer bankruptcy decision. *Journal of Finance* 54, no. 1: 403–20.

Douglas, Mary, and Baron Isherwood. 1978. *The world of goods: Towards an anthropology of consumption.* Harmondsworth: Penguin.

Dowding, Keith, Jurgen De Wispelaere, and Stuart White. 2003. *The ethics of stakeholding.* New York: Palgrave Macmillan.

Drakeford, Mark. 1998. Last rights? Funerals, poverty, and social exclusion. *Journal of Social Policy* 27:507–24.

Duflo, Esther, William Gale, Jeffrey Liebman, Peter Orszag, and Emmanuel Saez. 2005. Saving incentives for low- and middle-income families: Evidence from a field experiment with H&R Block. *Quarterly Journal of Economics* 121, no. 4 (November): 1311–46.

Dunham, Constance R. 2001. The role of banks and nonbanks in serving low- and moderate-income communities. In *Changing financial markets and community development,* ed. Jackson L. Blanton, Alicia Williams, and Sherie L. W. Rhine, 31–58. Richmond, VA: Federal Reserve Bank of Richmond.

Dunning, David, Dale W. Griffin, James D. Milojkovic, and Lee Ross. 1990. The overconfidence effect in social prediction. *Journal of Personality and Social Psychology* 58:568–81.

Dynan, Karen. 1993. The rate of time preference and shocks to wealth: Evidence from panel data. Working Paper 134, Board of Governors of the Federal Reserve, Washington, DC.

Economic and Social Research Council, ed. 2002. How people on low incomes manage their lives. Swindon: ESRC.

Economic Policy Institute. 2007. Living wage: Facts at a glance. Washington, DC: Economic Policy Institute. Available from http://epi.3cdn.net/6654f659599ce2fd22_qnm6b9ce8.pdf. [cited 17 June 2009].

Edin, Kathryn. 2001. More than money: The role of assets in the survival strategies and material well-being of the poor. In *Assets for the poor: The benefits of spreading asset ownership,* ed. Thomas M. Shapiro and Edward N. Wolff, 206–31. New York: Russell Sage Foundation.

Edin, Kathryn, and Laura Lein. 1997. *Making ends meet: How single mothers survive welfare and low-wage work.* New York: Russell Sage Foundation.

Ehrenreich, Barbara. 2001. *Nickel and dimed: On not getting by in America.* New York: Holt.

Ehrenreich, Barbara. 2009. Too poor to make the news. *New York Times* [online edition] 14 June. Available from http://www.nytimes.com/2009/06/14/opinion/14ehrenreich.html [cited June 15, 2009].

Elder, Glen H., Jr., Rand D. Conger, E. Michael Foster, and Monika Ardelt. 1992. Families under economic pressure. *Journal of Family Issues* 13:5–37.

Elliehausen, Gregory, and Edward C. Lawrence. 2001. Payday advance credit in America: An analysis of customer demand. Monograph no. 35, Georgetown University Credit Research Center, McDonough School of Business, Georgetown University, Washington, DC.

Elliott, William, III. 2008. Children's college aspirations and expectations: The potential role of children's development accounts (CDAs). *Children and Youth Services Review* 31, no. 2: 274–83.

Elliott, William, and Margaret Sherrard Sherraden. 2007. Specifying children's educational expectations: The potential impact of institutions. CSD Working Paper 10-17, Center for Social Development, Washington University, St. Louis.

Elliott, William, and Kristen Wagner. 2007. Increasing parent expectations via college savings: Closing the achievement gap. CSD Working Paper 07-08, Center for Social Development, Washington University, St. Louis.

Ellsworth, Scott. 1982. *Death in a promised land: The Tulsa race riot of 1921*. Baton Rouge: Louisiana State University Press.

Engel, Kathleen, and Patricia McCoy. 2007. Predatory lending and community development at loggerheads. In *Financing low-income communities: Models, obstacles, and future directions*, ed., Julia S. Rubin, 227–62. New York: Russell Sage Foundation.

Engen, Eric M., William G. Gale, and John Karl Scholz. 1994. Do saving incentives work? *Brookings Papers on Economic Activity* 1:85–151.

Ernst, Keith, John Farris, and Uriah King. 2004. Quantifying the economic cost of predatory payday lending. Center for Responsible Lending. December 18, 2003 (Revised February 24, 2004) Available from http://www.responsiblelending.org/paydaylending/research-analysis/CRLpaydaylendingstudy121803.pdf [cited 15 June 2009].

ESRC. 2002. *How people with low incomes manage their finances*, ed. Economic and Social Research Council (ESRC). Swindon: ESRC.

Essen, Juliet, Ken Fogelman, and Jenny Head. 1977. Childhood housing experiences and social achievements. *Child Care, Health, and Development* 4:41–58.

Etzioni, Amitai. 1988. *The moral dimension: Towards a new economics*. New York: Free Press.

Fan, Xitao, and Michael Chen. 2001. Parental involvement and students' academic achievement: A meta-analysis. *Educational Psychology Review* 13, no. 1: 1–22.

Federal Reserve Statistical Release. 2006. Consumer credit. 7 December. Available from http://www.federalreserve.gov/releases/g19/current/default.htm [cited 11 December 2006].

Feldstein, Martin. 1995. College scholarship rules and private saving. *American Economic Review* 85, no. 3: 552–66.

Fellowes, Matt. 2006. From poverty, opportunity: Putting the market to work for lower income families. Brookings Institution Policy Program Report, July. Brookings Institution, Washington, DC.

Financial Service Authority. 2005. Measuring financial capability: An exploratory study. *Consumer Research* 37. London: University of Bristol, Personal Finance Research Centre. Available from http://www.fsa.gov.uk/pubs/consumer-research/crpr37.pdf. [cited 1 May 2006].

Finnegan, William. 1998. *Cold new world: Growing up in a harder country.* New York: Random House.

Fischer, Claude. 1982. *To dwell among friends: Personal networks in town and country.* Chicago: University of Chicago Press.

Fisher, I. 1930. *The theory of interest.* London: Macmillan.

Fisher, Monica G., and Bruce A. Weber. 2004. *Does economic vulnerability depend on place of residence? Asset poverty across the rural-urban continuum.* RUPRI Rural Poverty Research Center Working Paper #04-01, March 2004. http://www.rupri.org/ productsarchive.php#9 [cited 15 June 2009]. Columbia, MO: Rural Poverty Research Center.

Folbre, Nancy. 1988. The black four of hearts: Toward a new paradigm of household economics. In *A home divided: Women and income in the Third World,* ed. Daisy Dwyer and Judith Bruce, 248–62. Stanford: Stanford University Press.

Friedman, Milton. 1957. *A theory of the consumption function.* National Bureau of Economic Research, General Series no. 63. Princeton: Princeton University Press.

Fry, Tim R. L., Sandra Mihajilo, Roslyn Russell, and Robert Brooks. 2008. The factors influencing saving in a matched savings program: Goals, knowledge of payment instruments, and other behavior. *Journal of Family Issues* 29:234–50.

Furnham, Adrian F. 1985. Why do people save? Attitudes to, and habits of, saving money in Britain. *Journal of Applied Social Psychology* 15, no. 4: 354–73.

Gale, William G., J. Mark Iwry, and Peter R. Orszag. 2004. *The saver's credit: Issues and options. Retirement Security Project.* April. Washington, DC: The Brookings Institution and George Washington University.

Gale, William G., and John Karl Scholz. 1992. Examining the evidence on IRAs and household saving. In *Personal saving, consumption, and tax policy,* ed. Marvin H. Kosters, 76–83. Washington, DC: AEI Press.

Galligan, Richard J., and Stephen J. Bahr. 1978. Economic well-being and marital stability: Implications for income maintenance programs. *Journal of Marriage and the Family* 40, no. 2 (May): 283–90.

Galster, George C. 1983. Empirical evidence on cross-tenure differences in home maintenance and conditions. *Land Economics* 59, no. 1: 107–13.

Galster, George C. 1987. *Homeowners and neighborhood reinvestment.* Durham: Duke University Press.

Gigerenzer, Gerd, and Peter M. Todd. 1999. *Simple heuristics that make us smart.* Oxford: Oxford University Press.

Gilderbloom, John I., and John P. Markham. 1995. The impact of homeownership on political beliefs. *Social Forces* 73, no. 4: 1589–1607.

Glennerster, Howard. 2006. Capital poor. *Benefits* 14, no. 10: 27–31.

Godwin, Deborah D. 1990. Family financial management. *Family Relations* 39:221–28.

Godwin, Deborah D., and Joan C. Koonce. 1992. Cash flow management of low-income newlyweds. *Financial Counseling and Planning* 3:17–42.

Goldberg, Fred. 2005. The universal piggy bank: Designing and implementing a system of savings accounts for children. In *Inclusion in the American dream: Assets, poverty, and public policy,* ed. Michael Sherraden, 303–22. New York: Oxford University Press.

Goldberg, Fred T., and Jodi Birk Cohen. 2000. The universal piggy bank: Designing and implementing a system of savings accounts for children. Paper presented at the "Inclusion in Asset Building: Research and Policy Symposium," Washington University, St. Louis, September.

Grable, John, and So-Hyun Joo. 1999. Gender and financial education: Changing financial knowledge and attitudes. *Journal of Family and Consumer Sciences* 91, no. 4: 29.

Granovetter, Mark. 1983. The strength of weak ties: A network theory revisited. *Sociological Theory* 1:201–33.

Green, Richard K., and Michelle J. White. 1997. Measuring the benefits of homeowning: Effects on children. *Journal of Urban Economics* 41:441–61.

Greene, Vernon L., and Jan I. Ondrich. 1990. Risk factors for nursing home admissions and exits: A discrete time hazard function approach. *Journals of Gerontology* 45, no. 6: S250–S258.

Greenspan, Alan. 2005. The importance of financial education today. *Social Education* 69, no. 2; 64–65.

Gregory, Lee, and Mark Drakeford. 2006. Social work, asset-based welfare, and the child trust fund. *British Journal of Social Work* 36, no. 10: 149–57.

Griffin, Dale W., David Dunning, and Lee Ross. 1990. The role of construal process in overconfident predictions about the self and others. *Journal of Personality and Social Psychology* 59:1128–39.

Grinstein-Weiss, Michal, Kristen Wagner, and Fred M. Ssewamala. 2006. Saving and asset accumulation among low-income families with children in IDAs. *Children and Youth Services Review* 28, no. 2: 193–211.

Grinstein-Weiss, Michal, Min Zhan, and Michael Sherraden. 2004. Saving performance in Individual Development Accounts: Does marital status matter? *Journal of Marriage and Family* 68 (February): 192–204.

Grinstein-Weiss, Michal, Yeong H. Yeo, Kate Irish, and Min Zhan. 2009. Parental assets: A pathway to positive child educational outcomes. *Journal of Sociology and Social Welfare* 36, no. 1:61–85.

Groenland, E. A. G., J. G. Bloem, and A. A. A. Kuylen. 1996. Prototypicality and structure of the saving concept for consumers. *Journal of Economic Psychology* 17, no. 6: 691–708.

Gruber, Jonathan, and Aaron Yelowitz. 1997. Public health insurance and private savings. NBER Working Paper 6041, National Bureau of Economic Research, Washington, DC.

Guest, Avery M., and R. S. Oropesa. 1986. Informal social ties and political activity in the metropolis. *Urban Affairs Quarterly* 21:550–74.

Gyourko, Joseph, Peter Linneman, and Susan M. Wachter. 1999. Analyzing the relationships among race, wealth, and home ownership in America. *Journal of Housing Economics* 8:63–89.

Hahn, Beth A. 1993. Marital status and women's health: The effect of economic marital acquisitions. *Journal of Marriage and the Family* 55 (May): 495–504.

Hall, Peter A., and Rosemary C. R. Taylor. 1996. Political science: The three new institutionalisms. *Political Studies* 44, no. 4: 936–57.

Halstead, Ted, and Michael Lind. 2001. *The radical center: The future of American politics.* New York: Doubleday.

Harkness, Joseph M., and Sandra Newman. 2003. The effects of homeownership on children: The role of neighborhood characteristics and family income. *Economic Policy Review* 9, no. 2, 87–107.

Harrod, Roy Forbes. 1948. *Towards a dynamic economics.* London: Macmillan.

Haurin, Donald R., Toby L. Parcel, and R. Jean Haurin. 2001. The impact of homeownership on child outcomes. Low Income Home Ownership Working Paper Series LIHO.01-14, Joint Center for Housing Studies, Harvard University, Cambridge.

Haveman, Robert. 1988. *Starting even: An equal opportunity program to combat the nation's new poverty.* New York: Simon and Schuster.

Haveman, Robert, and Edward N. Wolff. 2005. Who are the asset poor? Levels, trends, and composition, 1983–1998. In *Inclusion in the American dream: Assets, poverty, and public policy,* ed. Michael Sherraden, 61–86. Oxford: Oxford University Press.

Heath, Chip, and Jack B. Soll. 1996. Mental budgeting and consumer decisions. *Journal of Consumer Research* 23:40–52.

Helman, Ruth, and Variny Paladino. 2004. Will Americans ever become savers? The 14th Annual Retirement Confidence Survey. Issue Brief 268, Employee Benefit Research Institute, Washington, DC. Available from http://www.ebri.org/publications/ib/in dex.cfm?fa=ibDisp&content_id=496. [cited 11February 2007].

Henretta, John C. 1984. Parental status and child's home ownership. *American Sociological Review* 49, no. 1: 131–40.

Henretta, John C. 1987. Family transitions, housing market context, and first home purchase by young married households. *Social Forces* 66, no. 2: 520–36.

Henretta, John C., and Richard T. Campbell. 1978. Net worth as an aspect of states. *American Journal of Sociology* 83:1024–1223.

Heymann, Jody, with Joshua Cohen and Joel Rogers, eds. 2002. *Can working families ever win?* Boston: Beacon Press.

Hilgert, Marianne A., Jeanne M. Hogarth, and Sondra G. Beverly. 2003. Household financial management: The connection between knowledge and behavior. *Federal Reserve Bulletin* (July): 309–22.

Hill, Martha S., and Greg J. Duncan. 1987. Parental family income and the socioeconomic attainment of children. *Social Science Research* 16:39–73.

Hills, John, Rachel Smithies, and Abigail McKnight. 2006. Tracking income: How working families' incomes vary through the year. CASE Report 32, Centre for Analysis of Social Exclusion, London. Available from http://sticerd.lse.ac.uk/dps/case/cr/ CASEreport32.pdf. [cited 26 September 2007].

Himmelstein, David U., Elizabeth Warren, Deborah Thorne, and Steffie Woolhandler. 2005. Illness and injury as contributors to bankruptcy. *Health Affairs* 24, no. 1. Available from http://content.healthaffairs.org/cgi/content/full/hlthaff.w5.63/DC1. [cited 20 February 2005].

Himmelstein, David, Deobrah Thorne, Elizabeth Warren, and Steffie Woolhandler. 2009. Medical bankruptcy in the United States, 2007: Results of a National Study. *American Journal of Medicine.* Available from http://www.pnhp.org/new_bank ruptcy_study/Bankruptcy-2009.pdf [cited 15 June 2009].

Hinnant-Bernard, Thessaleneure, and Sue R. Crull. 2004. Subprime lending and reverse redlining. *Housing and Society* 31, no. 2: 169–86.

Hirad, Abdighani, and Peter M. Zorn. 2001. A little knowledge is a good thing: Empirical evidence of the effectiveness of pre-purchase homeownership counseling. Low

Income Homeownership Working Paper LIHO-01.4, Joint Center for Housing Studies, Harvard University, Cambridge.

Hirsch, James S. 2002. *Riot and remembrance: The Tulsa race war and its legacy.* Boston: Houghton Mifflin.

Hirschland, Madeline, ed. 2005. *Savings services for the poor: An operational guide.* Bloomfield, CT: Kumarian Press.

Hoch, Stephen J., and George F. Loewenstein. 1991. Time inconsistent preferences and consumer self-control. *Journal of Consumer Research* 17:492–507.

Hogan, M. Janice, Catherine Solheim, Susan Wolfgram, Busisiwe Nkosi, and Nicola Rodrigues. 2004. The working poor: From the economic margins to asset building. *Family Relations* 53:229–36.

Hogarth, Jeanne M. 2006. Financial education and economic development. Paper prepared for "Improving Financial Literacy," International Conference, Russian G8 Presidency in cooperation with the OECD. November 29–30. Available from: http://www.oecd.org/dataoecd/20/50/37742200.pdf [cited 20 April 2008].

Hogarth, Jeanne M., and Chris E. Anguelov. 2003. How much can the poor save? *Consumer Interest Annual* 49:1–18.

Hogarth, Jeanne M., Chris E. Anguelov, and Jinkook Lee. 2001. Who has a bank account? Changes over time in account ownership. *Consumer Interests Annual* 47:1–3.

Hogarth, Jeanne M., Chris E. Anguelov, and Jinkook Lee. 2004. Why don't households have a checking account? *Journal of Consumer Affairs* 38, no. 1: 1–26.

Hogarth, Jeanne M., and Keven H. O'Donnell. 1999. Banking relationships of lower-income families and the governmental trend toward electronic payments. *Federal Reserve Bulletin* 83:459–73.

Hogarth, Jeanne M., and Josephine Swanson. 1995. Using adult education principles in financial education for a low income audience. *Family Economics and Resources Management Biennial,* 139–46.

Hossler, Don, and Nick Vesper. 1993. An exploratory study of the factors associated with parental saving for postsecondary education. *Journal of Higher Education* 64, no. 2: 140–65.

Howard, Christopher. 1999. *The hidden welfare state: Tax expenditures and social policy in the welfare state.* Princeton: Princeton University Press.

Hrung, Warren B. 2002. Income uncertainty and IRAs. *International Tax and Public Finance* 9:591–99.

Hubbard, R. Glenn, and Jonathan S. Skinner. 1996. Assessing the effectiveness of saving incentives. *Journal of Economic Perspectives* 10, no. 4 (Fall): 73–90.

Hubbard, R. Glenn, Jonathan S. Skinner, and Stephen P. Zeldes. 1994. Why do people save? Expanding the life-cycle model: Precautionary saving and public policy. *American Economic Review* 84, no. 2: 174–79.

Hubbard, R. Glenn, Jonathan S. Skinner, and Stephen P. Zeldes. 1995. Precautionary saving and social insurance. *Journal of Political Economy* 103, no. 2 (April): 360–99.

Hudson, Michael, ed. 1996. *Merchants of misery.* Monroe, ME: Common Courage Press.

Hurst, Erik, and James P. Ziliak. 2006. Do welfare asset limits affect household saving? Evidence from welfare reform. *Journal of Human Resources* 41, no. 1 (Winter): 46–71.

Huston, Sandra J., and Y. Regina Chang. 1997. Adequate emergency fund holdings and family type. *Financial Counseling and Planning* 8, no. 1: 37–46.

Hutton, Patricia A., and James M. Holmes. 2005. Savings education: Learning the value of self-control. *Education Policy Analysis Archives* 13, no. 28. Available from: http://epaa.asu.edu/epaa/v13n28/v13n28.pdf [cited 15 June 2008].

Ifill, Roberto M., and Michael S. McPherson. 2004. When saving means losing: Weighing the benefits of college-savings plans. *Lumina Foundation for Education* 5, no. 2.

Immergluck, Dan. 2004. Hyper-segmentation and exclusion in financial services in the U.S.: The effects on low-income and minority neighborhoods. *Social Policy Journal* 3, no. 3: 25–44.

Jacob, Katy, Sharyl Hudson, and Malcolm Bush. 2000. Tools for survival: An analysis of financial literacy programs for lower-income families. January. Woodstock Institute.

James, William. 1890. *The principles of psychology*. New York: H. Holt.

Johnson, Elizabeth, James Hinterlong, and Michael Sherraden. 2001. New advances in technology for social work education and practice. *Journal of Technology in Human Services* 18, nos. 3–4: 5–22.

Johnson, Elizabeth, and Margaret S. Sherraden. 2007. From financial literacy to financial capability among youth. *Journal of Sociology and Social Welfare* 34, no. 3: 119–46.

Jolls, Christine, Cass R. Sunstein, and Richard Thaler. 1998. A behavioral approach to law and economics. *Stanford Law Review* 50:1471.

Joshi, Heather, and Susan Macran. 1991. Work, gender, and health. *Work, Employment, and Society* 5:451–69.

Kahneman, Daniel, Jack L. Knetsch, and Richard H. Thaler. 1991. Anomalies: The endowment effect, loss aversion, and status quo bias. *Journal of Economic Perspectives* 5, no. 1: 193–206.

Kahneman, Daniel, and Amos Tversky. 1979. Prospect theory: An analysis of decision under risk. *Econometrica* 47:263–91.

Kane, Thomas J. 1994. College entry by blacks since 1970: The role of college costs, family background, and the returns to education. *Journal of Political Economy* 102:878–907.

Karger, Howard. 2005. *Shortchanged: Life and debt in the fringe economy*. San Francisco: Berrett-Koehler.

Katona, George. 1974. Psychology and consumer economics. *Journal of Consumer Research* 1:1–18.

Katona, George. 1975. *Psychological economics*. New York: Elsevier.

Katona, George. 1980. *Essays on behavioral economics*. Ann Arbor: Institute for Social Research, University of Michigan.

Keister, Lisa A. 2000a. Race and wealth inequality: The impact of racial differences in asset ownership on the distribution of household wealth. *Social Science Research* 29, no. 4: 477–502.

Keister, Lisa A. 2000b. *Wealth in America*. New York: Cambridge University Press.

Keister, Lisa A. 2003. Religion and wealth: The role of religious affiliation and participation in early adult asset accumulation. *Social Forces* 82:175–207

Keister, Lisa A., and Stephanie Moller. 2000. Wealth inequality in the United States. *Annual Review of Sociology* 26:63–81.

Kempson, Elaine. 1996. *Life on a low income*. York: Joseph Rowntree Foundation.

Kempson, Elaine. 2006. Policy level response to financial exclusion in developed economies: Lessons for developing countries. Paper presented at the World Bank Access to Finance: Building Inclusive Financial Systems Conference, May.

Kempson, Elaine, Adele Atkinson, and Sharon Collard. 2006. Saving for children: A baseline survey at the inception of the Child Trust Fund. HM Revenue and Customs Research Report 18, London.

Kempson, Elaine, Stephen McKay, and Sharon Collard. 2003. Evaluation of the CFLI and Saving Gateway Pilot Projects: Interim report on the Saving Gateway Pilot Project. Bristol, United Kingdom: Personal Finance Research Centre, University of Bristol.

Kennickell, Arthur B. 2006. Currents and undercurrents: Changes in the distribution of wealth, 1989–2004. Available from http://www.federalreserve.gov/pubs/oss/oss2/pa pers/concentration.2004.5.pdf [cited 17 June 2009].

Kennickell, Arthur B., Martha Starr-McCluer, and Annika E. Sundén. 1997. Family finances in the U.S.: Recent evidence from the Survey of Consumer Finances. *Federal Reserve Bulletin* 83, no. 1: 20–24. Available from: http://www.federalreserve.gov/pubs/bulletin/1997/0197lead.pdf. [cited 30 December 2007].

Kennickell, Arthur B., Martha Starr-McCluer, and Brian Surrette. 2000. Recent changes in US family finances: Results from the 1998 Survey of Consumer Finances. *Federal Reserve Bulletin* 86 (January): 1–29.

Kingston, Paul W., and John C. Fries. 1994. Having a stake in the system: The sociopolitical ramifications of business and home ownership. *Social Science Quarterly* 75, no. 3: 679–86.

Kingwell, Paul, Michael Dowie, Barbara Holler, Carole Vincent, with David Gyarmati and Hongmei Cao. 2005. *Design and implementation of a program to help the poor save: The Learn$Ave Project*. Ottawa: Social Research and Demonstration Corporation.

Kirchler, Erich. 1999. Household decision making. In *The Elgar companion to consumer research and economic psychology*, ed. Peter E. Earl and Simon Kemp, 296–304. Cheltenham: Edward Elgar.

Knight, Jack. 1992. *Institutions and social conflict*. Cambridge: Cambridge University Press.

Kochhar, Rakesh. 2004. The wealth of Hispanic households, 1996 to 2002. Pew Hispanic Center Report, Washington, DC. Available from http://pewhispanic.org/reports/re port.php?ReportID=34. [cited 11 January 2007].

Koehler, Derek J., and Connie S. K. Poon. 2006. Self-predictions overweight strength of current intentions. *Journal of Experimental Social Psychology* 42, no. 4: 517–24.

Kojima, Sotohiro, and Yasuhisa Hama. 1982. Aspects of the psychology of spending. *Japanese Psychological Research* 24:29–38.

Kotlikoff, Laurence T., ed. 1989. *What determines savings?* Cambridge: MIT Press.

Kotlikoff, Laurence T., with B. Douglas Bernheim. 2001. Household financial planning and financial literacy: The need for new tools. In *Essays on saving, bequests, altruism, and life-cycle planning*, ed. Laurence J. Kotlikoff, 427–77. Cambridge: MIT Press.

Kotlikoff, Laurence, and Lawrence Summers. 1981. The role of intergenerational transfers in aggregate capital accumulation. *Journal of Political Economy* 89, no. 4: 706–32.

Kurz, Karin. 2004. Labour market position, intergenerational transfers, and home-ownership: A longitudinal analysis for West German birth cohorts. *European Sociological Review* 20:141–59.

Lackman, Conway, and John M. Lanasa. 1993. Family decision-making theory: An overview and assessment. *Psychology and Marketing* 10, no. 2: 81–93.

Lacko, James M., Signe McKernan, and Manoj Hastak. 2001. Rent-to-own: An empirical examination of customer experience. *Consumer Interests Annual* 46:103.

Laibson, David. 1997. Golden eggs and hyperbolic discounting. *Quarterly Journal of Economics* 112:443–77.

Laibson, David, Andrea Repetto, and Jeremy Tobacman. 1998. Self-control and saving for retirement. *Brookings Papers on Economic Activity* 1:91–196.

Laibson, David, Andrea Repetto, and Jeremy Tobacman. 2003. A debt puzzle. In *Knowledge, information, and expectations in modern economics: In honor of Edmund S. Phelps,* ed. Phillippe Aghion, Roman Frydman, Joseph Stiglitz, and Michael Woodford, 228–66. Princeton: Princeton University Press.

Lambert, Craig. 2006. The marketplace of perceptions. *Harvard Magazine* (March–April): 50–57, 93–95.

Lassarre, Dominique. 1986. Moving into home ownership. *Journal of Economic Psychology* 7, no. 2: 161–78.

Lassarre, Dominique, and Christine Roland-Levy. 1988. Understanding children's economic socialization. In *Understanding economic behaviour,* ed. Klaus G. Grünert and Folke Ölander, 347–68. Dordrecht, NL: Kluwer.

Lawrance, Emily. 1987. Transfers to the poor and long run savings. *Economic Inquiry* 25:459–78.

Lawrance, Emily. 1991. Poverty and the rate of time preference: Evidence from panel data. *Journal of Political Economy* 99, no. 1: 54–73.

Lea, Stephen E. G. 1999. Credit, debt, and problem debt. In *The Elgar companion to consumer research and economic psychology,* ed. Peter E. Earl and Simon Kemp, 139–44. Cheltenham: Edward Elgar.

Lea, Stephen E. G., Roger M. Tarpy, and Paul Webley. 1987. *The individual in the economy: A survey of economic psychology.* Cambridge: Cambridge University Press.

Lea, Stephen E. G., and Paul Webley. 2005. In search of the economic self. *Journal of Socio-economics* 34:585–604.

Lea, Stephen E. G., Paul Webley, and R. Mark Levine. 1993. The economic psychology of consumer debt. *Journal of Economic Psychology* 14:85–119.

Lea, Stephen E. G., Paul Webley, and Catherine M. Walker. 1995. Psychological factors in consumer debt: Money management, economic socialization, and credit use. *Journal of Economic Psychology* 16:111–34.

Le Grand, Julian, and David Nissan. 2003. A capital idea: Helping the young to help themselves. In *The ethics of stakeholding,* ed. Keith Dowding, Jurgen de Wisperlaere, and Stuart White, 29–41. Houndmills, Basingstoke, Hampshire, and New York: Palgrave Macmillan.

Lerman, Robert I. 2005. Are low-income households accumulating assets and avoiding unhealthy debt? A review of recent evidence. Urban Institute Opportunity and Ownership Project no. 1, Urban Institute, Washington, DC.

Lerman, Robert I., and Signe-Mary McKernan. 2008. Benefits and consequences of holding assets. In *Asset building and low-income families*, ed., Signe-Mary McKernan and Michael Sherraden, 175–206. Washington, DC: Urban Institute Press.

Levin, Laurence. 1998. Are assets fungible? Testing alternative theories of life-cycle savings. *Journal of Economic Behavior and Organization* 36, no. 1: 59–83.

Levitan, Sara, and Isaac Shapiro. 1987. *Working but poor: America's contradiction*. Baltimore: Johns Hopkins University Press.

Lewin, Kurt. 1951. *Field theory in social science: Selected theoretical papers*. New York: Harper and Brothers.

Lewis, Alan, Paul Webley, and Adrian F. Furnham. 1995. *The new economic mind*. Brighton, United Kingdom: Harvest Wheatsheaf.

Lewis, Oscar. 1959. *Five families: Mexican case studies in the culture of poverty*. Rev. ed. New York: Basic Books.

Lewis, R. Barry. 1998. ATLAS.ti and NUD*IST: A comparative review of two leading data analysis packages. *Cultural Anthropology Methods* 10:41–47.

Light, Ivan, and Carolyn Rosenstein. 1995. *Race, ethnicity, and entrepreneurship in urban America*. New York: Walter de Gruyter.

Lincoln, Yvonna S., and Egon G. Guba. 1985. *Naturalistic inquiry*. Beverly Hills, CA: Sage.

Lindh, Thomas, and Henry Ohlsson. 1998. Self-employment and wealth inequality. *Review of Income and Wealth* 44, no. 10: 25–42.

Lindsey, Duncan. 1994. *The welfare of children*. 1st ed. Oxford: Oxford University Press.

Lister, Ruth. 2006. Poverty, material insecurity, and income vulnerability: The role of savings. In *The saving gateway: From principles to practice*, ed. Sonia Sodha and Ruth Lister, 8–33. London: Institute for Public Policy Research.

Lloyd, Kim M., and Scott J. South. 1996. Contextual influences on young men's transition to first marriage. *Social Forces* 74, no. 3: 1097–1119.

Loewenstein, George F. 1996. Out of control: Visceral influences on behavior. *Organizational Behavior and Human Decision Processes* 65:272–92.

Loke, Vernon, and Michael Sherraden. 2006. Building assets from birth: A comparison of the policies and proposals on children savings accounts in Singapore, the United Kingdom, Canada, Korea, and the United States. CSD Working Paper 06-14, Center for Social Development, Washington University, St. Louis.

Lopez-Fernandini, Alejandra, Ellen Seidman, and Reid Cramer. 2008. AutoSave Overview. Washington, DC: New America Foundation, 16 July, 2 pp. Available from: http://www.newamerica.net/files/AutoSave%20Overview-Sept%202008.pdf [cited 15 August 2008].

Lovell, Phillip, and Julia Isaacs. 2009. The impact of the mortgage crisis on children and their education. *First Focus*, April: 1–5. Available from http://www.firstfocus.net/Download/HousingandChildrenFINAL.pdf [cited 15 June, 2009].

Lui, Meizhu, Barbara J. Robles, Betsy Leondar-Wright, Rose M. Brewer, and Rebecca Adamson. 2006. *The color of wealth: The story behind the U.S. racial wealth divide*. New York: New Press.

Lum, Terry. 2005. Health-wealth association among older Americans: Racial and ethnic differences. *Social Work Research* 28, no. 2: 106–116.

Lum, Yat-Sang, and Elizabeth Lightfoot. 2003. The effect of health on retirement saving among older workers. *Social Work Research* 27, no. 1: 31–44.

Lunt, Peter, and Adrian Furnham, eds. 1996. *Economic socialization: The economic beliefs and behaviours of young people.* Cheltenham, United Kingdom: Edward Elgar.

Lunt, Peter, and Sonia M. Livingstone. 1991a. Everyday explanations for personal debt: A network approach. *British Journal of Social Psychology* 30:309–23.

Lunt, Peter, and Sonia M. Livingstone. 1991b. Psychological, social, and economic determinants of saving: Comparing recurrent and total savings. *Journal of Economic Psychology* 12:621–41.

Lunt, Peter, and Sonia M. Livingstone. 1992. *Mass consumption and personal identity: Everyday economic experience.* Buckingham: Open University Press.

Luria, Daniel D. 1976. Wealth, capital, and power: The social meaning of home ownership. *Journal of Interdisciplinary History* 7, no. 2: 261–82.

Lusardi, Annamaria. 2000. *Explaining why so many families do not save.* Hanover, NH: Dartmouth College; Chicago: University of Chicago, Harris School of Public Policy Studies.

Lusardi, Annamaria, ed. 2008. *Overcoming the saving slump: How to increase the effectiveness of financial education and saving programs.* Chicago and London: University of Chicago Press.

Lyons, Angela C. 2003. How credit access has changed over time for U.S. households. *Journal of Consumer Interests* 37, no. 2: 231–55.

Lyons, Angela C., Yunhee Chang, and Erik M. Scherpf. 2006. Translating financial education into behavior change for low-income populations. *Financial Counseling and Planning* 17, no. 2: 27–45.

MacQueen, Kathleen M., Eleanor McLellan, Kelly Kay, and Bobby Milstein. 1998. Codebook development for team-based qualitative analysis. *Cultural Anthropology Methods* 10, no. 2: 31–36.

Madigan, Tim. 2001. *The burning: Massacre, destruction, and the Tulsa Race Riot of 1921.* New York: Thomas Dunne Books/St. Martin's Press.

Madrian, Brigitte C., and Dennis F. Shea. 2001. The power of suggestion: Inertia in 401(k) participation and savings behavior. *Quarterly Journal of Economics* 116, no. 4: 1149–87.

Maital, Sharone L., and Shlomo Maital. 1993. *Economics and psychology.* Aldershot: Edward Elgar.

Maital, Sharone L., and Shlomo Maital. 1994. Is the future what it used to be? A behavioral theory of the decline of saving in the West. *Journal of Socio-economics* 23, no. 1–2: 1–32.

Maital, Shlomo. 1982. *Minds, markets, and money.* New York: Basic Books.

Mandell, Lewis. 2004. Financial literacy: Are we improving? Results of the 2004 National Jump$tart Coalition Survey. Washington, DC: Jump$tart Coaliton for Personal Financial Literacy.

Manning, Robert D. 2000. *Credit card nation: The consequences of America's addiction to credit.* New York: Basic Books.

Marlowe, Julia, Deborah Godwin, and Esther Maddux. 1996. Barriers to effective financial management among welfare recipients. *Advancing the Consumer Interest* 8, no. 2: 1–7.

Masnick, George S. 2004. Homeownership and social inequality in the United States. In *Homeownership and social inequality in comparative perspective,* ed. Kevin Kurz and Hans-Peter Blossfeld, 304–37. Stanford: Stanford University Press.

Massey, Douglas S., and Nancy A. Denton. 1993. *American apartheid: Segregation and the making of the underclass.* Cambridge: Harvard University Press.

Matin, Imran, David Hulme, and Stuart Rutherford. 1999. Financial services for the poor and poorest: Deepening understanding to improve provision. Working Paper Series no. 9, Finance and Development Research Programme, University of Manchester, October.

Matin, Imran, David Hulme, and Stuart Rutherford. 2002. Finance for the poor: From microcredit to microfinancial services. *Journal of International Development* 14:273–94.

Maxwell, Joseph A. 1992. Understanding and validity in qualitative research. *Harvard Educational Review* 62, no. 3: 279–300.

Mayer, Neil S. 1981. Rehabilitation decisions in rental housing: An empirical analysis. *Journal of Urban Economics* 19:76–94.

Mayer, Susan, and Christopher Jencks. 1989. Poverty and the distribution of material hardship. *Journal of Human Resources* 24, no. 1: 88–114.

McBride, Amanda Moore, Margaret Lombe, and Sondra G. Beverly. 2003. The effects of Individual Development Account programs: Perceptions of participants. *Social Development Issues* 25, no. 1–2: 59–73.

McBride, Amanda Moore, Margaret S. Sherraden, and Suzanne Pritzker. 2006. Civic engagement among low-income and low-wealth families: In their words. *Family Relations* 55, no. 2: 151–62.

McCarthy, Mike, and Liz McWhirter. 2000. Are employees missing the big picture? Study shows need for ongoing financial education. *Benefits Quarterly* 16:25–31.

McClure, Samuel M., David I. Laibson, George Lowenstein, and Jonathan D. Cohen. 2004. Separate neural systems value immediate and delayed monetary rewards. *Science* 306 (15 October): 503–7.

McDonald, Gordon, Peter R. Orszag, and Gina Russell. n.d. The effect of asset tests on saving. Discussion Paper, Retirement Security Project, Washington, DC.

McGarry, Kathleen, and R. F. Schoeni. 1995. Transfer behavior in the health and retirement study: Measurement and the redistribution of resources within the family. *Journal of Human Resources* 30:S184–S226.

Megbolugbe, Isaac F., and Peter D. Linneman. 1993. Home ownership. *Urban Studies* 30, no. 4–5: 659–82.

Merton, Robert K., Marjorie F. Lowenthal, and Patricia L. Kendall. 1990. *The focused interview: A manual of problems and procedures.* 2nd ed. New York: Free Press.

Metcalfe, Janet, and Walter Mischel. 1999. A hot/cool-system analysis of delay of gratification: Dynamics of will power. *Psychological Review* 106, no. 1:3–19.

Midgley, James. 1995. *Social development: The developmental perspective in social welfare.* London: Sage Publications.

Miles, Matthew B., and A. Michael Huberman. 1994. *Qualitative data analysis*. Beverly Hills, CA: Sage Publications.

Miller, S. M., and Pamela A. Roby. 1970. *The future of inequality*. New York: Basic Books.

Miller-Adams, Michelle. 2002. *Owning up: Poverty, assets, and the American dream*. Washington, DC: Brookings Institution Press.

Mirowsky, John, and Catherine E. Ross. 1999. Economic hardship across the life course. *American Sociological Review* 64:548–69.

Modigliani, Franco, and Richard Brumberg. 1954. Utility analysis and the consumption function: An interpretation of cross-section data. In *Post-Keynesian economics*, ed. Kenneth K. Kurihara, 388–436. New Brunswick: Rutgers University Press.

Moore, Amanda, Sondra Beverly, Mark Schreiner, Michael Sherraden, Margaret Lombe, Esther Y. N. Cho, Lissa Johnson, and Rebecca Vonderlack. 2001. Saving, IDA programs, and effects of IDAs: A survey of participants. CSD Report, Center for Social Development, Washington University, St. Louis.

Morgenson, Gretchen. 2007. Mortgage maze may increase foreclosures. *New York Times* [online edition], 6 August. Available from http://www.nytimes.com/2007/08/06/business/06home.html#. [cited 7 August 2007].

Morgenson, Gretchen. 2008. Given a shovel, digging deeper into debt. *New York Times*, 20 July, 1A.

Morgenson, Gretchen, and Jonathan D. Glater. 2008. Foreclosure machine thrives on woes. *New York Times*, 30 March.

Morillas, Juan Rafael. 2007. Assets, earnings mobility, and the Black/White Gap. *Social Science Research* 36:808–33.

Mulder, Clara H. 2006. Home-ownership and family formation. *Journal of Housing and the Built Environment* 21:281–98.

Mulder, Clara H., and Jeroen Smits. 1999. First-time home-ownership of couples: The effect of inter-generational transmission. *European Sociological Review* 15, no. 3: 323–37.

Mulder, Clara H., and M. Wagner. 1998. First-time home-ownership in the family life course: A West German–Dutch comparison. *Urban Studies* 35, no. 4: 687–713.

Muñiz, Brenda, Eric Rodriguez, and Sonia M. Pérez. 2004. Financial education in Latino communities: An analysis of programs, products, and results/effects. Report, National Council of La Raza, Washington, DC.

Muske, Glenn, and Mary Winter. 1999. Cash flow management: A framework of daily family activities. *Financial Counseling and Planning* 19, no. 1: 1–12.

NAF (New America Foundation). 2008. Children's savings accounts. Available from http://www.newamerica.net/events/2006/childrens_savings_accounts [cited 17 June 2009].

Nam, Yunju. 2008. Welfare reform, asset limits, and financial asset accumulation among low-income households. *Social Science Quarterly* 89, no. 1: 133–54.

Nembhard, Jessica Gordon, and Anthony A. Blasingame. 2006. Wealth, civic engagement, and democratic practice. In *Wealth accumulation and communities of color in the United States*, ed. J. Gordon Nembhard and Ngina Chiteji, 326–42. Ann Arbor: University of Michigan Press.

Nembhard, J. Gordon, and Ngina Chiteji, eds. 2006. *Wealth accumulation and communities of color in the United States.* Ann Arbor: University of Michigan Press.

Neumark, David. 1995. Are rising earnings profiles a forced-savings mechanism? *Economic Journal* 105:95–106.

Newberger, Robin, and Michelle Coussens. 2008. Insurance and wealth building among lower-income households. *Essays on Issues,* no. 251, Federal Reserve Bank of Chicago, June.

Newman, Katherine S. 1999. *No shame in my game: The working poor in the inner city.* New York: Alfred A. Knopf and the Russell Sage Foundation.

Newman, Katherine S. 2006. *Chutes and ladders: Navigating the low-wage labor market.* New York: Russell Sage Foundation; Cambridge: Harvard University Press.

Newton, Jan M. 1977. Economic rationality of the poor. *Human Organization* 36, no. 1: 50–61.

Nissan, David, and Julian Le Grand. 2000. *A capital idea: Start-up grants for young people.* London: Fabian Society.

Nussbaum, Martha C. 2000. *Women and human development: The capabilities approach.* Cambridge: Cambridge University Press.

Nussbaum, Martha C. 2002. Capabilities and human rights. In *Global justice and transnational politics: Essays on the moral and political challenges of globalization,* ed. Pablo De Greiff and Ciaran Cronin, 117–49. Cambridge: MIT Press.

Nyhus, Ellen K., and Paul Webley. 2006. Discounting, self-control, and saving. In *Handbook of contemporary behavioral economics: Foundations and developments,* ed. Morris Altman, 297–325. Armonk, NY: M. E. Sharpe.

O'Curry, Suzanne. 1999. Budgeting and mental accounting. In *The Elgar companion to consumer research and economic psychology,* ed. Peter E. Earl and Simon Kemp, 63–67. Cheltenham, United Kingdom: Edward Elgar.

OECD (Organization for Economic Co-operation and Development). 2003. Asset building and the escape from poverty: An introduction to a new welfare policy debate. Paris: Local Economic and Employment Development, OECD. Available from http://www.tessproject.com/products/seminars&training/seminar%20series/Assets_Materials/Asset_Bulding_and_th e_Escape_from_Poverty.pdf [cited 13 June 2007].

Oliver, Melvin L., and Thomas M. Shapiro. 1995. *Black wealth/white wealth: A new perspective on racial inequality.* New York: Routledge.

Page-Adams, Deborah, and Michael Sherraden. 1996. What we know about effects of asset holding: Implications for research on asset-based anti-poverty initiatives. CSD Working Paper 96-1, Center for Social Development, Washington University, St. Louis.

Page-Adams, Deborah, and Nancy Vosler. 1996. Predictors of depression among workers at the time of a plant closing. *Journal of Sociology and Social Welfare* 23, no. 4: 25–42.

Pahl, Jan. 1980. Patterns of money management within marriage. *Journal of Social Policy* 9:313–35.

Pahl, Jan. 1989. *Money and marriage.* New York: Macmillan.

Pahl, Jan. 1995. His money, her money: Recent research on financial organization in marriage. *Journal of Economic Psychology* 16:361–76.

Paladino, Variny, and Ruth Helman. 2003. The 2003 Minority Retirement Confidence Survey: Summary of findings. *Retirement Confidence Survey, EBRI Notes* 21, no. 9 (July). Available from http://papers.ssrn.com/sol3/papers.cfm?abstract_id=434781. [cited 11 February 2007].

Pelletiere, Danilo. 2009. Renters in foreclosure: Defining the problem, identifying solutions. National Low-Income Housing Coalition, December. Available from http://www.nlihc.org/doc/renters-in-foreclosure.pdf [cited 15 June 2009].

Perin, Constance. 1977. *Everything in its place: Social order and land use in America.* Princeton: Princeton University Press.

Perkins, Douglas, Paul Florin, Richard C. Rich, Abraham Wandersman, and David M. Chavis. 1990. Participation and the social and physical environment of residential blocks: Crime and community context. *American Journal of Community Psychology* 18, no. 1: 83–115.

Perun, Pamela, and C. Eugene Steuerle. 2008. Why not a "super simple" saving plan for the United States? Washington, DC: Urban Institute. Available from http://www.urban.org/url.cfm?ID=411676 [cited 19 June 2008].

Poterba, James M., Steven F. Venti, and David A. Wise. 1998. Lump sum distributions from retirement savings plans: Receipt and utilization. In *Inquiries in the economics of aging*, ed. David A. Wise, 85–105. Chicago: University of Chicago Press.

Potter, Robert B., and John T. Coshall 1987. Socio-economic variations in perceived life domain satisfactions: A South West Wales case study. *Journal of Social Psychology* 127, no. 1: 77–82.

Powell, Walter W., and Paul J. DiMaggio, eds. 1991. *The New Institutionalism in organizational analysis.* Chicago: University of Chicago Press.

Prabhakar, Rajiv. 2009. *The assets agenda: Principles and policy.* Basingstroke: Palgrave-Macmillan.

Prabhakar, Rajiv, and Andrew Gamble. 2006. Assets and capital grants: The attitudes of young people towards capital grants. In *The new politics of ownership*, ed., Will Paxton and Stuart White, 107–19. Bristol: Policy Press.

Pratt, Geraldine. 1986. Housing tenure and social cleavages in urban Canada. *Annals of the Association of American Geographers* 76, no. 3: 366–80.

Prelec, Drazen, and George Loewenstein. 1998. The red and the black: Mental accounting of savings and debt. *Marketing Science* 17:4–28.

Pritchard, Mary E., Barbara Kimes Myers, and Deborah J. Cassidy. 1989. Factors associated with adolescent saving and spending patterns. *Adolescence* 24, no. 95: 711–23.

Pugh, Helena, Christine Power, Peter Goldblatt, and Sara Arber. 1991. Women's lung cancer mortality, socioeconomic status, and changing smoking patterns. *Social Science and Medicine* 32, no. 10: 1105–10.

Pulizzi, Henry T. 2009. Obama signs credit-card overhaul legislation into law. *Wall Street Journal* [online edition] 22 May. Available from http://online.wsj.com/article/SB124302235634548041.html [cited 15 June 2009].

Rainwater, Lee, Richard P. Coleman, and Gerald Handel. 1959. *Workingman's wife.* New York: Oceana Publications.

Rakoff, Robert. 1977. Ideology in everyday life: The meaning of the house. *Politics and Society* 7:85–104.

Rank, Mark R. 2005. *One nation, underprivileged: Why American poverty affects us all.* Oxford: Oxford University Press.

Ranyard, Rob, and Gill Craig. 1995. Evaluating and budgeting with installment credit: An interview study. *Journal of Economic Psychology* 16:449–67.

Rasmussen, David W., Isaac F. Megbolugbe, and Barbara A. Morgan. 1997. The reverse mortgage as an asset management tool. *Housing Policy Debate* 8, no. 1: 173–94.

Rawlings, Lynette, and Kerstin Gentsch. 2008. How households expect to cope in a financial emergency. Opportunity and Ownership Facts, no. 9, Urban Institute, Washington, DC. Available from http://www.urban.org/UploadedPDF/411621_financial_emergency.pdf [cited 19 June 2008].

Relman, John P., Fred Rivera, Meera Trehan, and Shilpa Satoskar. 2004. Designing federal legislation that works: Legal remedies for predatory lending. In *Why the poor pay more: How to stop predatory lending,* ed. Gregory D. Squires, 153–84. Westport, CN and London: Praeger.

Reutebuch, Timothy G. 2001. An exploration into Individual Development Accounts as an anti-poverty strategy. *Journal of Sociology and Social Welfare* 28, no. 3: 95–107.

Reuters. 2009. A record 5.4 million home loans behind or in foreclosure in Q4. *USA Today* [online edition] 5 March. Available from http://www.usatoday.com/money/economy/housing/2009-03-05-delinquent-home-loans-q4_N.htm [cited 15 June 2009].

Reynolds, Arthur J., and Sukhdeep Gill. 1994. The role of parental perspectives in the school adjustment of inner-city Black children. *Journal of Youth and Adolescence* 23, no. 6: 671–94.

Rhine, Sherrie L. W., and Maude Toussaint-Comeau. 1999. The use of formal and informal financial markets among Black households. *Consumer Interest Annual* 45:146–51.

Rhine, Sherrie L. W., Maude Toussaint-Comeau, and Jeanne M. Hogarth. 2001. The role of alternative financial service providers in serving LMI neighborhoods. Paper prepared for the Federal Reserve System Community Affairs Research Conference "Changing Financial Markets and Community Development," Washington, DC, April.

Robert, Stephanie, and James S. House. 1996. SES differentials in health by age and alternative indicators of SES. *Journal of Aging and Health* 8, no. 3: 359–88.

Rocha, Cynthia J. 1997. Factors that contribute to economic well-being in female-headed households. *Journal of Social Service Research* 23, no. 10: 1–17.

Rodgers, B. 1991. Socio-economic status, employment, and neurosis. *Social Psychiatry and Psychiatric Epidemiology* 26, no. 3: 104–14.

Rodin, Judith. 1990. Control by any other name: Definitions, concepts, and processes. In *Self-directedness: Cause and effects throughout the life course,* ed. Judith Rodin, Carmi Schooler, and K. Warner Schaie, 1–18. Hillsdale, NJ: Lawrence Erlbaum.

Rodriguez, Eric, and Deirdre Martinez. 2004. Pension coverage: A missing step in the wealth-building ladder for Latinos. National Council of La Raza Issue Brief No. 11, National Council of La Raza, Washington, DC. Available from http://www.nclr.org/content/publications/detail/1388/. [cited 11 February 2007].

Rohe, William M., and Victoria Basolo. 1997. Long-term effects of homeownership on the self-perceptions and social interaction of low-income persons. *Environment and Behavior* 29, no. 6: 793–819.

Rohe, William M., Shannon Van Zandt, and George W. McCarthy. 2001. The social benefits and costs of homeownership: A critical assessment of the research. Research Institute for Housing America Working Paper 01-01, Joint Center for Housing Studies, Harvard University, Cambridge, MA. Available from http://www.jchs.harvard.edu/publications/homeownership/liho01-12.pdf. [cited 26 September 2007].

Rohe, William M., Lucy Gorham, and Roberto G. Quercia. 2005. Individual Development Accounts: Participation characteristics and success. *Journal of Urban Affairs* 27, no. 5: 503–20.

Rohe, William M., and Michael Stegman. 1994a. The effects of home ownership on the self-esteem, perceived control, and life satisfaction of low-income people. *Journal of the American Planning Association* 60, no. 1: 173–84.

Rohe, William M., and Michael Stegman. 1994b. The impact of home ownership on the social and political involvement of low-income people. *Urban Affairs Quarterly* 30, no. 3: 152–72.

Rohe, William M., and Leslie Stewart. 1996. Homeownership and neighborhood stability. *Housing Policy Debate* 7, no. 1: 37–81.

Romich, Jennifer L., and Thomas Weisner. 2000. How families view and use the EITC: Advance payment versus lump sum delivery. *National Tax Journal* 53, no. 4: 1245–65.

Ross, Lee, and Richard E. Nisbett. 1991. *The person and the situation: Perspectives of social psychology.* New York: McGraw-Hill.

Rossi, Peter H., and Eleanor Weber. 1996. The social benefits of homeownership: Empirical evidence from national surveys. *Housing Policy Debate* 7:1–35.

Rubin, Herbert J., and Irene S. Rubin. 1995. *Qualitative interviewing: The art of hearing data.* Thousand Oaks, CA: Sage.

Rutherford, Stuart. 2000. *The poor and their money.* New Delhi: Oxford University Press.

Rutherford, Stuart. 2005. Why do the poor need savings services? What they get and what they might like. In *Savings services for the poor: An operational guide,* ed. M. Hirschland, 15–26. Bloomfield, CT: Kumarian Press.

Salisbury, Dallas L. 2008. July. EBRI policy forum: Defined contribution plans in a post–PPA environment. *EBRI Notes* 29, no. 7: 1–8.

Sanders, Cynthia. 2007. Domestic violence, economic abuse, and implications of a program for building economic resources for low-income women. CSD Research Report 07-12, Center for Social Development, Washington University, St. Louis.

Satterwhite, Aisha. 2000. Oklahoma's promised land. *American Legacy* (Summer): 45–52.

Saunders, Peter. 1990. *A nation of homeowners.* London: Unwin Hyman.

Sawhill, Isabel. 1989. The underclass: An overview. *Public Interest* 96 (Summer): 3–15.

Scanlon, Edward. 1998. Low-income homeownership policy as a community development strategy. In *Community economic development and social work,* ed. Margaret S. Sherraden and William A. Ninacs, 137–54. New York: Haworth Press.

Scanlon, Edward, and Deborah Page-Adams. 2001. Effects of asset holding on neighborhoods, families, and children: A review of research. In *Building assets: A report on the asset-development and IDA field,* ed. Ray Boshara, 25–49. Washington, DC: Corporation for Enterprise Development.

Scanlon, Edward, and Deborah Adams. 2009. Do assets affect well-being? Perceptions of youth in a matched savings program. *Journal of Social Service Research* 35, 33–46.

Scanlon, Edward, and Deborah Page-Adams. 2005. Homeownership and youth well being. In *Inclusion in the American dream: Assets, poverty, and public policy,* ed. Michael Sherraden, 128–48. Oxford: Oxford University Press.

Schelling, Thomas C. 1984. Self-command in practice, in policy, and in theory of rational choice. *American Economic Review* 74:1–11.

Schelling, Thomas C. 1992. Self command: A new discipline. In *Choice over time,* ed. George Loewenstein and Jon Elster, 167–76. New York: Russell Sage Foundation.

Schloemer, Ellen, Wei Li, Keith Ernst, and Kathleen Keest. 2006. Losing ground: Foreclosures in the subprime market and their cost to homeowners (December). Available from http://www.responsiblelending.org/mortgage-lending/research-analysis/losing-ground-foreclosures-in-the-subprime-market-and-their-cost-to-homeown ers.html [cited 18 May 2008].

Schneider, Daniel, and Peter Tufano, P. 2007. New savings from old innovations: Asset building for the less affluent. *Financing low-income communities: Models, obstacles, and future directions,* ed. Julia S. Rubin, 13–71. New York: Russell Sage Foundation.

Schoenbaum, Michael, and Timothy Waidmann. 1997. Race, socioeconomic status, and health: Accounting for race differences in health. *Journals of Gerontology,* ser. B, 52B, special issue: 61–73.

Schreiner, Mark. 2005. What does an IDA cost? Some measures from ADD. CSD Research Report 05-38, Center for Social Development, Washington University, St. Louis. http://csd.wustl.edu/Publications/Documents/RP05-38.pdf [cited 18 May 2008].

Schreiner, Mark, Margaret Clancy, and Michael Sherraden. 2002. Saving performance in the American Dream Demonstration: A national demonstration of Individual Development Accounts. CSD Report, Center for Social Development, Washington University, St. Louis.

Schreiner, Mark, and Michael Sherraden. 2007. *Can the poor save? Saving and asset building in Individual Development Accounts.* New Brunswick, NJ: Transaction Publishers.

Schwartz, Hugh. 2006. In-depth interviews as a means of understanding economic reasoning. In *Handbook of contemporary behavioral economics: Foundations and developments,* ed. Morris Altman, 356–75. Armonk, NY: M. E. Sharpe.

SEDI (Social and Enterprise Development Innovations). 2004. Financial capability and poverty: New approaches for addressing poverty and exclusion. SEDI Discussion Paper, Social and Enterprise Development Innovations, Toronto.

SEDI (Social and Enterprise Development Innovations). 2005. Why financial capability matters. *Synthesis report on Canadians and their money: A national symposium on financial capability.* June 9–10, 2005. Toronto: SEDI. Available from http://www.fcac _acfc.gc.ca/eng/publications/SurveyStudy/FinCapability/pdf/SEDI_FCAC_FinCa pability_eng.pdf [cited 18 May 2008].

Seidman, Laurence E. 2001. Assets and the tax code. In *Assets for the poor: The benefits of spreading asset ownership,* ed. Thomas M. Shapiro and Edward N. Wolff, 324–56. New York: Russell Sage Foundation.

Sen, Amartya. 1993. Capability and well-being. In *The quality of life*, ed. Martha Nussbaum and Amartya Sen, 30–53. Oxford: Clarendon Press.

Sen, Amartya. 1999. *Development as freedom*. New York: Anchor Books.

Shanks, Trina Williams. 2005. The Homestead Act: A major asset-building policy in American history. In *Inclusion in the American dream: Assets, poverty, and public policy*, ed. Michael Sherraden, 20–41. Oxford: Oxford University Press.

Shapiro, Thomas M. 2001. The importance of assets. In *Assets for the poor*, ed. Thomas M. Shapiro and Edward N. Wolff, 111–33. New York: Russell Sage Foundation.

Shapiro, Thomas M. 2004. *The hidden cost of being African American: How wealth perpetuates inequality*. Oxford: Oxford University Press.

Shapiro, Thomas M., and Heather Beth Johnson. 2005. Family assets and school access: Race and class in the structuring of educational opportunity. In *Inclusion in the American dream: Assets, poverty, and public policy*, ed. Michael Sherraden, 112–27. Oxford: Oxford University Press.

Shapiro, Thomas M., and Edward N. Wolff, eds. 2001. *Assets for the poor: The benefits of spreading asset ownership*. New York: Russell Sage Foundation.

Shefrin, Hersh M., and Richard H. Thaler. 1988. The behavioral life-cycle hypothesis. *Economic Inquiry* 26, no. 4: 609–41.

Shefrin, Hersh M., and Richard H. Thaler. 1992. Mental accounting, saving, and self-control. In *Choice over time*, ed. George Loewenstein and Jon Elster, 287–327. New York: Russell Sage Foundation.

Shelton, Gladys G., and Octavia L. Hill. 1995. First-time home buyers programs as an impetus for change in budget behavior. *Financial Counseling and Planning* 6:83–91.

Sherraden, Margaret S., Elizabeth Johnson, William Elliott III, Shirley Porterfield, and William Rainford. 2007. The *I Can Save* program: School-based children's saving accounts for college. *Children and Youth Services Review* 29, no. 3: 294–312.

Sherraden, Margaret S., Amanda Moore McBride, Stacie Hanson, and Lissa Johnson. 2006. Short-term and long-term savings in low income households: Evidence from Individual Development Accounts. *Journal of Income Distribution* 13, no. 3–4: 76–97.

Sherraden, Margaret S., Amanda Moore, and Philip H. Hong. 2000. Savers speak: Case studies of IDA participants. Society for Social Work Research, Charleston, SC, 31 January.

Sherraden, Margaret S., Cynthia K. Sanders, and Michael Sherraden. 2004. *Kitchen capitalism: Microenterprise in poor households*. Albany: State University of New York Press.

Sherraden, Margaret Sherrard, Trina Williams, Amanda Moore McBride, and Fred Ssewamala. 2004. Overcoming poverty: Supported saving as a household development strategy. CSD Working Paper 04-13, Center for Social Development, Washington University, St. Louis.

Sherraden, Michael. 1988. Rethinking social welfare: Toward assets. *Social Policy* 18, no. 3: 37–43.

Sherraden, Michael. 1991. *Assets and the poor: A new American welfare policy*. Armonk, NY: M. E. Sharpe.

Sherraden, Michael. 2001. Asset building policy and programs for the poor. In *Assets for the poor: The benefits of spreading asset ownership*, ed. Thomas M. Shapiro and Edward N. Wolff, 302–23. New York: Russell Sage Foundation.

Sherraden, Michael. 2002. Individual Development Accounts: Summary of research. CSD Report, Center for Social Development, Washington University, St. Louis.

Sherraden, Michael. 2005. Assets and public policy. In *Inclusion in the American dream: Assets, poverty, and public policy*, ed. Michael Sherraden, 3–19. Oxford: Oxford University Press.

Sherraden, Michael, and Michael S. Barr. 2005. Institutions and inclusion in saving policy. In *Building assets, building credit: Bridges and barriers to financial services in low-income communities*, ed. Nicolas Retsinas and Eric Belsky, 286–315. Washington, DC: Brookings Institution Press.

Sherraden, Michael, Deborah Page-Adams, and Elizabeth Johnson. 1999. Downpayments on the American Dream policy demonstration. CSD Report, Center for Social Development, Washington University, St. Louis. Available from: http://gwbweb.wustl.edu/csd/Publications/index.htm

Sherraden, Michael, Mark Schreiner, and Sondra Beverly. 2003. Income, institutions, and saving performance in Individual Development Accounts. *Economic Development Quarterly* 17, no. 1: 95–112.

Shipler, David K. 2004. *The working poor: Invisible in America.* New York: Vintage Books.

Shlay, Anne B. 2006. Low-income homeownership: American dream or delusion? *Urban Studies* 43, no. 3: 511–31.

Shobe, Marcia, and Suzanne A. Boyd. 2005. Relationships between assets and perceived economic strain: Findings from an anti-poverty policy demonstration. *Journal of Community Practice* 13, no. 2: 21–44.

Shobe, Marcia A., and Kameri Christy-McMullin. 2005. Savings experiences past and present: Narratives from low-income African American women. *Affilia* 20, no. 2: 222–37.

Shobe, Marcia, and Deborah Page-Adams. 2001. Assets, future orientation, and well-being: Exploring and extending Sherraden's framework. *Journal of Sociology and Social Welfare* 28, no. 3: 109–27.

Shockey, Susan S., and Sharon B. Seiling. 2004. Moving into action: Application of the transtheoretical model of behavior change to financial education. *Financial Counseling and Planning* 15, no. 1: 41–52.

Silver, Josh, and Marva Williams. 2006. A lifetime of assets. Asset preservation: Trends and interventions in asset stripping services and products. Woodstock Institute Research Report, Chicago. Available from http://www.communityinvestmentnetwork.org/nc/single-news-item-states/article/a-lifetime-of-assets-asset-preservation-trends-and-interventions-in-asset-stripping-services-and/?tx_ttnews%5 Bback-Pid%5D=760&cHash=33b93558e8&type=123. [cited 17 June 2009].

Simon, Herbert A. 1957. A behavioral model of rational choice. *Quarterly Journal of Economics* 69, no. 1: 99–117.

Smeeding, Timothy M., Katherine Ross Phillips, and Michael O'Connor. 2000. The EITC: Expectation, knowledge, use, and economic and social mobility. *National Tax Journal* 53, no. 4: 1187–1209.

Smeeding, Timothy M., and Jeffrey P. Thompson. 2007. Income from wealth and income from labor: Stocks, flows, and more complete measures of well being. Unpublished manuscript, Center for Policy Research, Syracuse University.

Smith, Kyle. 2003. Predatory lending in Native American communities. Fredericksburg, VA: Native Assets Research Center, First Nations Development Institute. Available from http://www.firstnations.org/publications/PredatoryLendinginNACommuni ties.pdf. [cited 11 February 2007].

Snyder, C. R. 2000a. *Handbook of hope*. San Diego, CA: Academic Press.

Snyder, C. R. 2000b. The past and future of hope. *Journal of Social and Clinical Psychology* 19, no. 1: 11–28.

Sodha, Sonia. 2006. Lessons from across the Atlantic: Asset-building in the U.K. Paper presented at the Lifetime of Assets Conference, Phoenix, AZ, September.

Sonuga-Barke, Edmund J. S., and Paul Webley. 1993. *Children's saving: A study in the development of economic behaviour*. Hove: Erlbaum.

Sørensen, Aage B. 2000. Toward a sounder basis for class analysis. *American Journal of Sociology* 105, no. 6: 1523–58.

South, Scott J., and Glenna Spitze. 1986. Determinants of divorce over the marital life course. *American Sociological Review* 51 (August): 583–90.

Spilerman, Seymour. 2000. Wealth and stratification processes. *Annual Review of Sociology* 26:497–524.

Spilerman, Seymour. 2001. Some observations on asset ownership, living standards, and poor families. In *Assets for the poor: The benefits of spreading asset ownership*, ed. Thomas M. Shapiro and Edward N. Wolff, 367–79. New York: Russell Sage Foundation.

Squires, Gregory D., ed. 2004. *Why the poor pay more: How to stop predatory lending*. Westport, CN and London: Praeger.

Squires, Gregory D., and Sally O'Connor. 1998. Fringe banking in Milwaukee: The rise of check-cashing businesses and the emergence of a two-tiered banking system. *Urban Affairs Review* 34, no. 1: 126–49.

Stack, Carol B. 1974. *All our kin: Strategies for survival in a Black community*. New York: Harper and Row.

Stavins, Joanna. 2000. Credit card borrowing, delinquency, and personal bankruptcy. *New England Economic Review* (July–August): 15–30.

Stegman, Michael A. 1999. *Savings for the poor: The hidden benefits of electronic banking*. Washington, DC: Brookings Institution Press.

Stegman, Michael A., and Robert Faris. 2003. Payday lending: A business model that encourages chronic borrowing. *Economic Development Quarterly* 17, no. 1: 8–32.

Steinberger, Peter J. 1981. Political participation and communality: A cultural/interpersonal approach. *Rural Sociology* 46, no. 1: 7–19.

Stern, Mark J. 2001. The un(credit)worthy poor: Historical perspectives on policies to expand assets and credit. In *Assets for the poor: The benefits of spreading asset ownership*, ed. Thomas M. Shapiro and Edward N. Wolff, 269–301. New York: Russell Sage Foundation.

Stewart, Sharla A. 2005. Can behavioral economics save us from ourselves? *University of Chicago Magazine* (February): 37–42.

Strauss, Anselm L., and Juliet M. Corbin. 1998. *Basics of qualitative research: Techniques and procedures for developing grounded theory.* 2nd ed. Newbury Park, CA: Sage.

Strotz, Robert H. 1956. Myopia and inconsistency in dynamic utility maximization. *Review of Economic Studies* 23, no. 3: 165–80.

Stuhldreher, Anne, and Jennifer Tescher. 2005. Breaking the savings barrier: How the federal government can build an inclusive financial system. Issue Brief, New America Foundation, Washington, DC.

Sullivan, Teresa A., Elizabeth Warren, and Jay Lawrence Westbrook. 2000a. *As we forgive our debtors: Bankruptcy and consumer credit in America.* New York: Oxford University Press.

Sullivan, Teresa A., Elizabeth Warren, and Jay Lawrence Westbrook. 2000b. *The fragile middle class: Americans in debt.* New Haven: Yale University Press.

Sunstein, Cass R., and Richard H. Thaler. 2003. Libertarian paternalism is not an oxymoron. *University of Chicago Law Review* 70:1159–1202.

Swartz, Thomas R., and Kathleen M. Weigert. 1995. *America's working poor.* Notre Dame: University of Notre Dame Press.

Swedberg, Richard. 2001. Max Weber's vision of economic sociology. In *The sociology of economic life,* 2nd ed., ed. Mark Granovetter and Richard Swedberg, 77–95. Boulder: Westview Press.

Terrell, Henry S. 1971. Wealth accumulation of black and white families: The empirical evidence. *Journal of Finance* 26:263–77.

Thaler, Richard H. 1985. Mental accounting and consumer choice. *Marketing Science* 4:199–214.

Thaler, Richard H. 1990. Anomalies: Savings, fungibility, and mental accounts. *Journal of Economic Perspectives* 4, no. 1:193–205.

Thaler, Richard H. 1992a. How to get real people to save. In *Personal saving, consumption, and tax policy,* ed. Marvin H. Koster, 143–50. Washington, DC: AEI Press.

Thaler, Richard H. 1992b. *The winner's curse: Paradoxes and anomalies of economic life.* New York: Free Press.

Thaler, Richard. 1999. Mental accounting matters. In *Choices, values, and frames,* ed. Daniel Kahneman and Amos Tversky, 209–23. Cambridge: Cambridge University Press and Russell Sage Foundation. First published in *Journal of Behavioral Decision Making* 12:183–206.

Thaler, Richard. 2000. From Homo economicus to Homo sapiens. *Journal of Economic Perspectives* 14, no. 1: 133–41.

Thaler, Richard H., and Shlomo Benartzi. 2004. Save More Tomorrow ™: Using behavioral economics to increase employee saving. *Journal of Political Economy* 112, no. 1: S164–S187.

Thaler, Richard H., and Hershel M. Shefrin. 1981. An economic theory of self-control. *Journal of Political Economy* 89, no. 2: 392–406.

Thaler, Richard H., and Cass R. Sunstein. 2008. *Nudge: Improving decisions about health, wealth, and happiness.* New Haven and London: Yale University Press.

Tin, Jan. 2000. Life-cycle hypothesis, propensities to save, and demand for financial assets. *Journal of Economics and Finance* 24, no. 2: 110–21.

Tobin, James. 1968. Raising the incomes of the poor. In *Agenda for the nation,* ed. Kermit Gordon, 77–116. Washington, DC: Brookings Institution.

Tversky, Amos, and Daniel Kahneman. 1974. Judgment under uncertainty: Heuristics and biases. *Science* 185, no. 4157:1124–31.

Tversky, Amos, and Daniel Kahneman. 1981. The framing of decisions and psychology of choice. *Science* 211, no. 30: 453–58.

Tversky, Amos, and Daniel Kahneman. 1986. Rational choice and the framing of decisions. In *Choices, values, and frames,* ed. Daniel Kahneman and Amos Tversky, 209–23. Cambridge: Cambridge University Press and Russell Sage Foundation. First published in *Journal of Business* 59, no. 4 (1986): S251–78.

Tversky, Amos, and Eldar Shafir. 1992. Choice under conflict: The dynamics of deferred decision. *Psychological Science* 3:358–61.

Twomey, Paul J. 1999. Habit. In *The Elgar companion to consumer research and economic psychology,* ed. Peter E. Earl and Simon Kemp, 271–75. Cheltenham: Edward Elgar.

U.K. Department for Work and Pensions. 2006. Personal accounts: A new way to save. Available from http://www.dwp.gov.uk/pensionsreform/new_way.asp. [cited 26 September 2007].

U.K. Financial Service Authority. 2005. Measuring financial capability: An exploratory study. *Consumer Research* 37 (June). London: University of Bristol, Personal Finance Research Centre. Available at http://www.fsa.gov.uk/pubs/consumer-research/crpr37 .pdf. [cited 17 June 2009].

U.S. Department of the Treasury. 2002. *Integrating financial education into school curricula: Giving America's youth the educational foundation for making effective financial decisions throughout their lives by teaching financial concepts as part of math and reading curricula in elementary, middle, and high schools.* (White Paper prepared by the United States Department of the Treasury Office of Financial Education, October 2002). Available from http://www.treas.gov/press/releases/docs/white.pdf [cited April 2, 2006].

U.S. Department of the Treasury, Office of Financial Education. 2006. *Taking ownership of the future: The national strategy for financial literacy.* Washington, DC. Available from http://www.mymoney.gov/pdfs/ownership.pdf. [cited 11 February 2007].

U.S. Department of the Treasury, 2009. School-based bank savings programs: Bringing financial education to students. *Insights,* April. Community Affairs Department, Comptroller of the Currency, Washington DC. Available from http://comptrol lerofthecurrency.gov/cdd/Insights-Schoolbasedbank.pdf [cited 15 June 2009].

U.S. Government Accountability Office (GAO). 2004. The federal government's role in improving financial literacy: Highlights of a GAO Forum. GAO-05-93SP, GAO, Washington, DC, November. Available from http://www.gao.gov/new.items/d0593sp .pdf. [cited 11 February 2007].

Varady, David P. 1986. *Neighborhood upgrading: A realistic assessment.* Albany: State University of New York.

Varcoe, Karen P. 1990. Financial events and coping strategies of households. *Journal of Consumer Studies and Home Economics* 14:57–69.

Veblen, Thorstein. 1899. *The theory of the leisure class.* New York: Macmillan.

Venkatesh, Sudhir Alladi. 2006. *Off the books: The underground economy of the urban poor.* Cambridge: Harvard University Press.

Venti, Steven F., and David A. Wise. 1992. Government policy and personal retirement savings. In *Tax policy and the economy,* ed. James A. Poterba, 6th ed., 1–41. Cambridge: MIT Press.

Vitt, Lois A., Carol Anderson, Jamie Kent, Deanna M. Lyter, Jurg K. Siegenthaler, and Jeremy Ward. 2000. *Personal finance and the rush to competence: Financial literacy education in the U.S.* Institute for Socio-Financial Studies, Middleberg, VA. Available from http://www.isfs.org/rep_finliteracy.pdf [cited 21 November 2005].

Vogler, Carolyn, and Jan Pahl. 1994. Money, power, and inequality within marriage. *Sociological Review* 42:263–88.

Voydanoff, Patricia, and Brenda W. Donnelly. 1988. Economic distress, family coping, and quality of family life. In *Families and economic distress: Coping strategies and social policy,* ed. Patricia A. Voydanoff and Brenda W. Donnelly, 97–116. Newbury Park, CA: Sage.

Wadhwani, R. Daniel. 2006. Protecting small savers: The political economy of economic security. *Journal of Policy History* 18, no. 1: 126–45.

Waldron, Tom, Brandon Roberts, and Andrew Reamer. 2004. Working hard, falling short: America's working families and the pursuit of economic security. Working Poor Families Project, Annie E. Casey Foundation, Ford Foundation, and Rockefeller Foundation, Washington, DC. Available from http://www.aecf.org/upload/publicationfiles/working%20hard.pdf. [cited 17 June 2009].

Walker, Catherine M. 1996. Financial management, coping, and debt in households under financial strain. *Journal of Economic Psychology* 17:789–807.

Walker, Michael. 1999. Gambling. In *The Elgar companion to consumer research and economic psychology,* ed. Peter E. Earl and Simon Kemp, 247–53. Cheltenham: Edward Elgar.

Wärneryd, Karl-Erik. 1999. *The psychology of saving: A study on economic psychology.* Cheltenham: Edward Elgar.

Warren, Elizabeth. 2008. Making credit safer: The case for regulation. *Harvard Magazine,* May–June, 34–37, 94.

Warren, Elizabeth, and Amelia Warren Tyagi. 2003. *The two-income trap: Why middle-class mothers and fathers are going broke.* New York: Basic Books.

Watson, Orson. 2006. The culture of money: A framework for understanding the impact of race, ethnicity, and color on the implementation of asset-building strategies. Washington, DC: Annie E. Casey Foundation. Available from www.aecf.org/upload/PublicationFiles/RE3622H5053.pdf [cited 11 May 2007].

Weber, Max. 1958. *The Protestant ethic and the spirit of capitalism.* New York: Scribner.

Webley, Paul. 1995. Accounts of accounts: En route to an economic psychology of personal finance. *Journal of Economic Psychology* 16:469–75.

Webley, Paul. 1999. Children's savings. In *The Elgar companion to consumer research and economic psychology,* ed. Peter E. Earl and Simon Kemp, 72–75. Cheltenham, UK: Edward Elgar.

Webley, Paul, Carole B. Burgoyne, Stephen E. G. Lea, and Brian M. Young. 2001. *The eco-*

nomic psychology of everyday life. East Sussex, United Kingdom: Psychology Press, Taylor and Francis.

Webley, Paul, and Ellen K. Nyhus. 2001. Life-cycle and dispositional routes into problem debt. *British Journal of Psychology* 92:423–46.

Webley, Paul, and Z. Plaisier. 1998. The development of mental accounts. *Children's Social and Economic Education* 3:55–64.

Whitbeck, Les B., Ronald L. Simons, Rand D. Conger, Frederick O. Lorenz, Shirley Huck, and Glen H. Elder Jr. 1991. Family economic hardship, parental support, and adolescent self-esteem. *Social Psychology Quarterly* 54:353–63.

Wilhelm, Mark O. 2001. The role of intergenerational transfers in spreading asset ownership. In *Assets for the poor: The benefits of spreading asset ownership,* ed. Thomas M. Shapiro and Edward N. Wolff, 132–61. New York: Russell Sage Foundation.

Williams Shanks, Trina R., and Destin, Mesmin. 2009. Parental expectations and educational outcomes for young African American adults: Do household assets matter? *Race and Social Problems* 1, no. 1: 27–35.

Willis, Lauren E. 2008. Against financial literacy education. Research Paper No. 08-10, Public Law and Legal Theory Research Paper Series, University of Pennsylvania Law School. Available from: http://papers.ssrn.com/sol3/papers.cfm?abstract_id= 1105384 [17 August 2008].

Wilson, Gail. 1987. *Money in the family: Financial organization and women's responsibility.* Aldershot: Avebury.

Winnett, Adrian, and Alan Lewis. 1995. Household accounts, mental accounts, and savings behaviour: Some old economics rediscovered? *Journal of Economic Psychology* 16:431–48.

Wolff, Edward N. 2007. Recent trends in household wealth in the United States: Rising debt and the middle-class squeeze. Working Paper no. 502, Levy Economics Institute of Bard College and Department of Economics, New York University.

Wolff, Edward N., and Ajit Zacharias. 2006. Household wealth and the measurement of economic well-being in the United States. Levy Economics Institute Working Paper no. 447, Levy Economics Institute, Annandale-on-Hudson, NY.

Woo, Lillian, William Schweke, and David Buchholz. 2004. Hidden in plain sight: A look at the $335 billion federal asset-building budget. Washington, DC: Center for Economic Development (CFED).

Xiao, Jiang-jian, and Geraldine I. Olson. 1993. Mental accounting and saving behavior. *Home Economics Research Journal* 22:92–109.

Yadama, Gautam, and Michael Sherraden. 1996. Effects of assets on attitudes and behaviors: Advance test of a social policy proposal. *Social Work Research* 20, no. 1: 3–11.

Zagorski, Jay L. 2006. Native Americans' wealth. In *Wealth accumulation and communities of color in the United States,* ed. J. Gordon Nembhard and Ngina Chiteji, 133–54. Ann Arbor: University of Michigan Press.

Zelizer, Viviana A. 1989. The social meaning of money: Special monies. *American Journal of Sociology* 95:342–77.

Zelizer, Viviana A. 1994. *The social meaning of money: Pin money, paychecks, poor relief, and other currencies.* New York: Basic Books.

Zelizer, Viviana A. 2001. Human values and the market: The case of life insurance and death in 19th-century America. In *The sociology of economic life*, ed. Mark Granovetter and Richard Swedberg, 146–62. Boulder: Westview Press.

Zhan, Min. 2006. Assets, parental expectations and involvement, and children's educational performance. *Children and Youth Services Review* 28, no. 8: 961–75.

Zhan, Min, Steven G. Anderson, and Jeff Scott. 2006. Financial knowledge of the low-income population: Effects of a financial education program. *Journal of Sociology and Social Welfare* 33, no. 1: 53–74.

Zhan, Min, and Michael Sherraden. 2003. Assets, expectations, and children's educational achievement in female-headed households. *Social Service Review* 77 (June): 191–211.

Ziliak, James P. 2003. Income transfers and assets of the poor. *Review of Economics and Statistics* 85, no. 1: 63–76.

Index

Page numbers in italics refer to tables in the text.